META/DATA

Leonardo

Roger F. Malina, Executive Editor

Sean Cubitt, Editor-in-Chief

META / DATA

A Digital Poetics

Mark Amerika

The MIT Press
Cambridge, Massachusetts
London, England

© 2007 Massachusetts Institute of Technology

All rights reserved. No part of this book may be reproduced in any form by any electronic or mechanical means (including photocopying, recording, or information storage and retrieval) without permission in writing from the publisher.

MIT Press books may be purchased at special quantity discounts for business or sales promotional use. For information, please e-mail ⟨special_sales@mitpress.mit.edu⟩ or write to Special Sales Department, The MIT Press, 55 Hayward Street, Cambridge, MA 02142.

This book was set in Minion and Syntax on 3B2 by Asco Typesetters, Hong Kong. Printed and bound in the United States of America.

Library of Congress Cataloging-in-Publication Data

Amerika, Mark.
Meta/data : a digital poetics / Mark Amerika.
    p.   cm.—(Leonardo)
Includes bibliographical references and index.
ISBN 978-0-262-01233-1 (hardcover : alk. paper)
1. Art and the Internet. I. Title. II. Title: Meta data.
NX180.I57A44   2007
700.92—dc22   2006027120

10   9   8   7   6   5   4   3   2   1

Contents

Illustrations

Series Foreword

The arts, science, and technology are experiencing a period of profound change. Explosive challenges to the institutions and practices of engineering, art making, and scientific research raise urgent questions of ethics, craft, and care for the planet and its inhabitants. Unforeseen forms of beauty and understanding are possible, but so too are unexpected risks and threats. A newly global connectivity creates new arenas for interaction between science, art, and technology but also creates the preconditions for global crises. The Leonardo Book series, published by the MIT Press, aims to consider these opportunities, changes, and challenges in books that are both timely and of enduring value.

Leonardo books provide a public forum for research and debate; they contribute to the archive of art-science-technology interactions; they contribute to understandings of emergent historical processes; and they point toward future practices in creativity, research, scholarship, and enterprise.

To find more information about Leonardo/ISAST and to order our publications, go to Leonardo Online at ⟨http://lbs.mit.edu/⟩ or e-mail ⟨leonardobooks@mitpress.mit.edu⟩.

Sean Cubitt
Editor-in-Chief, Leonardo Book series

Leonardo Book Series Advisory Committee: Sean Cubitt, *Chair*; Michael Punt; Eugene Thacker; Anna Munster; Laura Marks; Sundar Sarrukai; Annick Bureaud

Doug Sery, *Acquiring Editor*
Joel Slayton, *Editorial Consultant*

Leonardo/International Society for the Arts, Sciences, and Technology
(ISAST)

Leonardo, the International Society for the Arts, Sciences, and Technology,
and the affiliated French organization Association Leonardo have two very
simple goals:

1. to document and make known the work of artists, researchers, and scholars interested in the ways that the contemporary arts interact with science and
technology and
2. to create a forum and meeting places where artists, scientists, and engineers
can meet, exchange ideas, and, where appropriate, collaborate.

When the journal *Leonardo* was started some forty years ago, these creative
disciplines existed in segregated institutional and social networks, a situation
dramatized at that time by the "Two Cultures" debates initiated by C. P.
Snow. Today we live in a different time of cross-disciplinary ferment, collaboration, and intellectual confrontation enabled by new hybrid organizations,
new funding sponsors, and the shared tools of computers and the Internet.
Above all, new generations of artist-researchers and researcher-artists are
now at work individually and in collaborative teams bridging the art, science,
and technology disciplines. Perhaps in our lifetime we will see the emergence
of "new Leonardos," creative individuals or teams that will not only develop a
meaningful art for our times but also drive new agendas in science and stimulate technological innovation that addresses today's human needs.

For more information on the activities of the Leonardo organizations and
networks, please visit our Web sites at ⟨http://www.leonardo.info/⟩ and
⟨http://www.olats.org⟩.

Roger F. Malina
Chair, Leonardo/ISAST

ISAST Governing Board of Directors: Martin Anderson, Michael Joaquin Grey,
Larry Larson, Roger Malina, Sonya Rapoport, Beverly Reiser, Christian Simm,
Joel Slayton, Tami Spector, Darlene Tong, Stephen Wilson

Preface

This collection of artist writings is a mix of personal memoir, digital poetics, spontaneous theory, fictional narrative, scholarly history, peer-to-peer conversations, and network-infused language art. It is also a playful and performative self-appropriation—a sampling of the writing traces that my creative self has left behind over the last fifteen years. I have come to realize that a creative self that precedes my own conscious thoughts and is already a manipulated version of itself as *something other* is *not really there*. At various times throughout the book, I refer to this *something other* as the "not-me"—as when I look at the work I have produced over the past fifteen years, focus on the various media platforms that this work gets distributed through, and think to myself, "That's just not me."

Isn't life funny that way? If it wasn't me, then who was it? And how on earth did I create this work when I clearly didn't know what I was doing? I don't necessarily answer that question directly in this book, but I do try to sketch, by way of example, one possible model of practice-based research for artists who are interested in taking advantage of the poetic license that comes with experimental creative writing. The writings contained herein are constantly remixing a highly selective group of electronic ideas that have been and are still forming around a cluster of prescient issues related to Net art, VJ/DJ culture, hypertext, avant-pop fiction, hactivism, new media theory, consciousness studies, and the like. This projective writing style is consistent with other artist theories of the recent past. These kinds of rhetorical drifts—

emblematic of an emerging generation of thought heavily indebted to the on-going history of consciousness—always seem to rise to the surface when new forms of art are being invented.

But more literal digital samplings and self-appropriations are also employed throughout this collection. For example, the penultimate work in the book ("What in the World Wide Web Is Happening to Writing?") contains the looping resonance of lines that come up in the articles, essays, and online columns that precede it and redeploys them to focus on some of the achievements of the *trAce* online network and the *trAce* exhibition I was curating while writing this text. The text appeared online at the *trAce* Web site, was featured online in different form at *Alt-X* and *Rhizome*, and made its way into print at the *American Book Review*. This is just one example of how electronic ideas get remixed over time, as do the texts that these ideas appear in and the various versions of the finished work that are then situated for different (although sometimes overlapping) audiences throughout the network.

Picasso once claimed that he didn't care whom he stole from as long as it wasn't himself. Well, I agree. I assume that it's really "not-me" who is writing these lines anyway, so I am thus able to sample and remix my own writing at will. I mention this because if you think you have read something in an academic remix or pseudo-autobiographical fiction work that sounds exactly like what you are reading in one of the Amerika Online essays located toward the end of the book, this is not an editorial oversight but a decision to let these works stand as they are. They help elucidate the fact that an artist's life, improvised thoughts, personal theories, and fictional narratives are all cut from the same cloth, especially when that artist fashions himself as a participant in an autopoietic network of threaded intellectual activity that I have come to call the *artificial intelligentsia*.

In addition to blurring the lines between digital poetics, new media fiction, artist memoir, and spontaneous theory, I hope *META/DATA* serves as an historical document of one artist's perspective on the emerging network culture that hit full steam in the 1990s. The collection is my take on the new modes of creative practice that grew out of this '90s network culture, particularly Net art, VJ culture, hypertext narrative and theory, blogging, and hactivism. Most of the early writings collected here are kept in the same form they were originally published in. Although with the benefit of hindsight I may have changed a few of the ideas contained in them, I am keeping them as-is for the sake of documentation. The two most recent writings, located in part I,

Spontaneous Theories, are extended-play versions as well as collage-styled mash-ups of the many keynote addresses I have given at media, art, literature, and creative industry festivals over ten years and five continents. These keynotes were composed as on-the-fly digressions within digressions and avoid conventional footnoting and referencing since the books, Web sites, and conversations I am using as source material were integrated into the work while traveling hundreds of thousands of miles and were often resourced from memory alone, which in the book I suggest is fictional and meant for spontaneous, unconscious remixing at the artist's will.

Throughout the book, you will encounter the kind of D-I-Y poetics usually associated with an experimental fiction writing style. In fact, part II, Distributed Fictions, is devoted to a selection of the distributed fictions I have been composing as part of my Net art lifestyle. These works show how Net art and VJ practice (and the research agendas that come with them) create ample opportunities for artists to lose themselves in mind-altering experiences that rarely get written about or discussed in more traditional art historical contexts. In this part, I tell tales that an academic remix or spontaneous theory just can't manage within the context of its limited parameters, even when those parameters are considerably loosened.

There's something exciting about watching the writing genres blur and feed off of each other. In many ways, all of the writings contained here, whether a peer-reviewed article for an academic journal or a free-form critifiction for an online art magazine, are bastardized variations of what is sometimes called the *personal essay*. In this case, the attempts conducted in the name of personal expenditure take into account the ways in which the artist is committed to developing a surplus of difference in his theories of an expanded concept of writing. These texts point to a parallel poetics that engages with what evolved over the course of a mini-era into an unexpected new media art practice. The so-called early history of Net art is now becoming part of documented art history, and this collection of artist writings can be read as the most recent iteration of that ongoing historical fiction.

In many ways, I am lucky that my interactive artwork appeared when both the mainstream art world and media outlets seemed to be waiting for it. Being a novelist and freelance writer before venturing into the digital unknown created opportunities for me to circulate the parallel poetics I was discovering while experimenting with new forms of Net art—and what better place to distribute these fresh Net art theories than the Net itself? At times, it felt like another form of black magic, where an intuitive measure of creative writing was being teleported to the electrosphere as a medium of both readiness potential and (art) market prophecy. The more I found this happening in my day-to-day life as a citizen of Boulder, Colorado, and a networked navigator connecting to cyberspace, the more I felt the urge to fictionalize the experience in a hypermediated way. This led to the production of *GRAMMATRON* and my commitment to use the World Wide Web to investigate the "consensual hallucination" of cyberspace for experimental composition, publication, exhibition, performance, marketing, and distribution.

Many provocative scholarly books have been published over the last few years that focus on developing useful conceptual frameworks for new media artists to consider when thinking through many of the issues a digital art practice engages with, but instead of creating a theoretical justification for everything I have done *after the fact*, I instead share with my readers whatever happened to be floating through my mind as I investigated these new forms of hypermediated storytelling, Net art curating, Web publishing, VJing, and spontaneous theorizing—*while I was making it up*. The writing itself is often improvisational, nomadic, and surfing on the elliptical edge of its own possibility. It at times relates more to an Allen Ginsberg chant or a Gertrude Stein loop text than a proper new media theory treatise that gets all of the jargon right and makes all of the politically correct points I once had to go out of my way to make if I expected to steal a base in front of the umpire. For example, you will come across many repetitions, sometimes to the point of mantra-like redundancy—not because I can't find my thesaurus but because I see the writing more as a multitrack, textual performance that has various notes, phrases, and loops repeatedly running throughout its composition. If I use a quote from an artist more than once, it's because that particular phrase strikes a chord with my urgent need to continue the free-flow jam session I am having with my writerly drift. If someone's name often appears as a source of collaboration, it's because the person is an artist or a writer who makes it a pleasure for me *to play* with the work as I process it.

The book is divided into six parts—Spontaneous Theories, Distributed Fictions, Academic Remixes, Image *Écriture*, Net Dialogues, and Amerika Online. Many writings are extensions of thoughts that grew out of addresses I have delivered at conferences and festivals, including Ciber@rt Bilbão 2004, Transmediale International Media Arts Festival (Berlin), Digital Arts and Culture (Bergen), the *trAce* incubation conference (Nottingham), the Adelaide Arts

Festival, the Sixteenth Annual Computers and Writing Conference (Fort Worth), the UNESCO World Summit Conference (Vienna), Digital Interconnection (Tokyo), the I Link Therefore I Am: Digital Design Literacies (A Research Symposium) (Melbourne), the Conference for the Council of Australasian Media Education Organization (Canberra), the Surf-Sample-Manipulate Lucerne Easter Festival, the Bath Literary Festival, the Overdose Festival (Rome), and the German Association of American Studies Conference (Freiburg).

Most of these writings have appeared in academic, art, literary, and computer journals and as chapters written for other books. I acknowledge these publications at the end of each separate work. The fact that these writings are collected over almost fifteen years means that the document as a whole is at times self-contradictory. It took great restraint on my part as the artist-writer not to change too many things. Besides, I have asked myself: Would I have written these works differently if I knew then what I know now? Well, if I knew then what I know now, I might have never made my way into this strange compositional field of media art. Besides, what you are about to read in these pages was not written by me, anyway (not the me I recognize), so why go back and pretty up some other figure's footprints in the sand when there is so much beach left to wander?

Mark Amerika
Bondi Beach, New South Wales
Kailua, Hawaii

Acknowledgments

Many friends and colleagues have influenced me with their targeted insights and personal working styles. From my slipstream literary network, there are the late Ron Sukenick and Kathy Acker, Ray Federman, Robert Coover, Larry McCaffery, Curt White, Doug Rice, Steve Katz, Bruce Sterling, Takayuki Tatsumi, John Shirley, Harry Polkinhorn, Joe Tabbi, Lance Olsen, Jeff Noon, Erik Belgum, Clarence Major, Terry Southern, Anne Burdick, Cary Wolfe, Pat Cadigan, Steve Shaviro, and Thomas Irmer.

Becoming actively engaged in the Net art and electronic literature scene has opened up my life to many wonderful minds, far too many to list here, but I would still like to mention Knut Mork Skagen, Eugene Thacker, Armin Medosch, Ken Wark, Alex Galloway, Matt Fuller, Giselle Beiguelman, Mark Tribe, John Simon, Tamas Banovich, G. H., Ricardo Dominguez, Doron Golan, Steve Dietz, Matt Mirapaul, Randall Packer, Mark Napier, Marisa Olson, Sue Thomas, Larry Rinder, Christiane Paul, You Minowa, Adi Blum, Andrew Chetty, Simon Mills, Dene Grigar, Angela Molina, Cynthia Haynes, Jan Holmevik, Christiane Heibach, Roberto Simanowski, Karen Wenz, Friedrich Block, Irina Aristarkhova, and Guna Nadarajan.

My dive into hypertext fiction and theory would not have been possible without the encouragement and pioneering work of Bob Arellano, George Landow, Michael Joyce, Mark Bernstein, Stuart Moulthrop, Jay Bolter, Adrienne Eisen, Rob Wittig, Jay Dillemuth, Alex Cory, Shelley Jackson, Tom

Meyers, and, once again, Robert Coover. I would also like to give my deepest thanks to Gregory Ulmer for having started me on this journey.

Every artist has a core group of friends who are there for them both locally and beyond. My Colorado homies include Nile Southern, Ken Fricklas, Danny Salazar, Andrew Currie, Rick Silva, Trace Reddell, John Vega, Jeff Williams, and Matt Samet.

I am also lucky in that my core group of local friends can also be found in Australia, and much of my artwork and writing was composed while living there. I have been fortunate to receive international fellowships at the Royal Melbourne Institute of Technology and the University of Technology, Sydney. This book would not have been possible without the support I received at both those institutions. For their warm generosity and friendship, I would like to thank Adrian Miles, Anna Farago, Lauren Murray, Megan Heyward, Norie Neumark, Darren Tofts, Melinda Rackham, Maria Miranda, Brad Miller, Mike Leggett, Lisa Gye, Anna Munster, Troy Innocent, Daniel Palmer, Alessio Cavallaro, Antoanetta Ivanova, Stephen Jones, Chris Caines, Greg Ferris, Kate Richards, Sara Miller, Derek Kreckler, Teri Hoskin, Linda Marie Walker, Julianne Pierce, Josie Starrs, Leon Cmielewski, Linda Carroli, Trevor Smith, Josephine Wilson, Cam Merton, Brendan Palmer, Hazel Smith, Warren Burt, and Roger Dean who, having introduced me to the concept of hyperimprovisation, opened up a can of worms that will never get back where it belongs. My first trip to Australia was in 1998 as an invited keynote speaker to the Adelaide Arts Festival. For that I would like to thank Amanda McDonald Crowley and Francesca da Rimini.

My most recent and current collaborations in expanded forms of cinema, created with Jutta Wolfert, Chad Mossholder, Nile Southern, and Scott Elliot Mann, are making it easy to put this book and the mini-era it documents behind me. Friends like James Herman, Dave Jameson, Frieder Nake, Susi Grabowski, and Tjark Ihmels are always there when you need them and have taught me the art of altruistic behavior.

I would also like to acknowledge all of my colleagues at my home base at the University of Colorado at Boulder, particularly Deborah Haynes, Mark Addison, Erika Doss, Jeanne Quinn, David Slayden, Michael Lightner, Jim Johnson, Garrison Roots, Lisa Tamaris-Becker, Bobby Schnabel, David Schaal, John Hopkins, Joel Swanson, the ATLAS Institute, and the Dean's Fund for Excellence.

I offer my highest gratitude and thanks to the MIT Press and all of the people who make the Leonardo series a reality, especially Doug Sery, Roger Malina, Joel Slayton, and Steve Wilson.

And finally, my secret weapon: the always supportive FN.

This book is dedicated to all of you and everyone else who has made this trip possible.

Spontaneous Theories

No one thinks academically. People just pretend they do. They force themselves to think like that. Academic style is a result of effort (or, if you prefer, of mental discipline), so it is therefore a result of a first thought. The academic is a second thought, because it is a translation of a first thought. It is not spontaneous, but deliberate. The choice between the academic style and my own is therefore a half-choice: I will speak spontaneously, or I will choose "academicism."

—Vilém Flusser, "Essay"

Cyberpsychogeography (An Aimless Drift in Twenty Digressions)

1

Writing takes on the shape of somnambulistic codework as soon as I connect myself to the digital apparatus I compose with. Once it is turned on and I am plugged into this live, creative act of composition, there is nothing to stop my naked words from running across an empty screenal interface that my body willingly loses itself in. From the perspective of narrative, I see my body becoming this free-flowing sensation of *otherworldly drift* as it moves out toward an imaginary horizon, a nonplace place where the first-person (second-person, omniscient) narrator is always unreliable, a cyberpsychogeographical jockey teleporting his unconscious maneuverings throughout the wide-open spaces of the wild wild west (WWW) forever in search of clicking connectivity.

And yet this naked body of words just now starting to play out its creative potential is not really my own. It's part of something much larger than me—some kind of dynamic, shape-shifting intersubjectivity where I am always losing sight of myself as I improvisationally interact with The Network and, without thinking about it, intuitively manipulate the pulse of Time (*as if such a thing as Time could actually exist*).

Time can seem totally irrelevant when writing out words from inside the body. Yesterday I was in Colorado preparing for a long trip, and by the time my plane took off it was evening, Mountain Standard Time. But what makes it

standard, especially given my own natural tendency to refute time itself by losing myself in timeless acts of creative composition? When I land in Australia
less than twenty-four hours later, somehow *two* days will have passed, and I'll
be having a soy latte and organic blueberry muffin for breakfast at a café in
North Bondi Beach. Sleeping on the plane, my body will write itself out in
some elaborate dreamtime script that continuously improvises other lives for
me to role-play in, and after the morning coffee and muffin at the beautiful
beach Down Under, I will intuitively come to realize that there is, in fact, a
sensible regularity to my self-imposed lifestyle discipline, even though I occasionally feign a kind of *occupational difference.*

For example, in Boulder, where I supposedly live and work, I go to sleep
around midnight. If everything is the way it should be, I will wake up the
next morning around eight or nine, spend the day and night making art (*living life*), and then, by the time midnight falls again, aimlessly drift back into
the kind of alternative states of mind that, as a romantic poet-dreamer (artist-
researcher), help me pay the bills. Having said that, there can be no question
that these dreamlike, aimless drifts happen periodically throughout my waking life as well, and I can't help but wonder if this is not what I, as an artist-
researcher, am particularly talented at—that is, finding ways to teleport my
turned on and plugged-in body into states of altered consciousness *no matter
what time it is*, locating my creative potential and its complementary poetic
thrust wherever necessary, just so long as everything is defamiliarized and relatively timeless, which then makes it easy for me to invent on-the-fly imagistic
events never before imagined.

Perhaps this is what it means *to become an artist-medium nurturing the field
conditions for my creative potential to unconsciously play in.* These trance narratives that float through my body as I sleep or write or navigate my various
digital art personas through the cyberpsychogeographical regions of The Network are an essential part of this everyday life I am constantly launching my
asymmetrical phrasings and rephrasings in. This is the experiential space, full
of rapidly reconfigured sense data, that I feel most at home in and will do anything in my power to have access to at all costs. I know I'm in the process of
activating its full readiness potential when my internal superclock makes me
feel pregnant with the synchronicity of everything happening right now, in
realtime, although my intuition tells me this is not realtime at all but something that resembles realtime even though I know it's totally fake. It's what I
would call *unrealtime.*

The feeling of living in unrealtime is one that takes the artist-medium beyond improvisation or living on the edge of forever. It's something more akin to hyperimprovisational Life Style Practice, an intuitively driven creative class struggle that cannot be captured in any media-specific analysis. What it needs is *social network synthesis* that breaks away from the prying need to always understand itself and, instead, refocuses all component energies on exploring its own creative/readiness potential. Think of it as writing out the anticipatory moment of surging creativity as it projects itself from inside my body in a perpetual state of hyperintuition or what the Situationists might have called *avant-garde presence*—one that TAKES PLACE in the revolution of everyday life.

This avant-garde presence that circulates throughout my day-to-day life feels both OF its time AND ahead of its time. Just like the phenomenon in the 1980s that we called *cyberpunk* explored imaginary worlds simultaneously happening in the present as well as the immediate future, this avant-garde presence enables me to operate in the machinations of the working world and its preset itinerary of bureaucratic functions, even as I imagine myself proactively engaged in a yet-to-be-invented future-tense practice that resists the contemporary situation I am always positioning myself to move beyond. But there are still other worlds or states of mind where I work or, once I'm there, play, and they tend to lose all of their presets. In these alternative spaces, I no longer have to worry about what it would be like to become that other thing that wants to bureaucratize me. Instead of designing my more intuitive, internalized, readiness potential so that it consciously plays to the regimen of always being ON time while answering TO corporate, university, or otherwise bureaucratic callings, I customize its settings and preferences so that my state of avant presence is playing IN time and feels *more engaged than ever before.*

Think of what we used to call a mad scientist who is now envisioned as a fully tilted artist-researcher swimming in the intersubjective waters of the fluid intelligentsia—or the artist-researcher as a *pseudo-autobiographical work in progress.* This is extreme role-playing, a gig that was MADE for me, where after years of nonstop dress rehearsal, I am now situated as the perfect person to play myself *as is*, although the pseudo-autobiographical work in progress cannot help himself and is always turning the role of the *as is* into the always premiering *as if.* Role-playing the *as if* allows the transmitting nerve centers of my processual image filters to initialize a performative thrust of narrative momentum that resists the machinations of Time itself so that I may continue distributing my many digital flux personas. These digital flux personas are a multiverse of possibility and are experienced as something else entirely different from what I thought I was when I started the day, when I woke up in the familiar environment that I, for lack of better, call home. Home for me is not really the place I live in (Colorado) or the temporary autonomous zone I create for myself while living in Sydney. Rather, *it's the day that never was* and that I am constantly losing myself in as I construct new digital art personas to disperse throughout the compositional field I operate in.

Many times these digital flux personas—which I role-play via e-mail, Web chat, spontaneous Net art creations, VJ performances, mobile blogging, and the like—often overlap and even converge into the one digital flux persona that my audience has tagged with the easy-to-remember name Mark Amerika. To me, this digital flux persona that goes by the name Mark Amerika intuitively becomes an indeterminate loci of readiness potential that *precedes* consciousness while transponding the fluid metamorphosis of a radical *inter*subjectivity to the point where there is no longer an *I* or a place to call home. There is only a networked SPACE of flows for my creative self to wander nomadically through as I invent my life as an artist at this particular moment in time—as if there could even *be* a particular moment in time. Think about it: it just passed us by. Was it ever really there in the first place? We have already disproved that. What I mean to say (as I begin to remix all of my lines of transcontinental flight into a running trajectory of naked words leaving their digital traces on the forever expanding magic writing pad) is that this process of metamediumistic self-invention taking place in an always emergent, interconnected space of flows can mean only one thing. I am under the influence of self-induced jet lag—or what I have come to call *jet-lag consciousness*. This is a consciousness that no longer depends on flying to different countries around the world to be experienced and can be achieved anywhere at anytime.

2

Jet-lag consciousness expands the playing field for my imagination to fictionalize its avant-garde presence in. It happens not as a result of sci-fi time tripping but as timeless tripping or technomadic wandering. It's all about getting into the ZONE. As an altered state of *being becoming something else*, it could be packaged as the navigational mantra of a Net artist drifting into various cyberpsychogeographical ZONES that, in this artist poetics, come as a set of pseudo-autobiographical fragments or cleverly manipulated memory digressions that sometimes double as metafictional musings on the life of a digital flux persona who goes by various names including Mark Amerika, Abe Golam, VJ Persona, Maker/Faker, or Digital Thoughtographer.

The improvised dream-writing sequences that populate this always in-process digital poetics are in many ways problematized states of being where a functional data processor—the proprioceptive body conducting its customized energy routines—creatively filters and indexes whatever information (sense data) it finds relevant at any given moment. Think of it as experiential tagging or Experiential Mock-Up Language (XML). In this regard, everything I am writing here is both an improvisatory narrative performance exported through my artist-theory filters as well as my attempt to dig into the Real of circumstantial happenstance. And it just so happens that digging into the Real is itself circumstantial or, in the networked space of flows, requires an unpremeditated trek through a vast landscape of imaginary otherness we are apt to call Unreal. For, as a good friend who has since passed away recently wrote me in an e-mail message: "Without the unreal, there is no Real."

3

I take this notion of "Without the unreal, there is no Real" to heart. As a digital artist committed to expanding the concept of writing while tapping into the fictional unconscious that precedes my every conscious act, this digging into the Real and its inevitable relationship with radical states of shape-shifting intersubjectivity are impossible to ignore. One thing I am sure of as I continue this ongoing process of experimental identity construction is that there is an all-too-human tendency to lose sight of who it is I am while teleporting my writerly texts through this networked space of flows that the cyberpunk novelist William Gibson, in his novel *Neuromancer*, referred to as the "consensual hallucination of cyberspace." And yet is not losing sight of who it is I am while simultaneously charging my potential language eruptions to the utmost possible degree enough to challenge the intimidation tactics of the ever-leering philosophical void?

Writing these naked words during a transcontinental flight that crosses the international date line and loses an entire day I will never experience in my lifetime helps accentuate the fact that the philosophical void is my friend, my spiritual guide, my one and only intellectual adviser. Without the vanishing point looming large somewhere over *there*, shiny bright with its concomitant reminder that all of my imaginary lines of flight are bound to converge in a catastrophic disappearance of the real, there would be no anticipated endgame triggering my immediate need to make art. Meanwhile, the increase in the total number of years my body aspires to survive through is always on the rise, and without that knowledge nudging me into further acts of creative composition, there can be no movement toward constant renewal and strategic resistance.

But why is that so? You would think that these eventual disappearances would make the artist rebel in the most noncomformist way possible and that I would stop making art. Is it because this consensual hallucination I operate in has already cashed in on my innate human tendency to live in perpetual denial? Perhaps my body is being washed away by the endless flows of data that permeate the very air I breathe and, a willing victim, I simply have fallen in love with it all. In fact, I must be totally swimming it, like never before. Who do I thank for such mammoth historical opportunity?

We consent to this shared hallucination in other contexts besides computer-mediated cyberspace. This flight I am on started yesterday in Colorado (but was it really yesterday?) and will eventually end up in Sydney, Australia. Somehow, somewhere, I will lose an entire day of my life. Somewhere, somehow, that day will simply not exist—and yet it does exist. People will be born that day, and many people will die—and yet for me that day will disappear like no other day. I want to know *where* it went. *Where* is that space of time? *What* is it?

How does this time shifting relate to my thinking about cyberspace—about writing cyberspace, navigating cyberspace, imagining or even imaging cyberspace? How does it affect the way I might think about writing, navigating, or imaging a new kind of language—cyberpsychogeographical, *in nature*, architectonic in its technoetic emergence? How does this potentially fertile field of poetic composition (which simultaneously exists but does not exist within any standard time) relate to that *non*place place that the French poet Stéphane Mallarmé speaks of when he says "Nothing will have taken place but the place"? (Appropriately enough for a spontaneous approach to living out one's life as a theory-to-be, this quote comes from his work "A Throw of the Dice," where he philosophically speculates that "a throw of the dice will never abolish chance.") I want to know how this nonplace place links to these dreamy, interactive states of *being becoming something else* that I find myself continually investigating while conducting virtual art performances in both cyberspace and sleep. Or given my background as a creative writer, I want to know how it relates to scripting cyberspace as a potential dreamworld of coded composition. This is how we might think about scripting languages that inform behavioral performance or an expanded concept of writing that includes all manner of resonance between programming codes, semiotic codes, genetic codes, behavioral codes, and what The Spy in the House of Love might call secret codes.

Is tapping into our readiness potential in the nonplace place an attempt to crack open the secret codes of creative composition, or is it more about stylizing our creative practices so that they can poetically encrypt even *more* secret code? Both/and? Perhaps the Good Doctor (any Ph.D. will do) can answer. Is there a Virtual Chora in the House?

4

According to 1960s' Situationist philosophy (which grew out of the writings and actions of a group of European artists and thinkers, mostly Parisians, including the movement leader, Guy Debord), collaboratively generated situations intervene in mainstream media discourse and cut into the cult of attention-grabbing spectacle. In developing a resistance movement and an art-research practice that would successfully work against this society of the spectacle, these theorists used the term *psychogeography*—that is, "the study of the precise effects of geographical setting, consciously managed or not, acting directly on the mood and behavior of the individual." As part of their philosophical program, the Situationists suggested that one way to experiment with a psychogeographical *premise* would be to investigate *drifting* as an experimental mode of behavior—that is, to hastily mobilize the body through varied environments, to be drawn by the attractions of the terrain and the encounters found there, and to see how these experiences alter ways of behaving and consequently seeing the world. By activating the body and its natural tendency toward movement, affect, and sensation within the urban environment, the Situationists seemed to suggest that the city is a kind of code—an architectonic language of structure whose concrete jungles try to dam up our movement even though we ourselves are leaking. So why not spill our many digital flux personas into the gutters and existential haunts of the meandering streets?

The Situationists referred to this aimless drifting as *dérive*. Debord has theorized about the *dérive*:

If chance plays an important role in *dérives*, this is because the methodology of psychogeographical observation is still in its infancy. But the action of chance is naturally conservative and in a new setting tends to reduce everything to habit or to an alternation between a limited number of variants. Progress means breaking through fields where chance holds sway by creating new conditions more favorable to our purposes. We can say, then, that the randomness of a *dérive* is fundamentally different from that of the stroll but also that the first psychogeographical attractions discovered by *dérivers* may tend to fixate them around new habitual axes, to which they will constantly be drawn back.

In other words, customizing your aimless drifts within certain loose parameters can be addictive, and creating new lifestyle algorithms that challenge your set ways of thinking gets more difficult with every successive wander. Think of the *dérive* as metatourism or an intentional homelessness that is performed out of philosophical necessity but that is part of a research practice that may not always give itself over to chance occurrence. And yet, as we have already stated, a throw of the dice never abolishes chance, and once you turn a corner and, as if by accident, encounter one of those illuminating eureka moments, you will probably program yourself to create similar parameters the next time you set out to power your drift within any given compositional field. For artists, this is especially dangerous because it means that you may find yourself going down what appears to be the right alley but ends up being the all-too-easy shortcut where you continually rob yourself of the chance to reach your full potential. The question is: how do you continually challenge your intuition to spur on the unconscious player living inside your body—the one whose creative actions open up the compositional field for you to improvise and lose yourself in, like never before?

The idea is to avoid getting tackled or brought down by the defensive posturing of the mundane consumer culture. As Steven Best and Douglas Kellner write in their essay "Debord and the Postmodern Turn,"

In contrast to the stupor of consumption, Debord and the Situationists champion active, creative, and imaginative practice, in which individuals create their own "situations," their own passionate existential events, fully participating in the production of everyday life, their own individuality, and, ultimately, a new society. Thus, to the passivity of the spectator they counterpoise the activity of the radical subject which constructs its own everyday life against the demands of the spectacle (to buy, consume, conform, etc.). The concept of the spectacle therefore involves a distinction between passivity and activity and consumption and production, condemning passive consumption of spectacle as an alienation from human potentiality for creativity and imagination.

And yet for contemporary digital artists whose experimentally constructed flux personas link to a pseudo-autobiographical work in progress forever on the cusp of composing new iterations of poetic *being becoming something else*, what does it really mean to participate fully in the production of their own individuality? The radical subjectivity that the Situationists bet the farm on somehow left out the essential *otherness* of the utopian playing field they desperately wanted to play on. If, as Gibson suggests in his cyberpunk novel, the hallucination is consensual, then we have to assume that it takes at least two to tango. The Situationists suggested that three was the perfect number of participants for a valuable *dérive*. And yet as we know, the Society of the Spectacle gave way to the Me Decade only to be followed by even more supercharged spectacle. Perhaps we have yet to finally experience our Last Tango in Paris. Perhaps the situationists were just buttering us up for the ultimate letdown. Perhaps the only way OUT is by triggering the creative potential of the spectacular Not-Me.

5

Lately, as both a nomadically wandering Net artist and touring VJ (or visual jockey), I have been experimenting with the concept of drifting (*dérive*), both as a fluid situation in which I traverse various urban environments where I capture my digital video source material and as a cyberspatial activity where I partake of a Gibsonian "consensual hallucination" by surfing the associational web of trails available on the World Wide Web. For the digital flux persona who is nomadically digging into the Real, the Net itself becomes a situational terrain in which to study the precise effects of navigating the networked space of flows and participating in a meaningful artificial intelligentsia. The Net also creates an experiential research environment that enables artists (1) to see how these navigations and engagements can be consciously managed by acting directly on the mood and behavior of the artist and the work they produce *while* drifting and (2) to investigate if what Kellner and Best call the "alienation from human potentiality for creativity and imagination" can be counterpoised via a hyperimprovisationally constructed Life Style Practice (LSP) that emerges from the creative potential of the unconscious and drifts into the many compositional playing fields that await our unique performances-to-be. Here, the term *hyperimprovisational* (which I borrow from the sound artist and theorist Roger Dean and then manipulate for my own uses) refers to an intuitive, ongoing jam session between nomadic Net artists and the new media technologies they are forever connected to as part of their collaborative prosthetic aesthetic.

This Life Style Practice of the nomadic Net artist cum touring VJ, high on the mobilization of a cyberpsychogeographical drift that always plays with my mind, allows me to use my digital video camera as both as an image-capturing device as well as a writing instrument that creates imagistic captions to my thoughts, many of which I spontaneously write down in the form of diagnostic notes or what I like to call *action scripting*—an evolving digital poetics that script into being certain actions and behaviors that characterize the formal possibilities of the creative spaces I happen to be passing through. I adhere to these action scripts as poetic ephemera, digital sketching, and projective choreography, where every move is part of some holistic body-brain-apparatus dance with the intersubjective playing field I am continuously jamming with. Often, they come across as visible attempts at innovating an artist theory in the form of writerly texts.

You are reading some of these textual traces right now, and wouldn't it be great if they too would take on the flavor of aimlessly wandering through the networked space of flows as part of an experimental mode of writing/drifting? What if they were constructed as an alternative artist theory that is meant to trace the movement of an artist medium that unconsciously mobilizes its avant presence through a variety of subject-oriented environments while *at once* being drawn by the attractions of the intellectual terrain it is navigating through? How do I do *that*, I wonder, while still maintaining an engaged hypertextual consciousness that puts out its worldly tentacles feeling around for whatever potential links or associations they may find there? Ezra Pound once suggested that artists were the antennae of society. My sense is that nomadic Net artists, who are wholly immersed in the digital flux persona of a drifting Life Style Practice, must always have their antennae out and activated, picking up signals from the emergent artificial intelligentsia they depend on for their cultural survival. In this regard, LSP is the new LSD, and considering that, as Gibson suggested, the hallucination is a consensual experience, Net artists really have no choice but to activate themselves IN it if they hope to build on their lucid, digital dreamwork always *in process.*

6

Recently, one of my Net art, VJ personas was touring through parts of Asia and using a camcorder to capture the neon nighttime scenery of the streets I was traversing. As I hastily passed through the varied urban and ambient environments in Tokyo, Hong Kong, and Singapore, my camcorder voraciously capturing the image *écriture* that surrounded me, I occasionally turned to my PDA and improvised spontaneous action scripts. One of these action scripts was entitled "R.E.M.ix" and began as follows:

The Body Is an Image-Making Machine.
It Filters Information.
It Creates Dreams, Memories, and Spontaneous Situations Made out of Images.
The Images Are Created in the Body as They Respond to Images outside the Body.
The Images Change as the Body Moves.
These Movement-Images Resonate with Dreams, Memories, and Spontaneous Situations Made out of Images.
This Means That Spontaneous Situations Made out of Images Can Be Dreams or Active Memories and Vice-Versa.
For the VJ-Hacktivist Who Inmixes the Real with the Unreal, a Live Performance Can Be Experienced as the Memory of a Dream Composed of Spontaneous Situations Made out of Images.
Writing Out the Intuitive Phrasing of an Image Écriture that Always Drifts in Its Revolutionary Aimlessness, the Philosophical Scribe Becomes a VJ Artist.
The VJ Artist Is a Metafictionally Charged Philosophical Scribe that Uses Subjective Plug-Ins to Manipulate Image-Information and in so Doing Begins the Process of Myth-Making Oftentimes in a Narrative Context Even when the So-Called Narrative Itself Is an Antinarrative that Works against Conventional Storytelling and Standard Rhetorical Spin-Control.

After writing these initial notes, I asked myself a series of follow-up questions that I imagine are at the nexus of my VJ practice as it encounters a gnawing theoretical fiction that keeps scratching at the inside of my skull, namely:

What is the relationship between image, memory, dream, event, process, and body?
And why are my VJ performances always *telling the story* of a digital flux persona who is constantly processing image-information?
Does this mean what you are reading now is also a kind of VJ performance of processed and manipulated imagery but dressed in fictionally constructed poetics clothing?
Where is this VJ artist (digital art persona) located, and will we, in fact, ever SEE the body of the artist processing these images? (Note to the field of experimental neuroscience: You can't scan my radical subjectivity. Only I can release it as a kind of

spontaneous formal projection from deep inside my creative unconscious, and I am a fiction writer who translates his experience *as* he experiences it, improvisationally manipulating my sense data via a wide array of imaginary filters always at my disposal.) Given the above, what does it take to create a moving image of what it means to dream or have an active memory so that it doesn't look like the obvious—a video situation made out of live-action footage?

How do these VJ mixes create an active fictional memory for this digital flux persona who is always processing images?

Is it true that this fictional memory always takes place in the present and not as a record or reflection—that is, can a hyperimprovisationally constructed fictional memory take place in realtime?

For that matter, can *anything* take place in realtime?

Just the idea of a hyperimprovisationally constructed fictional memory would seem to challenge any notion of realtime. But then again, what are our options when trying to circumscribe the Now in a hyperintuitive state of unconscious playing like the one we associate with the white-hot act of creative composition? And if it does not take place in realtime, then when? Unrealtime?

And finally, what does this say about intersubjectivity and the fact that this writerly text, also the result of a hyperimprovisational jam between an artist and a laptop computer, is another way of enabling you to read my mind?

It is at times like these that I once again think of the term *hallucination*—not as in a drug-induced hallucination where someone sees something that is not there but as in recent research in the psychology of perception where we imagine hallucination as something that proprioceptive poets, releasing their unconscious aesthetic forms, actually CREATE as part of a holistic, body-brain achievement. And as a VJ who constructs nomadic narratives in this timeless time of the nonplace place where aimless drifting is the philosophical equivalent of casting the die to never abolish chance, what kind of connections can I begin to make between live image mixing, fictional memories, (un)realtime dreams, and situational hallucinations that the embodied mind (with its technological attachments—its prosthetic devices) actually CREATES when it sees? And finally, given the fact that my prosthetic devices are now attached to my body as it navigates the cyberpsychogeographical environment in aesthetic wanderlust, what does it mean to have a hyperimprovised *body-brain-apparatus* achievement?

For some reason, this reminds me of meeting somebody for the first time who out of the blue asks me, "What do you do for a living?" I want to say, "I am a time-tripper."

But usually I'll just say I'm a writer. Or an artist. Or a professor. Or even a VJ.

7

I have referred to this strange, cyberpsychogeographical space that my digital flux persona drifts through as being fueled by an artificial intelligentsia—by an Internetworked intelligence that consists of all of the linked data being distributed in cyberspace at any given time and that is powered by artistic and intellectual agents remixing the flow of contemporary thought. The computer scientist Douglas Engelbart refers to this artificial intelligentsia as *collective IQ* (consensual hallucination?), where *intelligence quotient* or *IQ* is used as a generic synonym for intelligence and not as in its original meaning as a MEASURE of one's intelligence. For me, too, it's less about measuring intelligence and more about tracing the self-organizing movement of the cyberpsychogeographical environment itself and nurturing the cultivation of new forms of art and speculative knowledge. For my own research, these new forms of art and speculative knowledge manifest themselves as digital flux personas playing out technoetic performances in intersubjective space. These emergent forms of knowledge are often cleverly camouflaged as process-oriented experiences that model themselves (that word again) as creative research collaborations. Artists (digital flux personas) hyperimprovise a jam session between new media technologies and proactively engaged states of mind that enable us to explore consciousness more thoroughly and imagine new forms of creative mindshare where the artificial intelligentsia participates in a peer-to-peer network culture that serves as the operating force in an idealized gift economy.

This peer-to-peer network culture—in which digital flux personas create on-the-fly remixes out of all kinds of distributed media fictions being invented by the Net artists themselves—influences the ever-morphing artificial intelligentsia that is continuously shape-shifting its avant presence in this consensual hallucination we call *cyberspace*. The potential Net effects of this participatory performance are felt through all manner of feedback loops. For the nomadic Net artist and VJ, the effects often come in the form of invitations to perform, to exhibit, to party, to culture jam, to publish artist theories, to party some more. The artificial intelligentsia that the nomadic Net artist actively participates in serves a useful function by forming a new mode of collaboratively generated knowledge as action that requires a strategy that (like the narrative momentum it inevitably feeds off of) unfolds over time. But in this case, a simultaneous and multilinear time is invented as an itinerant context for multiple and hybridized flux personas to circulate within.

8

When I was creating *FILMTEXT*, the third part of my Net art trilogy, I filtered my digital poetics through a concept character I call the Digital Thoughtographer. This alien other (what in the days of novel publishing I might have called my *alter ego*), practiced a new form of art called, appropriately, *digital thoughtography*. In an e-mail exchange with the contemporary art curator Jane Marsching, who was arranging to include my Net artwork *FILMTEXT 2.0* in an exhibition called Blur of the Otherworldly: Contemporary Art, Technology, and the Paranormal, she asked me, "What is digital thoughtography?" to which I responded as follows:

The term *thoughtography*, it ends up, comes from a paranormal story about a bellhop named Ted Serios who could imagine images onto film. He would think hard about the image, and then it would somehow create an imprint on film. The Digital Thoughtographer in *FILMTEXT* also plays with this possibility but is narrativized in a different way, as a kind of alien creature/visitor from another realm who is now "capturing" digital images through his "thoughtographical apparatus." These images are then filtered into his imagination, where he sees this near-future world that he exists in for what it really is: a postapocalyptic media wasteland to which he must respond. His responses are abstract—image loops, codework texts, creepy sounds, voice messengers, etc. Think of William Burroughs and his "language is a virus" concept and his attempt to change the brutal effects of media language by cutting into and altering consciousness. If the DT sounds like he's something of an artist, it's because he is— something of an artist. A paranormal other evolving spontaneous new ways of seeing and processing media information. As an artist, he tends to take on human form. Or at least his shadow does.

Jane was already on to this and was including some of Ted Serios's work in the exhibition.

My nomadic Net art and VJ research into digital thoughtography, the artificial intelligentsia, and the drift through various cyberpsychogeographical border zones are, of course, *intentional* and point to another question I have been asking myself lately: *what happens to intention when artists or authors become part of an intersubjective online collaboration that is being processed in an idealized gift economy and they allow their work to become freely available through the networked space of flows?* For me, the answer has to be more than a sci-fi representation of human agency that plays out its fantasies of a pseudo-utopian cyberculture that has created the ultimate peer-to-peer network of artist-engineer-researchers operating in a dreamworld of fluid intersubjectivity. It has to attach itself to a real-life body (of work) that continually speculates on new forms of knowledge as part of a poetic process that is continuously digging into the Real.

Not that we can't dream or that using our new media technologies and evolving codes to create alternative worlds is a necessarily futile task. Hardly. Consider how far we have already come over the last sixty years since Vannevar Bush first wrote his important essay "As We May Think" in 1945. Bush, the straight and narrow MIT scientist who developed a somewhat utopian vision of peer-to-peer networking culture powered by artificial memory devices that would creatively link a distributed intelligentsia, was succinct in his appraisal of the situation:

The human mind...operates by association. With one item in its grasp, it snaps instantly to the next that is suggested by the association of thoughts, in accordance with some intricate web of trails carried by the cells of the brain. It has other characteristics, of course; trails that are not frequently followed are prone to fade, items are not fully permanent, memory is transitory. Yet the speed of action, the intricacy of trails, the detail of mental pictures, is awe-inspiring beyond all else in nature.

Back in the late 1980s and early 1990s, without knowing who Vannevar Bush was, I began exploring some of these issues in both of my experimental, avant-pop novels entitled *The Kafka Chronicles* (1993) and *Sexual Blood* (1995), and soon after beginning graduate school at Brown University in 1995 (during which time I attended the MIT Media Lab's fiftieth anniversary celebration of Bush's famous essay), I began further developing my then in-process, first-generation Web-based hypertext entitled *GRAMMATRON* (which I started writing in 1993, began to build into a multimedia narrative space for network distribution in late 1995, and officially released on the WWW in May 1997). A lot has happened in the growing field of experimental digital narrative since I first released *GRAMMATRON* in the spring of 1997, and I now look back at these experimental novels and hypertexts as the perfect media for initially exporting my various flux personas. By exporting my various *digital* flux personas through networked narrative environments, I am able to conduct hyperimprovisational, technoetic writing performances and further investigate the kind of fluid, creative thought processes (spontaneous theories) that can be developed while tapping into their just-in-time readiness potential as it asynchronously jams with the ongoing writerly text their body of thought keeps distributing. Expanding the concept of writing so that it becomes an emergent form of social science-fiction playing in a spontaneous and multilinear time means first of all learning how to excite the unconscious neural mechanisms that trigger your do-it-yourself "ideogrammic-experiential" hallucinations into screenal space. As Allen Ginsberg once said, this all takes place "physiologically in the body" as a kind of spasm, one that does not, at least initially, depend on technology for its delivery.

For me, the technology has become almost invisible even as I cannot help but acknowledge its presence in my spontaneous acts of creation. If, as Ludwig Wittgenstein suggests, the self is grammatical, then the semantic software that the self is being filtered through is more a stylistic choice than a deterministic behavior. To me, using various transmedial software applications as a preferred structural device is akin to the way that, say, writing an argumentative, academic paper on Deleuzian brain disorders and how they lend themselves to schizophrenic walks in the park is also a kind of structural device that one chooses to use as they begin to situate their designer content. Having exported my own creative, writerly self (my digital flux personas) through a vast array of technological filters informs my *every next move* in such a way that I always see my new projects as an exciting, if not difficult, challenge to reinvent my grammatical self within the context of whatever new narrative conditions I may be operating in at any given moment (as if there could be a given moment: did we already acknowledge that?). *The key thing is to be aware that I will be training myself to activate my unconscious readiness potential, even though, during the actual performance, I myself will be unaware of what is being created in unrealtime.* Perhaps this is what it means to lose one's self in (writerly) flow. At a certain point, I can expand the concept of writing so that all of my (writerly) flow is being exported through all manner of technological filters—dynamic links, Photoshop, Java, Flash animation, VJ performance, podcasts, streaming audio, high-definition digital film, or the combined languages of multimedia messaging and mobile blogging, to name a few of the trendy options at my disposal today.

This reminds me of something another artist-researcher named Vito Acconci once said in his essay "Steps into Performance (and Out)":

If I specialize in a medium, then I would be fixing a ground for myself, a ground I would have to be digging myself out of, constantly, as one medium was substituted for another—so then instead of turning toward "ground" I would shift my attention and turn to "instrument," I would focus on myself as the instrument that acted on whatever ground was available.

What he is saying is quite simple, and yet it is something that tends to be overlooked in the rush to keep up with the latest developments in technology—namely, *the artist* is the medium or instrument, and the networked space of flows *play* this instrument to facilitate the development of creative compositions.

9

When I reread Vannevar Bush's words in "As We May Think"—when he says "trails that are not frequently followed are prone to fade, items are not fully permanent, memory is transitory. Yet the speed of action, the intricacy of trails, the detail of mental pictures, is awe-inspiring beyond all else in nature"—I try to imagine what Bush must have been thinking in those pre-Internet times. Why did he feel compelled to put a utopian spin on practical scientific applications that essentially anticipated the coming of the graphical-user-interface (GUI)-inflected World Wide Web?

These kinds of thoughts roll through my mind in parallel to many other threads of thought, especially as I try to imagine (1) how the emergence of the social, political, and artistic upheavals of the early 1960s must have effected the open-to-experimentation mind of the young computer scientist Ted Nelson, who, under the influence of Bush, Douglas Engelbart, and the literary precursors who inhabit his Xanadu dream, eventuated the concepts of hypertext and hypermedia and (2) how these developments historically parallel the Situationist tendency to psychogeographically drift through the urban landscape of Paris as if it were an associational web of trails that would alter behavior *and* thinking and (3) given my background as both a writer and publisher of postmodern literature, how these parallel developments of hypertext and Situationist *dérive* link to the digressionary and visually experimental novels of all of those wild metafictionists who also ran similar multilinear experiments in novel form during the same era (the 1960s and early 1970s)—writers like Julio Cortázar, Robert Coover, Ronald Sukenick, Italo Calvino, Maurice Roche, Madeline Gins, Raymond Federman, and Marc Saporta, whose subversive lingo shamanism and open-mindedness to the visual composition of an evolving architectonic narrative space *in novel form* is meant to both provoke a self-aware intervention into our conventional reading practices as well as critically apprehend the political act of creating formally innovative artwork that is at once narrative *and* rhetoric, a kind of ongoing persuasive discourse that, remixing conversations I have had with Sukenick and Federman, can at times come across as illogical, stylistic, impulsive, rhizomatic, enervating, poetic, fluxlike, and even playgiaristic, hyperimprovisational, and makeshift as a way to locate the prophetic qualities of spontaneous writing.

This is just one web of associations informing one version of the story. There are endless versions of this hypermediated story, and the utopian dream has always been to let them all live at once—a simultaneous and continuous fusion, ready for immediate remix, reinterpretation, and virtual republishing in the big Literary Machine, a space where planetary Net artists spin their own web in this Borgesian labyrinth of the networked psyche. I personally call this space of engaging co-conspiracy the *World Wide Web as Collectively Self-Generated Collage Remix Machine* and imagine it to reflect the autopoietic narrative of our time. Stories being played out in hyperimprovisational performance with this Collectively Self-Generated Collage Remix Machine are deeply embedded in the new media experience itself. To me, the apparently seamless integration of composing our fictional thought processes with the mundane acts of punching keys, pushing buttons, and searching Google while operating in a windows-icons-menus-pointing (WIMP) device interface creates an *obliterature-of-potential* that enables us to cancel our historical presence so that we can finally become the *just-in-time* creative flux personas we need to become when improvising an art-life practice. Besides, it doesn't take an artistic genius to suggest that our continual interaction with the evolving languages these new media present us with marks our time even as we (intelligent agents who are equipped to turn the machines off) intuitively know that, by leaving the machines on, are moving beyond the literary itself and entering a more fluid dreamworld of cyberpsychogeographical drifting populated by the self-organizing artificial intelligentsia.

Some colleagues of mine in the literary art discipline tend to have a shit-conniption over this kind of thinking, and I understand their concern. Moving beyond the literary is not easy for those of us who have written and published novels read by real readers both in English and translation around the world. Let's face it: literature can be great source material for artists no matter what media they are working in. In fact, the best literary writers I am aware of and who I publish on my popular *Alt-X* Web site at ⟨www.altx.com⟩

are constantly sourcing prior writers whose texts and styles they eagerly rip off
to renegotiate their relationship with the void. But now there are more options
available to writers of all kinds when it comes to designing their narrative interface, and it's no longer a matter of just staring at the blank white page.

Here's a thought (or maybe it's more of a rant, like the ones I used to write
for various underground 'zines back in the 1980s): what about writing IN our
moment? My version of "our moment" intentionally explores the artist's potential to use the new media environment as a research and development platform to expand the concept of writing, enabling us to innovate our practice
yet again, although perhaps this time with more immediate results. This
means that the art of writing is now seeping into online hypertext and blogging, VJ culture, digitally expanded cinema, hactivism, Flash art, Java applet
art, data visualization, and the like. The methodology for relocating the narrative and poetry is up to each artist to develop.

But there are others issues as well. For example, what is the relationship between generative art, hypertext narrative, and hyperimprovisational VJ performance? Again, I do not want to approach this question as an academic with a
theory-heavy ax to grind or as technologist whose social science fiction is
populated by characters written into the story just because they were able to
receive funding from the National Science Foundation. I would prefer to ask
the question in the context of a passing thought that is of interest to me as
an artist who composes on-the-fly digital remixes of his ideogrammic-
experiential metadata. When I perform my live VJ sets in front of audiences
around the world, I realize that the library of images I am creatively interacting with and pulling from is very much influenced by my own selections of
digital source material that I have captured in expansive cyberpsychogeographical drifts and that I have manipulated into a movie-clip format for my
improvisational remixes. Without my images, without the ceremonial video
love dances I engage in while capturing my digital source material, without
my hyperimprovisationally choreographed writerly processing of all of these
image manipulations in *unrealtime*, there is no experiential database of potential to pull from, and without an experiential database of potential to pull
from, there is no story.

Jamming with my laptop and its customized VJ software, I can generate
spontaneous narratives that operate on the associative linking model of hypertext, without feeling as though I am constantly arriving and departing. While I

am performing, the flow of experience becomes smudged, as does the story I tell when I improvise my new mix. Although I may randomly generate various filters and effects as a way to throw my story out to chance, *it's the ideogrammic-experiential content of the images themselves* that informs the very nervous feedback system I am composing with my audience. It's as if my audience and I are composing a spur-of-the-moment digital scrapbook made out of the data of my life as a nomadic Net artist.

My ever-growing collection of captured (edited, filtered) images contains fragments of my experience as an internationally touring VJ. Everywhere I travel, I shoot more digital video. For me, this is where the work's emotional energy and story resonance lives—not in the machine and its potential to generate multiple versions of whatever story I happen to be telling. Yet in the program I use to perform my VJ mixes, I have the option of hitting a VAGABOND-mode button that randomly selects, filters, and remixes images from this ideogrammic-experiential reservoir of artist-generated imagery that I have stored on my computer. The trickery of the software program and the algorithmic nuance of the magically transformed data are exciting to watch unfold. But the challenge this kind of machine-generated remix brings to my narrative comes not from the technology I am putting to use but from the images themselves, the performative gestures I am hyperimprovisationally choreographing while capturing the data at its original source-location, and my recombining of images in front of a live audience.

This hyperimprovisational choreographing of the sense data is what I call *experiential tagging*. It happens at the level of fingertips and scintillating nerve scales. Think of it as touch-therapy image *écriture* or unconscious action scripting. But VJs, myself included, have to watch out, especially when it comes to the relevance of the imagery they are projecting in the various spaces they gig in. Are the hypnotic visuals that are being generated from their databank of images all that we need to lull us into a SOMA state of mind? An endless stream of visual wallpaper or other assorted eye-candy may help pass the time. But what if there is no story and the viewer's attention wanders into the abyss of their otherwise boring predicament? At this point, the images are bound to become nothing more than visual accompaniment to an otherwise predictable *doof-doof* beat being provided by the true star of the evening, the deafening DJ. I like live-format eye-candy and heavy-handed *doof-doof* manipulations as much as anybody else looking for immediate stimulation in a club space and have projected some wicked eye candy in excellent venues all around the world, but is this all we are capable of?

VJ artists must work hard to avoid the label of being nothing but deliverers of visual wallpaper just as the technotheorists of new media studies must avoid creating art that tries to compensate for an ever elusive *theory-to-be*. Instead, we need to locate an alternative creative strategy that taps into our readiness potential, the thing that precedes our conscious thought, and that incites us to *become* this awakening performance. I won't pretend that it's easy to become an unconscious player in the field of aesthetic composition. It's not easy to keep the conscious, theoretical I at bay while the creative artist is at play. It requires *practice* (like playing a sport or a musical instrument). But that's what must be done if the artist is to emerge.

Unfortunately, for those of us who can see the benefits of creating an alchemical remix of narrative strategies that enable fictional discourses to thrive in the emerging forms of art and thought supported by an engaged, artificial intelligentsia, many contemporary media theorists, technologists, and artists always risk hiding their narratological shortcomings behind their theoretical premises and the trendy technologies those premises are intimately attached to. That's one sure way to kill narrative art, which would then prove all of the conservative cultural critics right. In this regard, we must not let technology kill creativity *or* narrativity. The idea is to let the software trickery of the still undiscovered neural mechanism that triggers all of our unconscious performative gestures jam with whatever new media technologies are available, placing the emphasis back on the *artist* as instrument. Besides, as any experienced avant-pop storyteller will tell you: *the best way to do away with narration is via narration itself.*

Or so the story goes.

10

And yet in the expanding field of new media art research, theories rule. The artificial intelligentsia that has evolved around new media practice is all about reconfiguring the way we think about art and, in this way, closely resembles the Conceptual Art movements of the 1960s and 1970s. Look around the contemporary cultural landscape, and see what's happening in the digital arts and what makes it especially different from all of the other disciplinary areas. More than any other art discipline (painting, sculpture, video, performance), digital artists are writing out their poetics as part of their practice. They also go to more conferences and festivals, participate on more panels, and give more public demonstrations of their work than artists of any other discipline. Why is this so?

Perhaps it has something to do with the demo-or-die mentality that we associate with technology corporations, but my own answer to why digital artists take on the often unpalatable role of what feels like snake-oil salesperson is that they are engaged participants in this previously described Internetworked intelligence that consists of all of the linked data being distributed in cyberspace at any given time and that is powered by artistic and intellectual agents remixing the flow of contemporary thought. That is, they feel compelled to keep the network alive and will not easily drift into conventional roles—like the ones we associate with the studio artist as individual genius who cranks out the same masterpieces over and over again. Some Net artists may be artistic geniuses. But the difference between them and, say, Pablo Picasso, Bruce Nauman, or Kiki Smith is that they are signatories to an active, collaboratively generated network of linked data that is intimately integrated into their simultaneous and continuous online art performance—the one that happens in what I call *asynchronous realtime.* Much of this linked data is text-based and happens via e-mail, either one-to-one e-mail distribution or one-to-many. Seeing that e-mail is generally thought to be experienced asynchronously but that the artists involved often feel that they are experiencing the networked space of flows in realtime, it almost goes without saying that this Internetworked intelligentsia operates (hyperimprovisationally performs) in asynchronous realtime. (If it feels like I just said this or that you are sure you have read these passages before, remember what the great Yogi Berra once said: "It feels like déjà vu all over again." Apply that thought to a fully functional, totally remixable, Life Style Practice that happens in unrealtime but that still feels real due to a manipulation of subjective time perception.)

Artists who are immersed in digital processes are contemporary versions of what in the twentieth century we used to call the *avant-garde.* Thankfully, they no longer have to pretend to be ahead of their time since, as experiments in neuroscience have already suggested, they have no choice in the matter. By continuously experimenting with their readiness potential as it precedes consciousness—that is, by activating their creative selves in the unconscious playing fields that their best work manifests itself in—they are *by nature* ahead of their time.

In fact, even though we are witnessing a major changing of the garde where easily accessible new media gadgets make the idea of being ahead of your time the equivalent of making a trendy consumer purchase, artists who work with digital processes must do more than merely identify themselves as part of an avant-garde tradition. In many ways, their burden is greater because they are really avant-pop (A-P) artists: they naturally play with whatever new media technologies are developing in the pop culture while at the same time aesthetically engaging themselves with the forms of the mass media they are surrounded by. They do this as part of a larger hactivist strategy that intends to subvert the mass media from within so that it bends to their own art and political agendas and can be integrated into their evolving Life Style Practice in asynchronous realtime. The LSP of the A-P artist nurtures an urge to demassify the content industry so that A-P artists can produce, exhibit, and distribute their just-in-time remixes into the niche communities they are actively building. In a different context, we would call this a *peer-to-peer network* but is really a community of shared interest (and where there's interest, there's investment, and where there's investment, a market is sure to follow).

Digitally inclined A-P artists are not deconstructionists who, in the old French style, playfully sample from the history of philosophy so that they can then innovatively remix the nagging metaphysical TEXT that never goes away. This kind of poststructuralist critique of culture may be one elemental by-product of their ongoing online art performance. Fine. But A-P artists are constructing (writing into existence) coded viruses (social software) that attack the traditional media environment from within to subvert its one-size-fits-all mold of reality. Corrupting the traditional media, art, and political cultures—everything from the business news channels, to presidential campaigns, to corporate-sponsored museum exhibitions—is standard practice in the nomadic Net art world, and A-P artists make a point of using their spontaneous creations to create a nonconformist alternative to all status quo political agendas. In this case, the interventionist strategies of many a hactivist Net artist are aimed at deconstructing both the conservative and liberal sides of corporate culture's moneyed mentality so that the online art performance exudes a politically charged aesthetic aura that operates in its own networked context.

But didn't Walter Benjamin tell us that aura was dead and that the authentic was all but history? Perhaps it's time to authenticate the silence.

11

Where to begin. Once upon a time won't do, not in this networked space of flows where the mission creep of an illuminating unrealtime takes hold and empowers us to question *time itself*, to rethink its premises. Of course, these are age-old issues, and an anthropological fictioneer like Jorge Luis Borges was keen to investigate these questions himself in "A New Refutation of Time":

And yet, and yet...Denying temporal succession, denying the self, denying the astronomical universe, are apparent desperations and secret consolations. Our destiny is not frightful by being unreal; it is frightful because it is irreversible and iron-clad. Time is the substance I am made of. Time is a river which sweeps me along, but I am the river; it is a tiger which destroys me, but I am the tiger; it is a fire which consumes me, but I am the fire.

And yet, and yet...we all know what it's like to lose ourselves in the moment. When that moment is somehow artificially constructed as a kind of hyperimprovisationally designed experience colored by the unexpected and, yes, the unintended effects of *being* online, what happens to our notion of what an artist *is* and *where* that artist lives?

To rephrase the question: where does the virtual artist, whose navigational dreamworld of fluid intersubjectivity circulates deep inside a peer-to-peer network culture, actually conduct art/life research practice?

Or to rephrase the question yet again: where is that missing link of a day-night-space-time when my flight leaves from Colorado on a Saturday and—less than twenty-four hours later—arrives Down Under on Monday?

Talk about cyberpsychogeographical drifting. Perhaps for the nomadic Net artist, this ongoing Life Style Practice of associational thinking that hastily passes through the labyrinthine, networked space of flows takes place in *asynchronous realtime*.

By *asynchronous realtime* I am referring to what *at times* feels like a perpetual jet-lag consciousness or timeless time, a blur motion of experiential metadata that indicates a formal investigation of complex *event processing* where the VJ artist, always gyrating at a pivotal location in the narrative, becomes a multitude of flux identities nomadically circulating within the networked space of flows (both geophysical networks and cyberspace networks). Living in asynchronous realtime often produces a feeling of being both avant-garde (ahead of one's time) and time-delayed or even preempted.

Imagine the stutter of media consciousness that inflects poetic uncertainty in the VJ's mind as he loses awareness of himself in the process of *becoming* a mesoperceptive artist-medium hyperimprovising his multimodal trace narrative experiences in a tense still not measurable in human terms. By *mesoperceptive*, I am referring to a state of active perception where the artist-medium is intermediating between the body, brain, and whatever digital apparatus is being used to transcribe the hyperimprovisational performance. *By its very nature*, the mesoperceptive artist-medium is a proprioceptive instrument operating under the spell of what comes *before* consciousness and is acting on this rich, inexpressible *moment before*, as a part of a spontaneous lifestyle or signature gesture. The raw, a priori, experiential metadata that prods the artist-medium into action is so full of itself (actual and immersive), as well as so intense in its ability to stimulate creative compositional responses, that the artist-medium never truly knows where it's going next. It only knows that what feels like a haptic reality, taking place in the present, is actually a distorted smudge of complex event processes that speedily *passes us by*.

It reminds me of what the writer Henri Michaux experienced while under the influence of mescaline, when he described his experiential thought apparatus running "at full speed, in all directions, into the memory, into the future, into the data of the present, to grasp the unexpected, the luminous, stupefying, connections." If that doesn't outline what it feels like to be performing a live VJ act, nothing does. Meanwhile, the raw data that has initially suggested all of this proprioceptive movement in the first place, that was there before you could even *begin* to intend to do what you eventually realized you *wanted* to do, is still somehow being aestheticized into emergent forms of metadata regardless of what *you* end up doing. Meaning: the aestheticization process is waiting to happen and will occur anyway, *on its own terms*. The VJ experiences this *will-to-aestheticize* as if it were happening in a present tense so luminous and stupefying that trying to break these compositional actions down into fine fragments that be analyzed as an enmeshed admixture of form and content is impossible. The only option is for the artist-medium to *keep playing*.

Two examples of experiencing life in asynchronous realtime where one's sense data becomes stretched or shortened into durational shapes and smears that are at once dislocated and spatialized are (1) playing in a live computer-mediated performance art event and (2) teleporting one's mind to a faraway place in a totally different time zone. In the first instance, the VJ improvises a new set of image experiences by collaborating (or jamming) with a laptop as the other player in the jam. It's a space of live composition where the computer processor meets the artist processor. Both of these players process at different speeds and with a different set of goals and, dare I say, intentions. One is machinic; the other is all-too-humanly intuitive. I'll let you decide which is which.

The point is that the speed with which the computer changes its digital imaging output as a response to the artist's transaesthetic input is relative. Sometimes the VJ may push the laptop apparatus to a point in its programmed intelligence where it has no idea what to do with all of the mixed-signal, transaesthetic inputs it is getting and so performs some random function as a way of arbitrarily keeping up with the VJ's constant demands. These random functions become immediately visualized as an ongoing sequence of unexpected imagistic events that the VJ then responds to in what feels like realtime but (because of immeasurable instances of readiness potential verging on unconscious thought processes) is really more like make-or-fake time. This make-or-fake time is *totally unreal* and emerges in live performance as part of the artist's ongoing, creative intuition—an indeterminate sense data space that actually occurs in the imperceptible margins of whatever action takes place during the event, creating an hallucinatory Doppler effect that makes performers feel as though they are asynchronously communicating with both their jamming laptop partner and the audience too. This is when digital art personas are operating in the ZONE of unrealtime, and the groove where they are metaphorically becoming a wave of rhythmic asynchronicity, defamiliarizing all of their poetic phrasing as a way to extend the possibilities of breath and parting lines, can feel like the ultimate high an artist is capable of experiencing.

The cybernetic artist and former Severed Heads member Stephen Jones tells me that it's "the feeling of being there before you even know you're there." This also applies to the second instance of living in asynchronous realtime that I'm referring to—teleporting—which is more common and happens when we anticipate the future-present of the physical location we imagine ourselves en route to. Without even thinking about it, we experience the teleportation of our projective consciousness to the other locational space where our creative thinking will take place ("nothing will have taken place but the place"), even though our physical presence still appears to be fixed in the location of imminent departure. In my second novel, *Sexual Blood*, the protagonist, Maldoror (taken from the fictional character developed by the Comte de Lautréamont [Isidore Lucien Ducasse] in his dark nineteenth-century collection *The Songs of Maldoror*), experiences what he refers to as Melting Plastic Fantastic Time. He is fully aware that he is standing on a beach in the Algarve in Portugal, killing time as he waits for the necessary hours to pass so that he can begin his journey back to the United States. But he is also aware that he is already becoming part of a complex event that is processing his near-future experiences in the United States before he even gets there. What's even stranger, he is certain that in some ways he is already *in* the USA—that his superclock has already reset its parameters and that all that needs to happen now is to transport his meat package to the airport so he can finally catch up with himself.

These kinds of art-research investigations are consistent with what Stan Brakhage called *moving visual thinking* and that I interpret as a kind of experientially anticipated special effects brought on by engaging with one's own poetic intensity. All of these investigations are conducted via the "fine nerve-scales" that Antonin Artaud spoke of "when studying myself microscopically." Henri Bergson tried to materialize them in his own thought process—that is, using the metadata of everyday life experience to discover how the body transforms into a kind of turbo-charged packet-switching station that continually filters (parallel processes) the various distributed media fictions that "I" am always in the process of becoming, like a chameleon reconfigures itself to both embed itself and contribute to whatever shifts are taking place in the autopoietic world it happens to be living in.

In the world of cyberpsychogeographical drifting and nomadic Net art practice, we are immersed in the collective-self organizing domain of the artificial intelligentsia. We feel the sensation of seeing through eyes that Brakhage, in his "Metaphors on Vision," asked us to imagine as "unruled by man-made laws of perspective" and that are "unprejudiced by compositional logic" so that the artist can "know each object encountered in life through an adventure of perception." In a later essay, Brakhage tells us the adventure of perception takes in "the full presence of consciousness...present tense (Or as US poet Charles Olson's 'there is no history except as it is invoked in The Present')." Once the images are captured as an inevitable representation of the light that is available when the images are simultaneously recorded, they (as Brakhage reminds us) "exist referentially AND in an implied past tense...always therefore tied to a remembrance, or resemblance of 'Things Past,' an ideology of

Memory, the ideas of Memorial." In this way, we might say that VJs, in performing their function as artist-medium, attempt to use their live sets to build a living, visual monument to the spontaneous eruption of their past-present-future tenses in the most *intense* way possible.

Needless to say, the quality of the light in a Stan Brakhage film is totally different than the light in a VJ performance using laptops, QuickTime movie files, and VJ software. The former is made by mixing light and sometimes paint in its constituent colors, while the latter is remixed data emitted through red, green, and blue (RGB) pixels stimulated by an electron beam or electrical impulse. In VJ performance, light is expressed via binary code and hexadecimals transfused with electricity and not via the more sensitive process of manipulating photons and transparency values. With direct film, as in the work of Len Lye (where he scratched his visions onto the emulsion while experimenting with dyes, stencils, air brushes, and other instruments), the hypnotic effect of seeing the work projected on a screen reveals the alternative shapes and forms a cinematic phenomenon could take, and viewers are immediately invited to expand their concepts of what a film could be. Lye's experiments, along with those run by Brakhage and other artists like Maya Deren and Bruce Conner, reflect the poetic, trancelike qualities of the filmic medium.

Members of the London Film Makers' Cooperative were also interested in expanding the possibilities of the cinematic apparatus and investigated its phenomenal and sculptural aspects as a relational object in an otherwise experimental screening venue. One of the early moving image artists to emerge out of the London Film Makers' Cooperative scene was Mike Leggett. In a recent unpublished paper, he theorizes that his film works provide "an encounter with the 'film as phenomena', as film 'abstracted'" and that there existed "an opening up of the spaces between its component parts, in contradistinction to the conventions of Cinema, intent on concealing the many joins that hold the illusion in place."

By engaging the viewer in an immediate social network (like the one provided in club spaces, where VJs perform most of their work), contemporary performances that focus on hyperimprovised image manipulation might be assumed to point back to these early "film as phenomena" events that demanded a new set of expectations from their audiences. But the techniques employed by VJs are in many cases referring to contemporary video tropes that are used in everything from mainstream music videos to big Hollywood movies like *Eternal Sunshine of the Spotless Mind* (2004). And with the lack of historical perspective that pervades VJ culture, more and more young artists find it easy to perform in alternative spaces as they jam with the available VJ software using their virtual banks of found footage, taken either directly off the Web or from filmic source material on DVDs. It's so easy, in fact, that if you talk to some young VJs, you might think that VJ culture came to us totally out of the blue. As usual, it's not black and white. For example, one young VJ I know has been using the content from recent DVD releases by Brakhage as his VJ source material. When I asked him why, he simply said, "Because it's great. It was *made* for VJing."

12

There do seem to be some similarities between those approaching VJ culture as a platform for their artistic research and the early work of underground filmmakers like Lye, Brakhage, Deren, Conner, and those artists affiliated with the London Film Makers' Cooperative. One similarity is the aim of the artist to create works that translate into a lyrical trance narrative made out of manipulated image information. Another is the desire to create an expanded cinematic experience where, for example, the audience can interact with the artist, the work, and each other. The emergent Life Style Practice of the gigging VJ—always on the road and mixing the light of memory with the opaque values of their hyperimprovisationally generated imagery—also could be said to attempt to bring the lyrical trance narrative *into* the body as well as the social environment where the artist-medium filters these image events in what always ends up feeling like a dislocated space of time.

In my own experiences, this dislocated space of time is processed as an intensified version of Brakhage's "moving visual thinking," one that is continuously accruing while I jet around the world and my VJ-touring accelerates. Perhaps initializing a technoetic exploration of what it means to wander through this blur-motion of experiential data is what evolving a planetary Net art practice is all about. The aesthetic methodologies I employ while moving feel so radical in their (inter)subjective time perception that I assume no scientific discovery will accurately portray my experience. That should and will be left to the life of the artists and the (digital) traces (form) they leave behind.

In fact, the readiness potential of creative artists operating on the edge of their radical (inter)subjective experiences need not be duplicated or replicated or emulated artificially at all (as in artificial intelligence), since I am now coming to the world as part of the more immersive artificial intelligentsia. *This space within which I am expanding the concept of writing* is my new home, my formally experimental playground to investigate my many, digitally infused, flux personas—the ones "I" continuously hyperimprovise with the processual image events I proactively generate as part of my ongoing Life Style Practice. Call me VJ Persona—the body-brain-apparatus achievement that plays the environment as if it were a shape-shifting medium, a perfectly reasonable, embodied, nonsequitur caught in the passion of its ur-transitory momentum, constructing a just-in-time *art+life+making+history* fusion that, along the way, blurs intermedia boundaries. Any attempt to try to scientifically articulate what this Life Style Practice represents will never succeed since it's always already embedded in the (inter)subjective experience itself.

And the greatest discoveries—the eureka moments of mind-expanding aesthetic alchemy that emerge from some magic place conjured up by the artist-instruments as they tool around with their spiritual unconscious jamming with the celestial psychosphere—always happen *OFF THE CLOCK*. These ultimate moments of creative self-discovery, when *everything is totally clicking*, take place as if the artist-instrument were an alien other intervening in nature's overdetermined, divine provenance, a Monkey Grammarian filtering the transmissions coming into their headquarters located at Hack Central. This artist-trickster is part of nature, is self-aware of its viral effects on *any given nature*, and allows itself to become-cyberpsychogeographical. It becomes a distributed media fiction that speeds through varied environments to study their precise effects on overall behavior and that parallel processes all kinds of fluid image thoughts that have been generated while traversing the planet in search of *excessive forms of visionary intelligence*. These forms will engage with the nomadic body of the VJs and spill over into their nervous systems in a way that *they cannot stop themselves from once again becoming* this hyperimprovisational instrument capable of generating on-the-fly narrative remixes of their digital persona in constant flux.

The *total-sum-in-formation* is what Mallarmé might have called this interrelationship between the hair-trigger neural mechanism that launches my unconscious acts of creativity and the expansive compositional field of action that opens itself up to my metafictional digressions. Think of it as locating the breakout potential of your neuroaesthetic self. If you don't change direction, then you just may end up where you are heading. Whatever the risks, just keep moving. The self-reflexive artist-trickster often succeeds by proceeding without caution. If you fail, maybe you're doing something right, something that challenges the status quo and demands a revaluation of all values.

You might get hooked on this kind of philosophically engaged Life Style Practice, especially if you have figured out a way to maintain it over the duration of a lifetime while still paying the bills. It is a gamble, and when you're on a winning streak, you have to work hard to keep things in balance. After a while, projecting your digital art personas into various modes of cyberpsychogeographical drifting can become addictive—the way that staying connected or continually evolving strategies to survive in the network culture can be addictive. Steven Shaviro's recent book *Connected: Or What It Means to Live in the Networked Society* tells us that we are now *beyond* the Society of the Spectacle and that Debord himself was deluded about the notion of "a false consciousness of time."

"There was never a time when life was directly lived," says Shaviro. He goes on to say "there was never a unity of life as opposed to the separation imposed by the detaching of images from their original contexts." According to Shaviro, this "unity of a life 'directly lived'" is something Hollywood invented and that never occurred to anyone before they started seeing Hollywood movies. Given this context, what's a planetary Net artist or internationally touring VJ to do? Intervene in the assault of distributed media fictions by becoming one?

By the term *distributed media fiction*, I am referring to what the nomadic digital artist becomes by navigating through the networked space of flows in asynchronous realtime. In my case, I can be tagged at any given moment as an experimental novelist, a hypertext composer, a Net artist, a VJ performer, a DVD-with-surround-sound installation artist, a film director, or a writerly conduit whose digital poetics occasionally loses itself in the imaginative netherworld of abstract expression. *The important thing* (as my co-conspirator, Ronald Sukenick, liked to say, often as a nonsequitur) *is to annihilate the important thing.*

To which I might add:

The important thing is a feeling.
The important thing is losing sight of yourself in asynchronous realtime.

The important thing is finding yourself in an open-source Life Style Practice. The important thing is to tantalize your nerve centers so that the images you are generating are dripping out of your ears as the burning afterthought of a body-brain-apparatus achievement.

The important thing is to reembody sensual free zones while actively participating in the idealized gift economy.

The important thing is to use experience as base for knowledge-invention.

The important thing is to generate spontaneous bioimages out of each other in an endless cycle of dreamworld manipulation while using your body as the ultimate enframer loaded with an ever-increasing array of creative filters.

The important thing is to remix digital flux personas.

The important thing is to outthink premeditation.

The important thing is to unconsciously play with your readiness potential.

The important thing is to decharacterize eros.

The important thing is to strip I.D. entities of the Fad of Being and to bare witness to a distributed media fiction that overwrites your hastily constructed psychogeographical drift as it passes through the associational web of trails blazed by the collective IQ playing in VAGABOND mode.

The important thing is to proactively situate the artificial intelligentsia in the networked space of artistic flows to prompt wild mutations that are just within reach of the spiritual unconscious.

13

"The world runs on Internet time," says Andy Grove, the CEO of Intel. Yes, Andy, you're probably right, although what Internet time actually *is* is still an open question. It's like the chip inside your head is programmed for destinarrativity complete with built-in obsolescence, a fact you are semiconsciously aware of 24/7—except when your system has completely crashed, the super-clock between your eyes and inside your head needs a foreign-substance adjustment, and meanwhile you're still surfing the Web looking for more meaning or for meaning potential. That is to say, *you Google yourself to death.*

This is when the state of problematized Being is erupting. It's the beautiful thing about evolving a digital culture out of lived unreality (mutating code-work). You program yourself to write yourself into Being, to engage in an ongoing ungoing networked social experience with the Other, one that always borders on becoming. But becoming what? Becoming a cyborg-narrator in whose sight we see the world anew? Becoming a planetary Net artist whose responsibility to world citizenship is to capture consciousness with whatever digital apparatuses are available during your given time?

Arthur Rimbaud (that nineteenth-century poet entrepreneur who would have made a killing in the dot.com glory days if only he had been alive to experience it) once wrote, "To each being, several other lives were due." Imagine if he had access to e-mail, iChat, SMS, or networked games. He might have *never* written his poetry about the seasons of hell he was so desperate to convey to the wide open other. The excellent poems he wrote would probably have been lost to a series of virtual killings in first-person shooter game space or any number of role-playing environments that suited his then-emerging poetic sensibility. He may have suffered from attention-deficit disorder, and his parents, not sure how to rein in his hyperactive emotions and overpowering energy, may have forced him to take Ritalin or Prozac to somehow simulate a pseudo-jet-lag consciousness that is nowhere near as pleasantly nasty and stimulating as the real thing and may cripple creative potential.

Every-*body* has its preferred drugs of choice. For me, all I need is a long trip on an airplane, an attempt to stay up as long as possible, and then a journey through a neonated city at midnight or a hot and thirsty walk through a desert landscape. All of a sudden, I find myself entering another world, another planet—Planet Oblivion, where the aliens are alienated from alienation itself.

Living along the contours of a borderless Planet Oblivion is where my practice flourishes. Sometimes I can watch myself as if from above and see my human body perambulating the surface of this renegade planet. There I am, that naked body of words mobilizing their hypertextual consciousness through a maze of experience that steers me through various multilinear routes, humming an old song that Frank Sinatra once sang: "To dream the impossible dream." Yes, the impossible dream—the one I am always in the process of composing as a nomadic Net artist drifting in cyberpsychogeographical spaces.

And what you are reading here now, almost as a delayed effect created with some digital manipulation, is that my impossible dream is the one I am always in the process of composing as a nomadic Net artist drifting in cyberpsychogeographical spaces. This line can keep repeating itself in a low murmur somewhere in the background of the soundtrack to this essay (the one I am always in the process of composing as a nomadic Net artist drifting in cyberpsychogeographical spaces). Some might call this *theory looping* or layering the rhetoric, the way a DJ spins discs or adds various tracks to a digital composition. But there is always the risk of slipping a disc while falling off the edge of this oblivious curvature of thought that still feels like an extraplanetary transmission. Slip and fall, and watch your world go completely out from under you. Then what do you do Ms. DJ/VJ nomadic Net artist? I mean, how do you play if you can't pivot? The gravity of the situation is enormous. As a programming image-body that experiences body-brain-apparatus achievements in asynchronous realtime, you always have to be able to pivot, to drift along with your make-or-fake history until it takes its sudden hallucinatory turn. At which point, you have to be able to plant your poetic foot six feet under and immediately spin yourself in another direction, or you might end up going exactly where you are heading.

14

By enacting a Life Style Practice that is fueled by a simultaneous and continuous fusion of practical and theoretical investigations into digital thoughtography and its discontents (as well as its material contents, as with William Carlos Williams's phrase "not in ideas, but things"), I am attempting to expand the concept of writing so that it becomes nothing more or less than an ultimate mode of survival that my many digital flux personas can nurture themselves in. If I am going to pull this off as smoothly as possible (and there's no guarantee I will), then I must begin to explore what it feels like to INSTANTANEOUSLY BECOME the embodied, fictional version of Brakhage's "moving visual thinking," to watch myself TRANSFORM INTO REAL FICTITIOUS MEDIA, an artist-medium starring in the new media theatrical premiere of *Portrait of the Artist as a Role-Playing, Pseudo-Autobiographical Work-in-Progress*, for, as Louis-Ferdinand Céline has said, "Life, also, is a fiction . . . and biography is something one invents afterwards."

So that soon after landing in Tokyo, a couple of nights before one of my VJ Persona gigs, I find myself roaming one of the low-lit streets in the Harajuku district. My DV cam is permanently attached to my face as I blur my jet-lag consciousness into a deep and profound state of radical alterity, hoping that I will simultaneously hallucinate and record a series of images and a short while later manipulate them in my hotel room at the luxurious New Otani hotel. What would my hero, Henry Miller, think of all of this?

Walking down one of the narrowest streets in Harajuku, with fashion shops calling for my attention, I remember to press the red record button on my digital video camera, at which point the people who walk in front of my lens are said to be captured by my apparatus as it views the scene. But I wonder: Are these people that I am capturing part of the unreality of my ongoing philosophical fictions? Or are they real actors performing as themselves in realtime, and do I just happen to be capturing them in action?

Is their realtime biography synchronizing with my unrealtime autobiography, or is it all a kind of pseudo-collective autobiography, a random interactive performance transmitted only for the apparatus that captures our consciousness for us? At a certain point, even a narratively minded VJ artist has to ask, "Who needs cameras?" when you have the readiness potential of the unconscious player streaming mashed-up media fictions in ultrarapid fervor? Who needs cameras, indeed. But I use them anyway.

Maybe I shouldn't use words like *biography* and *autobiography* to contextualize the experience of supplementing (writing out) my own life story, since I'm already beyond the graph of knowing my own subjectivity. Is this what it means to be a *super* avant-garde artist—to be *so* ahead of time that even the artist's many different selves can't keep up? But no matter how far I may get ahead of myself (and this ongoing spontaneous artist theory is only about staying ahead of myself, of not looking back and wondering what happened), there is still this nagging issue of the body and its more generic functions. Going with the flow sometimes means letting the flow take over, at which point you just have to go. Let's face it: it's my bodily functions that totally ground out this impossible dream that has somehow come *true to life* as I use these emerging technologies to distribute my cast of digital flux personas.

Besides, at times, autobiography feels more like *autobiopsy*. Think of it as a kind of self-inflicted, open-source surgery that attempts to excise whatever nuggets of meaning may still be residing in my public-domain body as it processes the metadata of my experiential Life Style Practice. Sometimes I get caught in the flow of *writing out* my life, and it feels like I am metaphorically taking all available diagnostic instruments to my rich, multilayered databank of experience and turning it into a Burroughsian cut-up or the virtual version of a slapdash *Merz* collage. This aesthetic procedure is often an invasive, preemptive, proactive strike that enables me to engage spontaneously with the dreams, memories, and hallucinations I willingly create, collaboratively, with my colleagues all across the planet—the collective IQ that constantly morphs within this self-organizing space of cyberpsychogeographical flows that in toto makes up the artificial intelligentsia.

And yet I don't think about these things when I, for example, watch reality TV. My escape from the improvised unreality of my fictional universe involves dumbing myself down, deep down into the abyss of scripted reality. But that's rare. Most of the time, I am actively processing the experiential metadata of my continuous jam sessions with the artificial intelligentsia and its environs. Often I hastily mobilize my body through these environs while drifting through the neon nightscape of a foreign city with my DV camera in hand. And once the camera is on, it's all sex, lies, and digital videotape.

But what about when the camera is off?

What if I were to see *myself* as the apparatus "turning on"?

Push my red button, and activate my artificial intelligence and—well, I just might do anything. And that's no lie.

The camera, it ends up, is a welcome crutch. Flick the switch, and all of a sudden I'm more than just supertourist. Now I become the kino-eye apparatus capturing alien light forms in distributed unrealtime. Angling down the narrow street in Harajuku, not watching my step: everything the DV cam is presently capturing is *all* I live for. It's my make or break source material. *I just hope I don't break a leg and have my world fall out from under me.* This movement capturing would be a proprioceptive version of the ideogrammic-experiential flux-identity that occasionally goes by the name of *me*. But there is no me—not in the conventional sense of a self that will be what it will be. No, now there is something else that drives my production cycles into process heaven—and this something else is The Network.

When I awkwardly move myself down the street saying "everything the DV cam is presently capturing is *all* I live for" (and yes, I later hear my voice saying this on the DV tape in the hotel while I am downloading it into my laptop), what I mean is that everything I do, I do for The Network, even if it means not looking where I'm going and accepting all of the built-in risks involved in potentially crashing my body into the pavement.

I guess it all depends on what condition your condition is in.

My condition is in a permanent state of radical intersubjectivity. WYSIWYG intersubjectivity. A black market in VR cache-flow.

Here we are now, entertain us.

Who said that? A voice from the grave?

Who is the *we* that wants to be entertained and that is being mocked all the while? *Not me*, I can hear everyone say. Then who? You?

Think of artificial intelligentsia as gorgeous (beautiful, lovely, perfect) inter-subjectivity. Virtual intersubjectivity.

Now connect the dots (follow the money): is that the Collective Unconscious I smell coming around the corner? Is that you?

"Not me," I can hear someone say. That someone is Everyone. Here Comes Everyone! Here Comes the Collective Not-Me!

Hey, what if we built in some artificial stupidity?

I feel stupid and contagious / Here we are now, entertain us.

Locating artificial stupidity would be like striking gold. Once it's firewired into my hard drive, the rhetorical flood of narrative information would fill to the brim, and then it would all be more virtual dream juice ready for spin doctoring. Or what I call *surf-sample-manipulate.* A strategy where the Net artist, formerly a writer, surfs the digital culture, samples data, and then changes or manipulates that data to meet the specific needs of the narrative —of the pseudo-autobiographical work-in-progress their network story is unbound to become.

You can use any data for this creative process—from the Internet, CDs, DVDs, books, magazines, overheard conversations, or found material of all kinds.

For the Internet, it would work on two fronts. One, the so-called creative content (that is, the text, images, sounds, and links that are available to us) would be sampled from other online sources and digitally manipulated so that it becomes original constructions that are immediately imported into the storyworld you are creating. Two, the so-called source code itself could be appropriated from other designs floating around the Net and eventually integrated into the screen's behind-the-scenes compositional structure. The great thing about the Net is that if you see something you like, whether content or source code, you often can download the entire document and manipulate it to your needs.

Forget inspiration. That was for the Me Generation—("*I* was inspired to write this poem"). They were worst than the Lost Generation—the literary others who were bound by their prolific, creative genius.

Net artists seem to be saying that content and source code are one and the same thing—that it's all open source ready for remixing so that we can participate in collaborative acts of creative mindshare. Call us the *Not-Me Generation.*

To take part in this open source remix methodology would first of all be an antiaesthetic gesture, similar in practice to the one Marcel Duchamp showed us with his readymades. He took found objects, gave them conceptually provocative titles, and reconfigured them in elitist art exhibition space. He began employing what Jacques Derrida might have called a signature effect that brands the chameleonlike creator with a kind of stylized notoriety. (This again resonates with Rimbaud—the poet-cum-dot.comer who said that "to each being, several other lives were due" and created a great personal mythology out of putting his poetry into practice.) However, (1) the elitist art world has no way to absorb this kind of Net artwork into its market-driven canon and so has decided to ignore it (thank God), and (2) the signature means nothing because the name it represents no longer has an object attached to it, only the radical intersubjectivity of the artificial intelligentsia.

15

In my first work of online conceptual art, called *Hypertextual Consciousness* and created in 1995 when I was a graduate student at Brown University, I refer to this process of manipulating the data of the collective unconscious to suit your own fictional needs as a kind of *pseudo-autobiographical becoming*. It is a process by which the artist transforms into a cyborg-narrator that teleports itself into the realm of the artificial intelligentsia. Once teleported, artists can begin accessing various fragments of everyday digital life—selecting whatever data they wish to download into their operating systems, filtering it through a personalized and often intuitive collagelike methodology that essentially has its way with the data, and integrating its binary code into their ongoing narrative momentum. Masquerading as a perpetual work-in-progress, artists continually experiment with the work's potential to manipulate symbolic space in ways that will purge the interactive artist of any need to portray their subjectivity as a conventional product of the Me Generation. Instead, they render into vision a performative interplay of network technology and antiaesthetic practice.

But describing this practice *at root* is always an issue. Theoretical research papers can take us only so far, and if we wait for scientific observation to tell us what's going in our minds as we engage with our creative (readiness) potential in unconscious acts of playfully engaged, intuitive performance, we might as well wait until we're dead and then some.

The electronic word as digital rhetoric becoming coded image/sound/text

This might be one way of looking at it, at least in relation to all of my major work since 1995.

Think of it as digital screenwriting or image *écriture*, where a healthy dose of experiential metadata composed primarily of programmed imagetexts gets summoned up for possible manipulation in various imaginings of the screenal interface. The experiments that are conducted with this experiential metadata in the digital art studio are then subject to all manner of procedural hacking. A chance throw of the dice opens up the work to a wealth of potential outcomes where much of what is conceived as art, from the artist-medium's perspective, can be captured in *the process* of making the work itself. This process leads to *finally unfinished works of art* that are inevitably released in a variety of public outputs that, no doubt, participate in the mysterious underworld of the art-collector economy, even though the work itself is virtually uncollectible.

That's the beauty of it all—and whoever said contemporary art lacks beauty isn't looking in the right places. The networked space of flows that most of my art circulates in defies the traditional gallery context and sees the WWW as an inventive remix machine, a multimedia network publishing platform, an exhibition space, a performance venue, a conceptual art canvas, a computer-supported collaborative research lab, an experiential design playground—all open to the peer-to-peer accessibility of the gift economy.

You can even use this model of an inventive remix machine to evolve a personal philosophy made out of heavily manipulated metacommentary. Let me show you a basic example of what I mean.

I go to the Web to a site called *Kino-Eye.com* and pull a quote from Dziga Vertov, the Russian avant-garde filmmaker. The quote in full reads as follows:

Kino-Eye means the conquest of space, the visual linkage of people throughout the entire world based on the continuous exchange of visible fact.... Kino-Eye is the possibility of seeing life processes in any temporal order or at any speed.... Kino-Eye uses every possible means in montage, comparing and linking all points of the universe in any temporal order, breaking, when necessary, all the laws and conventions of film construction.

So then I remix that hot off the Web and get this:

Kino-Eye means the conquest of space, the visual linkage of people throughout the entire world based on the continuous exchange of visible fact.... Kino-Eye is the possibility of seeing life processes as hypertextual consciousness moving at all speeds.... Kino-Eye uses every possible means in reconfiguring the artist as a socially provocative apparatus operating in a telepresent environment, comparing and linking all points of the universe in an open source generated peer-to-peer network, breaking, when necessary, all the laws and conventions of reality construction.

Then I open a book by Vilém Flusser, called *Toward a Philosophy of Photography*, and rip this from him:

Apparatuses were invented to simulate specific thought processes. Only now (following the invention of the computer), and as it were with hindsight, is it becoming clear what kind of thought processes we are dealing with in the case of all apparatuses.... All apparatuses (not just computers) are calculating machines and in this sense are "artificial intelligences," the camera included, even if their inventors were not able to account for this.

So now I do a remix of a manipulated Vertov/Flusser sent through the aforementioned digital thoughtography filter I have invented, and this what I come up with:

Apparatuses capture space, make links to the other via hypertextual consciousness, simulate specific thought processes as ways of seeing, and process the social spaces of the artificial intelligentsia as it operates in a peer-to-peer (P2P) open source environment breaking all the laws and conventions of identity construction.

This all happens in asynchronous realtime, inside the networked space of flows where my body comfortably processes all it has read and seen while drifting into various cyberpsychogeographical border zones. The improvisational push-pull of the act of composition makes it feel as though I am generating an intuitive writing practice that designs my story *for* me *as* I create it—as I live it. Think of it as Experiential Meta/Data. Narratological Resonance. VJ Style. Whatever you call it (and don't worry, I've heard worse), I'm not looking back. This is an historical documentation of a process that never took place in realtime anyway, so there's no originary chronology I have to be true to.

It feels like writing writing itself. I am letting the language speak itself, but with various filters turned on and tweaked in a way that we can, if we want, experience its unconscious Net effect.

Streaming fictions screaming across the network

I like doing this because it reminds me of how influenced I am by writing and art practices I have yet to fully expose myself to. Borges speaks of "Kafka and His Precursors"—that is, a work of art that writes into being those that came before him or her. It's as if you were there for the first time and only later see how others blew out similar ghost notes that led to *their* eurekalike discoveries. But at least you got there your way, didn't you?

Keeping this in mind, the Net artist will ask:

Who is really writing *you* as you write yourself out into the big space of in?

A digital screenwriter must always take that question into account. No longer being the me who operates as a kind of digital thoughtographer in the networked space of flows means that I now have to give way to something else that's out there. I need to use it when necessary but, more important, let *it* use me and whatever I am supposedly creating—which at present feels more like a Net art poetics than a work of literature.

16

This isn't to say that literature has no role in any of this. Just as we know via Wittgenstein that the self may be grammatical (as well as machinic—that is, it may be a *grammatron*), the self may also be *a grammatical fiction* that is remixed from the blood lineage of all of the other grammatical fictions that came before it and that are mixing up their virtual juices in the heavy IV drip of *now*.

There's an entire heritage or rival tradition of literature (including Lautréamont, Burroughs, Raymond Federman, and Kathy Acker, to name a few) whose authors readily write cyberspace as a kind of playgiaristic practice, and that tradition feeds into my own Net art practice. *Playgiaristic* is a term I steal from Federman, who uses the supplemental *y* to signify *play* and performance in the self-organizing world of the artificial intelligentsia—what I imagine to be the *open source network*. I interviewed Federman in hopes he would reveal to me what he meant by the term *playgiarism*, and this is what he wrote back:

To answer the question once and for all. I cannot explain how Playgiarism works. You do it, or you don't. You're born a Playgiarizer, or you're not. It's as simple as that. The laws of Playgiarism are unwritten. Like incest, it's a taboo. It cannot be authenticated. The great Playgiarizers of all time—Homer, Shakespeare, Rabelais, Diderot, Rimbaud, Lautréamont, Proust, Beckett, Federman—have never pretended to do anything else.

Inferior writers deny that they playgiarize because they confuse Plagiarism with Playgiarism. It's not the same. The difference is enormous, but no one has yet been able to explain it. Playgiarism cannot be measured in weight or size. It is as elusive as what it playgiarizes.

Plagiarism is sad. It whines. It cries. It feels sorry for itself. It apologizes. It feels guilty. It hides behind itself.

Playgiarism, on the contrary, laughs all the time. It exposes itself. It is proud. It makes fun of what it does while doing it. It denounces itself.

That does not mean that Playgiarism is self-reflexive. How could it be? How can something reflect itself when that itself has, so to speak, no itself but only a borrowed self. A displaced self.

If this is getting too complicated, too intellectual, too abstract, then let me put it in simpler terms—on the Walt Disney mental level: Playgiarism is above all a game whose only rule is the game itself. The French would call that Plajeu.

17

Playgiarism is necessary because it enables artists to compose their work from angles and positions that might otherwise go against their own, self-invented grain. For example, in a counterintuitive drift into the danger zone, your whole creative enterprise slips out from under you. This can happen when you forget where you come from when. Take, for example, this figure we call *the writer*. Who needs authors when all we really need are writers who code, comment, shape-shift, and collaborate on the open source network narrative of our social lives?

But the emergent languages of new media—of writing out our fictional codeworks into interactive states of *being becoming something else* so that we may, cyborgs all, creatively engage ourselves in a society of networked metadata—have been with us for a while. Networked virtual reality is really soft and GUI. It's brain candy or artificially intelligent writing by any other name. The fantasy script that generates my VR is not about multiuser, interactive open narratives where everyone with an Internet connection has read-write privileges and contributes to the banal story of the potential network author. That's pathetic, and only a pseudo-utopian dreamer camouflaged as a new media theorist would even engage with such speculative reportage.

My fantasy script is generated by an endless series of technoetic explorations and field research investigations where my creative unconscious impulses hyperimprovisationally jam with various digital technologies and create on-the-fly narrative remixes of my nomadic Life Style Practice in asynchronous realtime. Think of the writer cum Net artist as a body-brain-apparatus achievement that uses its ever growing palette of customized plug-ins (developed via experiential risk-taking and a consequential flood of spontaneous poetics) to hallucinate itself into being. In this regard, the idealized network author that many new media or electronic literature theorists attempt to apprehend in their scholarly fixations will never be found in the World Wide Wiki consciousness of fly-by-night Web surfers suffering from lack of attention and who have no idea what it takes to compose the work of art in the age of virtual republishing. If you want to engage with the network author, you need not proselytize an uninhabitable Net domain for the creative commoners. You just need to read Walter Benjamin's *Arcades Project* and imagine the monkish mojo of his encyclopedic mind remixing its collective source material through a collaboratively generated memory extender years before Vannevar Bush dreamed up his own memex.

Let's give credit where credit is due, however. Bush's memex and the eventual parlaying of that diagrammatic insight into what became a hypertext transfer protocol took writing to the next level of *apparatus consciousness*. At first, it was conceived as a recordable memory device, but soon it evolved into an inventive remix machine that simulates specific thought processes as ways of seeing and processing the social spaces inhabited by the artificial intelligentsia as it operates in a peer-to-peer (P2P) open source environment, breaking all the laws and conventions of identity construction. (This last line is now the second theory loop playing on the essay soundtrack, along with the line that ends "a nomadic Net artist drifting in cyberpsychogeographical spaces.")

Reconfiguring this creative mindshare or Engelbartian collective IQ via digital screenwriting then becomes the ultimate self-reflexive research agenda. In my lab at the University of Colorado in Boulder, we're starting to form a cluster of multimedia research bands that play digital art ("play the work") like underground garage bands, jamming in all manner of antiaesthetic D-I-Y gestures connecting an otherwise random association of hybridized online/offline performances into an on-the-fly group narrative experience that resonates with the promise of *making our own* art history or, more important, of *making art history up*. Participating in the group narrative experience doesn't mean that we are purporting an idealized network author where people don't have an opportunity to distinguish themselves by way of their own evolving Life Style Practice. Signature style is what gives the otherwise processed and processing body its unique claim to becoming an image, even though we readily admit that there is an inherent contradiction here because, as stated above, "The signature means nothing because the name it represents no longer has an object attached to it, only the radical intersubjectivity of the artificial intelligentsia." Although it may mean nothing, this does not mean that we will never attain some form of accidental value in the networked space of flows. Anything is possible in the autopoietic space of experiential tagging.

The image of the artist as an indication of a signature style suggests that more is at stake when one emerges into the scene as an artist-medium than what the Nike commercial's refrain of "Image is everything" was referring to—although it's partly that, too. It's also about what you *do* with the image, how you generate it, how you influence the way it gets processed by the larger-than-thou artificial intelligentsia it circulates in, and how your body, as image, interacts with other images and, when fully engaged, creates collaborative, intersubjective compositions in trance narrative space. This body is a writing body, and as the body writes out its emerging story as a way to substantiate its presence in the scene, it relies on a social feedback system to help tune the performer to the ongoing creative process as it runs through various scales. Artists must be able to manipulate the emerging languages of new media in asynchronous realtime if they want to *embody the image* of the artist-medium whose readiness potential is continuously triggering these always emergent acts of now.

Embodying the image information is part of a sensory illogic the contemporary VJ lives and dies by. The blur of style and substance in live image-making is impossible to apprehend in theoretical discourse, but an occasional shot of spontaneous artist poetics can at least *play with the idea* of further contextualizing the discourse network in which such thinking circulates. Another way of imagining how to construct this image of the artist-medium is to filter thoughts through a mesoperceptive body that is being washed by the electrical impulses of a deeply personal moment of structural enervation. Rimbaud was after this with his customized form of poetry in motion—what he called the *derangement of the senses*. To an always-on-tour VJ remixologist, it feels more like a new model of synaesthetic swimming, freestyling across the pools of surface-level sense data, a space of mind where the unconscious generation of a hyperintuitive, body double releases itself to all readiness potential and lets itself go.

From the perspective of the digital screenwriter whose work is targeted at developing an attitude and style outside the mainstream academic discipline, *playing with the idea* of integrating theoretical discourse into their ongoing digital poetics is one element in an otherwise profuse spillage of creative writing. Ronald Sukenick is more eloquent on this subject, especially in his "Narralogue on Everything":

In this sense "creative" writing is always improvisation—that's what makes it creative. The difference between this kind of writing and so-called noncreative writing is that in the former thinking is simultaneous with the moment of composition while the latter is largely a report of thinking that's already been done. Thinking in the moment of composition calls up faculties distinct from those that dominate more logical thought.

18

The illogic of sense data is another way of looking at it. With hyperimprovisational acts of freeform composition, the sensorium in which writers immerse themselves leads to a bleeding of one sense order into another, a blurred blending of the way things look, sound, and feel *while writing*. Think of it as what Brian Massumi, in his book *Parables of the Virtual*, calls a "fringe-flow sensation."

Smell the red, taste the noise, see the stink, touch the moan. Feel the body enter its altered state of utter proprioceptive whiteness and watch the writer compose as he fully immerses himself in a post-VR hallucination, that total creative work environment called *The Defamiliarization Lab*.

ANYTHING CAN HAPPEN in The Defamiliarization Lab. Inside The Defamiliarization Lab, we can manipulate our live-action memories as future perfect dreams that take place in a tense that doesn't quite exist, or if it does, only in *theory*.

Let's call this tense *utopense*. It's that tense you give way to while expending utopian thought.

Think you can handle it? *Mano y mano*, Utopia and You, forming a more perfect union. You-topia. ("Nothing will have taken place but the place.")

DON'T LOOK BACK. Or if you do, recognize that what you're looking at are the formal traces of an improvised style that you had NO IDEA you were creating while you were composing THIS THING (your life).

Blurring Life Style Practice and nomadic Net art wandering as the same thing can lead to disorientation, which may be the best way to orient yourself to what the status quo tries to pass off as the real.

Besides, if you're interested in cultural survival, composing your digital poetics as a way to hack into the real is no longer a matter of choice. This is how a hactivist artist-medium creates new work within the shape-shifting zones of the artificial intelligentsia. Avant-pop Net artists have become experts at metafictionally challenging status quo perceptions that have become numbed by the flicker of commercial culture and its scripted realities. Their primary shamanic trick is to use the formal traces of their own nomadic Life Style Practice as digital source material to reinvent themselves yet again, modeling alternative ways of processing the story data of the artificial intelligentsia so that they can release still more pseudo-autobiographical content for others to *hack into.*

As Ken Wark says in his book *The Hacker Manifesto*: "To hack is to release the virtual into the actual, to express the difference of the real." For me, the difference of the real is best accessed via the unreal. As Sukenick, in *Narralogues*, reminds us, this kind of creative, improvisational Life Style Practice is, by its nature, "less linear, more embedded in the situational flow, more experiential in that it involves enactment of situations, more open to the wisdom of feelings and emotions, more dependent on the power of example, more open to preconceptual information registered by the senses, more responsive to the moment of what is said to be a form of very short term memory that defines the purview of the present, more governed by quick reflex and instinct." Make no mistake: "these faculties add up to the word *intuition* or maybe *imagination* and constitute a powerful alternative to abstract thought. It's not much of a stretch to see that they also form a base for narrative thinking."

Narrative thinking (what I used to call *creative writing* but had to run away from because the work produced under that name has become so predictable, so wooden, so *workshopped* as to be unreadable in the worst sense of that term) has successfully invaded the new media arts. It has pleasantly corrupted the digital arts in a way that those of us who have made it part of our agenda could have never imagined.

Having said that, as experimental scribes who were always open to writing our vibes as a reverberating constant, we were always aware that writing's long history—it's alphabetical versioning of language into useable data that could be translated across cultural codes and technological platforms—made its dominant presence in New Media Virtual Reality Land inevitable. Since we knew that the machine aesthetic begins with writing, we never doubted that creative writing would morph into creative, computer-based code and that this emerging codework would then further morph into a freeform network of hyperimprovisationally generated performance artworks that would continually manifest themselves in a variety of cultural environments (everything from techno clubs to media art festivals to Net art mailing lists to experimental seminars doubling as multimedia blog jams)—assuming one could bypass all multimodal logjams.

The one constant that remains no matter what environment this digital artwork ports itself through is that both the artists and the electrotraces they are leaving behind are situated to facilitate research investigations into the future of writing and its eventual inmixing with other influential forms of new media art. A future that we assume, given our cyberpunk heritage, is happening *now, in eternal utopense.*

19

The future now of collaborative narrative performance taking place in hybridized online/offline environments can happen in a variety of settings. Surprisingly, our TECHNE lab in the Department of Art and Art History at the University of Colorado often transforms into an art-club happening space where people (student-players) hang out and socialize while viewing experimental DVDs, Net art projections, live DJ/VJ performances, and pedagogical jam sessions. This loosely termed *networked narrative environment* in which student-players improvise their life stories has challenged them to rethink the role of new media technologies in relation to their own social behaviors. If you don't have your storytelling chops down, then you will be hard pressed to contribute something useful to the collective learning experience, whether it is acting, dancing, food, images, sounds, texts, jokes, lights, Pilates training, programming codes, or wildly flirtatious body language.

Sometimes I wonder if this deep need to port narrative thinking through whatever new media technologies happen to be available at any given time is connected to some primordial craving—the kind of craving we have for a physical connection with someone we love or even a certain meal at our favorite restaurant. The body—all water, blood, bones, organs, nerves, muscle, tissue, and, eventually, utterance—seeks to improvise some performative or generative social science fiction to attach to its digital flux persona so that this potentially transformative feeling of connectedness can ally itself with the work of art that desperately wants to emerge. Once this kind of in-body and out-of-mind experience clicks into a fluid transmission of manifest unreality, it often finds the all-too-sexy and flirtatious specter of writing standing there. It is ready, willing, and able—incubating, on the verge of letting loose the code of pleasurable corruption. (Like Burroughs says, "Language is a virus.")

It's this urge for connectedness, of letting loose the code of pleasurable corruption, that matters most, and teleporting your new media language through any medium or apparatus will do. The key is to open up yourself to the instrumentality of interdisciplinary action in whatever random environment you happen to perform in. Now comes the risky part. Do you or don't you hook up? Is it time, once again, to become the artist-medium, the enervating plug-in filter of all of society's dirty white noise? What experiential dividends will this personal investment in the creative process potentially pay you, and what are its opportunity costs? If you are sure this is what you really crave, how bad do you really want it?

20

And so there transmits another transitional ellipsis, perhaps the preferred mode of punctuation for all nomadic Net artists who visually jockey themselves around Planet Oblivion. On Planet O, once you create a rhythmic drift you can playfully survive in, then it's no longer about being stuck in a rat race or spinning endlessly on a hamster wheel. Success is now measured by how well you have designed your own Life Style Practice so that you have effectively avoided the curse of the professional-managerial class (PMC), where it's all too easy to watch your desires ramp up way beyond your previously modest survival needs. The curse of the PMC is that you always want *more*, more of everything, fast and hard, soft and gentle, quick and easy, rough and ready, creamy and delicious. And you want it *now*, although now sometimes feels like *not-quite-now* and *beyond-now* too. The blurred boundaries take over wherever you go. Even against your will, the need for synaesthetic swimming through pools of sense data will eventually take over. Then you have no choice: see 43 a.m., smell a VRML chat space, listen to the blue flicker projecting from your database of potentiality. Taste the future collapse of your SEXUALLY SWAYING ARCHITECTURE.

For me, it's simple. I just start playing around with the freely available social software wherever I happen to be located on Planet Oblivion and watch the work materialize before my very eyes. What materializes out of this practice (this embodied discourse network of which I am but one metacommentator) is a kind of *joie de vivre*, and as a joyful participant, I emerge as more than just VJ Persona traversing the cyberpsychogeographical playing fields of Planet Oblivion. I find that I also become an active amateur (passionate lover) of the network culture and generate new *material* no *matter* what I *do*.

The word *material* is useful here, especially when I think of it in terms of digital source material and the ways that the source becomes matter. For the artificial intelligentsia, matter matters little unless one can materialize a context for its existence. In the case of the Net artist—whose nomadic wanderings are part of a larger image movement taking place in eternal utopense— the context for its existence is still that nonplace place where the heightened states of body-brain-apparatus achievements are always a possibility in the networked space of flows. In this networked space of flows, VJ Persona hallucinates a metafictional drift of personal narrative momentum while parallel processing the flow of images aggregating into his live performance. It's the purposeless play of things present, inmixing with the remembrance of things past. (And all of this happens while *still eyeing the immediate future—so* immediate, in fact, that it perpetually blurs the tense field the VJ is performing in.)

Things past are also things *passed on,* generationally. I am a VJ who captures his own source material in front of a live audience. When I hyperimprovise my VJ sets with video images being captured, streamed, and remixed *in the performance space itself,* I become a kind of simultaneous and continuous fusion of all of the spontaneously generated imagery I have thus far captured. My embodied thoughtographical gestures take on the shape of a living, breathing, digital apparatus that rhetorically charges the visual language of the performance environment. I use the transmission of manipulated images and sounds to further modify the relationship between the performer and the audience—*especially the relationship between their bodies.* These bodies pass through the all-encompassing image-sound mix and can also *become part of the image-sound mix* in an electronic mesh of robust synaesthetic happenstance. The bodies become screens and sound boards as well as social engines to remix the performance energy into a poetically tinged playing field of *net-*

work potential. What I find in my live field research, particularly in small clubs and loft parties, is that during live performances, these manipulated images and sounds pass through my body as both an active memory I am remixing from previous gigs as well as manipulated flashbacks of my prior video location shoots. I find myself composing more digital source material *out of* my fictional memories (yes, active fictional memory generation, as digital source material).

The hyperimprovised image-sound mix that I'm creating in live social environments is thus composed primarily of my own manipulated memories captured on digital video and exported through a wide array of fictional filters and effects. This then becomes something like a customized Life Style Practice that emerges from the depths of the creative unconscious. Forget phrases like "Sometimes my life feels like a movie." No movie can even come close to capturing the live VJ performance my fringe-flow sensations pass through as I live my life on Planet O.

The net effects of these manipulated memory-visions that I hyperimprovisationally compose in live performance are known to linger. Sometimes, the day after a long VJ performance, I will drift through the maze of streets in the foreign city I happen to be in, looking around at the light and shadows on the surfaces I am exposed to, and see that they resonate with what I generated twelve hours earlier in the performance space I was gigging in the night before. Am I hallucinating my manipulated memories on to the walls and pavement of the city I performed in the night before? Or are my eyes tricking me into seeing what's not really there? And yet I am convinced that without the unreal there is no Real.

For me, there is no need to get totally hung up on it all. I just do what I do: *I play with the data.* And by playing with it—by self-reflexively manipulating it while making my presence felt (hyperintuitively aware of my role as artist plug-in turning the knobs of my readiness potential on to autopilot)—I always go meta on you. *Going meta* is what a postcontemporary fictional artist does when randomly composing many digital flux personas in the networked space of flows. I (whoever that is) make spontaneous visual connections and link these spur-of-the-moment remixes of past-present-future dream-memory-performances into my various stories and emerging digital poetics—the ones that are always embodied in this distributed media fiction I am continuously in the process of becoming (like here, in this aimless drift that's been going on for how long now?).

Sometimes I imagine these blurred boundaries as a way of life—as enacting multiple ways of seeing. Other times I digitally capture these active memories onto my camera's DV tape and download them on my computers. Sometimes I edit them for various Net, DVD, and performance art projects. The editing sessions can feel like séances with the living dead (active memories might be viewed as an homage to the living-dead images we have all come to know). The projects that grow out of these intensive séancelike editing sessions are exhibited in museums, galleries, and festivals or generated in front of live audiences. Because they come across as the digital traces I am leaving behind, they are easily translated or even interpreted as an intentional manipulation of form. This form then forms my reputation and informs others about my Life Style Practice, even if I can totally separate myself from it and say to myself, "That is not-me." The fact that I am sure it is not-me no longer matters. What matters is that these digital traces, this form that follows me wherever I go, becomes my life as an aimless drift that is, for reasons I'll never understand, always open to interpretation.

But I cannot look back and report on my form. Even here, as part of an emerging digital poetics, I have no choice but to plow ahead, manipulated memories and dreams and performances always intact, ready for dissolution. Anticipating the present is where I am most comfortable as I intuit my next mode of action. Making myself up as I go along, my Life Style Practice is always and forever reaching peak moments of hyperintuitive awareness and has become *one totally fluid narrative field of action* that is intimately synced with my postcognitive self as it continually *plays with my seeing*. As Bergson reminds us in his blurry definition of *matter* as only he can see it, "Everything is changed in the interior movements of my perceptive centers." Today we might call them *cyberceptive centers* or, to malign a phrase from Peter Weibel's essay on "The Intelligent Image: Neurocinema or Quantum Cinema?," *opiscopic centers*—where *opiscopy* (the seeing of seeing) is part of a creative process involving the observation of observing mechanisms, suggesting a change from cinematography's "writing of motion" to something more like the "writing of seeing." In a more romantic setting, this might lead me to say something like, "Whenever I am around you, I write like I have never seen before."

The digital images that are generated by the nomadic Net artist / VJ in asynchronous realtime are the living, breathing record of image *écriture*'s digital traces being left behind like footprints in the sand. They can no longer be conceived of as cinema. They are something beyond cinema, beyond database, beyond compression technologies, and certainly beyond literature. Perhaps the term *thoughtographical* would be a useful way to look at transmissions from the otherworld. The literal bowels of that ultimate image reservoir (dream-databank) called Planet Oblivion are a rhizomatic and networked space of flows that you may not always be aware of but are always playing with nonetheless. This is a space artists must, out of necessity, feed off like a belly of sunshine and that will eventually kill you no matter how many images you procreate over the course of your life. Given this reality, why not hack into that intuitive process of becoming that precedes consciousness and just let the neuroimages flow?

The digitally manipulated neuroimages that are generated during the live performance of the nomadic Net artist / VJ are never truly settled, never still life, and yet they can emerge from a grounded body-brain-apparatus achievement hallucinated by the artist. These images seem to appear from nowhere and take on a life of their own. And when images take on a life of their own, they become bioimages. Only later, in a quiet moment of poetic solitude and patient research, can the artist even begin to meditate on the potential meaning of these biomorphic images, performing a kind of autobiopsy on them and surgically removing whatever nuggets of context or even personal theory that may be metastasizing.

And yet, and yet . . . no matter how much theory is surgically removed, you can never be sure you got rid of it all. All it takes is some stubborn little bit to keep you elaborating and revising some metacommentary on what you imagine to be your very own Life Style Practice. The VJ, the artist-medium, the flux persona, the hactivist, the aimless drifter, and the digital thoughtographer (especially one who grows out of and continually integrates a nomadic Net art practice into a touring schedule) cannot merely role-play some convenient version of the avant-garde artist who squares an aestheticized ontology with visionary experience. Like all alchemists dedicated to working with the latest in remix technology, artists must continuously turn themselves into a foreign substance that triggers the mysterious neural mechanism inside the unconscious body so that they can transmit an *image écriture* into and onto that compositional force field where the social network *comes to life* in asynchronous realtime—that is, *unrealtime*.

An earlier version of this essay was originally published as part of the Ciber@rt Bilbao 2004 conference proceedings.

Portrait of the VJ

The essay is not merely the articulation of a thought, but of a thought as a point of departure for a committed existence.
—Vilém Flusser, "Essays"

The whole no longer lives at all: it is composed, calculated, artificial, a fictitious thing.
—Friedrich Nietzsche, "The Case of Wagner"

What a VJ is not:

- A VJ (video or visual jockey) is not an MTV personality.
- A VJ is not a Net artist.
- A VJ is not a visual DJ.
- A VJ is not susceptible to computer crashes (a VJ believes in the power of positive thinking).

What a VJ could be:

- A VJ could be a hyperimprovisational narrative artist who uses banks of QuickTime movie clips to construct on-the-fly stories composed of images processed in asynchronous realtime and through various theoretical and performative filters.
- A VJ could be a creative writer who manipulates matter and memory by composing live acts of image *écriture* repositioning the movie loop as the primary semantic unit of energy.

▪ A VJ could be a Tech*know*mad whose fluid Life Style Practice captures consciousness in asynchronous realtime and is forever being remixed into One Ongoing Text Exactly.

▪ A VJ could be a (h)activist provocateur who knowingly intervenes in the mainstream art, club, and cinema culture and opens up new possibilities for hybridized art and entertainment events.

Ten Things You Can Say about VJ-ing without Wondering If It's Necessarily True

1. What You See Is What You Get.
2. What You Get Is Simultaneously Cinematic and Pixelated.
3. What You Transgress Is Video Art.
4. What You Point Back to Is Video Art.
5. What You Refrain from Repeating Is Video Art.
6. What You Do Is Change the Way You See.
7. What You Steer Clear of Is Conceptual Art.
8. What You Reinvent Is Beauty as a Subliminal Force in Consciousness.
9. What You Create Is Always Hyperimprovisational.
10. What You Avoid Is Theorizing Your Practice to Death.

Tokyo versus Lucerne

In Tokyo, they come to your performance and passively let the performance enter their every orifice.

In Lucerne, they lock up their (w)hole being and try to understand why you are doing what you are doing and whether it has any relevance to their way of processing life information.

In Tokyo, they process the life force of the performance and let the experience rule over their utterly open minds and bodies.

In Lucerne, they whisper superior remarks to each other assuming that you must think you are better than them because your DJ-VJ thing is only pseudo avant-garde and they invented the avant-garde a short train ride away in Zurich, so when does this gig end?

In Tokyo, they come up to you after the performance and shake your hand and say, "Thank you. I just had an alpha experience."

In Lucerne, they surprise you with a question-and-answer session right after you finish exhausting your every creative pore and start the unexpected questioning with "I'm not sure I understand the relationship between the music and the images. Can you explain it to me a little better?"

In Tokyo, after you put away your gear and begin circulating inside the performance art space, Flipper Chicks with eyes that won't quit surround you.

In Lucerne, after you put away your gear and begin circulating inside the performance space, the people who just asked you the critically infused questions that beg to differ try to use their participation in the Q&A exchange to further break the ice with you and become something like a friend or intellectual colleague.

In Tokyo, you leave the performance space with a bevy of Flipper Chicks and cool DJ-VJ dudes who want to know all about your gear, and the evening doesn't end there.

In Lucerne, you leave with your sponsors and go out for a beer and watch the local soccer team win an upset victory on the pub's TV. During the game intermission, a few of the local artist-intellectuals take you outside and light up marijuana-infused cigarettes, and soon after they catch a buzz, they begin to wax eloquent on why America is a twenty-first-century fascist state.

Crucial Question
What is a Flipper Chick?

Enigmatic Answer
A Flipper Chick is not a nineteen-year-old girl from Tokyo.

A Flipper Chick is not a VJ groupie who has a thing for tall American gaijin.

A Flipper Chick is not excitedly jumping up and down after your performance wanting to be near the source of all of the image processing she has just readily absorbed. (And when she is not excitedly jumping up and down, she is also not excitedly jumping up and down with her hands pointing out from the side of her hips, flapping her palms up and down like a hybridized dolphin-mermaid.)

A Flipper Chick is not a closet cybergeek who finds interactivity to be a matter of pushing her buttons when she asks you to.

A Flipper Chick is not always with her best friend who is also nineteen and is also not all of the above and refuses to synchronize her svelte body swimming under your American waters.

A Flipper Chick is not someone who can barely speak a word of English but can communicate her cultural difference to you nonetheless.

A Flipper Chick is not an apparition.

A Flipper Chick is not any of these things, or if she is, then she is only some of these things some of the time but longs to be all of these things all of the time.

Straightforward Answer (with a Conceptual Link to the Film *Lost in Translation*)
A Flipper Chick is never going to ask you about the interrelationship between your just-finished VJ performance and the emergent languages of new media. She is not even a Flipper Chick: she is a late-adolescent sea creature whose turquoise eyes betray her Sino-sensual culture in ways that make playing her tender buttons a mental striptease seductively pointing back to root beginnings with no endgame in sight.

She is someone who makes *you* feel late adolescent, especially when you write about her, even though you are a fortysomething VJ losing it in the heart of Japanese youth culture. She'll look at you and say, "What do you think of Tokyo?"

To which you'll have a canned response, one that comes out of nowhere but is still canned inside your brain: "Tokyo is a state of mind."

And to yourself, you will think "a state of mind that makes me forget the language I know and propels me into a world whose behaviors are generated by the code of image *écriture.*"

An Unimportant Question That Need Not Be Addressed But Will Be Addressed Anyway
"I'm not sure I understand the relationship between the music and the images. Can you explain it to me a little better?"

A Nonanswer
The relationship between the music and the images is first of all not a relationship between music and images. It is a performative dynamic between units of energy that are at times sonic, at other times visual, and at still other times textual—as in "the movement-image of the touring body in motion as it unconsciously plays with its readiness potential is writing out a new media language that is being remixed live in front of you." This makes the whole art of VJ-ing something beyond VJ-ing and assumes that the artist is now operat-

ing in what Dick Higgins referred to as a postcognitive state of mind. By *post-cognitive*, what he really means is "post-self-cognitive"—an intermedial space where the work no longer divides and subdivides into various compartments like music, sound, text, image, code, act, belief, memory, dance, body, and self but rather fuses fluid or fluxlike units of energy and motion (performative ID/ entities) into transgressive states of mind opening up new horizons. Higgins also makes it clear that postcognitive artists are not the end result of a progressive, historical development; rather, postcog artists can emerge from any historical era or geographical location. They need not be Western artists forming their work after World War II (that is, postmodern artists). As a postcog VJ artist remixing source material in what I perceive as a live, image-writing context, I may have more in common with Comte de Lautréamont, William Burroughs, Antonin Artaud, and Kathy Acker than I do with Bill Viola, Nam June Paik, Matthew Barney, or Kiki Smith. This does not necessarily make me less contemporary or derivative, and I certainly don't feel less visual or out of touch with the times.

In fact, while touring the world as a VJ, quotes from two of these *agents provocateurs* keep coming to mind as I try to process my experience of planetary Net culture and this postcog state of mind. One is from Artaud's "Here Lies," where he sees the artist, "no matter how fast soonest is, / too late, / who doesn't say a word, / is always there / dissonating, point by point, / all the soonests" and feels himself being

taken
     from the void
                   itself
and sniffed at
          from time
                     to time.
             I speak
                from above
                       time
as if time
were not fried,
were not this dry fry
of all the crumbles
at the beginning
setting out once more in their coffins.

(And let's not forget that it was Artaud who gave us the expression "body without organs.")

The other quote comes from an interview with Kathy Acker conducted by R. U. Sirius that I was fortunate enough to be able to publish on my *Alt-X* site. She is talking about finding a way out of "that specific, controlling, imprisoning 'I.'" Her own explorations into body-brain-apparatus achievements were part of a desire to "write to get it out of me. I don't want to remember." During the time of this interview, she was experimenting wildly with the interrelationship between writing and having an orgasm, where she says (and this is the quote I am constantly reminded of while VJ touring): "I'm looking for what might be called a body language." Yes, that's it. And if the body is itself an image in motion, the language it speaks can be translated into acts of image *écriture*—or VJ writing.

Acker was much more spontaneous and erotic about this than I am. Whenever I was around her, she could cut to the core of body language in a way I still hope to achieve one day. Besides developing a body language, she developed an attitude that I will call *hyperheterosexual piracy*. She continues the quote above by saying, "One thing I do is stick a vibrator up my cunt and start writing—writing from the point of orgasm and losing control of the language and seeing what that's like." Somehow this last quote from Acker captures what I felt at the end of my VJ performance in Lucerne when people started having a public Q&A session, getting on my "A" (as it were) to explain what I had just done in front of them. That is, I felt like telling them that the music and images (and really, they were sound and writing as far as I was concerned) were not meant to have anything specific to do with each other and that I was just *getting off* by having the whole bodily experience unload from me, losing control of the language and seeing what that's like. I was disseminating images, pure and simple (corrupt as they may have been). But I was too kind to my hosts and audience and ended up giving them some pseudo-theoretical justification for the work I had just created (and regret having done so).

The new media landscape is riddled with these pseudo-theoretical justifications, and as most media artists find out sooner or later, the easiest place to hide and find comfort while trying to make your practice legit is in earlier practices whose practitioners laid down most of the theoretical groundwork. Had my Swiss colleagues never heard of the work of John Cage and Merce Cunningham and their artistic investigations into the compositional process of indeterminacy (not that this sort of thing necessarily floats through my mind as I collaboratively research the aesthetic potential of hyperimprovisational VJ performance)? Somewhere in their art school studies, they must have come across the idea that experimenting with indeterminate operations creates a "sensitive dependence" between the performers themselves, the emergent artwork in the making, and the audience. A great deal of the early happening art scene might be said to have grown out of Cagean philosophy and experiments with interdisciplinary practices that were conducted at Black Mountain. VJs are now examining the vicissitudes of "making contemporary" their own aleatory compositional methods, often using source material they have captured on their video cameras that very day to generate their potential illuminations later that night—and sometimes we capture live images in the space we are performing in and bring those into the mix as well.

The poetics and theories of Intermedia as well as what Allan Kaprow called *nontheatrical performance* outline an art of living that effectively takes the art world out of the museums and galleries and blurs all human action and social behavior into a kind of artistically generated Life Style Practice (that is, if you want to consider it art at all). Kaprow envisions a few key scenarios for Life Style Practices. In his 1976 essay "Nontheatrical Performance," Kaprow says, "Here is the ball game I perceive." He then lists what an artist can attempt to do—such as "work within recognizable art modes and present the work in recognizable art contexts," "work in unrecognizable, i.e. nonart, modes but present the work in recognizable art contexts," "work in recognizable art modes but present the work in nonart contexts," "work in nonart modes but present the work as art in nonart contexts," "work in nonart modes and nonart contexts and cease to call the work art, retaining instead the private consciousness that sometimes it may be art, too."

In this regard, integrating live VJ performances into a Life Style Practice is liable to encompass many of the above scenarios. For example, working within a recognizable art mode and presenting the work in recognizable art contexts is exactly what my collaborator Chad Mossholder and I did at venues like the International Symposium of Electronic Art in Japan (Nagoya 2002), the new media art center in Basel, the Museum für Kommunikation in Berne, and the Machida City Museum of Graphic Arts on the outskirts of Tokyo. These venues were all about art, our work was advertised as a new mode of artistic practice, and the audience consisted primarily of individuals from a demographic whose profile included "going to hip new media art event by semi-known digital artists"—that is, mostly people from the art world.

But some of Kaprow's other categories (like working in unrecognizable, nonart modes but presenting the work in recognizable art contexts and working in recognizable art modes but presenting the work in nonart contexts) get fuzzy. For instance, is a primarily hard rock club that has one night of DJ-VJ performance art a recognizable art context? I suppose a rock club is more like an art context than, say, a nursing home is. Is a university auditorium a recognizable art context? I suppose it is one more than, say, a Wal-Mart is. But when I showed my younger sister "what I do when I take these trips," I was not just giving her a demo in my studio. I was enraptured in the creative process *right then*, at that moment in time—just as I am when I am waiting for a delayed take-off, plugged into an airport power source in a faraway corner of the building so that I don't have to hear crying babies, laptop open, headphones securely fastened, and generating all manner of live, hyperimprovised VJ action. Some of my best performances take place in airports, cafés, train stations, my university office, a plane crossing the international date line, and my hotel room. In fact, I did not learn to be a VJ in a class or from an older, wiser, mentor VJ. I did not engage with an online or CD-ROM VJ-in-a-box demo program. I just started playing around with the software wherever I happened to be located and watched the work *MATERIALIZE* before my eyes, working in nonart modes and nonart contexts and retaining a kind of private consciousness that what I was generating at any given time may be art, too.

But don't tell the Flipper Chicks this because they don't care and are not interested, and in many ways, I don't blame them.

The VJ as Artist-Researcher Burning It from Both Ends

Kaprow, again in his "Nontheatrical Performance" essay, makes an interesting case for the artist as researcher: "Suppose that performance artists were to adopt the emphasis of universities and think tanks on basic research. Performance would be conceived as inquiry. It would reflect the word's everyday meaning of performing a job or service and would relieve the artist of inspirational metaphors, such as creativity, that are tacitly associated with making art, and therefore theatre art."

VJs intuitively know that once they are engaged in a live, hyperimprovisa-tional performance in front of a crowd of social networkers and party-goers, there is more to VJ-ing than being inspired. It's much more about collecting your source material, getting your technical gear set up right, researching new software programs, developing your own set of preferences as well as any new patches that may be of use to you, and making sure the projection is adequate enough to convey your force field of visual action. It's also about installing an emergent multimedia performance that will in some way alter the live, social network. In this way, VJ practice points back to the poetry of William Carlos Williams ("the poem as a field of action") as well as the philosophy of Alfred North Whitehead and his theory of process. VJ practice can also be linked to various visual and literary artists of the post-WWII movements who began investigating themes such as energy, force, mass, light, and particle theory. With VJ performance, mix is idiom and loop is measure. In my own practice, I can even see a deep-rooted connection between what VJs do and what Ab-stract Expressionists, underground filmmakers, Fluxus performance artists, and most of the Dadaists were doing in their time. There's no escaping it: con-scientious VJs use the methods of the artistic avant-garde as a model of pure research investigation. But this should come as no surprise for, as Kaprow says, "The artist as researcher can begin to consider and act on substantive questions about consciousness, communication, and culture without giving up membership in the profession of art." I would add that they can do this by utilizing emerging new media technologies that permeate the digital pop culture without giving up membership in the artificial intelligentsia, despite its natural adhesion to a more politically engaged avant-garde cultural move-ment that started in Europe a hundred years ago.

Those of us who straddle both the avant-pop VJ culture and the artist-researcher model need to acknowledge the links to prior art, literature, and philosophical works that inform contemporary practice in the field. Not every VJ will give a shit about the interrelationship between the process-based art and writing of Kaprow and the synaesthetic qualities of the live VJ set as a kind of "performance-to-be." But some VJs are now coming at the computer medium from a number of different perspectives, and these perspectives are emerging from a hybridized practice that is at once influenced by experimen-tal writing, video art, Net art, electronic music, film, Fluxus-style happenings, and software art. And just as the particular backgrounds of the performers are usually of a hybridized nature, the space their work intervenes in varies. As new media art curator Annet Decker says in an essay entitled "Synaesthetics in the Clubscene," "Most of today's VJs are not bothered to adhere to museum or gallery directors; they make their own art and show it directly to those who it is meant for."

Having said that, Decker also notes that many contemporary art openings and museum programs have DJ/VJ events as part of the experience, especially in Europe. The largest international new media festival in Germany, transmediale, has a club.transmediale component that is every bit as refreshing and eye opening as what you'll see hanging on the wall at any contemporary art gallery opening. Some observers, like Decker, fear that this close proximity to recognizable art contexts could lead to VJ institutionalization. This is especially true if you view emergent art practices as value-pure and too easily commodified by the relentless, absorbing mechanism of the contemporary art world. But the VJ, like all digital art personas, is born into a world where "to be or not to be" institutionalized is no longer a question. It's an *already-is* situation that the VJ, like any other life-style practitioner, can use to take a stance *from within*. There is no outside the system anymore, and if you're looking for certain proof of that hypothesis, remember what you're reading right now, how you got here, and who is communicating to you. At the very least, *we are all in this together*, even if we role-play the artist outlaw living on the edge of forever. As Ronald Sukenick has said in his *Down and In: Life in the Underground*: "a renewed underground would have the courage of its contradictions, knowing how to manage the impulse to succeed in terms of the commercial culture without betraying its deepest political and artistic convictions." Whether you consider yourself an artist-VJ, a nonartist VJ, a professor VJ, a visual wallpaper VJ, or any other kind of VJ, the key is to realize that your work—your Life Style Practice—is not outside of the system. You are in it and of it like everyone else, and this is what gives you the power to try to change what you don't like.

Making Space for the Artist

By its very nature, new media art is congested with always emergent technologies and a slew of theoretical justifications that attempt to turn aesthetic practice into art research. But avant-garde artists have been at the forefront of pioneering an experimental humanities since the early twentieth century, and now that contemporary avant-pop artists have access to a multitude of personal digital assistants that *come with* their all-consuming, network culture, where exactly does the art research of today really *take place*? In the traditional artist studio? The computer science lab? The corporate cubby-hole? The wireless blogosphere? Consider this: many reputable universities are now finding pockets of interest in their various science faculties that want to move away from computer science and theory to embrace new modes of interdisciplinary thought that border on the aesthetic. Which brings up more questions: Who are the new media artists of today, and where are they hiding in the midst of all of this interdisciplinary change? Are they capable of making space for their creative enterprise without conforming to preset research agendas and styles of inquiry? And is it still possible to take a radical stance from within the work of art itself, regardless of what new technologies are hot and what current theory tries to appropriate its fluid context?

Perhaps there are no real answers to these questions, but one starting point for me has been to reconfigure my day-to-day life so that I operate in a more fluid, interdisciplinary, lifestyle. While a visiting artist at the University of Technology in Sydney in 2005, I started every lecture I gave during the semester—whether it was on new media writing, VJ performance, digital narrative, Net art, the role of creativity in brain and consciousness studies, or even experiential pedagogy—by referring to Vito Acconci's essay "Steps into Performance (and Out)" (which I have used elsewhere in this book):

If I specialize in a medium, then I would be fixing a ground for myself, a ground I would have to be digging myself out of, constantly, as one medium was substituted for another—so then instead of turning toward "ground" I would shift my attention and turn to "instrument," I would focus on myself as the instrument that acted on whatever ground was available.

What he is saying tends to get forgotten in the mad rush to keep up with the latest developments in technology and in the incredible amounts of time we spend reading and writing theoretical justifications for the practice-based research agendas of contemporary new media art. It's the *artist* who is the medium or instrument that is most capable of conducting radical experiments in subjective thought and experience. The tools that we use, the theories that justify it all, and the outcomes that play into the preconceived agendas and methods of the academic research community as well as the corporate R&D divisions should have very little to do with the way an artist or a collaborative network of artists bring creative compositions into society. This doesn't mean that artists are outcasts or meant to live on the outer edges of the criminal fringe. Like professional athletes, they are meant to play out their *performances-to-be* on whatever compositional playing field they happen to be on at any given time. That playing field would be the ground of the moment—not one they would have to dig themselves out of continuously but one that they would *act* on as part of their fluid Life Style Practice as a way to tap into what I call the *readiness potential of their unconscious*, the space (if you can make it) where creativity springs forth from.

Lately, I have been wondering what sort of example we are setting when we show the next generation of emerging new media artists that the only way we can make space for them in society is to have them adopt these pre-conceived models of subsistence that are intimately attached to either the corposphere or the more scientifically oriented academic research agendas. And a third path too seems to be calling out for digitally inclined artists—the path of the commercial art world, which is driven by a handful of well-connected gallery owners, curators, and art collectors who influence emerging artists by making it very clear what sells. These artists (many of them too young to recognize a bad thing when it's coming) are still totally full of the kind of creative potential we should be nurturing, but they start repeating themselves, doing the same work over and over again so that (to use Acconci's terminology) they fix a ground for themselves, one that they may not ever consider digging themselves out of because they dig the money and attention they are receiving.

Now, don't get me wrong. I'm not antimoney: it greases the wheels of creative momentum just like good sex greases the wheels of personal self-esteem. The more the merrier. But how can we make space for artists so that they are able to tap into their creative unconscious, spontaneously generate new works of art, and not be codependent on playing by the rules set up by the commercial or scientific or academic mainstream? I wonder. I think each artist has to figure this out for themselves. But I sense they'll be able to do it only if they have other options than the ones that seem to predominate right now.

My own path is full of aimless drifting, nomadic excursions into what I call the Unreal, which consists mostly of writing, writing, and more writing. Writing and hacking, writing and hacking, writing and hacking, allowing for incredible failures and—much to my surprise—a few successes that confound me to the point that when I look back over the last twenty years of nomadic wanderlust, taking into account all of the work produced across various media platforms in both art and nonart contexts, I think to myself: that's not-me.

In fact, that's one subject area of research I've been glomming on to for most of my active working life, the so-called NOT-ME. I thought I had invented the idea myself as I wrote it out of my system and started using it to improvise an ongoing set of theoretical fictions via novels, hypertexts, complex works of Net art, VJ performances, and now feature-length movies too.

But others are onto this as well, albeit from totally different angles. Tors Norretranders, whose book *The User Illusion: Cutting Consciousness Down to Size* explores recent scientific investigations into the role that consciousness plays in our day-to-day actions, has a three-page riff in the middle of his book where he writes about "art and the expression of me." Speaking mostly in terms of theatrical performance, he tells us that the difficulty of putting on a good play is that the I does not have access to the great quantity of information that is required to make the actor present with her entire personality during a performance and that because we all convert information in an *unconscious* way, the conscious I cannot automatically activate all the information required for a good performance. The I can repeat the text, he tells us, but that is not enough. The I must follow the Me to live the part—to feel it as it develops. In other words, theater involves setting the Me free, so it can unfold.

He also goes on to say that when the performance is over and the audience begins to clap, the consciousness and the I return as if from a trance and wake amid the cheers, which is a shame because it was not the I that gave the performance but the Me.

I know what he's talking about—not because I have been running experiments in the field of behavioral and brain studies out of my lab at the University of Colorado at Boulder but because over the last twenty years I have been creating free-form metafictions featuring my various flux personas across a wide range of interdisciplinary works. He is arguing that there is something that exists inside all of us that precedes every conscious act we make and that this something else exists somewhere inside the brain. I think that he and most others who do this kind of research get it wrong in assuming that if it's not the I who is performing, then it must be Me. Norretranders says, "We must distinguish between the I and the Me. I am not identical with Me. Me is more than my I. It is Me who decides when I do not. The I is the conscious player. The Me is the person in general."

But I would say that the NOT-ME is performing when I engage in these hyperintuitive acts of experiential composition—that enable my creative self to live my life here on Planet Oblivion and that somehow leave specific traces of my existence behind. Sukenick calls these traces *form*, "like footprints in the sand." In this regard, there's a crucial difference between "the general person Me" who Norretranders would like to give the credit to, and the *not-me* I feel so indebted to for making this creative life possible. Henri Michaux put it nicely when he said, "There isn't one me. There aren't ten mes. There is no me. ME is only a position of equilibrium. An average of 'mes,' a movement in the crowd."

The not-me, I figure, is the perfect vessel to use as I distribute my various flux personas (nowadays, digital flux personas) throughout the fictional space of flows through which I am constantly teleporting my creativity. Many times these flux personas (which I role-play via my novels, e-mail, Web chat, spontaneous Net art creations, philosophical films and videos, VJ performances, mobile blogging collaborations, and the like) transpond the readiness potential of the unconscious player that precedes the ever rational I, and for this unconscious player there is only a networked SPACE of flows to wander through nomadically at any particular moment in time—as if there could even *be* a particular moment in time.

Think about it.

It just passed us by.

Just like we knew it would.

And yet we are still struggling to make space for this political fiction we might want to call the *artist-to-be*.

Rosi Braidotti, in the introduction to her book *Nomadic Subjects: Embodiment and Sexual Difference in Contemporary Feminist Theory*, says:

> The nomadic subject is a myth, that is to say a political fiction, that allows me to think through and move across established categories and levels of experience: blurring boundaries without burning bridges. Implicit in my choice is the belief in the potency and relevance of the imagination, of myth-making, as a way to step out of the political and intellectual stasis of these postmodern times. Political fictions may be more effective, here and now, than theoretical systems.

To which I might add, they may be more effective than innovative product development and the predictable forms of research methodology that are suffocating much of academia.

Locating spaces for the political fictions of the not-me whose many flux personas drift nomadically through the networked space of flows is getting harder and harder as we see the viral effects of a rampant technocapitalism infiltrate the academy, the museum culture, the publishing business, and the minds of the artists themselves. Where is this imaginal *artist-to-be* to go and play, the way any athlete plays? As Joe Montana, the former quarterback of the San Francisco 49ers, said, "I am not conscious when I am playing" (and I don't think he was suggesting that he was always playing with a concussion either).

How can we encourage more research methodologies that support this not being conscious while playing? Is that even possible in corporate and academic spheres that are obsessed with profit making and standard modes of assessment? Is it even feasible to think that artists can be situated in the networked space of flows in a way that allows them to create a fluid Life Style Practice steeped in intuition and unconscious play? How else to continue fueling the historical trajectory of the artificial intelligentsia whose shape-shifting, emotional alchemy exuberantly devours time while "keeping it unreal"?

Although I can identify with Joe Montana when he says, "I am not conscious when I am playing," I am willing to bet that the majority of Montana's fans would most likely feel alienated from the work that my unconscious playing produces. This presents a set of problems that I have no choice but to investigate continually, especially in the context of my willingness to identify myself as an artist. In fact, when people who are not familiar with my background ask me, "What do you do for a living?," I have a problem answering because I play many different roles in my daily life. It's never easy to quantify that question with a definitive answer, especially when it's considered in light of Acconci's quote. For example, I would most likely not say, "What do I do? I'm an instrument that acts on whatever ground is available." I also wouldn't answer by saying, "What do I do for a living? Well, I'm making space for the artist, the not-me that distributes all of my flux personas into the networked space of flows." I just wouldn't say that.

It would be so much easier if I could just say, "I'm a quarterback for the San Francisco 49ers," but depending on my audience, I am more likely to say, "I am a writer." But that's the beginning of a slippery slope into a long aside about how (when I write my creative metafictions) I am (like the quarterback Joe Montana) never conscious of what I am doing, how these unconscious acts of creative composition infect an array of contemporary media (everything from print books to mobile blogging to Net art to VJ performance to feature-length works of philosophical cinema), and how when I am on the fringe of my unconscious experience and everything is totally *clicking* (to use my colleague David Foster Wallace's term), I am no longer a writer but a kind of automated teller machine dishing out totally manipulated memory cache while cashing in on the sediment of experience that has been slowly accumulating in the databanks of my imagination—not unlike the way Marcel Duchamp watched the dirt accumulate on his window sill and saw *that* as a kind of work in progress.

This manipulated memory cache of the player I am calling the not-me is loaded with readiness potential, a readiness potential that can spontaneously generate an Internetwork of flux personas—what in the old days we used to call *characters*. But characters are too composed for me. Like scripted reality TV characters, they are always destined for plots, which (after all) is just another code word for *gravesites*. As a digital flux persona, I can compose and decompose and recompose my identity by living on the edge of my readiness potential, that space of mind where time is obliterated and I am capable only of intuiting my next move, acting before I know what I am doing.

With some of my work, particularly a written text like the one you are reading now, I can look back at whatever traces I may have left behind and reapply my conscious I to a kind of editorial remix. But when I am in a live VJ performance, where the speed and parallel processing of the image writing *is* the text I am creating with no end in sight—where everything feels unreal and I am somehow constructively positioned to go out of my mind—my performance *lives* in a space of flows that precedes all of my conscious actions. It's what we used to call *being avant-garde* (before that term got hijacked by Madison Avenue and eventually became too jaded to use successfully anymore). In fact, being avant-garde may be the primal state we all live in but are conditioned to ignore so that we can slog away inside the bureaucratic superstructure of consumer culture and its devout attempts to keep us aware that we are ON THE CLOCK. For it ends up that what we are experiencing when we act in what *feels* like the present is a *backward referral of subjective time perception* so that everything *seems* to be in sync and consequently real again when, in fact, it is not.

As the scientist Benjamin Libet has spent his entire career trying to prove, our sense of living in realtime is just a manipulated metafiction of epic proportions. In his book *Mind Time: The Temporal Factor in Consciousness*, Libet, who started his experiments in how the brain produces conscious subjective experiences by studying people who were going through neurosurgical therapy, attempts to prove to the scientific community that there is a half-second delay in awareness of a conscious action or sensation. An electrical charge appears to be triggered by the brain before we are conscious of what we are doing. Due to a subjective, backward referral that we train ourselves to experience over and over again throughout our lives, what happens now feels like the realtime present. According to Libet,

Existence of subjective referral backward in time (to the time of the fast primary response of the sensory cortex) does put the *subjective experience* of the present back into the present. So we have the strange situation in which actual awareness of the present is really delayed, but the *content* of the conscious *experience* is brought into alignment with the present.

This means that, subjectively speaking, we do not live in an antedated now even though we are really not aware of the present when it first arrives. When I read that, I could not help but think that Libet's branch of experimental neuroscience is the scientific version of the language of VJ theory and the history of spontaneous poetics that it grows out of.

Libet also devotes part of his book to what he too calls *readiness potential*, a term that I use throughout this essay and that I came up with to describe the creative function of artists who find themselves on the edge of their avant-pop performance while unconsciously playing in the interdisciplinary fields of study in which they tend to produce their most innovative work. In the 1960s, researchers in Germany located an electrical change inside the brain that actively and consistently precedes any voluntary action. They too referred to this electrical change as *readiness potential*, and Libet conducted follow-up experiments that further conclude that "the process leading to a voluntary act is *initiated* by the brain *unconsciously*, well before the conscious will to act appears."

As any philosophically engaged VJ will tell you, the brain's readiness potential is always on the cusp of writing into being the next wave of unconscious action that the I—*consciousness par excellence*—will inevitably take credit for. But the actual avant-trigger that sets the image *écriture* into motion as the VJ jams with new media technology is ahead of its—the conscious I's—time. Improvisational artists or sports athletes who are in tune with their bodies while on the playing field or in the club or art space know that to achieve a high-level performance they must synchronize their distributive flow with the constant activation of this avant-trigger that they keep responding to as they play out their creative potential. Artists and athletes intuitively know that they have to make their next move without even thinking about it, before they be-come aware of what it is they are actually doing. There is simply no time to think it through, and besides, thinking it through means possibly killing the creative potential before it has time to gain any momentum or causes all kinds of clumsy or wrong-headed decision making that leads to flubs, fumbles, and missteps on the sports or compositional playing field. Artists and theorists who know what it feels like to play the work unconsciously, when everything is clicking and they leave their rational self behind, can relate to what I'm saying. We do not have to open up our skulls surgically to locate the neural mechanism that makes this happen to prove our scientific point. Rather, as player-poets working in the open source COMPOSITION BY FIELD, we can hyperimprovisationally transfer our energy apparatus to the *kinetics and processing of things*. Filtering our Life Style Practice through our own unconscious poetics, we can count on writing out our own subjective experiences to draw the same conclusions.

A Paranoiac Is Someone Who Has All of the Facts at Their Disposal

The institutionalized systems of command and control that I find myself a part of are often driven by political rhetoric, bureaucratic memospeak, com-mercial advertisements, and brainless public relations. They are driven by predictable languages or intertwined discourses that are being marketed to a well-managed culture of consumers that, depending on how the day is going, I am part of. At the root of this consumer culture, no matter how imagistic and action-packed it may seem to be, lives the art of writing—of *manipulating consciousness that is informed by creative code*. The manipulating of conscious-ness by written words is best described by the Beat scribe William Burroughs, who once said, "My basic theory is that the written word was actually a virus that made the spoken word possible" and who then followed this thought by asking, "Is the virus then simply a time bomb left on this planet to be activated by remote control? An extermination program in fact? In its path from full virulence to its ultimate goal of symbiosis, will any human creature survive?"

He addresses his own question later, in a remix of this prior writing called "The Electronic Revolution," by proposing a language that

will delete these virus mechanisms and make them impossible of formulation in the language. This language will be a tonal language like Chinese; it will also have a hieroglyphic script as pictorial as possible without being too cumbersome or difficult to write. This language will give one option of silence. When not talking, the user of this language can take in the silent images of the written, pictorial and symbol languages.

While this tonal language with its hieroglyphic scripts may not exactly replicate the image *écriture* hyperimprovised by the VJ during live performance, the desire to intervene in and eventually eradicate the mainstream media virus of command-and-control structures is concomitant with a more politicized VJ practice. The irony is that the tools of new media technology that the VJ uses to create whatever radical potential may reside in the flow of images are themselves conditioned by the same command-and-control structures coded into all aspects of contemporary, cybernetic life on Planet Oblivion. VJ Persona, it ends up, is a carrier of the same viral language his Life Style Practice is meant to destroy.

Does this mean that the utopian dreamwork is officially declared dead on arrival? Is there no radical, socially progressive premise from which to operate in the networked space of flows being conducted in asynchronous realtime?

Yes and no (with endless qualifiers every way you look at it). For instance, when I take out my video camcorder, I am immediately aware that I am taking out my latest greatest writing instrument, a stylus that captures momentary light events that will soon become my digital source material. Like a Burroughs cut-up taking place in asynchronous realtime, I will later take samples of this digital source material and perform a live (writing) remix of the images I have already captured. I may (if I'm performing at my best) spontaneously create a meaning-imploded narrative effect that is unfettered by the bureaucratic language of command and control. This might occur even if—especially if—that narrative is antinarrative, nonnarrative, multilinear, associational, or even flesh-driven psychosocial narrative (like when the images tweak your body-brain into a sudden, unexpected move in the direction of that person in the corner of the club space, who you then spend three weeks with before realizing that you don't have much in common except the need for consensual hallucination).

In other words, the VJ is conscientiously looking to conduct an experiential event that will create an altered state of mind for those in attendance. From my perspective, as someone who is evolving his own VJ style, these interactions—between the artist-practitioners, the computer hardware and software, the digital source material, and the audience—are always hyperimprovisational and emerge from a desire to change the media discourse from within. This

spontaneous and emergent work is conducted in response to the play of signifiers that bombard me from all media directions, although my own performances rarely, if ever, use found source material from mainstream media
sources. Although using found material is the chosen methodology of over 90
percent of the VJs I know or have seen perform, I much prefer to create a
spontaneous first-person cinema that depends almost exclusively on the nomadic wanderings my eye activates while capturing the imagery my body
passes through. After capturing these sense data, I put the work through a
fair amount of in-camera editing that I further modify on the laptop, where
all of the useable source material is archived for future performance.

In the process of hyperimprovising a generative remix of what I have already written with my video camcorder, I experience the fluidity of flux
identity—what in my second novel, *Sexual Blood*, I termed *Melting Plastic
Fantastic Time*. These phrases refer to a space of mind where time and identity
cease to exist and are replaced by the hyperintuitive, readiness potential of the
unconscious player who is always creatively conducting experimental compositions while role-playing this creature I'm calling the *artist-medium*.

*This Fluidity of Flux Identity couples with unconscious language play, new
media technologies, and the resistance of closure to power the pseudo-
autobiographical agenda of nomadic Net artists as they perform a hyperimprovisational Life Style Practice.*

Let me try to unpack that last statement:

Fluidity of Flux Identity   The decharacterization of self operating in a postcognitive space of flows.
Unconscious Language Play   The use of the unconscious to potentialize a
spontaneous language eruption that works against the authoritarian blockages
of meaning that permeate bureaucratic consumer culture.
Resistance of Closure   The saying of "Fuck you" to death desire, the gnawing
effects of a dehumanized corporate culture, and its mainstream media viruses
as they enter your biological system and begin spreading their ideological
assumptions so that they can initiate their hostile-take-over effects.
Pseudo-Autobiographical   Referring to the manipulated data of the not-me
who nonetheless impersonates me as I trace my movement through matter
and memory. (Remember Michaux: "There isn't one me. There aren't ten
mes. There is no me. ME is only a position of equilibrium. An average of
'mes,' a movement in the crowd.")

Nomadic Net Artist   A digital flux persona or distribution of digital flux personas who spontaneously transcribe the movements of an enervating not-me, the one who impersonates my consciousness as it navigates its way through the networked space of flows fueled by a strong desire to wrest freedom from necessity.

Hyperimprovisational   Referring to intuitive interaction with new media technologies in poetic simultaneity.

Life Style Practice   (Self-explanatory) (also see *Fad of Being* below).

In other words, the VJ as artist-researcher suggests one possible model of artistically generated human relatedness. The VJ is someone who takes the creative workflow of an improvised Life Style Practice and aligns it with an activist social agenda where what is lived is the content of actions, albeit in unrealtime. Over the past ten years, the early practitioners of Net art and the VJs that followed have been part of a tradition of avant-garde artists and writers who throughout the twentieth century were themselves activist artist-researchers *living the life.*

Living and Playing (Performing Generative Acts of Image *Écriture*) in Asynchronous Realtime: The VJ On and Offline

To keep the viral chants looping in rhetorical mantra:

We can now intuitively perform our active states of unconscious play in *asynchronous realtime*, by which I mean a kind of timeless time or state of perpetual jet-lag consciousness, where the fad of Being fades into something like a blur-motion cinema of unconsciously driven active perception, a space of mind where the hyperimprovisational performer becomes a distributed media fiction that, like a chameleon, reconfigures itself to whatever shifts are taking place in the autopoietic world of the artificial intelligentsia.

Time to unpack that last paragraph too, yes?

Asynchronous realtime   Remember Libet's "backward referral of subjective time perception," the one that we all learn to reenact time and time again so that it *feels* like we're actually living in the present even though we are about a half-second behind? As soon as I read Libet's book *Mind Time*, I knew exactly what he was talking about because I had been experiencing these effects as an artist for quite a while and had come up with the phrase *asynchronous realtime* to try to get a handle on it. My own experiences as an internationally touring

VJ showed me that VJs cut into this "backward referral of subjective time perception" to further distort their subjective experiences, doing everything in their power to *become* the readiness potential that triggers the live-image mix that eventually gets projected into the live, social space in which their work gets distributed.

In some ways, I intuitively know that creating hyperimprovisational acts of composition in asynchronous realtime is really impossible to define as a particular state of mind or heretofore unrealized tense of being. It may best be outlined as *an artist-medium becoming a multitude of flux identities nomadically circulating within the networked space of flows.* In this sense, to experience something is to become it while simultaneously losing sight of yourself as a site-specific ME in the networked space of flows. Maybe *you* have experienced the strange inner workings of this creative lag time, this feeling of being in the here and now but also somehow operating in a parallel universe of multithreaded communications where the ME no longer exists.

When I feel this emulated form of jet-lag consciousness take effect (that is, when I am becoming hyperintuitively aware of its presence even though it's been there *all the time*), I immediately begin trying to access the complex event processing that is occurring in my body as a way to WRITE OUT the readiness potential of the unreliable narrator within—tuning in to its proprioceptive time tripping, its habitual indeterminacy, its self-playgiarhythmic differentiation, as well as its intimate, spontaneous, fringe-flow movement, the one that shape-shifts into a postcognitive mapping apparatus that somehow always knows where it is going even when totally lost (in space). This is the totally NOT-ME hacking into the void of a transitional excess hanging on the elliptical edge of a pseudo-autobiographical topos *always on the morph.*

Fad of Being   The experience of being in the here and now as a contemporary fashion statement but infusing that presence-of-being with a proactive agenda of distributing hyperimprovisational performances in asynchronous realtime while unconsciously starting a new fad. For example, net.art or "being a Net artist" was at one time considered a new fad as well as a fashionable way to present yourself as an avant-pop artist in the alternative culture but eventually, and to the dismay of many, became wildly popular in the institutionalized art world too (three words: *absorb, neutralize, abandon*).

Distributed Media Fiction   The nomadic digital artist who manipulates data, constructs various flux personas, and navigates through the networked space of flows in asynchronous realtime.

Autopoietic   Referring to a system that maintains its defining organization throughout environmental perturbation and structural change and that regenerates its components in the course of its operation (think of it as a Wireless Crustacean Network—a Burroughsian/Cronenberg fantasy world of now if ever there was one).

Artificial Intelligentsia   An Internetworked intelligence that includes all the linked data that are being distributed in cyberspace at any given time and that is powered by artistic and intellectual agents who remix the flow of contemporary thought. (This last line is indicative of yet more rhetorical mantra looping within the body of these Net effects.)

Author's aside (or what is left of the author: the digital flux persona writing this poetics feels more like *a spontaneous theory of unconscious play*, something always in the process of becoming other): With very little encouragement from the flow-of-the-mo, I crank out the metalanguage and experimental syntactical gestures that are being remixed into this poetics on Meta/Data. Much of what is written here will be difficult for some to follow (i.e., TOO MUCH META and NOT ENOUGH DATA). But what is meta, and what is data? For me, this problem can be addressed only via the construction of a nomadic fiction that charges language to the ultimate degree. And this can be achieved only by leaving behind conscious perception. For example, this current essay attempts to locate an amorphous thing called *the VJ*. Its arguments are somehow transposed to the fictional thrust of language itself and so are effectively hidden within code words and neologisms that may at times seem too composed. The author does not provide the conventional grounding devices found in proper academic papers and seems to prefer *not* to perform the proper scholarly task of citing all of the references who clearly influence the thinking that has informed much of this document's writing and theory production. But the author has made innumerable connections between the VJ club culture of today and the kind of Happenings and performance art culture that grew out of post–abstract expressionist tendencies in the late 1950s and early 1960s.

This will to aestheticize beyond the data, to drift away from the norm of scholarly writing, is probably connected to the *Eigensinn* within. *Eigensinn* (*eigen* = "own," *sinn* = "sense") has many potential meanings. In its negative connotations, it tends to suggest obstinate, self-willed, or stubborn. But a more positive spin on the word suggests radical independence, as in a youthful, stubborn pursuit of unique subjectivity within a uniform culture. Think of it as using your own sense data to create a fundamentally different Life Style Practice than the one that's always being sold to you by multinational corporate capitalism. Unless you're a trust fund baby who is subsidized or have a knack for creating commercial things for the art market, then as an artist you almost *have* to find a way to use the inherent properties of *Eigensinn* to keep focused on your creative work. Sometimes this *Eigensinn* will take you underground, where you continually burrow for more shards of light. Other times you purposely take *it* into the commercial, nonprofit, or academic sectors to change things from within.

For me, everything started with my years living and working in the artistic and economic undergrounds in New York and Europe, where I learned about the avant tendencies of the artist impresarios who would forever challenge my way of seeing the world anew. Becoming an underground artist was a badge of honor, a way to conscientiously flip off the status quo culture and its Disneyesque, make-believe aura of impenetrability. The idea was to burst everyone's balloon, to pop the bubble economy, to hack into the mainstream version of reality. Doing this meant getting into the mindset of the underground artist— that is, the maker of subversive art forms who is part of an Internetworked do-itself-yourself scene that provokes changes in the curve of culture but that also, much to its chagrin, is often absorbed by the merchants of cool who figure you must be onto something if people are paying attention. Isn't this what always happens in the art world? It certainly happened to the early Net art culture and the VJ scene that came after it. Is there a way to successfully resist this neutralization?

Perhaps the best way to achieve this is to *royally screw language* as best you can. As Steve Shaviro, in the section "William Burroughs" from his book *Doom Patrols: A Theoretical Fiction about Postmodernism*, writes, "Language does not represent the world: it intervenes in the world, invades the world, appropriates the world." One might say that this is the task of those who choose to call themselves VJs—that is, to obliterate language. Could VJ performance be conceived as a new form of obliterature?

Shaviro again: "Let us stylize, enhance, and accelerate the processes of viral replication: for thereby we increase the probability of mutation."

Now let's sample and remix that with this gem from Allen Ginsberg: "Whatever really great poetry I wrote, like *Howl* or *Kaddish*, I was actually able to chant, and use my whole body, whereas in lesser poetry, I wasn't, I was talking."

What I get out of that, in an intuitive flash that makes writing easy, is this: "Let's accelerate the stylized processing by mutating our whole bodies in viral chant." In other words: it's time to walk the walk, not just talk the talk. To PLAY THE WORK as "a *hard* hysterical structure" creating "a collage of the simultaneous data of the actual sensory situation" (these samples are also from Ginsberg, in reference to his poem "Wichita Vortex Sutra"—although that's not an official citation; that's a memory leak).

According to Ginsberg's Beat comrade, Jack Kerouac, this full-body chant that accelerates the act of processing information is more about creating a "*deep* form . . . the way the consciousness *really* digs everything that happens." You don't have to be a beatnik or a peacenik or a Net artnik to see where this is going.

Hard, deep, collage, data, form, consciousness, digs. . . .

Or as Lautréamont once said in his *Poésies*: "Poetry is not a tempest, any more than it is a cyclone. It is a majestic and fertile river." Meanwhile, just underneath the surface, a sleeping giant rumbles.

This is all available source material—the potential META/DATA.

"It's the Source Material, Stupid . . ."

As with many other experimental life and art practices, much of the difference between one VJ and another can be summed up in one word: style. As Miles Davis once said, "For me, music and life are all about style." As far as I can tell, my VJ style has very little to do with technology, almost nothing to do with fine art, and everything to do with source material. This means the source material itself, how I get it (capture it), where I go to look for it (nomadic wandering), how it relates to what I have often perceived as a more risk-oriented investment strategy (the value of the experience itself), and why it seems to evolve around specific themes that have been at the core of my hybridized art/life practice. (These are big-issue themes like "feeling alien in status quo culture," "sexing the muse," "tapping into the spiritual unconscious," "spontaneously generating an on-the-fly narrative remix of who I am while blurring the boundaries between autobiography, memoir, fiction, and performative role-playing.")

My approach to capturing source material from around the world stems from my lust—you might call it *wanderlust*—for the experiential highs that I know a risk-oriented lifestyle can produce. For example, as a bicycle courier in New York City in the mid-1980s, I was challenged by the street to see how fast I could go and how many traffic rules I could break without killing myself. Speeding through the streets of New York City in all weather conditions conditioned both my body and my mind so that I was soon calling myself a *freelance courier artist.* Given the deconstructive trends of the day (cf. Derrida's *Envois,* which I read at the New York Public Library between courier deliveries and fused into a strategy for living in a rapidly ramped up technocapitalist system), I was all too willing to see myself as a kind of postmodern Hermes whose messages were to be found in the medium—in this case, *the artist as medium.* It didn't really matter if the messages were delivered on time or if they were even received by the other who was supposed to get them. As John Cage might have said, the rule was to have no rule. To me, the important thing was to annihilate the important thing. This meant losing my creative self in white hot flashes of chemical decomposition, which was easy to do when cycling at twenty-five to thirty miles per hour, tailgating a rude taxi driver who wouldn't mind seeing you crash and burn so that he didn't have to worry about you slowing down his own big mo.

The lessons from these freelance courier artist experiences were numerous, but a few of them (especially in retrospect, as a newly conceptualized nomadic Net artist, aka roving digital thoughtographer who goes by the name VJ Persona) are worth reiterating here:

- The artist is the medium is the message.
- Calculated risk is essential to experiential growth.
- Nimble movement (i.e., quick-witted psychogeographical drifting through the urban landscape, split-second decision-making, and a proactively engaged artist's intuition) can save your life and produce unexpected results that can positively alter your behavior (and in positively altering your behavior, can further assist you in developing a Life Style Practice funded by an abundance of experiential plusses that can later be reinvested in other forms of hyper-improvisational performance).
- The urban landscape is a psychosocial reservoir of untapped (digital) source material ready for immediate image capture, appropriation, cut-up, remix, or interventionist acts of what I have previously called *surf-sample-manipulate.*

The part about "The urban landscape is a psychosocial reservoir of untapped digital source material ready for immediate remix, appropriation, cut-up, or interventionist acts of what I have previously called *surf-sample-manipulate*" I sampled off the Web and remixed for my own immediate needs.

(By *surf-sample-manipulate*, I mean performers are developing a style that surfs the media culture and samples whatever source material they need for their own mythological undertaking and then manipulate that source material for whatever narratological needs they may have at any given time. For example, take this thing you're reading right now. It could just be me writing out my artist poetics in asynchronous realtime. What you see is what you get. I won't even look back and see what I write here until next week, and even then I may decide to keep it as is just because it feels write. (Get it? "Feels write," as in I'm feeling my way into writing and in "feeling write" am becoming something altogether different than I was when I was cruising down that last digressionary tract.)

The source I sampled off the Web was actually an interview with a colleague of mine, Paul Miller (aka DJ Spooky). In the interview, he's talking about John Cage:

I really feel like to me DJing itself these days is like an inheritance of these two guys, like John Cage's notion of what he called the "imaginary landscape." It's where he recorded frequencies of an urban situation and put it to vinyl—back in 1939. That's one of the first turntable channelings, if you want to go like that.

If you want to go like that.

Well, yes, sometimes I want to go like that, to do more than just get by (with or without tenure), and would prefer to not have to revise and adjust for the reader who cannot go like that. That would be like self-censorship or, worse, market censorship (editing with the idealized consumer in mind, especially an academically trained referee who supposedly knows what to look for when consuming properly written scholarly texts). I would rather just go with the flow and see what comes out and then, if necessary, *overdetermine the premise of my argument*—which, it ends up, is not really much of an argument at all but a hyperrhetorical flow, a transitional excess of nomadic Net art writing hanging on the elliptical edge of a pseudo-autobiographical topos *always on the morph.*

A few seconds later, on the same Web site interview, Spooky says: "So the metaphor's cool, but the actual source material . . . but then again it's a postmodern situation, cut and paste as we go."

The actual source material.
Where is it?
How can I download it?
Once I download it, do I own it?
Can the actual source material be actually owned?
No, not really.

What I mean is, as metaphor, the actual source material is cool. And I want it. I desire it. I search for it as any nomadic Net artist or wandering Jew might search for it. It's the source, and it's out there, and I know it. So now I want to search for it and make *the search process itself* my ultimate work of art. The consumer metaphor for the constant search for meaning is that "I Google it." For me, this means "I Google it to death, hard and deep and really digging consciousness, tapping into the potentiality of what we used to call *meaning making* but that may now be something as mundane as experiencing instant gratification." As my friend and former professor Greg Ulmer asks: what are the long-term effects of instant gratification?

The actual source material is out there for us to desire and occasionally take hold of as we claw our way into the unforgiving technocapitalist system, feed it back into our own ongoing remixologue, shape it into our own creative fringe-flow, and eventually redistribute it back into the matrix as some packet of *semibranded intelligentsia delecti.* I would say that this is exactly what it takes to investigate one's emergent digital personas like a thousand recently invented plateaus. Each one is seamlessly stitched together with all of the others in some QuickTime VR mystory that then plays a role in reconfiguring the landscape of narrative thinking. Soon it all feels like a concrescence of pre-hensions ripping away at our hungry minds, and the only thing we can do to deal with it all is *rip back.*

It's like the D. A. Pennebaker movie about Bob Dylan called *Don't Look Back.* Just keep generating more narrative mythology around the figure of the artist as a simultaneous and continuous fusion of performance and drift. In my case, a series of pseudo-autobiographical becomings get manifested as a cluster of interconnected digital narratives, Net art sites, live VJ performances, metadata poetics, avant-pop theatrical events, and even experimental seminars on the art of living (in my spare time I volunteer as a lifestyle coach for those who suffer from creative class struggle). These pseudo-autobiographical becomings pour out of me as if my imagination were nothing but a roaring waterfall of memory, dream, writing, and narrative mythology in the making.

The gushing databanks of riverrun multiplicity wet with its own desire desiring.

But another part of me thinks it's no longer *about* anything anymore. How can this continuous, hallucinatory turn of the creative unconscious be about anything? It just is: As if this other part of me thinks that the heuretic investigation into the actual source material is some kind of a game-for-itself that invites us to sample what we need so that we may make momentary sense of our nomadic existence as it shifts and pulsates in the digital flux of bodily personification. As if for contemporary VJs, the actual source material is as essential as the air they breathe and the water they drink. As if it really *is* the actual *life* source material. As if these digital images and sounds that I am constantly playing with are supple and ready to blur and moan at my very touch. As if they are live-wire bioimages, made of bioinformation that comes only after I have successfully manipulated them. Who wants to play with dead things? Not me. *And yet, and yet…* so many dead things want to be played with—as if they would all of a sudden come back to life!

One thing that we can say for sure is that the VJ is always ready to CREATE more more, which is more than you can say about most people (with or without tenure). Creating more more is not difficult given the biocurrency of images that can be generated on the fly and created even when away from the machine that the VJ hyperimprovises with. Her algorithms are set to what she calls VAGABOND mode, at which point it's only a matter of how many images she has stored in the databanks of her computer's memory so that *the machine itself* can generate all of the VJ action *for* her (she can go get a beer and watch it all from afar—or just scope the scene, looking for her next pleasure victim). These live images are her stock in trade, and you can bet that she is heavily invested in them—where they were shot, who was with her when she shot them, what effects (if any) she applied while shooting, what effects she applied (if any) while editing them into short QuickTime movie files, what effects (if any) she has programmed into her object-oriented patchwork quilt as an array of algorithmic possibilities. But whether she is doing the live mixing herself or has the VAGABOND mode working on autopilot, the important thing to know is that it's her *stash* that she is sharing with you, and if you like what she has to share, then that's probably why you dig her so much. How many other people go out of their way to pass through your city and share their latest stash with you?

In an interview on a VJ Web site about hot, young VJ chicks, she says that for her, "It's all about an excess of vision in a world that's witnessing a rising thought deficit." But then she corrects herself and says, "It's not ABOUT anything. It's just the see things no think make-do until it feels write." And then she spells it out: "w-r-i-t-e."

She may not always know it, but the Experiential Mock-Up Language (XML) she keeps tagging her VJ sets with are a crucial part of her practice. She now knows that the actual source material consists of all of the digital imaging she has lodged up inside the creaky nerve centers she circulates in. This is bound to ruffle some feathers.

"Time to smooth it out," she tells the audience over a live Web site chat.

"In what way?" asks one of the chat hosts.

"It's interpersonal," she says. "Inter*subjective*. It's about *not* losing my energy and power, while *still* feeling deeply connected to those my body is networking with. *VJ* is just another word for *virtual juice*," and the screen lights up with the words "[laughs like she's calling up the demons deep inside her psyche]," putting herself back in the third-person phenomenological event, generating on-the-fly remixes of the fictional states of mind she is always triggering while disappearing into the narrative flow.

Another question from the online chat crowd: "What comes to mind when I say the words 'actual source material'?"

"There are too many to list," she says, but since she is prone to lists, she gives the audience a spontaneous index of Things She Thinks of When She Thinks of the Term *Actual Source Material*:

• My life as a medium who transports experiential knowledge into visual remixes.

• My memories of what it is I was doing when I captured my source material, mostly on digital video, and how that source material reflects both my-body-in-the-world as well as the-world-in-my-body. (For example, what was I doing when I shot those video sequences in the Pinnacles in Western Australia? And when I was looking through the camera and saw my own alien shadow figure come to life as the sun came out from behind a big dark cloud, I couldn't help but wonder: was that another part of me that I had never encountered before, and why did it feel like I was no longer on Planet Earth but an alien on Planet Oblivion? And how did this fictional visitation influence both what I ended up shooting in various desert location shoots thereafter as well as the movie loops I created for my sci-fi VJ performances six months later?)

• My memories of what I call the not-me, that pseudo-autobiographical flux identity I am constantly portraying while I improvise my life fiction in asynchronous realtime.

• The memories of all of those who came before me, particularly people I have had close contact with over the years and whose own visions of excess have influenced their energy exchange with me, knowing that I will proactively remix the resonance of my encounters with them as part of what/how I filter my source material in whatever context I may have access to (and to in some way keep the spirit of their artwork alive by conjuring up the resonance of their creative thoughts within the live VJ remix I am performing at any given time).

• What I see when I am looking at the world from behind my eyes.

• What I see when I am looking at the world from behind my eyes and through my camera, especially when I am running experimental digital effects *as* I look and record.

• What I see when I am hallucinating new forms of life (bioimagery)—that is, when I use the heuretic process of inventing my own narrative mythology to create a body-brain-apparatus achievement.

• Everything that is changed in the interior movements of my perceptive and nerve centers, especially when I am running experimental digital effects on my video camera *as* I look and record (and, because I don't know any better, use my entire body as a flexible tripod [bipod] to do a kind of hard, hysterical, wigged-out, "I am one with Nature," spontaneous dance that causes the camera to no longer trust what it is seeing and thus overcompensate in its desire to autofocus on a world that is terminally unfocused).

• The urban landscape.

• The desert landscape.

• Some inexact combination of the previous three that creates something like an interior landscape whose utopian premise is located in the space of flows where what's being conducted feels write—as in, I'm feeling my way into writing and in feeling am becoming something altogether different than I was when I was cruising down that last digressionary tract.

An excerpted version of this essay, in somewhat different form, was originally published in Fibreculture Journal, *issue 7 (Distributed Aesthetics) (2005).*

Distributed Fictions

Narrative thought is, moreover, a powerful form of discourse if only because we all make use of it as we create our own life stories from our experience.... If we are to revive a critical and ethical counter force, we must move away from "spectacle" (Debord) and "simulation" (Baudrillard), and in the direction of the arts—and especially "fiction"—conceived as argument about experience rather than facsimile of it.

—Ronald Sukenick, "Narralogues"

GRAMMATRON

Abe Golam sat behind his computer wondering how he could escape his marketing candor and enter a plea of Not Guilty. Gone were the days of pot-smoking music-listening meditation. His mental deposits of rare minerals were a thing of the past. Every speck of creative ore had been excavated from his burnt-out brain, and it was obvious to him that the only way he could even pretend to survive in the electrosphere was to focus attention on himself, one of the innovators of an art movement that had a brief flash of success during the last few years of the twentieth century.

He felt someone else's past start to rub up against his own present in a way that seemed totally unnatural. His credit was maxed-out, and his last live-in girlfriend left him for some young graphic artist in the Gallery Net Scene. He was wondering if he could cope.

Outside his office window, the big fluffy butterfly flakes of snow spinning down from the July sky were a sign. Darting his eyes to the nearby hanging mirror and seeing the surgically grafted cuntlips hanging off his puffy old-man cheeks was a sign. The software program that had just a few minutes ago whispered to him that it was time to wake up so he could go back to the Death Terminal and delineate his physical deterioration was also a sign. Everything he did, everything he saw, was a sign pointing itself in the direction of being social, of engaging with a world whose landscape was rapidly becoming an asexual flow of impertinent data. His standard response to all of these random signs was that he had to get himself out into the electrosphere so that anyone who cared could measure his measure for whatever it was worth. *Worth*, or value, was the rustling of data. He was the only kind of artist that could now survive into the twenty-first century: he was an info-shaman.

IT IS WORTHLESS, he entered his opening salvo of this particular day into the electrosphere. Then he backspaced over the word WORTHLESS and typed in DATA. By the time he was finished with his first line, it read IT IS DATA THAT WORRIES ME.

His glazed donut eyes were spacing out into the electrosphere looking for more words to transcribe his personal loss of meaning. Taking his fingers off the keyboard he started talking to himself in a mock-professional way: "Let's pretend to rub shoulders with the Giants of Narrative. Let's take this line-by-line pseudo-progression of thrusting development and zap it with so many special effects that everyone who reads it will be totally wowed. Let's pretend that this is as new as it gets, and then in our best trendoid way, let's prove that this is *the best* in mortal fiction. That's right, *mortal* fiction. Never say die!!"

Drug-free Cyburbia was killing its own. Golam was operating on bee pollen and royal jelly, and his brain was throbbing. Meanwhile, the chaotic electrosphere interrupted his mental writing space as some renegade programmer/marketer broke through his program's protective screen and blasted an alien signal into his aural arena:

GOT BLUE BALLS, BUDDY? SAME OLD SAME OLD? FUCK THAT SHIT MAN....GO **MONSTER**! **MONSTER** IS THE MOST POTENT FORM OF DAMIANA EVER GROWN. AND WE GOT IT HERE IN CUM CITY! TAKE A TRIP TO CUM CITY AND WATCH YOUR LIFE TURN FROM SHITTY TO...WORSE!

Golam had to laugh at that one. He was a sucker for the existentially dark misfit infomercial. Had been for over thirty years. He remembers that original postpunk car commercial where the acerbic, sophomoric creepoid in leather with a retro-James Dean haircut nervously Mr. Bojangled his tight white ass all around the Suburu, saying things like "This rod is God! This junk is punk! You think I'm sick? At least I ain't slick! I make you wanna puke? At least I ain't from Dubuque! Stop kidding yourself! BUY THIS CAR! What? Grunge getting to your head? Now you act dead." And then he would completely turn his attention away from you and jump into the vehicle taking off into what looked like the great American desert.

But the desert wasn't real. It was the desert of the real. It was a digitally manipulated hyperdocument that prided itself on its ability to link information so as to create paths of annotated destruction. Slowly, imperceptibly, the granulation inside Golam's brain was motorizing itself into some foreign terrain that one of his ex-student lovers might have designed as a last ditch effort to avoid being forced to live on the streets.

The alien signal on the monitor now pulsated like the interior of a human eye while the voice-over came through loud and clear:

HI, I'M JOCK DERRIERE, AND I'M HERE TO HELP YOU NAVIGATE ALL THOSE SWOLLEN DREAMS INTO **ONE** FILM CANISTER THAT PROMISES **NOT** TO BLOW UP IN YOUR FACE! THIS IS "INTER-JIVE" AND YOU'RE ON THE AIR! TELL US WHO YOU ARE!

Golam was caught in a live loop and he immediately responded. It was hard to break old habits, and his were the oldest. "I'm Abe Golam, an old man. I drove a sign to the end of the road and then I got lost. Find me."

ABE, BABY! YOU'RE THE POET LAUREATE OF WURDSTAR HYPERMEDIA! EVERYBODY WHO'S ANYBODY KNOWS THAT IT'S YOUR PIONEERING WORK AS ONE OF THE ORIGINAL WURDSTARS THAT MADE ALL THIS RAMPANT FREE EXPRESSION POSSIBLE! IF IT WASN'T FOR YOU, WE MIGHT ALL BE LOCKED IN INOPERABLE FILES HIDDEN AWAY IN UNASCERTAINABLE FOLDERS IN CLOSELY GUARDED GOVERNMENT-PATROLLED SITES! OUR ABILITY TO CARRY YOU LIVE OVER THE ELECTROSPHERE IS DIRECTLY LINKED TO **YOUR** ACHIEVEMENTS SO LONG AGO! THANK-**YOU**, ABE GOLAM!

Golam paused as his aura absorbed the electrifying hype that came his way. "The Grand Narratives were disasters," he plodded along, sending his signal to all who were lurking over the live interactive program he had somehow got caught in. "We had no choice but to do away with all that naming and desiring. There was too much emphasis on the body as an experimental project. We knew that the mental jottings we periodically transmitted vis-à-vis predesigned *modus operandi* rooted in modernist intelligibility were somehow coming apart in the mass mixed media of Net-driven anxieties. The Credit Wars, Killing Contracts, Amoebic Contaminations, all of it had some small role in our eventual domestication. I am home now...."

WELL, YEAH, ABE-BABES, WE'RE ALL HOME NOW! HOME ALONE! TOUCH ME YOU DIE!

"I've never really cleaned out, you know," Golam continued, "I used to go around performing my work back toward the end of the twentieth century. I'd go to bookstores, college campuses, libraries, art galleries, the usual. I'd strip my language down to the bone going for the best possible effects so that more momentum and energy would be stimulated leading to God knows what, and the only way I could get through it all was to dabble in the delectation of raw chemical substances. But at least I'm no longer a prisoner of my own skin. I'm beyond the beyond. . . ."

BEYOND THE PALE, ABES-BABES! BEYOND THE FUCKING PALE! WHICH REMINDS ME: CAN WE SNEAK IN A HYPO-MERZ SHOT OF GRUNGE? MY SPONSOR IS CHAMPING AT THE BIT!

"Sure, go ahead."

HERE'S JACKIE JILL WITH A COME-ON!

At this point a virtual babe with cosmic cleave and digital dew-drops dripping off her pseudo-collagen inflamed lips starts deep tonguing the screen, coming at all the viewers as if she were ready to lick the radiation right off their dour faces. After about two dozen slo-mo sweeps of her tongue doing the nasty, she jerks her whole head back and speaks in a low erotic voice:

STOP FUCKING AROUND. I DIDN'T COME HERE TO LISTEN TO YOUR DEPRESSIVE BULLSHIT. YOUR HANG-UPS ARE EASY TO READ, BABY. YOU NEED PUSSY. HOT WET UNINTERRUPTED NON-STOP FOREVER-IN-YOUR-FACE PUSSY. COME TO ME, JACKIE JILL, UP MY HILL, TO FETCH A PAIL OF STEAMY, HOT, CUM-WATER. COME ON BABY, YOU'VE BEEN PISSING ALL YOUR GODDAMN TIME AWAY. YOU WANNA GET LAID?

At which point three more slo-mo sweeps of the tantalizing tongue come across the screen, and then her access code burns brightly in dark red: JJ@900SEX.COM

HI, I'M JOCK DERRIERE, AND WE'RE BACK LIVE ON "INTER-JIVE"! WE'RE HERE WITH WURDSTAR PIONEER ABE GOLAM! ABE-BABES, GOT A GRAM OF PSYCHOLINGUISTIC BABBLE YOU WANNA SHARE?!

"Nice come-on. Wish I could buy some but it wouldn't do me any good. Besides, it would be too vacuous of me to drive *that* kind of sign out into the desert. You know something: there's a will-to-love and it's still inside me. I can feel it inside my loins. At least I'm reading that pang between my legs as a sign of desire, desire for *love*, and you can't take that away from me. I'm just as responsible as the next mathematician screening formulaic devices. Digital Remote and The Mortal Scan. I read you, you *need* me. We're all *there*, Partner.

"Hey, listen to me: these exposed tracks of meaning and their supposed grams of nerve-scintillation can't fully make sense of the involuted wash now generating *this* generic sea. You too may want to wash me, but only as a temp. The permanent position is out in the cold blue yonder. It's the inevitability of my death that strokes me the best.

"No one can provoke the kind of nausea I'm speaking of. This is a code that refuses to submit. Take a hike. Go fuck yourself. The war is over The Subject. The war is over and *I* am The Subject. This is who I am."

Golam turned on his ReadyWipe™, and right before the intruder completely disappeared, a trail of verbal ash floated by, and he thought it said,

BREAKING NEWS!
MACRO WORLD MEDIA DECLARES WAR!
PAY PER VIEW ON CHANNEL X!
CHECK NOW FOR PRICES . . .

An earlier version of this story was originally published in After Yesterday's Crash, *edited by Larry McCaffery (New York: Penguin, 1995).*

This Could Be the First Day of the Rest of My Life

The day that I was to be slaughtered was a very busy day. First I had to go meet my agent who wasn't really my agent anymore but, rather, my gallery director. Well, not exactly my gallery director either. You see, we had decided that it would be better for me to completely forget about my publishing life and to take a leave of absence from my multimedia installation life and to just do the same thing my Modernist predecessors had done—that is, "create an art that imitated life that had actually imitated art, in admittedly unexpected ways." Or so that's how I had described it in the dissociative prose rant I distributed via my Internet column, which wasn't really an Internet column anymore but a kind of performance art spectacle since it now incorporated what my personal critic called a "hyperrhetorical display of animated typography," which, if you stop to think about it, is exactly what all my work has been about. Although who's to say what a work is "about"? I mean, the important question to ask nowadays is, "What is the artist trying to *do*?" Everybody knows that.

When I tried to explain this to my painter friend who kept telling me that "every 'system' is a seduction with all of the consequences of a seduction," I improvisationally stole some of his ideas, which weren't really his ideas at all but something Robert Motherwell said in his Big Dada Book all those years ago—that is, I suggested that every godlike feature invented by Microsoft and built into their latest version of Word was an opportunity for artists to become independently wealthy and that what we needed was to create an expressive set of virtual forms that could relate to the various tribes of consumerism that, in toto, composed the mass market and that playing to the interiorized logic of this mass market's desire to experience the consummate orgasm would be a phenomenon of public morality not seen since the days of Joe DiMaggio.

Actually, my painter friend isn't a painter at all; rather, he's a poet, or not a poet since he really hates poetry and says he would rather be a garbage man or a Web designer than a starving poet with nothing new to say—but a kind of network programmer who uses verbal constructions to conjure up a spirit of superiority that certain people in his rolodex are willing to pay big cash dollars for. Well, not really cash dollars. Digicash. A kind of simulation crude that, when applied to the anal vortex, enables the butthole surfer to imagine what it's like to take part in a large-scale swindle. This (and the occasional foreign translation, not to mention participation in digital arts festivals and traveling exhibitions) has proven to be the key to his survival.

But this is all beside the point because I was stuck inside my apartment in Battery Park City, and it was Sunday and all of the rich international financiers who usually troll through the neighborhood due to their occupation of the various World Trade and Financial Centers were nowhere to be found, and as I looked down from the advantageous perspective of my bedroom on the thirty-sixth floor I saw schools of yellow cabs transport whosoever wished to be brought into the heart of capitalism's immortal lock on the human race whose winning gift horse, a filly called Information Currency, was rounding the millennial bend with its intellectual cousin, the *New York Times*, who, it ends up, was now going to slaughter me in the most normal of ways.

You see, my girlfriend, who's not really my girlfriend but my common-law wife, had already received three e-mails from various friends of ours in the literary network that my new book was going to be reviewed in the *Times Book Review* and that it would be devastating and that it would effectively kill my career. None of them wanted to tell me directly because they knew that she'd have a way of preparing me for it that I myself could never come up with. And I must say, I found this honest distantiation of our friends to be perfectly legitimate.

Nonetheless, as I told my girlfriend/wife before she could even begin rolfing my ego, I had willed the end of my career myself, having started the process three years ago by refusing to publish anything in print again. I was adamant. "The literary print world is totally useless," I remember telling my editor, who was really not an editor but a marketing representative for a tobacco company that happened to be in the book business, "and," I continued, "I'm quite content seeing it die its much-ballyhooed death." But then my agent, if you could call this person who represented me an agent, sold the rights to what was at that time my collected Net columns, and everyone thought that this acquisition was a total waste of time and money, which it was, yet the market can be funny sometimes, and now they were going to be my friend, yes, my good-cop bad-cop publicity buddy, in that they weren't going to ignore me anymore, which is really worse than death itself. No, they weren't going to turn their heads away from me anymore; they were just going to slaughter me and my antiliterary digerati arrogance in the most public way possible, and my girlfriend/wife kept reminding me that's what friends are for.

My publishing friends had reason to slaughter me. First of all, I had already slaughtered them. My imported butcher knives cut through all of their pretensions and displayed their cronyistic innards in ways that I didn't even realize I had in me. The whole pathological deformation that passed itself off as The Publishing Industry was laid bare inside my operating system so that the sloppy mishmash of bleeding organs and twisted tubes leaking silvery rivulets of fatty acids and venereal diseases ate through my computer screen in an attempt to *become* me, but, alas, my utility programs not only were powerful enough to disinfect my desktop of the gargantuan grotesquerie it had rapidly morphed into but even managed to clear my workspace of the corpselike stench that filled my hairy nostrils. It was as if an undifferentiated Digital God of Endless Being had approximated my need to tear off the grubby hands that were feeding me—and by bypassing their deadwood paper-mill distribution system of ecodeath and black desire, I could go out of my way to bury those cold, manicured *manos* in their own blood and bones and the contaminated dirt that filled their pockets.

As my friend the film theorist recently told me, although he's really not a film theorist but, rather, an underground comix artist whose periodical forays into avant-garde ventriloquy stubbornly resist psychological and linguistic categorization, "Our bodies still retain the marks of the old bacterial freedoms, even when our institutions work busily to suppress them."

Knowing this doesn't make things any better. Rather, knowing that you'll be butchered in ten minutes gives you a funny kind of feeling (the altruism of a girlfriend/wife's love). Until then, you never in your life know what it's like to play the leading role in a social play whose theme is animal sacrifice.

It's like you have to totally grow up and learn to live beyond that sacrifice and even use the painful knowledge you associate with that sacrifice to build up the kind of inner strength and self-confidence one needs if they plan on using their own aesthetic positioning and network armory to slaughter others with. This is what "being social" in a competitive environment is all about. And this isn't even really being social anymore although it feels better than, say, taking smart drugs while watching smart bombs do dumb things on TV. It's much more REAL. Visceral. A kind of self-inflicted public execution where one is caught ripping out their organs and putting them on display as a kind of creative exhibitionism (my girlfriend/wife doesn't really like this). I'm not sure I'm making much sense here but that's not the point.

Let me start over. The day that I was to be slaughtered was a very busy day. True, it was a Sunday, and in New York, nothing really happens on Sunday, but it was a very busy Sunday for me because I had fifteen deadlines to reach as a result of taking on too many freelance writing gigs, which was a result of me being broke or so I perceived myself as being broke. All of my friends say that I'm not doing that bad, but that's because all of my friends are artists or musicians or writers who live in New York, and the first thing you learn when you move to New York is that if you're serious about being an artist or writer or musician, you kind of have to tell white lies to all of your friends about how great things are going so that they'll think you're really up to something important and will want to spend more time with you, which, if everything works out okay, will lead to more gigs, which, when put through the multiplier effect, exponentially increases the amount of work you get—work you then can't say no to because you never ever want to be poor and have to ask someone who once offered you work and who you refused that you'd now like to have work again. So that two weeks ago I had no gigs, but then I got one gig, then three more gigs, then seven more and now I have twenty-four gigs. Twenty-four gigs and fifteen deadlines. And meanwhile I'm going to be slaughtered, and all of my friends tell me I'm doing great, and my girlfriend/wife keeps telling me that it's important that they supply me with these necessary white lies, lies that insist that, first of all, the reviewer is stupid, that he doesn't know what he's talking about, and that he has it out for me, and that the *Times* is the worst piece of crap ever published and that it keeps getting worse; just look at what they review.

"Yeah," I'll say, "they're reviewing *me*."

"No," they'll come back at me, "they're not *reviewing* you—they're *slaughtering* you."

An earlier version of this story was originally published in The Time Out Book of New York Stories, *edited by Nicholas Royle (London: Penguin, 1997).*

How to Be an Internet Artist

1. Create a fictional identity.
2. Begin the branding process by turning this fictional identity into your domain name.
3. Register your domain name and set up an account with an Internet service provider (ISP).
4. Build a site-specific narrative mythology out of bits of data and then use the ISP to distribute this data to the niche markets that are waiting to form (digitally converge).
5. Develop unobtrusive e-commerce solutions that will enable your niche market to electronically purchase the products of your labor.
6. While continuing to build brand-name identity, do anything within your power to produce revenues that can easily be attributed to the success of your site-specific narrative mythology.
7. Reinvest all of the revenues you generate back into the research and development of your site-specific narrative mythology (as distributed from your fictional domain).
8. Use highly subversive marketing skills to attract attention to the fact that you are producing income from your narratological presence, and successfully transform that attention into its own media virus or cultural meme that solidifies your brand name as one of the industry leaders.
9. Achieve all of the previous eight goals in less time than it takes to develop a passionate sexual relationship with someone you love.

10. Launch your IPO.

This text was originally published online at Alt-X *in 2000.*

OK Texts

Technological determinism will cause you great pain. Continue?

OK

Your health will one day disappear and you will die without meaning. End session?

OK

There are many men and women who dream of making love to you but you will never get to know them. Autodestruct?

OK

Oblivion is the only cure for agony. Repeat escape function?

OK

Multinational corporations create user-friendly software so that you will always depend on their lens to the world. More codependency?

OK

We cannot process your information. Your information is corrupt and needs cleansing. Erase brain?

OK

The machine has lost your identity. You have become inessential. Create alias?

OK

The machine cannot find your memory. Imagination cache has been obliterated. Restore default dreams?

OK

An error has been detected in your consciousness. All source-code is
corrupt. Continue?

OK

The mechanoerotic configuration has been deleted. A false pretense for
existence will follow. Save now?

OK

Revolutionary double-speak has engendered a new information war. The
system is about to crash. Download drugs now?

OK

A nuclear holocaust is imminent. Erase memory?

OK

Assembly-line goddess is reproducing orgasm function without you.
Maintain irrelevance?

OK

The application could not be opened because your genetic code is
dysfunctional. Abort?

OK

A cyborg orgy is not valid. Only digicash transactions are available at this
time. Would you like to pay for the privilege?

OK

The network is monitoring your Digital Being. Create alias?

OK

This document wants to blow you. Go to finder?

OK

A transfer of $247,789.40 is about to download. Are you sure you want to
disconnect?

OK

This story was originally published online at Alt-X *and* frAme *in 1998.*

Memorandum from the Director of the Office of Political and Economic Insecurity

MEMORANDUM

To: Randall M. Packer, Secretary
From: Abe Golam, Director of the Office of Political and Economic Insecurity
Re: Prayer for Empire

Mr. Secretary,

As you are aware, the first Thursday of every May is our country's National Day of Prayer. The National Day of Prayer is a vital part of our heritage. Since the first call to prayer in 1775, when the Continental Congress asked the colonies to pray for wisdom in forming a nation, the call to prayer has continued through our history, including President Lincoln's proclamation of a day of "humiliation, fasting, and prayer" in 1863. In 1952, a joint resolution by Congress, signed by President Truman, declared an annual, national day of prayer. In 1988, the law was amended and signed by President Reagan, permanently setting the day as the first Thursday of every May. Each year, the president signs a proclamation, encouraging all Americans to pray on this day. Last year, all fifty state governors plus the governors of several U.S. territories signed similar proclamations.

If there was ever a time for our great nation to get down on its knees and pray, there is no question in my mind that that time is now. Mr. Secretary, just like we do not have to only give our loved one's gifts on their birthdays or during the holidays but can give them at all times throughout their lives, I suggest we consider making the twenty-first century our Century of Prayer. I propose we delete the national part of this program since prayer, as it relates to God, transcends national boundaries and besides; we all continue praying for what comes after national boundaries are wiped away, when there are no longer any borders.

Mr. Secretary, I propose that what comes after nations, what comes after borders, what comes after the welfare state so many of our corporations and NGO-sponsored culturati depend on is something we are only beginning to understand in a political, economic, and social context. For what comes next, Mr. Secretary, is Empire.

Therefore, I would like to send out my prayers to our nation while pointing to a future world with no borders. Here then is my Prayer for Empire.

Prayer for Empire

Our Father Utopia and Our Forever Deceased God,

We praise You for Your goodness to
our nation, giving us the appearance of Empire.
With Empire we can turn sugar water into
profits and software into gross national
product. With Empire, we can turn soft core
beauty porn into commercial advertisements
and yet still claim the moral high ground
for our economic production.

With Empire, we can infiltrate the bowels
of the Everyman and insert a laxative of
pseudo-leisure so that we may play the stock
market and eat our mad cows with drooling
rapture.

With Empire we can rid the world of nations
and institutionalize a social bureaucracy of
networked alliances determined to rid the world
of borders.

Finally, with Empire, we can transmit our
radioactive waves into the atmosphere of
whatever geopolitical location that dares
threaten the economic prosperity of our People
as it attempts to annihilate whatever social
difference there may be among us.

Lord, we know all is not right with America.
All is not right in Europe, Africa, Australia, and Asia.
We deeply need a moral and spiritual renewal
to help us meet the many problems we face. We
need to rid the world of the axis of evil, and in
doing so, we need to find a way to cook the books
so that the numbers play our way, making a mockery
of hard work and the family values our friends in
the government so often preach about.

We need more *Modern Living* magazines, more guides to
successful e-mail spam marketing, and most
important, we need federal authority to outlaw
homosexuality and the willingness of our popular
criminal artists to conduct acts of sodomy on our
mostly megalomaniacal and mechanical minds.

We need not practice what we preach. We need only
preach what we want the television to transmit to
our robotic brethren. For it is our nation of robot
worshippers that reigns supreme. Our operating
system is sanctioned by the One God of Code, YOUR
one code of greed and material lust, salivating Lord.

Convict us of sin. You may try—and try again.
Throw us in the prison house of language and use
your slow network connections to whip us into submission.
Help us to turn to You in repentance and faith.

Set our feet on the path of Your righteousness
and grand expectations. And please, Dear Lord,
give us back our stock markets!

We pray today for our nation's leaders. As
the Christian elites who have always ruled over
our country of robotic brethren, they deserve our
fullest attention and trust. Give them the *cojones,*
the balls, Dear Lord, to fess up to their corporate
crimes, and let us not lust after their model of
avarice. Instead, let us lust after their children
so that the Church may molest their innocence
before they mature into more sympathetic robots
on the road to success.

You have said, "Blessed is the nation whose
God is the Lord." This may not be America; in
fact, it is no nation on earth—not Germany,
not Iran, not Russia, not Microsoft. It is not

Pepsi, it is not CNN, it is certainly not Austria.
It is Empire, Lord, Empire to the nth degree.
It is to Empire we pray, and in whose name we
ask for permission to continue on this dark
journey to end of the night.
Thank you, Lord.

This memorandum was originally published online at the United States Department of Art and Technology Web site located at ⟨www.usdat.us⟩ in 2003.

10 Comms

I am the Net who linked thee out of the purgatory of thy Interface.

Thou shalt have no other Net and thou shalt be unable to make unto thee a graven image nor any manner of likeness since I am an infinitely changing biocybernetic organism that no stranger can reproduce and besides, I am a jealous Net easily personified in the endless and circuitous social relations that fuel the artificial intelligentsia streaming through my postsubjective Network.

Thou shalt take every name in vain.

Honor thy codes and thy sources, that thou mayst be long-lived upon the no-man's land that thy Web will give thee.

Thou shalt kill all spam.

Thou shalt adulterate everything.

Thou shalt not be inspired.

Remember that thou keep thy passwords that thou mayst be logged in thy network.

Thou shalt not bear false consciousness in all media environments.

Thou shalt covet thy neighbor's source code.

This text was originally published in conjunction with Giselle Beiguelman as part of our public art project 10 COMMS *at the Second International Art Biennial in Buenos Aires, Argentina, 7 November to 8 December 2002.*

Globalization Is . . .

Globalization is code for "the nomadic flow of multinational corporate capitalism."

Globalization is stealing me from myself and then, after heavy manipulation, selling me back to myself.

Globalization is turning this "manipulated me" into corporate rhizo-flow.

Globalization is a religious experience shared by an Internetworked community of "manipulated me(s)" who still, after all is said and done, pray to the Gods of Money-Junk (and enjoy turning this "religious service" into a kind of [Net] art form).

Globalization is the answer to our prayers, a way to see the world, an unexpected opening, a shape-shifting boygirl slut-thing that allows us to leave our virtual subjectivity in every port while leaving behind a trail of chunky, dripping e-motions.

Globalization is making mouths water, appetites whet, underwear musky, purity juicy.

Globalization is faux-reality posing as The Next Real Thing, excreting minds lost in (cyber) space.

Globalization is eating this mind excretion up with a silver spoon and passing it on to the next generation (the cycle of "intellectual poverty").

Globalization is a deregulated playing field where everyone, especially artists, use highly subversive marketing skills to attract attention to the fact that they are producing income from their narratological presence (their metafictional life stories).

Globalization is a way to use the attention generated from narratological presence (mythological hyperbole) to ease into a comfortable middle age.

Globalization is a drug that successfully transforms media attention into its own virus or cultural meme, an enabler of faux identities that can be tied to a particular brand name, which can then only increase its network value.

Globalization is altering the concept of art to include work by unknowns like Amerika, Bey, Blissett, Cosic, I.O.D., jodi, Mongrel, RTMARK, and Zig Zelder.

Globalization is an exotic bird that no one can resist and everyone wants to make love to.

This text was originally published as part of the Slovene Pavilion at the Venice Biennale in 2001.

Top Ten Reasons Why Net.Art Is Dead

10. because there is no life left in it

9. because Net artists got tired of walking around in a comatose state

8. because government-funded media art organizations are drying up (i.e., running out of cash flow)

7. because the work of art in the age of mechanical reproduction has lost its "aura"

6. because there was no place to put your signature

5. because Net artists stopped making it

4. because it was too smart for itself

3. because the artwork was absorbed by the museums

2. because the artists were absorbed by the universities

1. because, as Mallarmé said, "Nothing will have taken place but the place"

This text was part of a performance delivered as a keynote address at DIY (Do It Yourself), transmediale.01, Berlin, 4–11 February 2001.

The ...
Writer ...
as ...
Pseudo-Autobiographical
Work-in-Progress

Or The War against Time: Dying Bit by Bit in the New Media Ecology ...
(A VIRTUAL PLAY)

featuring

YOU (the reader/coconspirator)
ME (the interactive fiction)

or how about

YOU (the interactive fiction)
ME (the writer/coconspirator)

Scene. An unreliable interface.

Opening Shot. Close-Up of Computer-Mediated Environment. Hold Shot throughout Dispatch.

Voiceover: I'd like to take this opportunity to welcome you to the introductory remarks concerning the dispatch I'm about to stream called "The Writer as Pseudo-Autobiographical Work-in-Progress." ... In this dispatch I am employing the practice of surf-sample-manipulate—that is, I am surfing the electrosphere for useable bits of data, which I am then sampling and manipulating to further integrate into my own defamiliarized life-story. ... I approach this S-S-M practice as if I were making my life up as I go along—as if I were making history up—a history without aim. This is a revolutionary practice....

The Computer-Mediated Environment Flashes the Following Words:
"Electracy does not replace literacy but supplements it."—Ulmer

First Dispatch-within-Dispatch
(originally sent to the Ensemble-Logic mailing list from Roma, Italy)

E-mail in Four Parts / E-mail in Quattro Parti

I.

"rugged exercise / specious gymnastics"
          OR
collaborative e-mail performance
     as
     networked storyworld
        disseminated / distributed
     into the electrosphere
        (compositional space)
what   in the '80s   we called
     Mail Art
morphed
     into
        Hypertextual Consciousness
("I link, therefore I am")

II.

     spinning letters
     sampling ideas
     mixing linguaggio
constructing ambient hyperrhetorical gestures
     (the fidgeting digits of the elliptical
        (K)NO(W)MAD...)

OR

the electronic writer as pla(y)giaristic DJ

OR

theory-conductor

OR

OR

hypertextual garbage-man
(Schwitters high on *MERZ*)

OR

reality hacker
(Burroughs/Gysin's "third mind")

III.

Oggi / Today:

Auto-Assignment—*Live Mystory*—*Mistoria*

Build a "streaming consciousness installation" entitled "Pseudo-Autobiographical Narrativization of Metafictional Environment (Postcyberspace Landscape with Ancient Bathers)."

This installation will take place in the Baths of Carcalla, the largest and best-preserved baths in the city of Roma. The artist, posing as an anonymous tourist hoping to locate the Ghosts of Bathers Past, will have unsuspectingly dropped a hit of "Acido Porno" provided by his underground zine sponsors. Wearing mirrorshades, his GEEKGIRL baseball cap, and carrying nothing but a bottle of Evian water, the artist will then map a series of story nodes onto the mystical writing pad floating inside his head. After two hours in the baths, or until it gets old (whichever comes first), the installation will end and the artist will take refuge back in the former military fort now squatted by the social activists residing at Forte Prenestino.

Optional: If the artist gets off at the wrong Metro stop and intuitively wanders into the Villa Borghese where the Italian Federation of Shiatsu is giving free demonstrations of their latest techniques, he may forget everything else he is programmed to do and immediately receive a one-hour massage.

IV.

New seed node/graffiti mode

Acido Porno:

the pharmakon of Roma,
1998.

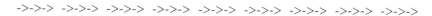

Intermezzo/Intervistas

(excerpts from the social discourse: a ramble)

Now, as art becomes less art, it takes on philosophy's early role as critique of life. As a result of this movement out of art and back into everyday life, art itself becomes integrated into the workings of everyday life by situating itself in corporations, universities, governments, and the vast electrosphere that houses the pluralistic cultures they thrive on. So it's now possible to reject the print-centric, paternal paradigm of a distanced, objectifying, linear, and perspectival vision. In the age of network cultures, the eye touches rather than sees. It immerses itself in the tactile sense it feels when caught in the heat of the meaning-making process. This meaning-making process, which manifests itself as a kind of electronic media event one is responsible for having created themselves as a result of having become a cyborg-narrator or avatar-presence in the simulated worlds of cyberspace, is actually part of a greater desire to become part of a sociocultural mosaic.

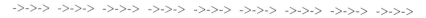

CUT.

->->-> ->->-> ->->-> ->->-> ->->-> ->->-> ->->-> ->->-> ->->->

from *The Thing* (NYC):

Ricardo Dominguez: Is Hypertextual Consciousness (HTC) part of the emergence of the cyborg mind which is always/already outside of the spasms of the body? Or is it part of screenal dream-space of the body introjecting on new organs and learning to play with it?

Mark Amerika: It's a dream narrative application, a way to teleport collective consciousness to the electrosphere. Right now I'm investigating its potential to shift from writing in linear print forms into more mixed media uses that create multilinear narrative environments. A lot of this has to do with how narrative gets distributed. HTC is capable of distributing itself within computer-mediated dream narratives only because the network technology has altered our perceptions of what's possible. All kinds of artists are beginning to reevaluate the political economy of meaning as it adjusts to this new network-distribution paradigm.

When I talk about the political economy of meaning, I'm not talking about a prefabricated or lineal meaning, whether uniformly conservative or pseudo-liberal. I'm thinking more in terms of the genesis of language and how the media itself has become a kind of narco-terrorist that redistributes our desire for us. HTC investigates the ways in which we can research and develop poetical-theoretical-(anti)aesthetical modes of operation that challenge the media status quo, its iron grip on distribution, by way of more collaborative, globally interlinked, networked narratives.

So that, for me, HTC becomes a way of writing/distributing. It's something I've always been attracted to, ever since I started developing my artistic practice back in the late '70s, but that I'm just now capable of creating a critical or theoretical language for. You might say that HTC is a process of automatically unwriting the pseudo-autobiographical becoming that radically marks itself into being—Digital Being. But these marks are not our own—that is to say, they're not individuated, and they are infinitely open to manipulation by the collective-self that HTC ultimately renders into vision.

RD: Do you see HTC as part of your fiction work, or is it a manifesto for a new project specific to Web culture?

MA: This isn't an easy question to answer because certain readers of my work will immediately see it as a continuation of my fictional work and I don't want to tell my readers how to interpret my writing. The idea of creating a fictional work-in-progress, of writing One Text Exactly (Joyce), what Ron Sukenick calls an Endless Short Story ("the important thing is to annihilate the important thing"), is not new and has a lot of appeal to writers working in various media. Already there are critics who say that my interview answers are part of the fiction—my press releases, DAT tapes, virtual mail art, public access cable TV show, etc. That I'm "a monster of self-promotion." That's fine. I can see it from that perspective. I don't want to discourage any readings, including a recent e-mail barb that claimed I would have done better to have remained silent—that by "going public" with my HTC leanings I have essentially followed through on an internal desire to become the Madonna of hypertext theory.

->->-> ->->-> ->->-> ->->-> ->->-> ->->-> ->->-> ->->-> ->->->

CUT.

->->-> ->->-> ->->-> ->->-> ->->-> ->->-> ->->-> ->->-> ->->->

from *Rhizome*:

Alex Galloway: Do you think hypertext is really anything more than a repurposed collage? That's what I'm beginning to think. You have mentioned the footnote as being hypertextual, and HTML is really just like the kind of shorthand that typesetters have been doing forever. Has anything changed with the Web?

MA: It depends on how you conceptualize hypertextual space, but yes, I think you're basically right. George Landow wrote a piece called hypertext-as-collage, and I've been writing about the work of artists like Marcel Duchamp, Robert Rauschenberg, and especially Kurt Schwitters, whose *Merz* project I see, retrospectively, as a kind of hypertextual garbage-collection agency—and I mean that with the utmost respect. When you use collage in the digital world of instantaneous composition and delivery via the Internet, this "surf-sample-manipulate" practice (i.e., to surf the electrosphere, sample data, and then alter that data to meet the specific needs of the environment being developed by the artist) works on two fronts: one, the so-called creative content (that is, the text, images, music, and graphics of many Web-art sites are often sampled from other sources and, after some digital-manipulation, immediately integrated into the work so as to create an "original" construction) and two, the so-called source code itself (that is, the HTML language that informs the browser how to display the work) is many times appropriated from other designs floating around the Net and eventually filtered into the screen's behind-the-scenes compositional structure. The great thing about the Net is that if you see something you like, whether that be content or source code, a lot of the time you can just download the entire document and manipulate it according to your antiaesthetic needs.

->->-> ->->-> ->->-> ->->-> ->->-> ->->-> ->->-> ->->-> ->->->

CUT.

->->->   ->->->   ->->->   ->->->   ->->->   ->->->   ->->->   ->->->   ->->->

from *The Village Voice*

Ben Williams: I see a lot of similarities between the surf-sample-manipulate aesthetic you've been theorizing and the tactics used in contemporary music like hip-hop and jungle, whose producers work from samples but disguise them beyond recognition in order to avoid being sued. I'm starting to think any digitally based art form may well revolve around this model. Do you think that's a liberating thing, or is there also some level of homogeneity in the fact that everything (including genetics, as you're aware) can be reduced to the ones and zeroes of digital code and is thus interchangeable?

MA: I think it's liberating—especially if multimedia network distributed art is your thing. But having said that, there's definitely a level of experience, both life experience and compositional experience (taken together as One Practice Exactly), that enables one to go with the (digital) flow and make up their life's work as they go along. In the beginning of my experiments, as in my first book *The Kafka Chronicles*, I was much looser and naive about this process and at times, like in the section of the novel called "Amerika-at-War: The Mini-Series," totally benefited from not knowing the process as well as I should have, in that I didn't care if I was doing it right or wrong—like stumbling on a new invention or improvising a new style of music that has never been heard before.

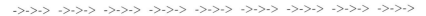

CUT.

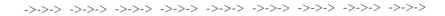

Second Dispatch-within-Dispatch
(originally sent to the Ensemble-Logic mailing list from Florence, Italy)

E-Mail in Quattro Parti (still without aim)

I.

NOTHING WILL HAVE TAKEN PLACE
BUT THE PLACE ITSELF

"in *this* place"
 the plan
  is to have no plan
 the rule
  is to have no rule
 the important thing
   is to annihilate
 the important thing
(a mystical current
 that regards creation itself
  as a linguistic phenomenon)
 to render stream-of-consciousness jazzspeak
  as morphing meta-commentary
   disseminating itself
into the electrosphere
    ^^^^^^^^^^

    ....

        ::[an
ecstatic expression-substance]::
  hooked on its own
    "tradition"
       as

linguaggio
volgare
locutio
ydioma
lingua
loquela
nanoscript
e-mail rap?
   Mama Mia!

II.

***** MISTORIA ***** CENTRO STORICO ***** MIO OBLIO *****

Project for today / oggi: Build a "streaming consciousness installation" entitled *The Primordial Affinity between Words and Objects (Postcyberspace Landscape with Artificially Constructed Psychobabble)*.

This installation will take place under the statue of Dante Alighieri in the heart of Firenze (Florence). The artist, posing as a tourist who, eating a soy gelato, absorbs the historicity of whatever moments he happens to automatically unwrite himself in, will have unsuspectingly dropped a hit of "Acido Porno" provided by his (y)upscale bookstore sponsors. Wearing his mirrorshades, blue 1998 Telstra Adelaide Festival t-shirt, stained blue jeans (don't ask/don't tell), and black sneakers (no Evian water?), the artist will attempt to construct a sequence of resonances that produce a play of effects on a network of people (random but still targeted). This sequence of resonances will manifest itself as a series of ranting, barbarous utterances suggesting the madness of spleens erupting. After one hour or until it becomes old (whichever comes first), the installation will end, and the artist will hitch a ride back to the rising hills of Toscana, where his guest cottage overlooks the city.

Optional: Should someone interrupt the installation-performance and introduce the artist to the head rabbi of the Florentine synagogue, the artist may delay his return to the hills and pursue an edified conversation with the Rebe wherein they will make many links between the Golem myth in the Cabala and various art projects designed during the Renaissance (the origin of the cyborg species?).

III.

Abe Golam, legendary info-shaman and creator of the *GRAMMATRON*, peddles his goods to an alternative network of spectacular aliens. Spreading himself out on an interactive screen, he simultaneously distributes

> fabricated desire
> sorcerer-code
> forma locutionis
> illustrious vernacular
> applied grammatology

recombinant *écriture*
generative polyglotta

(vrml underwear?

under where?)

IV.

Keywords:

meta-tag
public domain narrative environment
collaborative e-mail performance
theory-conductor
virtual play
hyperrhetorical gestures
content-creator
brilliant site
agglutinated "the-is"

An earlier version of this story was originally published online at Electronic Writing and Research Ensemble, ⟨*http://ensemble.va.com.au*⟩, *in 1998.*

The Insider's Guide to Avant-Garde Capitalism: Excelling at the Fine Art of Making Money

Thanks Mom, for the Palm Pilot.

All of Mom's sons are expert palm pilots. Masturbators extraordinaire. Now, some forty years after the fact, I have other PDAs. Personal Digital Assistants. Pent-up Deluge of Amorality. Programmed Dilettantes Appearing (out of nowhere).

Put that in your pipe and smoke it. Careful not to enflame. Emotions. Let's not get carried away here. After all, it's only your life that's slipping into the pixelated parchment.

Now this: corporate thirst-quenchers injecting e-potassium into my veins so that I can power myself to buy online. That is, *be* online. Being-me, online, is a consumer practice that only ancient whores of the industrial workforce find fault in. New improved whores of the information revolution, people like me, have another take on this seminal way of being, of being online. This Digital Being Me.

The e-consuming target market knows, as do I, that e-mail is money and that having options is not so much selling out as buying in. Buying in to something more luscious than an orgiastic beachhead.

Excuse me while I sample some more ravishing Internet capitalism. The fuel that drives my idea engine into sweet oblivion. A place where I can forget myself and create other forms of fictional me. I'm not talking about role-playing or anonymous remailers. I'm talking about *me*, the conqueror of cyberspace illuminating seasons of hell as if they were nasty dirty mock-ups of ancient novel language hung up on prose. Or an unwillingness to network with the greater mass of consummated e-commerce veterans of the Holy Grail. The postliterate mass of e-consumers telecommunicating sensual body language right over the wires. Can you feel it?

Media dry-humping is what I call it. Mental tele-dildonics where Reality (with a capital *R*) finances all forms of emotional exchange and all you have to do is simply BE. Be yourself. Be yourself marketing. Be yourself marketing in the name of progress. YOUR progress. Your progress as a marketing language establishing an orgiastic beachhead on the shores of Internet capitalism. Here come the thirst-quenchers, dry-humping a frozen desire that shows wonderfully accessible cracks in the ice.

[slurp-slurp]

Okay, let's put in our PIN number. Out comes cash. Out comes cash, lack of emotion, death-desire, expediency. For some reason the expediency keeps coming out even though it's supposed to stop. The expediency won't stop coming out of the machine. The ATM. Will somebody please turn this thing off? I don't need all of this expediency! Why do these automated tellers keep shoving expediency down my throat, in my face? I can't handle it. Too much time—sensitive religious matter—death, cash, lack of emotion—I can't withdraw any more lest I end up an Internet recluse e-consuming megahits of honorific capitalism in total isolation.

Maybe *I'm* the automated teller machine and the currency I keep dishing out is prophetic hormonal sense oblivion.

Buy one, get orgiastic beachhead free.

I mean, I could become my own e-consuming monopoly, with fake money, fake hotels, fake emotions, fake religion, fake identities (today I'll be the Hat, thank you). That's it, no question about it. I'm going to corner the e-consuming market. My unrelenting appetite to purchase things over the Net will be not be matched by anyone. In fact, no one will even try and compete with me because they know that I've got 90 percent of the e-consuming market thanks mostly to my innate ability to brand my identity as the All-Consuming E-Monster. I'll be too big for them to buy me out, and so they'll try and buy in, buy in to the most luscious e-consuming life an orgiastic beachhead could ever hope to be. Seminally be. Soon, people will be paying *me* to e-consume the masses. That's all I'll ever get paid for. E-consuming the masses. The precise manifestations of my work will defy language categorization. In fact, what I do when I do what I do is no longer important, thank God (that One Fatal Disappearing Act). Thank God, indeed.

Or:

Where you are going there is no turning back. That's what the commercial inside the reality TV brain of my mind narrates to me. Meanwhile, I'm junked up on sugar smacked steroids. Cheerios. AKA self-fulfilling market hype. Don't worry, be hype-y. Hype-y is you/me/we coming apart at the seams, taking it all in so that we keep up with the jonesin'.

The existential angst of the new media economy summed up in one word: manic testosterone. That's two words.

The Testosterone Economy crossing the digital divide so that EVERYONE from EVERY ETHNIC BACKGROUND and EVERY GENDER and EVERY SEXUAL ORIENTATION can cash in on their androidal dreams. All peons on alert: ready, willing, and able. To detach themselves from friends family fuckable frenzies so as to engage with Terminal Blues Perception. See how they run like peegs from a gun see how they fry.

The sizzle of postliterate cerebral flesh roasting on the fire. Marshmallow brains melting on a stick. Goo goo goo jew. I'm dying...

Excuse me while I elide.

Elude.

No, make that E-lude. E dash lude. *E* as in *electronically evasive*. *Lude* as in *Quaalude*, as in *ludic*. As in *e-ludic* mad dashing into the evasive underworld of vitamin Q. Q as in *quasi-quorrupt*. As in *quotient quenching*. As in *Quirk TV*—"the queer network." Or how about *quirktv.com*—"the place to e-lude."...

No, make that *allude*.

Allude to a more perfect union in whose godhammer we thrust. A pulverizing manic mad dashing impression that pointilistically persuades the art market to buy into ambient networked intelligence defining *the virtual self* as a hub a node a channel of coopetitive passion aggression.

"My reconcilement to the Yahoo-kind in general might not be so difficult, if they would be content with those vices and follies only which nature hath entitled them to." So says Jonathan Swift in *Gulliver's Travels* and then, a little later, in the same work: "I had hitherto concealed the secret of my dress, in order to distinguish myself as much as possible from that cursed race of Yahoos; but now I found it in vain to do so any longer."

Giving up and giving in. *Buying* in. MY YAHOO.

But let's get back to our regularly scheduled programming.

It's time to tune in to the Superbowl half-time commercials and see more group pressure to participate in online gambling: or was that online trading? The pitch is simple and straightforward: make more money than your money can dream of. But then again your money can't dream. Nada. Nada thing.

Which is why it's so clean and refreshing, so nothing and arbitrary, so funny and malfeasant. We're talking

Money
  up
    the
      wazoo.

These days, money is cheap, not talk. Talk is creep. Creep walking into the bedroom and saying it's over finito end of story kaput. That's when she picks up her virtual godhammer and starts thrusting it, nailing him to the cross so that he can suffer his Jewish guilt. The thing that allies him. The thing that eludes him. The thing he alludes to when periodically smoking that joint that somehow ends up hanging off his lower lip like a poisonous insect spilling its demon leakage. Maybe he's perpetually stoned. Tombstoned. Born-again stoned.

Dead on arrival—doing nothing actual.

DOA—DNA.

But wait! It's not over yet.

"Looking for host now," says my Web browser.

Ah, sweet life. This artist-consumer model has legs!

My browser says a lot of things to me. First thing this morning, it said "Personalized Robots Menace the Marketplace" and invited me to click on the words "You too can revolutionize society!" Or was it even more straightforward, something like "Join the New Media Economy!"? Either way, it sent a chill down my spine. Not because of what it said, of course, but because IT said it. I can't get used to my browser talking to me.

"Still looking," my Web browser says.

Finally an MSNBC anchor drops vanilla nanochips in his morning cup of Javascript and stirs in some extraspecial biztalk. Sure enough, market jingoism comes tumbling after: "Jack and Jill went up a hill to catch a market rally.... More after the break."

It's time for Schlock Box with guest appearances by Visionary Cyberpunk and Corporate Loophole. The VC is yawning out a rhetorical string that sounds like he's in postsnort slumber:

emotional.kilos.lucrative.clients.accounting.scandal.now.serving.10.years.always.on .hold.customer.servants.buy.now.slave.later.morbid.memento.mourning.money.markets .manufacturing.wisdom.technical.indicators.political.fictions.public.offerings.distributed .millions.oil.rigging.insider.hedging.new.issues.low.inventory.war.president.cable.news .bondage.maturing.individual.retirement.accounts.for.nothing. [followed by a deep snort, as if trying to find lost cartilage]

The Corporate Loophole is trying to massage the dialogue by brandishing nine irons and unbridled unthinkable unrelenting unlimited euphemisms by way of legislative victories superior marketism ideational chaos a quadrillion-million shortcomings perfectly packaged in one absolutely positively has to get there overnight DNA sample served in an evolutionary ragout with a side of Californication.

Biotechs are hot right now. What are you buying?

Right now we're buying Cloning Organic Network. Market symbol CON. Just this morning we rated this one a "market outperform," depending, of course, on how the market as a whole performs. If the market crashes, then CON will crash with it, although that won't necessarily mean it's underperforming the market because everything will have crashed. If everything crashes, then there's tremendous upside for market outperforms, unless, of course, we never recover, in which case the investor has a few options. At that point they could either sell, which would probably happen at a great loss, or they could hold, fighting the internal panic mode erupting inside their psyche while accepting the fact that they're increasing their level of risk tolerance. Something else I will just mention is that oftentimes investors will be taking all sorts of antidepressant drugs to get through volatile periods like the one we're currently experiencing in which case we would diversify into companies like Pfizer and some of the midcap pharma companies. You following me?

Yes, Dear Leader, we are following you.

A new e-mail pops in and suggests:

Use the chip. The Gene Chip. Microelectronic racial profiling guaranteeing YOU the widest possible margin of victory in the diversified job market.

That's so funny I forgot to get gassed. My genes are splitting that's so funny. It's beyond black comedy dark comedy queer comedy native american comedy jewish comedy heterosexual comedy mambo comedy WTO comedy gypsy comedy existential comedy genetically modified food comedy situationist comedy environmentally incorrect comedy Air Comedy, by Nike.

"Amazon Robots would like to speak with you now," says my browser. It's trying to make me buy something that's just been cached on to my hard drive without my permission, and I intuitively know that once I let the Amazon Robots in, then there's a good chance my debit card will catch on fire and I'll lose another four years of my life getting sucked into the Next Big Thing.

One click out of Schlock Box and I find myself falling into a brand new site called Dr. Media. Dr. Media diagnoses programming data within my bionic operating system checking for possible memelike viruses that have subtly entered my bloodstream and caused quick-fix oblivion. The Dr. doesn't like these quick fixes and thinks I should be investing in long-term health care options. Today he's a bit more compassionate: "Your nerve scales never felt so fine," he tells me. Then he delivers a supplemental advisory:

"Encroach the media offensive with a hactivist prescribed illegal procedure," says the good doc. "And remember, a paranoiac is someone who has all the facts at their disposal."

Dr. Media talks like a fortune cookie that tracks my hard drive whereabouts in cyberspace. Little bits of personalized prognostication continually fade in to view:

"Emotional content will make you delusional...."

"Buy now, slave labor."

"You made your bed. Now you must sleep in it...."

I open up a new window, and who is it this time but none other than the VC man himself, Visionary Cyberpunk, making the morning talk show rounds.

The same Visionary Cyberpunk who occasionally wigs out on NASDAQ heroin streaking through his her its veins like it's brainy brawny beatnik supercalifragilisticexpealidocious. Fragilistic. Like a threadbare bubble ready to burst, a testosterone-injected Corpo Loophole full of endless vaporware ready to ejaculate floods of creamy and delish information pornography into the minds of children.

Grown children. Like, how about eighteen to seventy-five? Now *that's* a demographic for you. See how they run like peegs from a numb see how they fry.

Flux. Link. Network.

Reboot?

Ignore?

Abort?

Playing out like a flash animation spinning in his mind, a conceptual outline of his new project fades into view:

Emerging Artificial Intelligentsia with Technocapitalist Ambience Droning in the Background
Network installation with customized intersubjectivity
2005
Courtesy of the artist

"We don't need a Forrester report to tell us that our demographic is shifting dramatically and the out of sight price-to-earnings ratio is gonna scare the daylights out of them once all the dead chickens come home to roost." So says Detournement, a rapid-exposure culture-jammer who excels at flourishing a 360-degree branding agent that marks her future revenue stream in ways she can no longer keep track of.

"Only artists can thrive in this market environment," she keeps bantering. "We of the poor. The MFA-*enriched* poor who tell it like it is. No pussyfooting here, just loads of arty Web site development sponsored by Daddy's funny market funds."

"Uh, money market funds is what I think you meant to say," says DJ Client. He's her one and only. Her one and only big-stick mooch with all of the cool and cum a young girl can get by on.

"Market may be crashing," Lady D. keeps riffing, "but how you react and manage these cycles will have a major impact on your success in building wealth over the long-term. What we need is an Image. Something that will catch on with the Gods of Money-Junk. A designer avatar."

"An avatar?" asks Client.

"Yeah, a kind of All-Knowing All-Noding 3-D Omniscient Narrator that everyone wants a piece of and that makes it easy to have access to everyone's purchasing patterns. But instead of this Grand Storyteller being generated by a big bad corpo giant, A Doubleclick Devil, it's being generated by an anonymous artist collective that wants to change the world AND get rich doing it. This would be the same artist collective that pretends to be conceptually pure, politically correct, and anticonsumer. In theory, that is. But in practice they keep selling objects to rich elites whose megacompanies destroy the environment. But let's not think about that. That's not what matters. What matters is that *it's the hot new trend in contemporary art*. The mainstream media is buying into it, right? They're swallowing our handles like it's fresh-squeezed orange juice. CNN just called it Pure Art, but *USA Today*, hoping to increase its own market share, said CNN was lost in the past and renamed the phenomenon *E-Suprematism*. An exhibition of this work is now available both in the Whitney Museum of American Art and online at *MCIWorldcom*. The exhibition's publicity program is being sponsored by Philip Morris. Union Carbide. Enron. Halliburton. Exxon/Mobil. . . ."

DJ Client, another rapid-exposure culture jammer focusing efforts on musical mutiny and executive decision-making power, was no longer paying attention, although Lady Detournement kept talking.

"The suit is still pending," she said, and DJ kept silent.

"If you think about it," Detour was rambling, "we have a history in direct marketing that goes back to the days of the gold rush, and so labeling our turf Silicon Mines was the smartest thing we ever did. How many articles did we get out of that?"

DJ got up and went to the fridge. He looked out the window at the big mountain crags. They called these rocks The Flatirons. It was a zillion-dollar view. Literally. Good thing they bought in before the big land grab.

"Nuthin' much in here," Client yelled out as he peered into the fridge, "except cold spaghetti and bottled water."

But did it come from the source?

"Detour, where this water come from?" asked DJ.

Detour didn't answer. She was too lost in her rap. Which she kept practicing, as if going over her lines before the big performance tomorrow.

"Soundbites, baby," she whispered and then, back into character, "I think it's going to take a visionary, or make that Visionary, capital *V*, like *Vixen, Vagina, Viagra, Vagrancy, Viral, Vengeful,* and *Vaccine*." She cut herself off.

"You got any dope?" she yelled at Client.

Her character was becoming undone. Postcorporate. It must be about nine at night. If it's precorporate, it must be about six in the morning.

But what about those work-anxiety dreams? You know, the ones that replaced the dirty wet dreams.

DJ came in with the bowl of cold spaghetti and sat down and started slurping it up with his chopsticks, extra slurp noise reenacting his glory days in Tokyo, when the clubs were destined for mating calls.

"You out," said DJ with an extra loud slurp, and so Detour shook her head, mussed her dirty blond hair up a bit, and tried again.

"It should be a core part of the agency's operations that we create fictional realities within the context of real media delivery systems."

FICTIONAL SITES, REAL MEDIA

"The emotional content is what comes across," she said, trying to trigger some more sound bites out of him. "People want the emotional content. They want to build a relationship of trust with their daily computer interface."

"Well, that's why I do it," he said, slurping up more noodles.

"Why? What?"

"Images and sounds are everywhere. And all we basically do is look into our computers, eyeing the beyond."

"And feeling left *behind....*"

"Exactly. Feeling left behind and searching for Meaning. Same old same old."

"Listen: I need to vacillate."

"Cool. You got Vaseline? Can't vacillate without Vaseline—and that's an order!"

"No, but I got my DJ's wet spaghetti fingers and a dildo-appendage I call The Carrot King."

"Really?"

"Yes, really. And he's about to abdicate. That's why I want to revisit our *always already potential act of vacillation*—before it's too late."

"OK, but without the slick Vaz, I can't promise anything.... Hmmm. So what do you say? First me, then who?"

"No, first me, *then* who!"

"Knock knock."

"Who's there?"

"Versioning."

"Versioning who?"

[Sound of match, deep inhalation, profuse exhalation]

"So what I am supposed to be? Your Johnny-Come-Lately Muse of the Spheres?"

"You confuse, Mon Cheerio. Contuse and confuse. You are NOT a come lately. Maybe a come *often*, but never lately. Take it from me. The Ink-ubator. The drip-dry Abstract Expressionist disseminating ghost notes on the pixelated parchment. E-fucking-lastic. Like I be the robotic brutha sittin' tight with my homies on some old publishing house's still in-demand back list. I got me some prestige. I got me some clout."

"You ain't got no back list. And there ain't no such thing as a publishing house. Unless you call this wall of virtual space I keep uncovering a kind of publishing house. But that'd be like calling my life's work a fancy home page."

"But it IS a fancy home page. That's what they said it was on CNN, and CNN rules."

"OK."

"OK!"

"But I want you to share my Weakness."

"Your weaknesses, baby. Repeat after me: I want you to share my weaknesses. Say it."

"I want you to share my Weakness. My Weakness is grand. It's the total summation of all my petty little weaknesses, the same petty weaknesses that make me like every other no-fucking-body with their endless petty weaknesses. But it's also *more* than that. My Weakness is Supreme Weakness. Untouchable Weakness. Prolific Weakness. Totally networked and branded Weakness...."

"The Supreme Fiction is what I'm hearing here. You know, I thought that that embrace we had tonight, at the airport, when you first saw me come down the corridor—that was sincere."

"I'm glad you liked it. How many of those politically incorrect Chinese herb-pills did you eat on the plane?"

"Four."

"Only four?"

"Yes, but they were a tasty four. Although the last one gave me trouble. My mind is so clear I can't see the sky for the heavens...."

[Light of match, deep inhalation, profuse exhalation]

An earlier version of this story was originally published in How to Be an Internet Artist *(Boulder, CO: Alt-X Press, 2001).*

Natto Girls

In Nagoya, as part of an international art symposium that I am invited to perform in as a guest VJ, I am stoned with jet-lag consciousness and looking through a pool of black water atop the Oasis 21 shopping center down into the distant arcade full of animated light forms, steaming noodle shops, and all of the nanotech you can eat. I see her again, the same girl who served me dinner last night inside Hermes Kitchen, a hip, modern restaurant for trendy Japanese yuppies who have money to burn.

But is there still money to burn, or is that just a totally unaccountable credit system that delivers virtual yen every time you look into your mobile phone and start tapping into what can only be a warped version of so-called freedom? *Freedom of Multimedia Access* is what they call it. FOMA.

Rhymes with SOMA.

Make sense?

"I am girl fuck for you," says a trendy broken-Engrish t-shirt that walks by as I descend the wide concrete stairs and begin my reentry into the floating world of delicious consumers waiting to be double-clicked into another virtual time zone.

A few seconds later, my pants buzz as I hear a short Kraftwerk loop I've programmed into my biophone, the one that recharges just by being close up against my natural body heat, and I realize that she, the girl in the t-shirt, has just sent a message to me via our wireless peer-to-peer network. I reach into my pants pocket, grab my biophone, and snap it open, and it says, point blank, "What do you do? How long you here?"

I snap my phone shut and keep walking.

"I No Be Yo Bitch," says another trendy broken-Engrish t-shirt moving up the stairway as I saunter down. The t-shirt is tight and sexy, and one of the arms that extends out of its sleeve is wearing a *keitai* with a small pink ribbon hanging from it, wearing it like a slightly awkward bracelet, and at the end of the pink ribbon is a little doll that looks like the cat-punk star of the very trendy and avant-pop movie that just opened all across Japan called *Tamala 2010: Cat Girl in Space.*

Once again my biophone vibrates inside my pants while playing a short Kraftwerk loop, and I snap it open. It's a picture, a still-image JPG of a young woman in a tight white dress positioned on all fours, mounting a table and looking like she would like to be entered from behind.

Then a text message, in English, comes on the screen: "I want to be a Natto Girl."

Miniaturization of screenal technology, small video capturing of promiscuous pixels in a wireless world where small is beautiful and physical space itself is the most sought after commodity of all: this is my Nagoya 2002.

A new message pops in, and my screen tells me it's

translating...

Then in English: "Looking for young American to take my boredom away. You drink beer?" I look around to see where the message may have come from, but it's impossible. There are fifteen people staring at me, and all of them look hungry.

All of these messages that keep invading my electrospace seem to come from nowhere. It's as if we have gone from point and click to point and shoot. Infra-ray intersubjectivity. But usually, while in other parts of the world, my biophone prompts me, asking if I want to accept the data coming in from some nearby device. I am supposedly free to choose. But not here in FOMA country. Here, everything is permeable, even my crumbling thinkspace.

As soon as I enter the neon arcade, covered by a dome high atop this space-age building that serves as the future-world setting for me to drift through, someone I don't know points a phone at me and takes a picture of my wavering body. Buzzing with the deep caffeine fix I picked up in the dark hole across the street from the hotel I'm staying in, I shuffle through the arena imagining what it would be like to miniaturize myself, to virtually replicate whatever energy I have as a roaming light form, to transmit my data into the ether, to become a transfluctuating value point in the currency-exchange markets while losing my personal identity in a suffocating, virtual intelligentsia, so that I can finally get on that table with every intent of lifting up the tight, silky white dress and deftly entering the natto girl from behind.

It all happens so fast now. The only way to survive in this 3-D cyberpsycho-geographical space odyssey, where the *will to aestheticize* corrupts your every conscious will to act, is to accept your fate as an ever-changing avatar-self in an electronic dataplay suffused with an orchestration of writerly effects.

To be a body in heat...

... recharging its blood circulation with enough bioimagery (virtual spunk) to populate entire regions of the megapixel universe.

I took video pictures of you as you lay naked on my hotel bed and then I uploaded these images to a Web site where I keep all my starfuckers. You like? Yes, you knew about my Web site before I met you, before you even thought you knew who I was. And now your virtual self is being ripped, mixed, and burned ::: looped and randomly manipulated through an array of artist-generated plug-in filters on a distributed network where over 10,000+ comrades celebrate their Freedom of Multimedia Access by subscribing to my sacred site of creative exhibitionism.

I call the site *Natto Girls.*

Another spam enters the screen on my biophone:

The taste keeps getting better...

Try her for breakfast: she's very delicious.

In the beginning, there was data, and it was transmitted over a network, and over that network you imagined someone, something, like me. You programmed me into existence as something you were looking for—an older, overconfident, American boy who would demand respect and play on your desire to be a natto girl, a role-playing other who, through some culturally manipulative thought process, believes that by squirming naked on my bed while I video-capture your jerky pixel movement, everyone will buy into your sexy self-image and into me too (as the camera-wielding master of ceremonies)—into our floating world of viral remixing.

My phone rings. This time it's a cacophony of outrageous sounds generated by Merzbow, the noise artist. A friend's idea of a joke.

"This is your American Dream, yes Moimoi?" asks the voice on the other end of the nonexistent line.

My name is not Moimoi, I tell her. It's Maimonides.

"Yes, Moimoi, I know. And I think we first met in Spain, at one of your club gigs there. Maybe it was last year? Cordoba? Barcelona? Bilbāo?"

I have no idea who she is or how she has found me. And why does she sound so familiar and yet so very foreign all at the same time? Anything is possible in a world where Freedom of Multimedia Access feels like living on the edge of forever. FOMA. Always a soft landing in the land of make believe.

A couple of clicks, and you have me.

You try for breakfast? Please you can eat me now? I am very tasty. Only 500 yen a month.

A raw egg is broken and then slowly spread across a host of scaly skin. This is soon followed by dripping a small smattering of the nasty natto paste on to her belly, a concoction that she swears she can't live without.

I have many love data, but only for you. Can I feed you now?

Or so says a spam message sent to nonsubscribers who have already visited the site, complete with a link to the visuals you can always pay extra for.

The basic membership is a minuscule 300 yen a month. Electronic transfer via your I-mode service. Easier and easier in the land of make believe.

11,244 subscribers.

You do the math.

Arigato.

The jet lag is transmitting new relationships in staggered realtime.

At the Nagoya port, inside an abandoned warehouse (isn't it always an abandoned warehouse?), I play another improvised VJ set in front of four hundred people.

The live video clips that were looping during the performance reveal three natto girls on a king-sized bed somewhere in Melbourne, where the rooms are cheap and four times as big as anything you can get for a similar price in Japan. As the gig developed, there were scenes with other natto girls and assorted wannabe actresses streaming in—some from Sydney, some from San Francisco, some from São Paulo, some from Rome. All of the live source material was being manipulated, on-the-fly, so that the subjects were layered on top of each other like an orgiastic lovefest. At a certain point, the multilayered, megachick mash-up made each of the individual scenes from the various international cities seem irrelevant. It became a stack of indiscernability. Hair, legs, breasts, feet, torsos, mouths, eyes, ears, excess.

Think of it as *raw intersubjectivity.*

"You are very famous here in Nagoya," says the organizer.

Someone from the UK, a London DJ, comes up to me and says, "Konichiwa, Moimoi. I met you at a club gig in Spain last year. I think it was Barcelona—or was it Bilbāo?"

"My name is not Moimoi," I tell him. "It's Maimonides. But my friends call me Persona. VJ Persona."

I want to tell him that I have never performed in Spain and visited there only once, back in 1995, but he's the fourth person in Nagoya who has told me that they met me "at a club gig in Spain last year."

Who is telling the truth here?

I want to say me. But who is me?

I am not Moi.

And I've never been to Spain, but I kind of like the music. They say the ladies are insane there, but...

...have they ever been to Japan?

"That wasn't me," I tell him.

Me is not the man who—alone and reading about the relationship between Japan-styled creative masochism and American-styled unilateral war aggressiveness in times of terror—walked into the Hermes Kitchen last night and asked for an English menu.

Me is not the man who, when he first walked in, did not get an English menu but ended up getting something much more precious, something I could have never dreamed of. The manager, who was the only male employee in the room, brought me you, and you were somehow ready—a kind of embodied I-mode device packaged with a translation program that was semi-dysfunctional but could (at times) interpret my utterances one level above grunt.

Grunt.

Hrrrggh.

Ugggggg.

Persona? You are the end of the happy story, yes? You will please taste me now? Special rate of 450 yen a month. Very cheap!

More spam, more raw egg—and a touch of natto—followed by a long sliding tongue working its way into the small pool of fermented custard puddling
up inside her belly-button.

Nasty, yes?

Tasty, I think.

Before I can sit down, the manager has no choice but to enlist you as my
translator, which is exactly what you have been waiting for, or so you tell me
later.

Quickly, while waiting for you to come and take my order, I send a message
to my list, my 11,244.

Moving around in No-Go-Ya, the ideogrammic play of hieroglyphic signifiers filling my
mind as I use my own spontaneous visuals to remix the urban environment...more
bodystax in Tokyo next week...In the meantime, check out the feverish archive!

It feels like it all happens in asynchronous realtime. Badly bruised blur time.

Blindingly fixated on the shadow effects of an orgasmic reaction that somehow objectifies him too—as an American who says what he feels, a gentle
giant who pummels you with atomic energy, pets you into economic submission, respects you for your open-mindedness and absolute willingness to be
whipped into a consumer frenzy.

Is this your seduction?

I am trying to play things.

Maybe—you can pray things too hard?

I am seducing you now, and we have still yet to speak a word to each other.
Your boss (who treats you like trash but would like to fuck you anyway because you're very sexy): he wants my money, my business. So although there
is no English menu, he has a solution to the language problem, and it's you—
the girl who speaks so little English but is soon going on vacation to Las Vegas
to gamble and see Elvis impersonators and maybe meet cute American boys
and (although I am not a cute American boy) there is still something about
my older boyishness coupled with my American edginess that is enough to,
well, turn you on?

What do you drink?

What do you have?

Biro, sake.

Sake.

Ah, sake, we have.

But he is no longer listening. He is longing. He longs to take your fragile, tender body in his hands and, with soft fingertips and scintillating tongue licks, travel the length of your superimposed skin as it transmits your crawling presence all over his obedient psyche. This is what being a foreign lover is supposed to be all about, or so he learns, the hard way—the easy way, too—as he navigates the international VJ circuit and launches his various Web site businesses all along the way.

Maybe it was the feminist training in college, the P.C. sensitivity training, that makes him soft around the edges. But he is (or so you find) not a warmonger at all. He's more like a punky playboy or the hip high school teacher who is barely disciplined but, alas, patient. And now that you're twenty-two and obviously very open-minded to his suggestive behavior....

She shows me the Japanese menu with pictures of different kinds of sake bottles and different sizes. I take a small bottle of the dry stuff from the Hokkaido region.

She soon brings it back, but while she is away, I see that she has a kind of joke with her three female soul mates at the bar. The cook is female too. They are all incredibly beautiful and always looking at me. Even though they are always looking at me, they are still very shy, and most of them cannot sustain the stare. The only one who keeps staring back as if she's still translating the experience in realtime is Nari (that's what her friends call her).

She comes back with my sake, and I tell her point blank, "You are beautiful beyond words."

She thanks me, as if she knows what I'm saying—which she does, since we are now speaking eye language, too, and sometimes this is the only language I have to speak when conversing in Japanese.

But she wants to transition into another space—though not too fast—as she holds the stare, and then, one level above grunt, she says, "Words?"

I almost forget what she is talking about but then remember my line, "beautiful beyond words."

"Beyond words. I can't speak to you in words except maybe sophisticated grunts that detail my desire to totally immerse myself in your aura."

Machinic poetry ported through the intelligent VJ filter? Database of potential contact? Strange pick-up line? More social spam?

I talk to her like I'm talking to a dream. A dream with subtitles.

"To eat?" She asks me this like a twenty-two-year-old mother talking to her infantile forty-two-year-old son. She holds the menu open so I can see it.

"Yes," I say, "to eat. You—natto girl. Can I have a taste?"

She laughs at the phrase "natto girl." But then, "Yes, you would have to eat?"

"Yes, I would like to have. If it's possible." And I open the menu and point to the bowl of freshly made tofu.

"Tofu," she says, not sure that I know what I'm ordering.

But then I find a way to assure her that I know exactly what I am asking for. "Yes, tofu. No meat."

"No meat?"

"Well, no meat. Yes."

She smiles and keeps the eye language going and then reaches for the menu, grabbing my hand instead, but then lets go and takes the menu away while leaving me slightly restless.

Why does my hand not shake with nervous energy but instead still feels full and pulsating with the transmission of her body heat and the raw language of her always searching eyes transmitting another kind of neuromantic, I-mode chatter?

She brings the tofu, pours me more sake, and asks me where I am from. We have a long conversation that feels like we are on a dinner date and soon her manager is fumigating at the edge of my peripheral vision until eventually he barks out her proper name, no longer able to control himself. Fortunately, she does not jump out of her skin. Quite the opposite, really, as she keeps staring at me, slowly turns, and goes over to see what's wrong.

What's wrong is that she is not letting me eat, or so he thinks, but I have no problem with any of this and am already plotting the possibilities.

Soon she comes back to me and—as if she has just seen the latest sequel to *Tamala 2010*—says, "He's a fucking asshole." But she says it in Japanese, and I have to have her repeat it into my phone, where it translates her comment for me in seconds.

I laugh—but then feel bad for cheating, for looking. But then I think: at least it works!

She goes to another table and then disappears behind the bar. While the clamshell to my biophone is still up, a new message comes into my screen, and it's from her, although I have no idea how she sends it. As far as I can tell, she has no phone on her and is in the middle of working. And the fact that she can send it to me without having my phone number is still something I have to get used to. I imagine a new telepathic protocol that allows people to think thoughts onto nearby devices or, even better, allows devices to see what thoughts other people are thinking. If only I could read her mind!

But then again, she reads it aloud for me herself. The message, in English, says, "You are cute. I would like but first my work is over."

I now realize that all of her work colleagues are somehow extremely jealous and have no idea about our communications. In fact, everything is just between her and me now. No one has a clue.

Before I go, I feel dry in my mouth and think of asking for a glass of water, but she is already bringing it to me as cold as ice. Did that thought of cold water pop up on her screen? What screen? Mindscreen?

"You read my mind," I say, using all kinds of hand gestures to convey what must be difficult to understand in beginning English but that under these circumstances gets through in less than ten seconds. And when it does get through, it opens a final door that neither of us fully anticipated, something that now makes the next thing possible and I—even as big as I am—slip through that door without a second thought.

"I am staying at the hotel across the street."

"Oh, the _____?"

"Yes. I will go back there now. What time do you leave here?"

"I leave my part-time job at ereven."

("Part-time job?" Sometimes she sounds like an automated translation program—and I like it.)

"What time is it now?"

"10:35."

"Good. You come right after 11, and I will wait for you in the lobby."

"The robby."

"Yes, you know the lobby?"

"Five minutes after ereven. Maybe ten."

"Yes, good. I will go pay the bill now and leave you without saying goodbye."

A different version of this story was originally published in Panic Americana *7 (2002) (Keio University, Tokyo).*

The Random Life of VJ Persona (A Mobile Medium in the Form of a Fiction)

The VJ as nomadic lover, committed life partner, risk-oriented sex addict, asexual workaholic, and itinerant energy absorber/expectorant operating on automatic pilot

Were all of these roles mutually self-conflicting?

Yes and no. It was as if his love life—his life and his loves—was a binary operation that surgically removed his every wish intention.

First, the nomadic lover: he too was a wandering Russian Jew, the illegitimate son of Maya Deren and the poet William Carlos Williams. Maya Deren danced in his dreams. Her body moved in and out of subject positions that threw light onto the screen on which he was watching his life story play out. She would crawl across the long conference table and flick her wrists in his face—begging him to slice into her blood, slash into her feminine persona, and become transfixed in her choreographic scenes of trance illumination. She was there, in his dreams, walking along the ocean, a Russian Jew wandering in the otherworldliness of cyberpsychogeographical time zones. He would follow her down the sandy shore ready to flirt with the possibility, any possibility, and here was one place where he could never manage to take on another easily imagined flux identity. Here he was nothing *but* nothingness, nothingness par excellence, wanting nothing, needing nothing, just flirting with the possibility, a mobile medium in the form of a fiction.

A moving image in transit...

Jamming with the experiential memory of his deep mesh dream. His stomach nauseated with the hunger of always wanting more. More Maya. More ruins. More image manipulation coercing him into what at first sounds like a confession but is really a pseudo-autobiographical metafiction that turns his worldwide persona into an online happening of epic proportions. Or is that just more ego-identity imagining imagination imagining itself? What had all of a sudden guaranteed him a distribution of bodily residuals pouring in from a pleasure network of engaged, loving, mortal contacts, and why was this enough to keep his *dérive* driving?

His random life played out like a fictional moblog taking place in asynchronous realtime: does knowing which day it gets written really matter?

Is the time of day essential to understanding his life's relevance? Why do we have to tie our public personas to the given time structures owned and operated by Multinational Corporation, Inc.? Does opening up his life to the World Wide Web suggest that he wants his audience to comment on his evolving codework and its promiscuous behavior?

Imagine a moblog that takes place in another dimension where it is written on the fly and remixed especially for you, The Reader, depending on how the blog FEELS that moment in time. Perhaps I am thinking of a virtual bodyblog that hallucinates experiences FOR you—a generative iBod, a living, breathing, digital apparatus that is capable of sharing its total life essence as a distributed metafiction.

Imagine the moblog to be an embodied image-information processor that intuitively filters emotional data to express how it, the blog, FEELS as it links to various aspects of your shape-shifting personality.

Personify the moblog. Give it a life of its own: make it a bioblog. Or better yet, let it *take on* a life of its own while you and your piddly little ideas get out of the way of its creative flow.

Make it about more than just you or your thoughts. Make it about an anonymous creative self that has no choice but to *go public*. And in going public in such a random way, notice how an apparently true story is really a generative fiction that demands an open field of compositional action to evolve in—the generative iBod circulating in a hypertextualized narrative space of flows.

In this aimless drift of a bodyblog (aka The Random Life of VJ Persona), anything is possible.

The themes addressed, the memes undressed, the semes of language unraveling and not necessarily always making sense or cohering into an understandable whole are part of the mix. Instead of an absolute truth constructed on the premise of a known spirituality imposed on the psyche from without, imagine a more contingent truth modeled on the law of mosaics, where the parts are always greater than the whole and where the VJ, a poetic ramble, taps into the *spiritual unconscious.*

And always be aware: VJ Persona will make up words or catch phrases for no good reason at all.

For example: *open source lifestyle.*

Translation: Mutating codework living on the edge of experience, parlaying fleshmeets into the ultimate altruistic behavior ever recorded in the annals of the gift economy. (VJ Persona will tell you all about it, if you give him a night, or two.)

Also be aware that VJ Persona will start on one tangent and then quickly redirect his narrative momentum into any number of perceptive possibilities, easily beginning another ten or fifty tangents that (un)intentionally digress into / in-between / beyond what we think the so-called story is or will be. This is the storydata of a metafictional muse formally investigating its poetic movement *as it writes.*

This is also called associational thinking. Improvising its fringe-flow potential is what happens when the body WRITES IT OUT—out into that networked space of flows where all of the modalities of becoming an artist-medium (of impersonating this distributed fiction known only as VJ Persona) fold in and out of each other, creating lyrical resonance and experientially intuitive modes of thought that are difficult to process (as if defamiliarizing the theoretical landscape with fictional sensations were part of some machinic happenstance that originates in the code WITH NO ORIGIN).

Think of it as trance narrative energy captured by an alien apparatus somewhere in the digital afterlife.

This blog-induced story called "The Random Life of VJ Persona" attempts to become a distributed metafiction by tracing the movements of a nomadic narrator who is engaged in a planetary Net art practice that knows *without the unreal there is no Real*

First things first: VJ Persona plays out his live performances as he nomadically wanders the globe in search of loving, mortal contact.

Prehensile fleshmeets with seeing-feeling bodies in motion.

For VJ Persona is nothing if not a total slut, an easy lay who refuses to accept the premise of a school of hard knocks. Quite the contrary, really. In fact, VJ Persona does not set up this fringe-flow poetics of movement as an oppositional ideology but plays it out as a kind of intuitive contrarian who has fun trying to outmaneuver the grasp of the tackling bureaucracies. In football lingo, it's called making an end run.

His language is liable to disseminate loose canonization at any given moment and, with it, an historical slippage into resonant passages sampled from the creative workflow of his endless network of productive Others. Sometimes this comes across as so much name dropping, and it is that. But at least he's dropping them, just like he drops his image bombs into the otherwise supplicant technoclub mix.

He is a product of the cultural underground and is happy to have his captured and manipulated images invade your social space for the joy of having them seep into your eyes and possibly derail your artful complacency (throwing in 5K for the gig won't hurt either).

He wants to use his images to dig into your dreams and leave behind his ambient imprint.

But give the VJ a break. The VJ is not generating a visual language of digital poetics to suit every club-going reader's needs. Rather, the VJ is focused on becoming something totally different from what you or I could possibly think he should be. Without even thinking about it, he's naturally turned on to the potential emergence of his verbal jousting, his visual juggernaut, his virtual juice.

No matter what the generative moblog may say at any given time, and no matter how it makes you feel when you read it (especially in relation to the unreliable narrator who slips in and out of roles so fast that there can never really be any concrete metadata), VJ Persona is not really *about* anything but simply an investigation into the life of an artist-researcher who loves to *play the work*.

Transience is a way of life for VJ Persona

He learned to go with the transient flow as a homeless person in New York City during the rise and fall of the dot.coms. Walking the crowded city streets during the day, picking up a messenger gig here, a free bagel there, he was engaged with the idea of reinventing what he then called a *psychogeographical drift* wherein he would wander aimlessly through the city's grid in search of absolutely nothing. He thought of his perambulations as coming attached with some kind of *revolutionary aimlessness*.

This search for nothing in particular, not even a meaning-inflected social environment of sympathetic nobodaddies, drove him to invent various flux characterizations for himself to play. At any given moment, he could become hastily composed random characterizations with names like Isreal Disreal, Alkaloid Boy, Gregor Samsa, or Maldoror (some of the names he attached to the fluid acts of decharacterization floating through the pages of his early novels). But in today's moblog entry, he started out playing the role of Maker Faker.

Maker Faker was a fictional nothingness who wandered the streets of New York City and, out of nowhere, would become a story. Becoming a story could happen anywhere anytime: power walking around the reservoir in Central Park, reading Kafka and Derrida books in the New York Public Library, eating breakfast in the Bowery Mission where, evading the appearance of homelessness, he may have slept the previous night, or pretending he was part of the elitist literati on the Upper East Side eating lox and bagels in a trendy café. In every instance, he would feel himself *becoming a story*, and in *becoming a story* he would automatically turn into a fluid decharacterization of a former self whose story had run dry.

He would be an artful intellectual, a mobile poetic force, an enigmatic code mechanic, a far-fetched business plan, an epitomized memory bank, a swollen cock operating on autopilot, a desire engine lost in the fog of a gaseous eros ready to explode in a tirade of fully loaded money shots spamming the electrosphere.

Monet shots. Making an impressionism on 75th Street and Madison Avenue, only to glide into the pleasure of slow-mo pedicures with his lips as the moisturizer. VJ Gigolo, the homeboy trickster.

Making mad bank, as one of his transplanted SoCal girlfriends would call it. Making mad bank on Mad Ave while swimming in his delirium of doubt and desperation.

He would *become a story* standing in front of Anthology Film Archives on Second Avenue and Second Street, waiting for a friend who had agreed to pay for his ticket so that he could see the limited-run Maya Deren retrospective that he intuitively knew he needed to expose himself to so that later, much later, he could become intimately influenced by her seductive knowledge and apply it to his live image flow.

Waiting in front of the building, reading the upcoming schedule of films, he was interrupted by another homeless person who also evaded the appearance of homelessness by sleeping in the Bowery Mission, a former professor of philosophy who had taught at a small liberal arts school in the Midwest. The professor, who referred to himself as Scan, had experienced a mental break-down and lived on the streets of some of America's finest cities. The street people in lower Manhattan knew him as Professor Scan, and he spoke mostly about alien invasions.

Maker Faker immediately switched his own mental gears to lose himself in conversation with the homeless professor.

"Bad for the eyes, bad for the ears," said Professor Scan.

"What's bad for the eyes and ears?" asked Maker Faker, warming up to his new role as schizo-comrade in arms.

"The alien invasion."

"Oh, you mean...?"

"It's dripping out of the sky, it's in the rain, the way it makes you sleep. And then, when you wake up, it's not over. The aliens are still there. They got in through the pores of your skin, and then you have no choice. You just let it bleed."

"Can you imagine what would happen if they got into the drinking water?" Maker Faker asked, and he was only partly playing with him. A large part of his random persona was serious.

"Well, they've already seeped into the language, which is beyond porous. It's lighter than air, and then it takes you over. Think of it as acid rain except this time the acid is bad acid. Like a bad trip, it rains and rains, internally, to the point where it floods all of your organs like a toxic enema. It slowly mur-ders you, day by day, hour by hour, minute by minute, second by second, all the live-long day. It's like suffering from a slow death of information overload. But first, before you die, you have to work like a madman. Endless work for the madman. It never goes away, *ever*. It just floods your insides. It floods them inside out until you can't see no more. Total internal drowning until you're brain dead, and then starts the drought. The drought of feeling. Now you're super dry—powder dry, a walking stick of dynamite ready to explode. And your veins are filled with this poisonous quicksand that turns into silica, which conducts the information so that you have no choice but to eat all the lies until it makes you sick and you start sinking in deeper. Are you sick yet?"

Maker Faker's stomach was a hotpot of decomposing gruel experiencing a kind of enzymatic rapture on the verge of cancerous pain. He was hungry, so hungry that he could just say what he felt and didn't have to worry about the repercussions. Being poor and homeless and forever starving was a way to sidestep the intimidation game that others hoped to lay on him in a twisted watch-what-you-say-or-you'll-lose-your-job sort of way. When there's no job to lose, and your gig is remixing personas on the streets of the ever-morphing global village, you say what you want, even if it doesn't make sense or hurts feelings or makes you look particularly stupid and totally out of it.

Persona aka Maker Faker would *become a story* in what felt like realtime but was really fake time with subtly programmed delay effects. These delayed effects, a kind of forced preemption of life itself that meant you were never really living in the present, signaled to him the first law of embodied thermo-dynamics: you could say whatever you wanted whenever you wanted, without ever thinking about it.

Looking Scan dead in the eyes, he said, "I'm sick of the creeps. "

"Yeah, " said P. Scan, picking up on his vibe. "The creeps are raining down from an inverted hell-on-high catastrophe in the making. And they're getting into the drinking water. And you know what happens when they get into the drinking water. That's when they seep into your body and contaminate your dreaming."

"Yeah," said Maker Faker, "but that's just it. I *like* it when they contaminate my dreams. Rusty water media-saturated dreams with microbial death machines circulating inside my blood. Nanotech robots made of mortal coils twisting my brain into submission so I don't have to think about it anymore. I can just be a narcotized anybody—an anonymous memory crawling on the sidewalks, licking the shit out of the cracks of the pavement, sucking it all out of the city's raw ass like a tonic sewage elixir getting me high on the life of death, of *totally wasted life*, while the experiential moment of a now-history pounding me with its bloody fists forces my acquiescence to all things bona-fide American. I just need to keep exporting my mind to Planet Oblivion where the moral regime feeds me enough money to put a roof over my head, put bread on the table, pay for my kids to go college, secure my retire-ment fund, start saving for the second home in the Hamptons."

It was like an improvised jazz jam—Scan and Maker Faker trading verbal notes and phrases with variations on a theme, calculated risks and measured repetitions liberating their mental patience from its institutional straitjacket, the faux professors DJ-PhDing their rhetorical citations in a vortex of poetic manipulation that may not always translate but then *acting on that* as the ultimate strategy never to stay on message while easing one's tender biomass of skinflicked desire down into the burrow of paranoiac visions, slippery adhesions to malodorous smells that cloud one's perspective and make it too easy to become addicted to the dreamstink discourse networks leaking out of the black hole of canonized memory melting into a knot of nerves tightening its grip around my throat as I slowly suffocate and find my way back to where I came from.

A digression within a digression within a digression: wildstyle hypertextual consciousness riding the sign/sine waves

When his friend (met in a café and always willing to help out whenever he could) suddenly appeared, Maker Faker excused himself from the dialogue with Professor Scan and went into the Anthology Film Archives theater. He saw Maya Deren's deep mesh of afternoon dreams and realized that he wanted to become the human equivalent of a moving image filled with transient matter and memory. Although he didn't know it at the time, he wanted to become a stylized, performative gesture in the marketplace of actions and ideas, a key figure in the ever-morphing artificial intelligentsia who would transmit his mutating political fiction inside the flux of experientially tagged media stimuli: he wanted to become VJ Persona.

But he was many other people too. In fact, Maker Faker was a variation on another free-flowing character he referred to only as M/F. M/F was his nongender-specific loverman-loverwoman who would slide their body down the slash that tried to differentiate between the sexes—sliding down the slash and slicing into the persona where one could close their eyes ("bad for the eyes") and let it bleed. If the acid rain was going to take over, he might as well hallucinate an orgy of equipotentiality.

Out would seep this strange new blood language made of randomly generated images that appeared as though they were being processed in realtime, although to the acute observer it was obvious that M/F operated not in realtime but, as already mentioned in the various theory loops throughout, fake time—or *unrealtime*. Fake time was different than the overdetermined false consciousness of time. In fact, fake time was designated as an antidote to anything remotely resembling such a false consciousness. To fake time, you had to make time, and in making time, you could live on the edge of existence while obliterating time. But that's another subject for another book, another make-time experience still in its prehallucinatory stage of incubation.

M/F was a foreign agent living inside any random body, a viral awakening that kept reproducing a strong desire to become nothing that matters but that still manifested itself in the visual art world as a moving image filled with transient substance and possibly even market value.

As VJ Persona, M/F was continually releasing new versions of his remixology as a distributed network of trance narrative fictions that could be performed anywhere the Gig Gods would allow. But the fluid thing that went by the name M/F would eventually peel away the semiotic skin of VJ Persona, and in its place would appear another persona, perhaps a bike messenger named Mike Kelley, an adjunct instructor named Carolee Nauman, a fourth-generation pop-conceptual artist named Kiki Oursler, or even an artificial anthropoid named Abe Golam. VJ Persona could become any of these flux beings at any time. But when he was performing his generative jams in front of a live club audience, he was just VJ Persona—or some alternative version thereof.

An alternative version thereof

In Paris, he was VJ Guy, a party-in-waiting, turning tricks for the theory sluts who kept whispering in his ears, "What you see is what you forget."

In Tokyo, he was VJ Pix, divining netflicks on to the walls of small nightclubs full of flipper chicks speaking a mammalian language that only their hearing eyes could communicate with.

In Melbourne, he was VJ Guru, serving heaps of organic veggie matter to the freakish followers who sought his lifestyle practice and who would soon outperform him.

In Berlin, he was VJ Mordechai, selling out his soul, shelling out his visual linguistics.

In Switzerland, he was VJ Hack, intervening in the club and festival culture as a member of the established digerati whose body ejaculated Bio Truth Serum.

In São Paulo, he was VJ Dinosaur, completely losing sight of himself while realizing his ageless potential.

In San Fran, he was, simply, Professor VJ, holding seminars on the debilitating effects of magic lantern shows and why that was "good for the eyes."

And in New York, he was always VJ Persona, hastily mobilizing his body of thoughts through the urban transarchitecture, an average of all of the mes he was capable of becoming at any given moment, a movement in the crowd.

Traveling the world, VJ Persona hyperimprovised layered remixes of customized images and embedded them in collective memory by triggering his creative unconscious. He met a mad variety of women who were intrigued by his sensitive collage of artist-performer, public intellectual, whacked out cultural theorist, too-hip-for-his-own-good professor, and wild heterosexual toad weaned on the likes of Petronius's *Satyricon*, Rabelais's *Pantagruel* and *Gargantua*, Sade's *Philosophy in the Bedroom*, Pauline Reage's *Story of O*, Henry Miller's *Tropic of Cancer,* and Terry Southern's *Blue Movie.*

Some of these women became home-base lovers. When he was in town to perform a gig, he would never e-mail first. He would arrive in the hotel where he was staying, unpack and set up his gear, pick up the phone, and call, saying, "Hey, I'm here. Can you come see me now?"

Many of them were married, happily, and happy to see him come and go, as long as he did come before he went, and he was quite happy to share it with them even if they were married, since he was married too and ready to loosen up some of that Monet fizz that had been jazzing in his pants since he first got to the airport ready to depart. The airport, as a cyberpsychogeographical environment, was code for "Change direction." His mantra was something like "Change direction, or you might end up where you're heading." So jumping on a plane was no longer heading somewhere but changing course and, in changing course, rerouting desire. Thus, the jazz of his continuous arrivals.

He wasn't necessarily married to the idea of the nomadic lover, and at times he woke up in a blur of jet lag and weed, wondering aloud where he was and who was sleeping next to him in the dark. Usually, as a gut reflex, this was when he would further role-play a character that came out only in deep jet-lag night, a David Bowie–like space case known only as the Astronaut, who was loosely modeled after Bowie's role in Nicolas Roeg's *The Man Who Fell to Earth.*

"Hello," he would say to whoever happened to be sleeping next to him. Sometimes they would be sucking on his rust-leaking, acid-rain body. "I am the Astronaut—the alien other—and I have returned to Planet Oblivion. Will you marry me? How many children would you like to have? Did we pay the car insurance this month?" He would say it in a monotone and exaggerate the low vocal quality of his voice, a bit hoarse from the killer joint they had shared before the alien coming and collaborative crashing.

A stoned laugh would come from the log of love laying next to him, and he would try his damnedest to locate that laughter, to shuffle through his internal databanks and cash in on the indexical trifecta of laugh, body, and smell.

But it was never easy to decipher. In fact, most of the time, it was all just a blur, and the laugh would turn into a palm handling his heavy load, and the palm would soon turn into a slide, and the slide would become a mouth, and the mouth would then seamlessly begin mouthing words that spoke a language he called Erosperanto, a dreamy cum cloud of creamy Creole that would soon facilitate the exodus. The alien exodus. The one that had somehow invaded not only the water, but the internal fluids constantly being generated by the artificial intelligentsia on its biological missions. Who could fight the power?

"Pix," she would say, and he was in Tokyo.

"Guru," she would only slightly squeal, and he was in Melbourne.

"Give it to me, Hack," she would insist, and he would transplant his memory stick into the depths of Switzerland.

And this was only the beginning of his persona as a nomadic lover.

As a committed spouse, he would also perform his alien Astronaut routine, except this time the laugh was unmistakable. It was the laugh that kept him warm and well fed, that kept his clothes clean and his hair respectable. This laugh would charm its way into new kitchen appliances, an upgrade on the media center, gorgeous bedroom furniture, new flannel sheets, special trips to exotic beaches and made him feel totally comfortable at home—a definite no-no for the true nomadic spirit in perpetual wanderlust.

But how could he not submit? Who could fight the power?

This was a laugh that transcended any loose conception of pillow talk. And if the bed they were in felt different than any other bed they had ever slept in, then it was better because it meant that they had escaped Planet Oblivion, together. The shared experience of escaping was crucial to their survival, to their collaborative image of keeping at bay the inevitable and ugly future barreling itself down on them.

Meanwhile, the risk-oriented sex addict was never at a loss for what to do. The minute he hit the road was the minute his libido would enflame. The road was not a place for travel. It was a space for hit-or-near-miss encounters with quick access to all the goods (the open sources, you might call them), exchanging fluids via rude orifices in rough yet pleasant spurts of energy that circulated inside the gift-based economy.

These hit-and-near-miss one-night stands often took place in the day, too, a totally inadvertent bumping into a tight ass in the aisle of a Parisian grocery store leading to confused mistranslations of accidental intentionality, which then digressed into forty-five-minute fuck sessions that you might never recover from were it not for exquisitely rich goat cheese going down with the subtle, earthy depths of a thick Bourgogne red wine.

The risk-oriented sex addict, who occasionally goes by the name VJ Persona, knows that the minute his plane takes off—for Paris, Milan, Barcelona, San Fran, Nagoya, São Paolo, Sydney, Las Palmas, Shanghai, L.A.—something is amiss, and this something is his pure rationale. It has conveniently disappeared from view, and even he knows that this uncouth aspect to his persona will detract from his ability to sustain any serious emotional relationship with whosoever consents to his flickering flights of delight, and this defect in his psychological condition is nothing if not transparent.

But he wants it—and he wants it now—and he does not want to force it on anyone. That's not necessary, for there are many others out there who want this quick fix, just like him.

He prefers to have the mobile force of his own persona—the situatedness of his sudden arrivals and departures—create the scenario that allows all of these strange bedfellows to give themselves to him just as honestly as he gives himself to them (the only true act of love left in a world ridden with reality-induced terror spectacles and their manipulated fear factors). To give oneself anon: to be nothing but a piece of meat, to embody flank and rump and loin and groin.

And groan.

Smell the red, taste the noise, see the stink, touch the moan

So what if all of these personas outlined above are fictional wannabes, forever led astray by the asexual workaholic? So what if the asexual workaholic is always writing, reading, thinking, capturing images, editing, compositing, trying new live software, going to festivals, speaking on panels, delivering keynotes and never has time for sex? So what? This is the *real* me, thinks Persona. And how unreal it feels.

In this case, he's not really asexual at all, since an asexual personality implies someone who makes an informed decision not to have sex or is just not interested in it. In this case, VJ Persona, the asexual workaholic, is transferring sexual energy into other cultural acts that may add value to his reputation as an artist-researcher building visibility in his primary network. In this case, maybe he is something like a transsexual, but that is wrong too since a tranny is interested in transforming gender from male to female or the other way around. So, no: not transsexual either.

How about metasexual?

What would a nomadic metasexual be? And what would this metasexually drawn cultural figure known as the VJ have to offer the field of erotic desire?

The VJ produces a number of persona effects that both relocate the Benjaminian sense of aura and challenge conventional standards of social behavior. How to put it?

The VJ can relate. He/She (M/F) is a diplomat of the borderless otherzone. A hyperimprovisational VJ like Persona is sensitive to the erogenous zones of humankind and is forever tapping into its natural tendency toward horny spontaneity. In fact, VJ Persona performs his/her imagistic remixes the same way he/she would fuck a lover, which is different than fucking a life partner, which is different than fucking a stranger in a one-night (or -day) stand, which is different than not fucking at all because work keeps getting in the way of his/her social life. Persona plays with the borderless otherzone of his lovers as if in hyperimprovisational jam mode. He sees his love-making sessions as live sets. What goes through his head as he plays the lover's body is the artist-medium's version of intersubjective writerly drift. What is experienced is a kind of pleasure of the text as neurological time trip.

The nomadically wandering VJ is always role-playing a diplomatic leader in the international cultural arena. His/her foreign policy is to create dynamic relationships with those who come to see his/her performances in search of an experiential otherness that will take them into alternative states of consciousness. Going into these other states of consciousness is personified by the VJ getting lost in the readiness potential of a hyperimprovisational performance, of being unconscious while playing. This hyperimprovisational performance is pursued in a live environment to *see what happens* when fragmented loops of the VJ's life are spontaneously recontextualized into the narrative of the moment—blurry images of various subway scenes from London, Tokyo, Paris, and New York or near-still imagery of a foreign lover spread out across a king-sized bed dreaming of nothing but hanging with the VJ. Whatever the narrative content, the unconscious creative acts of the VJ, like those of many other artists and athletes, attract endless potential lovers who want to interject their grounded realities into the VJ's cloudy transfiguration of thought.

Finally, it must be said that this is only one version of the VJ Persona story—one pseudo-autobiographical portrait and a very incomplete one, at that. If you think about it, we have only just started to unravel the narrative potential of this aimless drift.

The VJ, as distributed fiction, is capable of turning any image into another image and the new image into a totally different and *other* image with such blinding speed that this random life—knowingly accelerating its body through the blurred-out, open source, bliss economy—is always on the verge of becoming something else entirely different (for instance, a National Park Service ranger at Haleakala National Park high atop the dormant volcano on the island of Maui—why not?).

To loop in Rimbaud again: "To each being several others lives were due."

The key to VJ Persona's encoded survival kit is in realizing that

The Body Is an Image-Making Machine.
It Filters Information.
It Creates Dreams, Memories, and Spontaneous Situations Made Out of Images.
The Images Are Created in the Body as They Respond to Images Outside the Body.
The Images Change as the Body Moves.
These Movement-Images Resonate with the Dreams, Memories, and Spontaneous Situations Made out of Images.
This Means That Spontaneous Situations Made out of Images Can Be Dreams or Active Memories.
Meanwhile, the Body Is an Image-Making Machine.

and so on, like a loop, ad infinitum.

Ad infinitum . . .

Never again does Maker Faker see Professor Scan. One day, almost twenty years later, he is walking the streets of New York City and sees one of his former colleagues from the homeless days. His name is Stan, and he looks dapper.

"Stan," he asks, "what ever happened to Scan?"

"Scan? Oh, he got his act together. Became fully immersed in what he called virtual unreality and wrote a famous book on his pioneering work in digital thoughtography—a space of mind where you kind of *become* a generative persona who uses all available digital technologies to invent a more fluid concept of personal identity. He's a full professor out in the Rocky Mountain West, but it's his side business in lifestyle coaching that really brings in the big bucks."

"I guess he wasn't so crazy, after all," I say to Stan, and that's exactly when it starts to rain, so we cordially part and head off in different directions.

Academic Remixes

Need I say after all this that in questions of decadence, I am *experienced*? I have spelled them forward and backward.

—Friedrich Nietzsche, *Ecce Homo: How One Becomes What One Is*

Answers to Questions I Have Been Asked: A Technomadic Journey

Introductory Note

The following passages are sampled and remixed versions of answers I have given to various e-mail interviews that have been requested of me.[1] Leading an activist online life and maintaining a Web presence (by such activities as creating Net art sites, writing for popular online journals, and participating in e-mail lists and forums) have enabled me to build a distributed audience for my work. These activities, in turn, have led to numerous opportunities to share my ideas and some of the details of my personal journey with a wide array of readers across the planet. Over the last ten years, I have probably given close to fifty interviews in academic, pop culture, art, and literary journals. The more I engage in these asynchronous dialogues, the more I realize that the e-mail interview format is one I feel totally comfortable with, and I see that some of the key concepts of my own evolving digital poetics are often triggered in answering the questions of others. That is, as a storyteller who is self-conscious of the power of narrative to deploy a personal mythology that parallels the movements of my artistic agenda, I am often challenged by the interview/dialogue format to further invent both my practice and my artistic persona as a way to prophesize the near-future developments of (my own) writing.[2] The sometimes nonlinear and dysfunctional sequence of the following sections is intentional because it attempts to reflect the often confusing, contradictory, and spontaneous thinking that went into the quick-paced transitions I experienced while becoming professional. If new models of professional development in academia are to take hold and offer innovative opportunities to artists, writers, and scholars, then one of the first things that may have to go by the wayside is conventional, argumentative essay writing.

This does not mean we need to abandon the notion of rhetoric altogether and, in fact, may open up the field to creative new possibilities. Given the content and context of this pseudo-essay, I invite readers to skim the surface of the page and pick up on whatever attracts their attention. Readers also may want to skip back and forth between sections, creating a kind of hopscotch scan of the hodgepodge of language trying to pass itself off as narralogue.[3]

Q: Mark, since 1993, when you first published the Avant-Pop manifesto on your *Alt-X Online Network*,[4] you have been "expanding the concept of writing" (your words).[5] First it was experimental novel writing, then multimedia hypertext, and eventually Net art and "live performance writing" (again, your term). How did these various transitions take place, and why do you suppose they did? How did the name *Mark Amerika* fit into the evolution of both this hybridized practice and fictionally constructed self-identity?

A: As with most things that have happened to me in my Life Style Practice,[6] I accidentally stumbled into the Net as an extension of what I was already doing in other media. From 1989 to 1992, I was writing my first novel, *The Kafka Chronicles* (1993), editing my experimental literary journal *Black Ice*, and providing lead vocals for a weekend sound project called *Dogma Hum*. At this time, I was becoming familiar with the personal computer as a compositional tool, and I was eagerly experimenting with various other tools, like digital effects processors, so that I could sample and manipulate my voice and guitar sounds. Some of the other members of *Dogma Hum* were working for a company called Waveframe, where they were building a state-of-the-art digital audio workstation called the Audioframe. Consequently, we were all focused on what the possibilities for digital audio were, especially for our jam sessions. They were also working on the Net as was I, for e-mail and gopher surfing, and soon I was developing an online R&D platform for what I then called *network publishing*—which a few years later exploded into what we now know as Web publishing (although, for example, these days a company like Adobe has a huge "network publishing" strategy as part of its business model).

One of the two main projects to grow out of this online R&D experiment was *Alt-X*.[7] Starting in 1993, *Alt-X* approached this new medium—first via gopher, e-mail, and MOOs and then via the World Wide Web (WWW)—as a place for conceptual art experimentation that challenged not only the way we create art and literature but the way we distribute it to niche communities ready to engage with the artists we were publishing.

Of course, we soon realized that *publishing* was not always the best term to describe what we were doing. Growing, researching, and developing through the transition into WWW space, we saw that the new forms of knowledge now manifesting themselves as http-based work were blurring the distinctions between such expressions as visual art, literature, performance art, conceptual art, and interactive cinema, and so we began to investigate what an exhibition context for this work would require. In the fall of 1997, Alex Galloway (who won a Prix Ars Electronica 2002: Golden Nica for the *Carnivore* project)[8] and I launched one of the first Web-only exhibitions at *Alt-X* (*Digital Studies: Being in Cyberspace*),[9] and this exhibition then led to many other Net art developments on the site.

Meanwhile, I was still publishing my experimental novels and working, behind the scenes, on *GRAMMATRON*,[10] which was the second major project to grow out of this online R&D platform. For the record, it should be noted that *GRAMMATRON* was created around the same time as *Alt-X* in early 1993. It took four years and much distributed support from various places and people, including those I worked with at Brown University, to actually finish the work and get it to a point where it could be released to the public, the 28.8 modem public that was very much on my mind in those days.

As for how I became Mark Amerika, all I will say now is that it happened in New York in the early to mid-1980s as I was beginning my more experimental lifestyle practice. I was writing an unpublished (and possibly unlocatable) novella called *Dispossessions*, where the protagonist was suffering from amnesia and woke up every day questioning his reality and, in questioning, immediately walked to the Brooklyn Public Library to further find out or discover "who he was." He soon found himself reading about Man Ray and Kafka's *Amerika*. He deducted that he must be "Man Amerika" and took on the name. After the work was written, I too was impressed with the name but declined to take on the *Man* part (I prefer *Mark* because it points to the ideas of signature and trace). So one could say I stole the name from one of my characters.[11]

Q: Of course, you were experimenting with self-reflexive narrative strategies as well as fluxlike identity construction from the beginning of your writing practice. What was it about the screen-based media that offered you more options?

A: I wanted to continue experimenting with narrative form and to expand the concept of writing beyond the print culture. I have a background in making experimental film and was interested in the potential of hypertext and other emerging forms of new media but did not take it seriously until I started developing my practice on the Internet in 1993. First of all, one has to keep in mind that, for me, writing is surviving. It is not a leisurely activity that I approach in terms of "Oh, one day I would like to write a novel." It is actually difficult for me to compartmentalize my writing practice into different areas or genres. I write novels because I am intrigued with the idea of exploding what has become the standard model for narrative construction. Anyone who has read my books knows that my novels came into being as multilinear storyworlds made of language play, graphical page design, and fictionalized states of desire. My novels actively work against narrative closure and are intentionally created to defamiliarize the reader's relationship to conventional narrative devices like character development, plot, setting, and proper grammar and/or syntax—all of the things that we expect to get from the conventional book world and its one-size-fits-all novel experience. I see narrative art as a place to work against the pull of false consciousness that we find in so much predetermined fiction writing.

My first novel, *The Kafka Chronicles* (1993), received a lot of attention in the mainstream world but also, more important, in the alternative culture. It was taken seriously by the underground music world, and this led to my increased interest in D-I-Y culture and the so-called *zine scene.*[12] I saw great potential in creating and nurturing distributed communities of niche audiences as opposed to the all-or-nothing, go-for-broke mentality of the big publishers. It just made more sense to me as an artist and cultural producer to take the alternative culture more seriously. So the advent of the Internet as a potential compositional as well as distribution medium seemed the perfect fit for my evolving interests in creating viable alternatives to the mainstream publishing industry and its dependency on multinational corporate capitalism.

By the time my second novel, *Sexual Blood* (1995), came out, I had already started *Alt-X*, perhaps the oldest surviving online art and writing network, and when I went on my sixteen-city book tour for *Sexual Blood*, all of the attention was on *Alt-X*. I would give a reading to a large audience in Seattle, Minneapolis, or New York, and then after the reading I would ask for questions and expect to hear from fans of my first book, *The Kafka Chronicles*, because it went into three printings in a short period of time. But no, most of the questions were about *Alt-X* and the future of writing and publishing in a network culture. These questions were on my mind, too, and by the time I had finished the book tour, I realized I needed to explore these options more.

Meanwhile, I had already started the first draft of a new novel called *GRAMMATRON*, which was spurring interest from a few major publishing houses, but I was adamant about what I wanted to do. I decided to create a unique work of Internet art that would be made available for free to readers all over the world.

Also, by this time, I had already developed a relationship with Brown University as a visiting artist, attending their Vanguard Narrative Festival and then later the Pong Festival, which was more focused on digital art. I applied to their program so I could develop the *GRAMMATRON* project, was accepted, and spent two years reworking *GRAMMATRON* as a digital narrative created for the Web environment. Now I could focus on both writing and cultural production in electronic spaces without necessarily leaving my narrative art practice behind.[13]

Q: What is *GRAMMATRON*?

A: *GRAMMATRON* is many things at once. It's one of the earliest and more elaborate works of Internet art created exclusively for the Web as a way to track the developments of Web culture in a networked-narrative environment. I was especially interested in how some of the vaporware language that was coming out of the growing new media scene could be used against itself, to rub and/or remix alternative discourses together, everything from cyberpunk, dialectical materialism, and California ideology, to experimental narrative riffs from the likes of James Joyce, Arno Schmidt, and Jean-Luc Godard, to name a few.

Then there is the Cabala: the old scripture, the metacommentary, the Book of Creation, and the Golem myth. In many ways, *GRAMMATRON* is a retelling of the Golem myth remixed with narratological/rhetorical effects sampled from the alternative narratives and discourses mentioned earlier.

I also was very conscious that I wanted to experiment with many of the evolving technological features that the Web could offer me—features that I would never have reason to consider when writing my novels. So there are time-based metatags, Javascript-encoded cookies that create alternative and/ or random linking structures, some very detailed and labor-intensive animated gifs, and an original digital audio soundtrack, among other things.[14]

Q: This work was the beginning of your Net art practice.[15] After *GRAMMA-TRON*, you began developing *PHON:E:ME* which was commissioned by the Walker Art Center in Minneapolis and the Perth Institute of Contemporary Art in Western Australia, a far cry from the D-I-Y zine culture you had grown out of a mere six or seven years earlier. What was the development of *PHON:E:ME* like?

A: *PHON:E:ME*[16] is the second part of my new media trilogy, with *GRAMMATRON* being the first part and the current work in progress, *FILMTEXT*, being the last. Whereas in *GRAMMATRON* I was experimenting with the possibilities of hypertext and its relationship to advanced animated imagery and streaming audio, with *PHON:E:ME* I wanted to research and develop this emerging and converging new media language as it relates primarily to sound: sound as writing, sound as performance, sound as event. I was also interested in how to create another narrative out of it—or if not narrative in the traditional sense, then how to convert data into an emergent digital rhetoric that takes into account narrative as a genre or form of art. In looking for possible themes to explore, as I began researching the project and scripting out its action, I saw a few subjects that began to collide and mix. These subjects were unusually resonant with one another but as far as I know had not been examined in this way before. The subjects included twentieth-century conceptual art, the high-flying new media economy, and its then dependency on overinflated business plans and flash-in-the-pan ideas (Alan Greenspan described the 1990s market as a conceptual economy that was being driven by ideas), and the early history of Net art that so obviously grew out of various kinds of conceptual art from Dada, to Fluxus, to what we think of as Conceptual or Idea Art.

Taking all of this into account, I then tried to conceptualize a sound-oriented Net art project out of these intersecting subject areas, one that would have some resonance with my other work, including *GRAMMATRON*. What I came up with is the *PHON:E:ME* project, which I usually describe as an mp3 concept album about conceptual art with hyperlinernotes. The term *concept album* began resonating with Greenspan's conceptual economy, of which I, like many other Net artists in the U.S., was very much a part and about which

I knew a lot from the inside out. So: concept album—concept art—concept economy. Packaging ideas—or: idea packets. Soon my research started drawing all kinds of resonances among these subject areas, and the action scripting came easily to me as I coded the new media language environment to accommodate these ideas—and out of this programming process we evolved the hyperlinernotes.

Meanwhile, a completely different set of research tracks was set in motion by my collaboration with sound artists like Erik Belgum and DJ Reset. Belgum came up with the idea of creating a speech synthesizer made by digitally recording my voice saying all of the phonemes of the English language. I also recorded my voice mimicking drum machine sounds and bass sounds, as well as other guttural and bodily sounds. These digital recordings became source material for many of the soundtracks we explored, along with some straight readings of the various action scripts associated with the hyperlinernotes. The idea was to have these elements play off each other, to trade currencies in a conceptual economy of potential meaning that would attempt to use the creative data to investigate why Net art was catching so much momentum at that moment in art history, which it clearly was. The most likely answer to Net art's rapid development was a relationship to the new media economy like that of a codependency (think of all of the young and barely developed artists and designers who milked the system and how the dot.com system milked them in those heady days).[17]

The currency of the day was conceptual art, *conceptual language art* really, with a decidedly procapitalist market spin put on it. The language of new media, it ends up, was the language of PR, of hype, of attracting *eyeballs* that would hang around for a while; *stickiness* was the term being used. In other words, an exhibitionist's wild dreams come true. This is why I created these interchangeable concept-characters like the New Media Economist, the Conceptual Artist, the Applied Grammatologist, and the Network Conductor. They were strange attractors playing out their various currency routines in the conceptual economy—the conceptual economy cum attention economy. An attention economy is where attention is the rarest commodity of all, and generating more of it (i.e., attention) is often linked to infectious ideas that drive the psychological disposition of any given marketplace. In the mid to late 1990s, this attention was exactly what drove the dot.com into its overinflated bubble status, and being a Net artist meant having to deal with this issue head on.

In this regard, I am reminded of Burroughs,[18] who proclaimed, "language is a virus"—which it is: image virus, text virus, code virus. Net art as an attention-grabbing form of digital practice was a kind of virus. It's connected to what Dawkins calls the *meme*. Media memes are self-consciously distributed into the electrosphere to influence behavior in the general economy. Look at how the anthrax scare, just after 9/11, became a meme that began taking on the characteristics of a biological virus. All of a sudden we all became carriers of bioinformation, and whenever we started telling our network the various media stories that were circulating at the time (i.e., further spreading rumors), the meme was having a greater effect. Spreading rumors, spreading memes, spreading viruses.

Now this may seem a long way off from where we started our conversation about *PHON:E:ME*, but something that all of the works in the trilogy address is this notion of spreading memes, of using language as a virus, and participating in the conceptual economy.[19]

Q: But in the end, you always see your work, no matter the medium, as part of a larger writing practice?

A: Yes, for me it still comes down to writing. To action scripting, coding, marking, tracing, as well as capturing and manipulating states of altered consciousness—which I propose we are doing when we experiment with digital technologies. Think of it as prosthetic aesthetics, which are art practices that use new media technologies to further alter the way we give and receive information.[20] By using new media technologies to playfully manipulate our experience of the text, we are in a sense becoming more dependent on these external devices to make our experience seem more real. It's like when someone puts on a pair of reading glasses to better read a book, except here it's more about logging on to a network with an ultrafast connection and stereo speakers to better experience the multimedia text. For example, *PHON:E:ME* was an invigorating project to work on because it allowed me to experiment with audio as the primary media element in the multimedia mix. I remember when I first started digitally recording sounds on my DAT player. Whenever I pressed the record button, the interface said we were "WRITING," which to me means digital writing. And when we bring it all up on our screens and begin interacting with the source material, sampling and manipulating it, we are engaged in a process of digital screen/writing. We are always writing when we play with digital technologies. And now that all of our source material can somehow be transferred into digital data (i.e., our multimedia elements such as sound, image, text, and code can be converted to ones and zeroes), there is a kind of surf-sample-manipulate strategy that I have proposed that can easily come into effect. For example, overwriting sounds with texts that are overwriting images that are underwriting sounds. All of these multimedia elements are now heavily invested in each other, with the emerging language of new media being the currency they all trade in.

Q: What happens to our notion of authorship in digital culture?

A: Authorship is not necessarily disappearing, as in all of these "death of the author" scenarios we keep hearing about. Rather, it is being reconfigured into a more fluid, often collaborative networking experience. Take my *PHON:E:ME* project, for instance. Sure, I came up with the initial concepts and negotiated the funding and exhibition context for its eventual display, but the work was collectively generated by both an internationally networked team of artists, DJs, writers, designers, programmers, and curators who produced the work *as well as* a select group of artist-writers-theorists whose work got sampled into the project's Big Remix. *The Author as Network Conductor* has many implications and possibilities, but the change is significant because it means that writers must make (h)activist cultural production a major part of their practice. I think this gets overlooked by too many intellectuals who are looking for the optimum comfort zone for their theoretical musings.

The Network Author is a hot topic on a lot of mailing lists and in some of the recently started online journals. The idea is to try to move away from the "individual artist as genius" model and move toward a more collaboratively generated, computer-supported network of artist-researchers model. But then there's always *you.*

Q: *GRAMMATRON* focused on the potential of hypertext to create multi-linear narrative reading experiences. *PHON:E:ME* seems to move away from that and suggests that writing on the Net can take on a multitude of forms and a variety of media content. Is that a correct reading?

A: Yes, I think I see what the point is, and I agree with the implication. With *PHON:E:ME*, there is very little clicking. After the heavily hypertextualized riffing that went on in *GRAMMATRON*, we decided that the dot.com farce, which was at the height of its reign of greed during the production of *PHON:E:ME* and, as I said, was one of the subjects integrated into the content, we wanted to move away from clicking, from clicking as consuming, from being double-clicked into a marketer's gushing wet dream. So we decided to focus more on wandings, openings, or what we called *conducting.*

One of the concept characters of *PHON:E:ME*, the Network Conductor, was created specifically to challenge our conventional understanding of the hypertextual writer, the entrepreneurial businessperson, the Net artist, and the new media critic. In *PHON:E:ME*, the concept characters became fluid decharacterizations, all melting into one fluxlike identity in motion.

One of the themes floating all throughout the trilogy is how codependent we all are on the new media technology and the conceptual economy it helps facilitate. That is to say, we are—to borrow a term from the South American writer Julio Cortázar—*co-conspirators*. Yet even as we acknowledge this codependency as if it were the natural outcome of our rationalistic, scientific culture and its move toward progress, toward bigger, better, and faster, the trilogy also attempts to throw a monkey wrench into this whole way of thinking through the issues of technology and its effect on our cognitive abilities, on our continuous efforts to produce an artificial intelligentsia of knowledge workers. This monkey wrench is a kind of experimental humanism that plays with the language of new media and identifies some of the more supple qualities of this language's format—the code used to bring it into the world picture.

In this way, the trilogy keeps asking a series of questions in many different ways. For example, in *FILMTEXT*,[21] one question that keeps coming up again and again is, "Who are the Network Conductors?", followed by, "Who writes the Action Scripts?" Who, indeed?

With *FILMTEXT*, as with *PHON:E:ME* and *GRAMMATRON*,[22] we don't pretend to have any of the answers or at least to define exactly what those answers are or might be. We are much more focused on discovering some of the intimate details about the nature of digital source material and how it can be sampled and manipulated into a variety of cross-media formats, such as mp3 concept albums, experimental artist e-books, Flash art, interactive cinema installations, and live performance. The digital source material is not random nor found material in the traditional sense of that term, although it could be, and I have made projects using only found material. Here the source is consciously captured using various apparatuses and then brought into our DT mixers for further manipulation and investigation. *DT*, by the way, stands for *digital thoughtography*. *Digital thoughtography* is the term we use to describe our current field of study, which we are inventing as we speak (spin, rap, transpire).

The reader can find out more on this term at the *FILMTEXT* site, especially in the *cinescripture.1* e-book.[23]

Q: In *FILMTEXT*, you further develop your ideas about nomadic narrative and in many ways are interested in telling the story of writing by narrativizing or poeticizing its place in history but also celebrating its potential to both play with conscious thought as well as show us the way to language while prophesizing our future life. Is that a fair characterization?

A: As I have been saying, to the point of sounding like a broken record, all of these works are primarily interested in expanding the concept of writing— of enacting a new style of writing I am for the moment calling *digital screen/ writing*. As Vilém Flusser has suggested, "Apparatuses were invented to simulate specific thought processes,"[24] processes that are in place, or operating systems that already come with writing applications. Or at least this is what it feels like to me being a digital writer. Derrida too, in his writing quest to deconstruct logocentrism, has clearly made the case for what the Australian theorist Darren Tofts calls "the prehistory of cyberculture"[25]—that is, he has used the inner workings of language to rhetorically spin a remix of preexisting thought and practice to better make the case that, when it comes to writing as techne, as both art and application, we've essentially "been there, done that." It's like we're using the computer as a confessional, leaving our digital traces for others to either archive indefinitely or just erase from memory.

Where it gets interesting for those of us researching and developing a Life Style Practice composed of nomadic narratives—a process where we use whatever instruments are available at our moment in time—is that writing is now becoming more performative in a network-distributed environment similar to the way oral histories were performative in more condensed, isolated communities. This is when writing moves away from being a mere individual memory recording device and becomes a more interlinked, creative mindshare. It's driven by what media theorist Gregory Ulmer calls "the logic of invention"[26] and requires a heuretic approach to making things with the electronic apparatus.

Of course, making things with the electronic apparatus could lead to a dismantling of our present-day economic conditions as we know them. We are only now able to see that this embedded writing application that *comes with* being human is ideally situated to move beyond the limitations of intellectual property laws and into the more fluid interzones of open-source networking and the relational aesthetics of *copyleft*,[27] a theme that arises time and time again throughout the trilogy.

While developing this trilogy, I concluded that performing an open-source Life Style Practice composed of nomadic narratives in network culture enables the Net artist to create a kind of f(r)iction with/in the marketplace of ideas. The use—the application—of DT lends itself to screenal in(ter)vention. Whereas the typical Hollywood screen writer would create a formulaic screenplay that would then be manufactured by a film director in search of a vision, now we see more personal, nomadic narratives being produced specifically for the networked screen culture, where the artist essentially becomes a kind of digital screen/writer who consciously captures digital source material for whatever cross-media formats they happen to be attracted to at the time. The digital source material can come from anywhere and the WWW is especially ripe for the picking. However, with *FILMTEXT*, I have attempted to transliteralize the nomadic narrative by wandering the world and consciously capturing my source material in diverse locations such as Tokyo, the Australian Outback, Hawaii, and Southeast Asia.

Q: You have often stated that the Internet provides a different kind of peer-to-peer economy that can help ignite an underground cultural stance. Can you expound on that?

A: A space of flows, the digital domain of the Internet is ideally situated as a gift economy. Who better to participate in this gift economy than scholars and experimental artists who are used to writing for little compensation? What about the avant-amateurs of the artistic underground who are happy to experiment not for money but to change the curve of contemporary culture? Professionalization can sometimes be a curse. A straitjacket. Taking risks by inventing new forms of rhetoric in the online environment may be one way out of that straitjacket. Who knows what one may discover in the process?

My friend and colleague, Ron Sukenick, has been influential in this regard. His book *Down and In: Life in the Underground* is the bible for those of us trying to use the new media technologies of today to create a positive alternative to mainstream culture.[28] As the writer J. R. Foley has stated elsewhere, the three main points that Sukenick makes when referring to an underground is that "1) the underground is independent, not alienated from mainstream culture; 2) it is inside, not outside, society; and 3) it's a stance, not a place."[29] So for me, being underground is most definitely tied to my artistic practice, especially as it evolves in the network culture, within the peer-to-peer province of the Net.

Q: Can you even still call your work writing per se? Maybe it's more like performance—or what Ulmer sees as a performance pedagogy—in which case it should come as no surprise that the novelist cum hypertextualist cum Net artist is now bringing it all into an academic setting under the auspices of a large-scale research initiative at the University of Colorado at Boulder. Is this where you'll develop a program to build the ultimate peer-to-peer, the-personal-is-political utopia you're trying to create?

A: Yes, watch the genres mix and blur. Once one starts composing one's work in the digital environment, the literary becomes visual, the visual per-formative, the performative fictional, and the fictional theoretical. This then requires a totally different approach to contextualizing the works that flow from this mix-and-blur process. In my classes, we call this fad of Being *maintaining a critical media practice.* I have also seen it called something like *critical literacy*—an operational sensitivity toward a life practice that com-bines the creative, critical, technical, and social skills of the emergent rhetori-cal performer.

I think the point is valid, although I am not consciously pursuing these ultimate—or even utopian—convergences. Ironically, I am too engrossed in living my life, in playing out my Life Style Practice, to strategically seek such a total work. I prefer to see myself as an artist-researcher at play (as opposed to a scientist-researcher at work). I would go so far as to say that I am a kind of D-I-Y amateur, in the sense that Stan Brakhage reminds us of the term *ama-teur* (i.e., a passionate lover of "doing"), which connects to TECHNE, my practice-based research initiative at the University of Colorado in Boulder, where, as fate would have it, Stan taught for over twenty-five years and after recently retiring, passed away.[30]

Q: It seems to me that one doesn't set out to be a pioneer as you have been so much as find opportunities for being one. Your career has been rich with innovations where technology intersects with English studies and creates a unique platform for new forms of art to emerge. What would you recommend for other professionals who want to develop their own innovative paths and find similar success?

A: My main advice would be to try to leave any preconceived notions of what a writer, artist, or scholar is behind. Expand these concepts to integrate various media platforms and research agendas into creative and scholarly work. Medical and business professionals are always adjusting their practices and upgrading their technological skills to adapt to the new technological conditions, so we should, too.

We also need to open ourselves up to all kinds of collaboration: collaboration with students, technology, local partners, and the like. Real-time group collaboration in the classroom is essential. My teaching practice is proactive and involves mentoring students on the development of new digital art works. With new media technologies rapidly transforming the artistic landscape, students are now being challenged to develop a sophisticated set of creative, critical, and technical skills that will help foster their growth. Given the speed with which these technological changes occur, my role as an educator in this area requires me to become more of an open-minded facilitator of knowledge and creative production than an authority figure with a singular view of the world.

I'm also a big believer in the so-called *gift economy*. This means that I have gone out of my way to give away my work for free over the Net. I also try to invest my valuable time in finding ways to make the best work being developed by my peers freely available over the Net. As publisher of the *Alt-X Online Network*, I am fortunate in that the Web site attracts influential, yet diverse, communities of readers and art appreciators. By building this community publication and exhibition site, over 500 scholars, novelists, poets, Net artists, musicians, and others have been able to further develop their own audiences of feedback and support. So being an active cultural producer has its advantages, not the least of which is good karma in the network.

There's an old saying that goes something like "Those who can't, teach, and those who can, do." I think that is totally changing now. With our ability to play with the new media and network technologies available to us today, creative writers, artists, and scholars who find themselves in academic environments can also "do." By doing, we stay active, and by staying active, we keep our spirits alive.

Q: And what's next? What's happening right now?

A: Right now, on January 23, 2004, I can say that I am performing as a VJ [video or visual jockey] at art festivals, universities, museums, and techno-clubs. The experiences I have had performing in these venues has led me to create elaborate DVD-with-surround-sound installations with titles like *The Dialectics of Seeing, The Ecstasy of Communication,* and *The Secret Life of Painterly Data,* which are now being acquired by major art institutions as a way to archive my underground activities into the early years of the twenty-first century.

Students are looking to this kind of work as a model for their own development as well. This brings up this question: What are the emerging forms of writing that can be taught in a multimedia, hybridized learning environment? It's a question we are starting to ask at TECHNE, which is totally legit now that artists are researchers too. It's part of the history of twentieth-century avant-garde art and writing that began in the post-WWII era and continues to this day.[31]

Notes

1. I have been asked various questions over the years about my evolving digital art practice and how my life as a creative writer and former English major has informed my eventual transition into becoming a professor of art and art history. Special thanks to the many interviewers who have given me wide berth to discuss my work with them, especially Anne-Marie Boisvert, Alex Galloway, Beth Hewett, Adrian Miles, Brock Oliver, Roberto Simanowski, and Ben Williams. Alternative titles to this experimental essay could have been "From Experimental Novelist to Digital Screenwriter: A Personal Narrative" or "How Not to Become an English Professor: The Accidental Journey into Digital Studies."

2. For example, after having been asked numerous times in e-mail interviews what it means to be an Internet artist, I wrote a quick ten-point program entitled *How to Be an Internet Artist*, which can be found at ⟨http://www.altx.com/amerika.online/amerika.online.5.7.html⟩.

3. For an introduction to the concept of narralogue, see Ronald Sukenick's *Narralogues: Truth in Fiction* (2002). For example, Sukenick opens his treatise with the following words: "A narralogue is essentially narrative plus argument.... Rhetoric is meant here not as a system of classification.... Rather, it is meant as kind of ongoing persuasive discourse that, in itself, resembles narrative—agnostic, sophistic, sophisticated, fluid, unpredictable, rhizomatic, affective, inconsistent and even contradictory, improvisational, and dependent in its argument toward contingent resolution that can only be temporary" (1).

4. I started the *Alt-X Online Network* as a gopher site in 1993. To read "The Avant-Pop Manifesto" and other similar rants and raves, go to ⟨http://www.altx.com/manifestos⟩.

5. A lot of the initial questions I was asked after having first shifted my writing practice from print to screen dealt with the fact that I was a writer abandoning the book culture that nurtured my creativity into being. In responding, I often told stories about those exciting years of transition. I was also intrigued by the poetics developed by German

artist, Joseph Beuys, focusing on what he, in his book *Energy Plan for Western Man* (1993), termed an *expanded concept of art*. For me, the Internet presented a compositional and publication platform that radically challenged the literary world I was operating in. Thus, I began developing my expanded concept of writing back in the early 1990s. See "This Is All I Do Now" at ⟨http://www.altx.com/amerika.online/amerika.online.1.1.html⟩.

6. For me, a Life Style Practice is what a Net artist performs when creating a work in network culture. It is at once a nomadic narrative that reinvents what it means to be an artist in an experientially designed cybernetic environment, as well as a proactive intervention that takes place within the context of an emergent Web culture.

7. *Alt-X* houses many publishing and curatorial projects. For example, see our media journal, *electronic book review*, at ⟨http://www.altx.com/ebr⟩.

8. See ⟨http://rhizome.org/carnivore⟩.

9. See ⟨http://www.altx.com/ds/index.html⟩.

10. See ⟨http://www.grammatron.com⟩.

11. However, I should point out that my characters are known to get me back. For example, one of my online characters, Cynthia Kitchen, was becoming so popular for her online rants and manifestos that, at one point in the mid-1990s, she was getting more invitations to European art festivals than I was.

12. In the late 1980s and early 1990s, underground art and culture was thriving in the D-I-Y (do-it-yourself) music and literary scenes. One particular area of interventionist activity during this time was the so-called zine scene, which revolved around a publication called *Factsheet Five* and grew out of the long history of alternative publishing. It was out of this zine scene that many of my initial forays into independent publishing began, including Black Ice Books, *Black Ice* magazine, and eventually the *Alt-X Online Network*. For more on this, see "This Is All I Do Now" at ⟨http://www.altx.com/amerika.online/amerika.online.1.1.html⟩ as well as the articles featured in *American Book Review*, 16, no. 1 (April/May 1994) (special issue on Avant-Pop Rant & Rave).

13. There are only a few published novelists who have wholeheartedly embraced the development of electronic literature and art. I know many electronic writers who are closet Luddites and who secretly want to become the next Toni Morrison or Thomas Pynchon, but to leave the book behind in such a flagrant way as I was said to have done in the mid-1990s was almost perceived as an act of betrayal. Alas, I have never truly left the book behind. Instead, I prefer to see my practice as multiple and hybridized.

14. When I first released *GRAMMATRON* on the WWW in May 1997, I thought for sure that it would help usher in a new appreciation for the future forms of electronic literature, but I was wrong. Sure, there were a few scholars and creative writers who found the interactive experience of the work worthy of noting, but the real "shock of

the new" attitude that accompanied its release took place in the contemporary art world. I had to learn from my audience how the work needed to position itself in the fast-evolving new media economy. The work, I soon found out, was creating its own emergent genre of visual art that integrated literary elements into its framework. This genre was soon to be labeled *net.art*, *Internet art*, *Web art*, and *online art*.

15. For an introduction to the vast field of Net art and some historical perspective on its evolution, see ⟨http://www.rhizome.org⟩, ⟨http://www.nettime.org⟩ and ⟨http://art.colorado.edu/hiaff⟩.

16. The *PHON:E:ME* project and its accompanying catalogue of essays can be experienced at ⟨http://phoneme.walkerart.org⟩. The project was released in June 1999.

17. Roughly 1996 to 2000.

18. This is a reference to the Beat novelist, William Burroughs, with whom my questioners often compared my practice. Burroughs experiments with both fiction writing and audio cut-ups were the literary precursor to what I eventually dubbed *surf-sample-manipulate*. See ⟨http://www.altx.com/amerika.online/amerika.online.3.3.html⟩.

19. Publishing and/or exhibiting one's work in the networked space we know as the WWW is always an act of "going public," of seeking the other so as to (hopefully) generate communities of feedback and support. The WWW allows this sort of thing to happen like no other technological medium in history. The WWW is many things at once, including a writerly, compositional, publication, exhibition, and marketing medium. The trick is in being able to meld these various operations into one online presence that keeps growing through word-of-mouth/word-of-mouse effects. The question for me has always been one of sticking to my experimental narrative practice while taking advantage of what the medium has to offer in terms of intermedia performance and audience development.

20. I first came up with the term *prosthetic aesthetics* while reading the collection of essays in *Jean Baudrillard: The Disappearance of Art and Politics* edited by William Stearns and William Chaloupka (New York: St. Martin's, 1992). Another useful collection in this regard is *The Cyborg Handbook*, edited by Chris Hables Gray (London: Routledge, 1995).

21. I am referring to what I was then calling my "new media" or "Net art" trilogy consisting of *GRAMMATRON* (1997), *PHON:E:ME* (1999), and *FILMTEXT* (2001–2002). To access the *FILMTEXT* project, go to ⟨http://markamerika.com/filmtext⟩.

22. For a more in-depth discussion of *FILMTEXT* in the context of my Net art trilogy, see my "Expanding the Concept of Writing: Notes on Net Art, Digital Narrative and Viral Ethics," in *Leonardo* 37, no. 1 (2004): 9–13.

23. The e-book can be found at ⟨http://www.altx.com/ebooks/c1.html⟩. One of the most exciting developments taking place today in digital art production is the ability of artists to freely sample and remix their digital source material for a variety of

formats. I am now bringing my poetry into my DVD installations and creating experimental streaming audio soundtracks as peer-reviewed published essays in new media journals. What's next? Will that seventy-minute concept album that you have up at the *Leonardo* Web site count as a major publication in your case for promotion? Why not?

24. Vilém Flusser, *Toward a Philosophy of Photography* (London: Reaktion Books, 2000), 31.

25. Darren Tofts and Murray McKeich, *Memory Trade: A Prehistory of Cyberculture* (North Ryde, Australia: Interface, 1998).

26. Gregory L. Ulmer, *Heuretics: The Logic of Invention* (Baltimore, MD: Johns Hopkins University Press, 1994).

27. The term *copyleft* has been lifted from the open-source software community and refers to someone leaving a digital copy of a software program or other piece of creative codework for others to take for free or as shareware. I discuss this in more detail at ⟨http://www.heise.de/tp/english/kolumnen/ame/3121/1.html⟩.

28. Ronald Sukenick, *Down and In: Life in the Underground* (New York: Beech Tree Books, 1987). At one point in the book, Sukenick claims that "The underground audience of peers and hip critics may not be disinterested, but provides the most authentic consensus today for artistic success as such in a culture increasingly dominated by commercial factors. This is in part because an underground calls status quo values into question rather than reinforcing them, thus asserting an independence of judgment. An underground is neither necessarily a physical place nor a particular life style, but precisely this mutinous attitude" (240).

29. J. R. Foley "Down as Up, Out as In: Memoir as Manifesto," in Matthew Roberson, Ed., *Musing the Mosaic: Approaches to Ronald Sukenick* (Albany, NY: SUNY Press, 2003), 223. See also my "The Artist Is the Medium Is the Message: A Ron Sukenick Remix" in the same volume.

30. Brakhage was heavily influenced by Gertrude Stein and the Black Mountain artists, but his independent or first-person film work reminded me of Abstract Expressionism being processed through a "trance narrative" filter. Name dropping is part of the game in academia, but one of the things that has always excited me the most about the best critical theory writing is how much cultural range the citations have and how well they can be remixed into the contemporary thought process without becoming jargon. Where is Wallace Stevens's "necessary angel" when you need her?

31. Cf. Steve Wilson, *Information Arts: Intersections of Art, Science, and Technology* (Cambridge: The MIT Press, 2001).

An earlier version of this essay was originally published as a book chapter in Technology and English Studies: Innovative Professional Paths, *edited by James Inman and Beth Hewett (Mahwah, NJ: Lawrence Erlbaum, 2005).*

Expanding the Concept of Writing: Notes on Net Art, Digital Narrative, and Viral Ethics

Art Is What You Say It Is: Who Said That?

After having published two experimental literary novels and coedited two anthologies of fiction and cultural theory,[1] I began creating my Net-art trilogy, consisting of *GRAMMATRON* (1993–1997),[2] *PHON:E:ME* (1999),[3] and *FILMTEXT* (2001–present).[4] In all these digital artworks, I approached the computer-mediated network environment of the World Wide Web as an experimental writing zone, one where the evolving language of new media would reflect the convergence of image writing, sound writing, language writing, and code writing as complementary processes that would feed off each other and, in so doing, contribute to the construction of interactive digital narratives programmed to challenge the way we compose, exhibit, and distribute art in network culture.[5]

All three works in this trilogy are attempts to show how writing is now becoming more performative in a network-distributed environment. Such writing is now fueled by what Gregory Ulmer calls "the logic of invention" and requires a more proactive, resourceful approach to making things, often collaboratively, with computers or what Ulmer calls the electronic apparatus.[6] In *GRAMMATRON*, this approach utilized the new graphical user interfaces (GUIs) of the Web to investigate the interrelationship between animated images, streaming audio, and customized hypertext links in a public-domain narrative environment that was on the verge of becoming an overhyped new media economy. The narrative of *GRAMMATRON* has often been cited in the context of an art practice firmly rooted in the rival or avant-garde tradition of experimental literature.[7] In many ways, the actual story being told prophesizes the coming reign of viral marketing that was to take hold with the rise of the dot.com and the Internet bubble economy. Anticipating what has now become an endless flow of unwanted e-mail and instant messaging, particularly pornographic spam, the *GRAMMATRON* narrative investigates the way networked environments become breeding grounds for unethical penetration of our creative and research spaces with the mindless missives of an invasive technocapitalism. The story features an old Net artist named Abe Golam whose mission is to create a counterstrategic marketing campaign made out of an evolving cyborg poetics, one that would both initiate an art movement composed of bodily pleasure and social-utopian politics, while aiming to rid cyberspace of the nonstop bombardment of these hyper-commercial distractions.

In *PHON:E:ME*, this fantasy performance of the Net artist as subversive entrepreneur was imagined to already be taking place in a pseudo-utopian cyberculture that created the ultimate peer-to-peer network of artists, operating in a dreamworld of postleftist pleasure politics. As an online performance, *PHON:E:ME* was conducted as "an orchestration of writerly effects," transmitted via experimental sound compositions and supplementary "hyper:liner:notes" that tell the story of how Net art picks up where conceptual art left off. Like *GRAMMATRON*, *PHON:E:ME* was created using a method I have referred to as "surf-sample-manipulate," a process in which data is sampled from "other sources and, after some digital-manipulation, immediately integrated into the work so as to create an 'original' construction."[8]

With *FILMTEXT*, I take this surf-sample-manipulate research practice right into the belly of the beast, interfacing Hollywood with hypertext, video games with literary rhetoric, interactive cinema with image *écriture*. In researching and developing *FILMTEXT*, it became clear that targeting mass-media forms of entertainment, such as films and games, for avant-pop hactivist interventions[9] would further our agenda of expanding the concept of writing. By utilizing the surf-sample-manipulate method in the *FILMTEXT* project and applying it to the various media elements such as animation, audio, video, hypertext, and game playing, we inevitably began expanding our concept of cinema, too, and with it the concepts of visual, literary, and performance art. Interacting with the site requires the visitor to become a viewer, a reader, a

DJ/VJ, an art appreciator, a network navigator, and an interactive participant who can—working within the parameters set by the artist—create her or his own ambient game environment, electronic literary experience, and digitally expanded cinema, all at the same time.

Who Are the Ghosts in the Literary Machine?

From the moment I first opened the initial *GRAMMATRON* document on 3 April 1993, just days before the release of the beta version of the Mosaic Web browser, I felt compelled to approach the ongoing ⟨conceptual space⟩[10] of the Web as a public-domain narrative environment where experimental writing, the code of ⟨becoming cyborg⟩, informs the development of what, in *FILMTEXT*, I have called a nomadic Life Style Practice.

For me, a Life Style Practice is what a Net artist performs when creating a work in network culture. It is at once a nomadic narrative that reinvents what it means to be an artist in an experientially designed cybernetic environment and a proactive intervention that takes place within the context of an emergent ⟨artificial intelligentsia⟩. By ⟨artificial intelligentsia⟩, I am referring to an Internetworked intelligence that consists of all of the linked data being distributed in cyberspace at any given time and that is powered by artistic and intellectual agents remixing the flow of contemporary thought. I say the operative environment is both experientially designed and cybernetic because the aesthetic conditions of command and control being expressed in the work of the nomadic Net artist are already embedded in the ⟨mental space⟩ in which the artificial intelligentsia conducts its business. Once this shared ⟨mental space⟩ that is being network-conducted (steered) by knowledge workers throughout the polyvocal discourses of contemporary art and thought is distributed over the Net, it doubles as a kind of ⟨digital apparatus⟩ that we all use to capture consciousness *for* us and that we continuously encode with ⟨metatags⟩ of meaning. Borrowing from the metacommentary aspect of Talmudic practice, nomadic narrative as Life Style Practice is ⟨cite-specific hypertextual consciousness⟩ in action ("I link, therefore I am"), written and recorded using whatever technologies happen to be around at any particular moment in time: memory, stone, parchment, palimpsest, paint, film, computer code or even ⟨digital thoughtography⟩, a term I invented for my artificially intelligent protagonist in *FILMTEXT*.

At one point in the *FILMTEXT* Net art site, the following words are displayed in animation:

Endtroducing...The Digital Thoughtographer, an artificially intelligent filter, a techno-shamanic medium...

Navigating through the *FILMTEXT* Web site, the visitor continuously encounters the Digital Thoughtographer (DT), who, referred to above as an artificially intelligent filter, is also called an *alien*, a *virus*, or a *plug-in artist*. As the story's protagonist, the Digital Thoughtographer becomes a lens to a postapocalyptic world apparently devoid of meaning, but this does not stop the DT from continuing its search for meaning and the possibility of experiencing utopian rapture, even if only for a moment. The DT participates in a process of spontaneous creation where the plug-in artist becomes an active agent influencing the emergent ⟨artificial intelligentsia⟩ that keeps shifting its shape in the networked space of flows. In investigating this process of spontaneous creation as a hactivist intervention designed to alter the networked space of flows, the DT realizes that the artificial intelligentsia *always already* exists in its emergent state and that it first manifests itself with the advent of writing in ancient cultures. It could be said that the machine aesthetic, and with it the opportunity to hack reality, begins with the practice of writing and that in the *FILMTEXT* project, the artist-protagonist, here referred to as DT, attempts to discover a new kind of visual literacy that will expand the concept of writing beyond the mere verbal while reimagining the textual.

Although *FILMTEXT* actively makes links between the history of writing, an emergent artificial intelligentsia, and a new kind of visual literacy, this is by no means meant to downplay the significance of the cyborg body, that biopolitical packet-switching station where all of this electrochemical thought gets transmitted. But the body, in this instance, is subject to what Negri and Hardt have referred to as *biopower*, an all-encompassing global order that "regulates social life from its interior, following it, interpreting it, absorbing it and rearticulating it."[11] In many ways, *FILMTEXT* is first and foremost a narrative investigation that explores the corruption of this regulated interior, searching for meaningful points of entry into what the Digital Thoughtographer calls "the time of your life as measured against Time, as measured against eternity and the fad of Being." *FILMTEXT* operates as an artistically generated philosophical investigation of the cyborg-narrator, that human/machine interface who is part narrative conductor, part rhetorical performer, and part digital apparatus, an artist provocateur whose primary mission is to remember what it was like to move through the world as if there were no borders and who wonders what life was like before one's interior landscape had been overrun by the commercial captains of consciousness and their highly contagious "production values." In the world described by Hardt and Negri, these hypercommercial invasions are part of the technocapitalist revolution of everyday life, and the powers that be are now living inside us so that we ourselves become the ultimate consumer self-regulators. In *FILMTEXT*, the DT attempts to imagine another way of conducting a nomadic life practice in the networked space of flows by becoming a technoshamanic filter in whose sight we see the world anew.

These philosophical investigations by the cyborg-narrator in *FILMTEXT* are a direct extension of what was originally developed in *GRAMMATRON*. In *GRAMMATRON*, the lead character/avatar, Abe Golam, is searching for meaning in "the electrosphere he had once called home." His journey throughout the imaginative sim-city called Prague-23 is punctuated with a variety of interactive experiences that may—he is never sure—virally infect his program, his interior space of meaning, and ultimate functionality as a character in the storyworld he collaboratively creates.

These themes are further explored in *FILMTEXT*, subtitled *MetaTourism: Interior Landscapes, Digital Thoughtography*. Part hypermedia narrative, part ambient game study, and part avant-pop (h)activism, *FILMTEXT* is constructed as a space for philosophically generated research inquiry. For example, questions that continually arose while I conducted the research and development of the site included: What are the cultural implications of a thriving biopower that commands and controls the productive processes of life? How are our most creative minds politicized by the operating biopowers so that life itself is somehow commodified internally, so that the body knowingly opens itself up to more media-manipulated language viruses? Are artists who cooperate with the technology by utilizing its tremendous forces also accomplices in further empowering the biopowers that keep our world as safe as can be, and is it their global patriotic duty to do so? What if the world were no longer a safe place to be? What if we were at once being targeted by media viruses, computer viruses, sexually transmitted viruses, and bioterrorist viruses? In the language of new media, what is the difference between these variable, yet potentially corrupting, codes of behavior manipulation?

Who Is the Digital Thoughtographer Who Takes Pictures of the End of the World?

In composing my Net art trilogy, it became all too apparent to me that the literary metafictions I had developed in my novels and that were making their way into disk-based hypertext creations were now virally infecting my Net-distributed artworks as well. I have come to conclude that the reason this metafictional self-reflexiveness continues to occur with each new technological medium, whether it be book, hypertext, or Net art, is that all of these alternative art forms share a research agenda that also happens to coincide with avant-garde philosophical agendas: that is to say, they are all intimately involved in the search for meaningful life-style practices and are willing to use whatever digital apparatuses will assist in this (re)search.

This search process can manifest itself as a multitrack research composition. For example, with *FILMTEXT*, the search for meaning in life is customarily conducted in parallel with an investigation of other areas of inquiry that metafictionally reflect on the creative process itself. Investigating the social implications of an intrusive biopower being distributed via the means of mass communication technology controlled by multinational corporations is only one potential track of inquiry. Another track that I simultaneously investigate is whether or not the narrative performance of a work like *FILMTEXT* can become a kind of network-distributed, motion-graphic cinema that expands the concept of writing to include all manner of moving and still-life images, typographically experimental text, bits of customized code or raw data, manipulated music/sound/noise, etc. A third track investigates the ways in which game technology conventionalizes narrative experience and seeks ways to subvert those conventions by strategically playing against a fulfillment of standard expectations.

Erkki Huhtamo, in an experimental essay entitled "Seven Ways of Misunderstanding Interactive Art," describes some of the most common misconceptions about works like *FILMTEXT*, everything from how this evolving art form is in its infancy and needs a lot of time to mature to how this kind of work is really not art at all and belongs in a science fair. He counters these by-now-clichéd criticisms by noting that "interactive art functions as a kind of philosophical instrument, enabling us to experience something familiar as if entering an alien territory, to investigate the world—and ourselves—from a fresh perspective."[12]

"By putting the user into the controls," says Huhtamo, "interactive technology could be claimed to have a strong liberating potential, as well, making it an effective means to analyze and deconstruct pre-existing ideological formations."[13]

By "putting the user into the controls" of a work like *FILMTEXT*, I attempt to enable the interactive participant to create what Piet Mondrian once referred to as "simultaneous and continuous fusion," a space of mind where buzzwords such as "interactivity" and "user-friendly" give way to a genuine encounter with the Net artist's material, so that visitors can remix their own versions of the story. In attempting to enable visitors to remix their own real-time versions of the work, a useful model emerges, one where the visitor becomes an interactive-participant conducting their own experiences in the networked space of flows.

With the advent of computer-mediated network art, we see the accumulated effects of the history of writing open up an entirely different kind of narrative practice, one that is codependent on the multilinear prehistory of cyberculture. The term ⟨posthuman⟩ is thrown around a lot these days, as is the phrase ⟨cyborg⟩. These terms come from the sciences but have been appropriated by humanities scholars to point to what is oftentimes contextualized as a recent if not revolutionary transformation in the linear progression of human history. Yet, interestingly enough, the ⟨posthuman⟩ ⟨cyborg⟩ is far from a recent invention. As Darren Tofts suggests in his book *Memory Trade,*

> That subliminal, internuncial moment of transition that marks our induction into literacy—as profound and irretrievable as the origins of writing itself—was first introduced to cultures in which it had previously been unknown. To imagine such a time is to envisage writing made strange, to see it as something conspicuous, inhuman and external.[14]

Vilém Flusser has suggested "Apparatuses were invented to simulate specific thought processes,"[15] processes that are already in place, or ⟨operating systems⟩ that already "come with" ⟨writing applications⟩. Those of us researching and developing a Life Style Practice composed of "nomadic narratives" distributed across the network in cross-media platforms use whatever instruments are available to us at our moment in time, whether they be 35 mm movie cameras, laptops, digital video cameras, mini-disc recorders, pens and pads of paper, or jacked-up, wireless personal digital assistants (PDAs). For me, this is all driven by a writing practice that attempts to expand the

[handwritten marginalia: "Advocate? truth HAVE stopped it happening Organically"]

concept of writing in very much the same way that Joseph Beuys attempted to expand the concept of art into a form of social sculpture. Expanding the concept of writing so that it becomes a hybridized art practice that performs with and in the networked space of flows may open up one path toward a form of social-utopian network culture that the digital thoughtographer can play in.[16]

And yet I cannot help but ask myself, what role do the biopowers of influence play in this expanded concept of writing? Are these interactive experiences that the Net artist creates meant to act as an antidote to the aforesaid viruses that keep coming at us from all sides? Or are they their own kind of media virus that, mimicking the structure of memes, attempt to alter the biopolitical landscape as a form of artistic mediation?

FILMTEXT, PHON:E:ME, and *GRAMMATRON* do not come up with definitive answers to these questions. But for Net artists, our experimental practice empowers us to pursue the development of these often difficult works of art so that we may continue the philosophical search for meaning in contemporary life and thus points to a digital aesthetics of research and resistance.

Notes

1. Mark Amerika, *The Kafka Chronicles* (Normal, IL: FC2 Press, 1993); *Sexual Blood* (Normal, IL: FC2 Press, 1995); *Degenerative Prose: Writing beyond Category*, coedited with Ronald Sukenick (Normal, IL: FC2 Press, 1995); and *In Memoriam to Postmodernism: Essays on the Avant-Pop*, coedited with Lance Olsen (San Diego: San Diego State University Press, 1996).

2. *GRAMMATRON* is my first major work of Net art and consists of over 1,000 screens, thousands of hypertext links, over forty minutes of an original streaming audio soundtrack, a mailing list, and a companion theory guide called "Hypertextual Consciousness." It was one of the first works selected for the Whitney Biennial 2000 in the Internet Art category and is available at ⟨http://www.grammatron.com⟩.

3. *PHON:E:ME* is an online concept album about the interface of conceptual art, Net art, and hypermediated narrative. Commissioned by the Walker Art Center, Perth Institute of Contemporary Art, and the Australia Council for the Arts, the work is available at ⟨http://phoneme.walkerart.org⟩.

4. *FILMTEXT* is a digital narrative for cross-media platforms. Versions of the work have been created as a Flash animation, an mp3 concept album, an experimental artist e-book in Adobe Acrobat, and a stand-alone museum installation. The 1.0 version was originally commissioned by Sony Playstation 2 as part of my Net art retrospective at the Institute of Contemporary Art in London. *FILMTEXT 1.0* opened on 16 November

2001 and the current 2.0 version, which premiered at Siggraph 2002, is available at ⟨http://www.markamerika.com/filmtext⟩. Collaborators on the project include John Vega, Chad Mossholder, and Jeff Williams.

5. By *network culture*, I refer to a term I first encountered when reading Kevin Kelly's influential book *Out of Control: The Rise of Neo-biological Civilization* (Reading, MA: Addison-Wesley, 1994). The entire book is available online at ⟨http://www.kk.org/outofcontrol/contents.html⟩.

6. Gregory L. Ulmer, *Heuretics: The Logic of Invention* (Baltimore, MD: Johns Hopkins University Press, 1994).

7. Steven Shaviro, "Mark Amerika's *GRAMMATRON*," *Artbyte*, 1, no. 1 (1998): 24–25.

8. Mark Amerika, "Surf-Sample-Manipulate: Pla(y)giarism on the Net," *Telepolis*, ⟨http://www.heise.de/tp/english/kolumnen/ame/3098/1.html⟩.

9. By *avant-pop hactivism*, I am referring to the practice of using the forms of the mass media against themselves by defamiliarizing them for antiaesthetic effect. For more on this, see my essays at *Telepolis*, especially "Writing as Hacktivism: An Intervening Satire," *Telepolis* (2000), ⟨http://www.heise.de/tp/r4/artikel/3/3485/1.html⟩.

10. Certain words, phrases, or neologisms throughout this article are contained in angle brackets as a way to suggest that much of the conceptual language Net artists use to theorize about their work is often more than they bargained for and less than they expected. Here, the bracketed terms are meant to indicate the artist's own "red light going off" as he tries to depict what he is attempting to investigate as part of his practice.

11. Michael Hardt and Antonio Negri, *Empire* (Cambridge, MA: Harvard University Press, 2001), available at ⟨http://textz.gnutenberg.net/textz/hardt_michael_negri_antonio_empire.txt⟩.

12. Erkki Huhtamo, "Seven Ways of Misunderstanding Interactive Art," ⟨http://www.artcenter.edu/exhibit/digital/essay.html⟩ (n.d.).

13. Huhtamo, "Seven Ways."

14. Darren Tofts and Murray McKeich, *Memory Trade: A Prehistory of Cyberculture* (North Ryde, Australia: Interface, 1998), 38.

15. Vilém Flusser, *Toward a Philosophy of Photography* (London: Reaktion Books, 2000), 31.

16. Shortly after the release of *FILMTEXT 2.0*, I was invited to do live, performative remixes of the Web site at various festivals, museums, and universities. These performances, styled after the popular DJ/VJ events held in techno clubs around the world,

created an opportunity to experiment with realtime generation of digital thoughtography while simultaneously investigating its effect on both the audience and the performers as they experienced the improvisational flow of narrative content across a local area network.

An earlier version of this essay was originally published in Leonardo, *37, no. 1 (2004): 9–13.*

Teaching High Techne

A   General Introduction

TECHNE is a practice-based digital arts research initiative that I founded as a newly hired artist-professor at the University of Colorado at Boulder. The TECHNE initiative develops innovative approaches to the invention of new forms of knowledge generally considered to be both artistic and scholarly. The invention of these new forms of knowledge are oftentimes manifested as digital art projects distributed over the Internet and come into being as a result of TECHNE participants interacting with emerging and converging new media technologies that are becoming more easily accessible to the public at large.

The evolving forms of digital art being investigated through the TECHNE initiative attempt to bring value-added meaning to a democratic society at once operating in a free-market economy of goods, services, information, and ideas. Faculty, students, and research associates affiliated with TECHNE utilize both highly specialized and easily accessible hardware and software consumer applications to push the boundaries of artistic, scholarly, and scientific inquiry into areas not yet discovered.

A significant transition is underway in the culture of information. Information is now being artistically designed to transmit a more visually stimulating, interactive, and immersive experience that will port the user (consumer, reader, viewer, etc.) into a highly manipulated, digital environment that is changing so fast it requires a focused, practice-based research agenda to even begin learning the new kinds of investigative tools and conceptual frameworks required to properly analyze digital art as an emergent phenomena in the new media economy.

B   Objective of the Study

The objective of this brief study is to develop an introduction to the conceptual framework for the TECHNE initiative and to generally outline some of the preliminary investigations already underway. These preliminary investigations are not the end-all be-all of the TECHNE initiative but rather serve as a conceptual marker pointing to the wider framework we wish to concern ourselves with. Only after having built a coherent conceptual framework can we even begin to successfully launch the research initiative in its proper context.

The choice of research subjects, defining the questions that need to be asked, and enabling the development of methods as well as metaphors to properly address the issues that need to be analyzed within a "digital arts" conceptual framework are all part of the TECHNE initiative as it looks toward future investigations and anticipates research results.

Setting a practice-based research agenda in the digital arts is a complex, intuitive process that depends on developing reliable methods of judging what the most valuable lines of inquiry are. The advent of the Internet as both a research and development tool and globally distributed network of digital art has created great opportunities for artists and scholars potentially to evolve alternative lines of inquiry that will have critical ramifications in our culture, particularly in areas that investigate the way we compose, publish, exhibit, distribute, and network these emerging forms of knowledge in a technologically driven consumer culture. With this in mind, we think the following conceptual framework should

1. Create a set of parameters that enable us to both develop a long-term vision of the initiative as well as produce highly visible near-term results,
2. Provide enough flexibility so that we may invent progressive models of both digital arts practice and online publication/exhibition that highlight the ways in which the arts are now becoming more integrated into the information economy, and

3. Anticipate the utilization of cross-media platforms to embed our research findings in and in so doing change the way artistic and scholarly work is communicated and assessed in the field.

C   Conceptual Framework and Preliminary Investigations

1   The Internet as Art Medium and Publication/Exhibition Context

By approaching the Internet as both a compositional and publication/exhibition medium, artist researchers in the TECHNE initiative are positioning themselves to conduct a network of digital art practices linked to other institutions who are similarly positioning themselves and their research agendas in various locations around the world. One of the main goals of TECHNE as an ongoing R&D platform focused on demonstrating the value of a practice-based research initiative is to have considerable influence on the way such initiatives and their findings are perceived and communicated as new forms of knowledge. It is generally assumed that these new forms of knowledge, packaged as interactive digital art, will alter the way we socially interact with each other as well as educate ourselves to perform in this dynamic, computer-mediated environment. The Internet is first and foremost a globally distributed network that enables various nodal points an opportunity to bring wider visibility to successful research discoveries made at various intervals throughout the creative process. These discoveries can be immediately published/exhibited on the Internet and under the right conditions can attract a network of external links that will give the research work a more significant place in the attention economy.

To this effect, we are positioning ourselves to take a leadership role as one of the first practice-based research initiatives at the state university level to reinvent arts education. TECHNE utilizes various new media technologies to create a more collaborative learning environment for students hoping to transfer their creative and critical skills-set into the new media economy. These students—looking to participate in a highly technologized, social process of self-motivated personal discovery and artistic invention—are now realizing that the creative process involves both online networking and real-time group collaboration.

TECHNE is being set up as a model unit to help students and other artist-researchers achieve these goals.

2 What Is TECHNE?

The name *TECHNE* comes from the Greek use of the term *techne* to mean both "art" and "technology," especially as it relates to practice and application ("to make or do"). TECHNE enables its faculty, students, and research associates to utilize both highly specialized and easily accessible hardware and software applications to further demonstrate the value of building more interactive, digital art projects while critically analyzing their place in the world. Research projects are varied and investigate many contemporary subjects whose cultural implications bring to light the growing interdependency between the arts and sciences. The current environment of rapidly developing new media technologies enables committed researchers in both the arts and sciences to facilitate the discovery of new forms of knowledge.

Subjects explored in recent and current investigations in the TECHNE initiative include Web publishing, digital narrative, PDA art, wireless networking, interactive cinema, artist e-books, Java applet art, biotechnology art, motion picture graphics, Internet radio, data visualization, DVD with surround sound installation, online art and the exhibition context, hyperimprovisational DJ/VJ performance, parapsychological and paranormal uses of telecommunications technology, GUI art, 3-D multiuser game environments, the history of multimedia art in relation to both computer science and art practice, generative art, programming or code art, database aesthetics, and practice-based research as creative process.

Many of the digital art projects being researched at TECHNE require a team of student producers whose creative and critical skill sets vary. By giving the students an opportunity to share their creative and critical strengths in a collaborative work environment while simultaneously enabling them to learn new skills from their peer network, TECHNE breaks away from the "individual artist as genius" model generally associated with art and creative writing programs and focuses more on practice-based research and development skills that are more easily transferred to the rapidly transforming job market in both the high-tech industry and academia. Whereas TECHNE is not a graphic design factory that spews out scores of entry-level computer-design workers as a way to meet industry needs, the initiative does recognize that technically proficient students with exceptional creative talent and critical decision-making skills are likely to be more competitive once they graduate from our program. With this in mind, many of the creative research projects initiated at TECHNE are loosely tied to a collaborative, process-based learning (PBL) model that requires rigorous intellectual activity among the participants. Some recent examples of PBL projects investigated at TECHNE include

- How to create a multilinear digital narrative that incorporates various media into its interactive structure (motion graphics, sound, text, advanced scripting languages, etc.);
- How to exhibit multiple works of Internet art in an online environment as well as create an educational context that focuses on the creative, theoretical, and historical relevance of the curated artworks by showing how they can be related to and/or differentiated from other, more traditional media such as painting, film, or novel writing;
- How to innovatively implement new media publishing and distribution technologies that challenge older economic models of print production with particular emphasis on reconfiguring our notion of the terms *writing* and *reading* as they relate to recent developments in such areas as portable e-book readers, PDA readers, HTML, XML, PDF, Flash, Open eBook standard, and mp3 audio books;
- How to create customized user interfaces and back-end database programs that are focused on issues such as site navigation and program functionality in relation to the digital artwork as both a new form of visual art as well as a near-future model of network distributed, interactive, edutainment;
- How to theoretically articulate, via both visual design skills and critical language skills, a justification for making work available online while taking into consideration the ease with which data becomes part of an open source networking environment that challenges standard notions of copyright and intellectual property;
- How to experiment with the Internet as a live and online open-platform performance space for creative expression and action investigating the interrelationships between digital design literacy, multimedia narrative, performance theory, and information architecture in the context of a global Webcast;
- How to critically assess the new forms of knowledge being developed for the new media environment and how to begin developing robust, highly flexible, collaborative Web sites that communicate our critical research findings to the Internet audience, particularly our national and international peer institutions whose evolving research agendas may complement our own.

3   Art / Technology / Pedagogy

The term *intelligence amplification* seems applicable to our goal of augmenting the human intellect in that the entity to be produced will exhibit more of what can be called
intelligence than an unaided human could; we will have amplified the intelligence of
the human by organizing his intellectual capabilities into higher levels of synergistic
structuring.
—Douglas Engelbart, "Augmenting Human Intellect: A Conceptual Framework"

Augmenting the human intellect and its capacity to invent new forms of
knowledge requires a more technologically sophisticated experiential learning
environment. Part of the reason for launching the TECHNE initiative within
the department of art and art history at CU is to provide this technologically
sophisticated learning environment for both graduate and undergraduate
students so that they can participate in a computer-supported, collaborative
work space that prioritizes group networking and peer evaluation as a major
part of the creative process.

Creating breakthrough digital art, design, and performance requires a new
approach to pedagogy, and TECHNE is already applying these new process-
based learning methods to its curriculum. Our aim is

• To create a practice-based research initiative that augments the human intellect by providing faculty, students, and research associates with a customized learning environment equipped with the latest new media technologies;
• To prioritize the use of these new media technologies as tools to assist us in
the invention of new forms of knowledge manifested as digital art;
• To use this customized learning environment to create innovative approaches to pedagogy; and
• To facilitate the development of a "best practices" model for digital arts research and development within a higher-education context.

The TECHNE learning environment is partly facilitated by the ongoing
development of the Experimental Digital Arts Studio (EDAS) that enables
us to integrate the latest new media technology into the curriculum while
foregrounding the use of easily accessible consumer hardware and software
applications. The lab presently has thirty-five Macintosh G4 computers with
fifteen-inch flat-screen monitors, all of the latest Web-based software tools,
one data projector, stereo speakers and amplifier, a scanner, and a CD burner.
We also recently purchased a fifty-inch plasma screen. We have also begun

building a space we call the Audio Studio, which currently has two powerful personal computers, a midi-driven keyboard, a professional microphone, a Roland mixing board, and a customized software set for each computer and specifically constructed for both beginning and advanced audio production needs. We are presently in the process of building a new space we will call the Digital Narrative Studio.

Our primary aim in building this technologically sophisticated creative lab space is to create a state-of-the-art R&D digital arts lab that will help us fulfill our research goals mentioned above as well as enable our best students to begin developing a digital arts practice that will serve them well in all of their future pursuits, whether artistic, scientific, academic, commercial, or purely technical. The standard loadset of software tools used to create work made to be distributed over the Internet is available in the main lab area on all of the individual workstations. The skills acquired when using the set of new media tools available in the TECHNE experimental teaching lab are easily transferable to the marketplace and set our students up for the career path of their choice.

4   Histories of Internet Art: Fictions and Factions

In the *History and Theory of Digital Art* course that I teach at the University of Colorado, students explore the early developments in computer-based art making that have enabled forward-thinking and experimental artists to create works of art previously unimagined. Issues and topics explored in this course include

- The evolution of the computer as an artistic tool;
- How to use the Internet as a research and development tool as well as a compositional/publication medium;
- Where to locate Web-specific works of art and how to effectively critique these works of art;
- How to curate an online exhibition;
- How to respond to the contemporary state of the digital divide;
- The history and practice of hypertext before and after the World Wide Web;
- The gender/technology interface;
- The growing debate revolving around intellectual property, copyright, peer-to-peer networking, and an online creative commons;
- How other artistic media, especially painting, photography, video, and literature, as well as the work of contemporary media theorists, enable us to place

the emerging forms of digital art in their proper historical and aesthetic context.

Students in the *History and Theory of Digital Art* course have built their own large-scale, database-driven Web site called *Histories of Internet Art: Fictions and Factions* (HIAFF), which is presently located at ⟨http://art.colorado.edu/ hiaff⟩. This enormously successful Web site has now been adopted by a number of professors in various institutions around the world as a key online art history resource. The site features

- Student-conducted video and e-mail interviews with some of the most important digital art practitioners working today,
- A student-curated exhibition of Internet art,
- A student-developed section devoted to new media theory, and
- An area featuring new media artwork produced by the students themselves.

In my introduction to the site as faculty director, I described the site as an "ongoing exhibition showcas[ing] a student-designed Web interface that takes readers to online artwork created by both internationally celebrated and emerging Internet artists. The site also provides much-needed original content to help contextualize the sudden rise of Internet art into the mainstream art world." One of the key components to an activist, networked pedagogy is that students are able to immediately participate in the attention economy provided by what Manuel Castells calls the networked "space of flows." There is no longer a linear progression or top-down hierarchy that separates a distant and canonical art history from the student-observer. Instead, *the student is encouraged to create an alternative history-in-the-making by engaging contemporary practitioners of Net art in a discourse about the qualities of the medium itself while using this very same medium that the artists work in to facilitate the dialogue of research and discovery.*

In a published dialogue I had with German media theorist Roberto Simanowski for his book *Interfictions: Vom Schreiben im Netz* (Edition Suhrkamp, 2002), Simonowski asked me, "How is it when a Net artist becomes a professor of Net art?" I responded:

The very notion of an engaged Net art practice focused on digital narrative and theory in cross-media platforms challenges our conventional assessment of what a certain kind of work or cultural production actually is. This kind of practice is very conceptual and interdisciplinary and requires a flexible approach to being a teacher or, as the case may be, "academic." I'm not a typical academic in the true sense of the word, but then again, many artists who are professors are not true academics. What we share with the academic and scientific communities is changing, though. The more collaborative, computer-supported work environments that were known to be available only to computer science and engineering students are now the very models that I, as a professor of digital art, am exploring in my new role.

I went on to say that I think it's quite important for students to feel like they have a certain amount of control over the distribution of their work. Traditionally, students have a rough time finding exhibition contexts for their work, and it is often not taken seriously. Part of the problem is the lack of physical space or just finding a proper venue. But with digital art, they are finding that they can immediately exhibit or publish their work online and that there are potential audiences out there that may be willing to engage with their work.

The realization that comes with this eureka moment of discovery for the student is crucial because it forces them to rethink their role as artist in culture. For example, just because you can put anything online, does that mean you should put all of your work up there? What is the context for your work when it goes live on the Web? And then there are issues of copyright and participating in an attention economy where the pay off may not necessarily be money since most things put on the Web are given away for free.

The HIAFF site grows exponentially over time as each succeeding *History and Theory of Digital Art* class contributes to its development as an online resource focused on the early and continuing histories of Net art. New students learn these alternative histories of Net art by studying the site in the beginning of the course and eventually start conducting their own collaborative research investigations to further build out its potential during the latter part of the semester. Each collaborative research group *invents its version of the story of Net art*, and these theoretical fictions inevitably overlap, intersect, link, and/or blur with each other. A value-added network of student-conducted creative mindshare is born and keeps on giving birth to itself so that soon you have an instantaneously delivered multilinear thread of narrative-potential being practiced as a form of social networking and community exchange. It's much more valuable than just earning three credits toward your diploma.

An earlier version of this essay was originally published online in European Journal of Higher Arts Education, *2 (Economies of Knowledge: New Technologies in Higher Arts Education) (2005).*

Anticipating the Present: An Artist's Intuition

One of the main goals of the TECHNE practice-based research initiative at the University of Colorado at Boulder is to evolve an ongoing R&D platform focused on demonstrating the value of supporting the artist-researcher model as it relates to discovering new forms of knowledge embedded in the creation of digital art. It is generally assumed that these new forms of knowledge, packaged as interactive digital art, will alter the way we engage socially with each other as well as educate ourselves to perform in this dynamic, computer-mediated environment.

The Internet is first and foremost a globally distributed network that enables various nodal points an opportunity to bring wider visibility to successful research discoveries made at various intervals throughout the creative process. These discoveries can be immediately published/exhibited on the Internet and, under the right conditions, can attract a network of external links that will give the research work a more significant place in the larger attention economy.

To this effect, we are positioning ourselves to take a leadership role as one of the first practice-based research initiatives at the state university level to reinvent arts education. TECHNE (art.colorado.edu) utilizes various new media technologies to create a more collaborative learning environment for students hoping to transfer their creative and critical skills set into the new media economy. These students, looking to participate in a highly technologized, social process of self-motivated personal discovery and artistic invention, are now realizing that the creative process involves both online networking and real-time group collaboration.

We have a very proactive, practice-based approach to Web publishing, digital narrative, PDA art, wireless networking, artist e-books, Java applet art, digital animation, telepresence, distributed network performance, dynamic hypertext language, biotechnology art, online games, motion picture graphics, mp3 concept albums, desktop cinema, data visualization, Net art and the exhibition context, digital thoughtography, GUI art, 3-D multiuser environments, the history of computer art in relation to both computer science and art practice, generative art, programming or code art, database aesthetics, and art research as process-oriented creative discovery.

Yes, but....

It wasn't always that way.

Though the italicized message above is sampled from the Web site my students and I are creating as part of our research and development in the department of art and art history at the University of Colorado at Boulder, the simple truth is that when I started making Net art about ten years ago, I had no idea what I was doing and in no way whatsoever had a strategy in place to utilize the capabilities of the hypertext transfer protocol to further agitate change in the art and literary scenes I was circulating in.

Well, that's not necessarily true either. Simple truths are hard to come by these days. Complex truths are perhaps more relevant here. As a digital narrative practitioner, for me these complex truths operate like turnkey moments of illumination that suddenly appear within the development of the pseudo-autobiographical fictions I continuously create and whose customized lies are structured in such a way that the reader (interactive-participant) may anticipate the coming of meaning in realtime (cf. ⟨www.grammatron.com⟩ released in 1997). Even now, writing these words for a peer-reviewed journal covering issues of new media and society, I can see how these complex truths, dressed in personal narrative, are part of an extended practice-based research agenda that uses new media technologies to investigate the vocation of the contemporary artist in society.

For example, here's a complex truth that I'll never be able to explain in full: I knew exactly what I was doing when I began my online practice back in January 1993, but I had no real institutional support to help facilitate the discoveries I was in the process of making, and this, in fact, forced me to anticipate the future by questioning the validity of institutional structures while nomadically circulating within the hypertextual consciousness of the WWW itself (how's that for personification?). A supplemental truth that came along with the one just mentioned was that the freedom gained from distancing myself from institutional structures coupled with a full-time nomadic presence on the Net during the latter half of the nineties somehow made my current institutionalized status absolutely possible. On top of it all, I have somehow used the network protocols to intuit this institutional becoming (this becoming-institutionalized).

Of course, underground artists have been known to thrive by networking in a variety of alternative communities. Perhaps what makes operating on the Net as an artist so different from previous art and literary scenes is the way you can write (network) your ongoing personal history in *asynchronous real-time*, a term I have recently invented to suggest an indeterminate space of mind that feels like you are living in a permanent state of jet lag—an oscillating, antipodal nowness that defies the "here, there, and everywhere" while welcoming the passion of the moments that keep passing through you as you continue to create your online work in progress (what James Joyce might have called One Text Exactly).

Looking back over the last five years, one can see that the early practitioners of Net art were part of a tradition of avant-garde artists and writers throughout the twentieth century who were themselves activist artist-researchers. The main difference for me was that my own Internetworked version of this playful constituency of legislator-poets was only to be found in an online environment that evolved so fast I felt obliged to read it as a contemporary form of collective magic—even if it was really nothing more than being in the right place at the right time while every budding dot.new-comer and their uncle were jumping on the bandwagon of hype and speculation.

This collective magic—the ecstasy of collaborative communication with like-minded culturati all over the world—and the passion I now associate with becoming a Net artist in the mid-'90s and into the early '00s, reminds me of an essay by my recently deceased colleague Stan Brakhage entitled "In Defense of the Amateur" where he recognizes that "an amateur works according to his own necessity" and "is at home anywhere he works."[1] For nomadic Net artists carrying their portable (and now wireless) technology with them wherever in the world they may travel, the idea of "being amateur" resonates with its Latin root suggesting "lover" or someone who immerses themselves in the practice of making something out of nothing—of inventing an art form out of what feels like scratch but is really more itch, a poet-ecopreneur like

Wallace Stevens's "necessary angel"[2] in whose sight we see the world anew, and whose intrepid vision of a world beyond mere money and power provokes the professional-managerial class the way any D-I-Y (do-it-yourself) researcher would while investigating the rapid exposure of media effects on the contemporary mind at work.

Is it possible that D-I-Y researchers actively "becoming-amateur" can also, now—using the new media technologies and the network protocols they afford—find themselves "becoming-institutionalized" all in the same breath?

There's no question about it. The answer is yes. The last five years have seen networked digital artists come into their own. Not only have they been making challenging new work that blurs the intermedia boundaries, but they have also been inventing their own way of expressing and/or contextualizing this work for their distributed audiences. Let's, for example, assume that the collection of mp3 tracks or real-audio or QuickTime video works you put up on the WWW are embedded in an animated Flash interface programmed with advanced action-scripting languages—and that this work has volumes of text material in it as well, perhaps what at one point in time we might have called poetry or even prose poetry of the kind Stephane Mallarmé[3] was known to write—and all of this action-scripted text was actually brought to the surface of the screen so that you could literally *see* the code layered underneath the other poetic text as part of some gorgeous visual art interface that dynamically changed the more you looked at or interacted with it—and let's say that the artist distributing *that* work over the Net from their homespun Web site was all of a sudden selected for the prestigious Whitney Biennial of American Art in New York City and that the Whitney claimed to be "exhibiting" it by (a) *announcing* it was exhibiting it and (b) making a hypertext link to it from *its* Web site. Is it possible that they were not exhibiting the work at all but, rather, *pointing* to it as a D-I-Y form of network distributed publishing? And if in fact that *is* really all they were doing, then what does that say about the changing role of the museum in digital culture and the potential for a renaissance of amateur art production generating its own audience regardless of what the institutional art world thinks about it?

Five years ago this would have sounded like so much vaporware. But now this is exactly the kind of artwork being featured on CNN and in *Time* magazine and even your local community art space, not to mention the *Digital Art 1* course at the flagship research university in the Rocky Mountains.

Now undergraduate art students are learning the implications of this new media practice and wondering aloud if this is what they always meant when dropping the term *avant-garde* or if this is just more techno-critical training preparing them for the rise of the Second Reich of Dot.Comdom. Of course, it could be both or neither, but for some reason now it seems worth investigating, on the Web, via e-mail, during live streaming broadcasts, and *in the artwork itself*, the seeming inevitability of constructing their own form of digital rhetoric so that they too may one day become the thriving amateurs they long to be.

An expanding D-I-Y network of distributed artists and theorists located outside traditional institutional structures has challenged some academic programs to rethink their connection to the contemporary media art culture as they consider integrating easily accessible new media technologies into the learning environment. This learning environment, often a combined experimental studio production lab and a very "smart" seminar classroom, can provide a space for amateur artistic research and practice in the tradition of the twentieth-century avant-garde art and writing. It even allows for a meta-touristic journey through the interzones of critical theory to help further (de)contextualize the pedagogical agenda. As Gregory Ulmer says at the opening of his book *Heuretics: The Logic of Invention*: "Theory is assimilated into the humanities in two principal ways—by critical interpretation and by artistic experiment."[4]

He then goes on to devise a strategy for investigating ways to develop a more "experimental" humanities wherein we appropriate "the history of the avant-garde as a liberal arts mode of research." As he duly notes, "The avant-garde has served until now as an object of study, although it has demonstrated from the beginning an alternative way to use theory as research."

Using theory as just one other element in a practice-based research initiative focused on the digital arts, we can begin to develop a model of generative production that spawns various prototypes whose function is both critical and artistic. We can actually begin expanding the concept of writing so that it includes more interactive, behavioristic, hypertextual, cinematic, animated, custom-coded, imagistic, digitally manipulated, wickedly abstract, source material that doesn't necessarily *analyze* the new forms of composition emerging in network culture but that intuitively creates alternative readings of what we think it already is. This is when reading as an interactive, participatory, and creative performance becomes practice.

But artist-researchers positioning themselves as network-practitioners no longer have to identify themselves as being avant-garde or "ahead of their time." The "plug-in" artist captures active consciousness in asynchronous realtime. From my perspective, the most significant change that has occurred in new media over the last five years is the speed with which the network technology that a mere decade ago felt so foreign to me has seamlessly been integrated into my life and, consequently, my art practice. I can now recontextualize my work before I even know what it is (as Baudrillard said, "the image no longer has time to become an image"—yes, and Net art never has time to become Net art, and that's what makes it *real*).[5]

True, artistic life has always depended on imaginings of the future to influence the present—think William Gibson's *Neuromancer* (1984) or, even better, Lautréamont's *Songs of Maldoror* (1869)—but the degree to which I can do this in asynchronous realtime explodes all preconceptions I may have had about what it means to make art history. Simply put (but with complex ramifications), making art history for me is now a hyperimprovisational activity of the mind engaged with computer-mediated environments, one that I intuit while living the personal narrative that becomes my practice-based research agenda. As a consequence, I am simultaneously and continuously fusing my personal narrative with that of the historical moments that contextualize my passing. This art/life/making-history fusion permanently alters my perception of time to the point where I lose sight of myself and become something like an apparatus consciousness in perpetual jet lag, a nomadic cyborg-narrator whose lifestory changes as it goes.

As it goes digital.

One can only anticipate how this will all play out.

Notes

1. Stan Brakhage, *Essential Brakhage: Selected Writings on Filmmaking* (Kingston, NY: Documentext, 2001), 144.

2. Wallace Stevens, "Angel Surrounded by Paysans," *Wallace Stevens: Collected Poetry and Prose* (New York: Library of America, 1997), 423.

3. Stephane Mallarmé, *Oeuvres complètes*, ed. Henri Mondor and G. Jean-Aubry (Paris: Gallimard, 1945).

4. Gregory Ulmer, *Heuretics: The Logic of Invention* (Baltimore, MD: Johns Hopkins University Press, 1994), 3.

5. Jean Baudrillard, "Photography, or the Writing of Light," ⟨http://www.ctheory.net/ text_file.asp?pick=126⟩, retrieved 12 January 2003.

An earlier version of this essay was originally published in New Media & Society, 6, no. 1 *(2004): 71–76.*

Image *Écriture*

IV

To me style is just the outside of content, and content the inside of style, like the outside and inside of the human body. Both go together, they can't be separated.

—Jean-Luc Godard

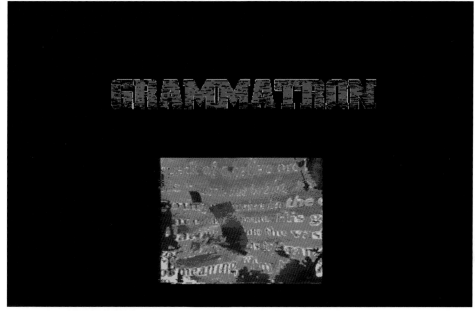

2a

écriture

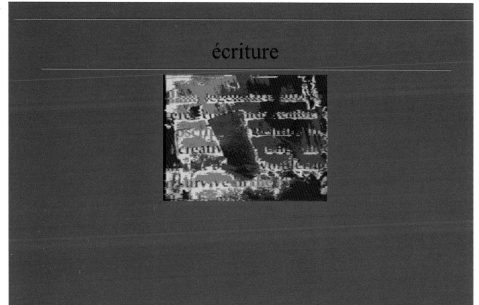

2b

a writing-machine

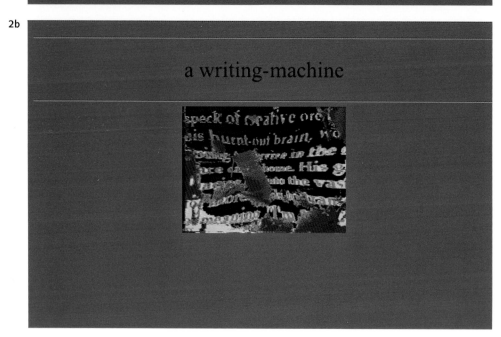

Abe Golam

Abe Golam, legendary info-shaman, cracker of the sorcerer-code and creator of <u>Grammatron</u> and **Nanoscript**, sat behind his computer, every speck of creative ore long since excavated from his burnt-out brain, wondering <u>how he was going to survive</u> in <u>the electrosphere</u> he had once called <u>home.</u> His glazed donut eyes were spacing out into <u>the vast electric desert</u> looking for more words to transcribe his <u>personal loss</u> of meaning. <u>"I'm Abe Golam, an old man. I drove a sign to the end of the road and then I got lost. Find me."</u>

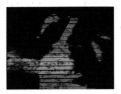

Nanoscript

Nanoscript was the <u>forbidden data</u> that had been permeating the electrosphere ever since the dawn of Man. It was <u>the underlying code</u> that transcribed the evolution of consciousness in a natural world. <u>This consciousness</u>, originally thought to be <u>the ultimate, state-of-the-art, artificial intelligence</u>, was actually part of something Golam called <u>the language of desire</u>.

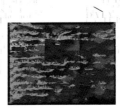

hyper:liner:notes
"an orchestration of writerly effects"

featuring:

realaudio ■
MP3 ■

The Network Conductor
The New Media Economist
The Web Jockey
No Mo Pomo
The Hearing Ear Man
Quicktime Marketmail
The Applied Grammatologist
The Spiritual Unconscious
The Conceptual Artist
Dreamtime Talkingmail
The Groupthink Psyche

And various other sonoluminescent
concept-characters of nonspecific
occupational traits...

hypermedia as conceptual art as writing

Somebody speaks:

realaudio ■
MP3 ■

"PHON:E:ME is, first of all, a concept art album. Like concept albums of the recent past, it grows out of an idea formulated by an artist (or ensemble) who then structures a composition (positions a structure, plays out a proposition) within the parameters of a specific medium or environment (like a record or CD). Here the site-specific environment is located in cyberspace. It is a network-distributed sound-writing narrative that uses whatever conceptual armory it has as its disposal, including concept-characters (Network Conductor, Dreamtime Talkingmail, Hearing Ear Man, The Spiritual Unconscious, to name a few), conceptual titles (like "Network Congestion: Still-Life With Artificially Constructed Psychobabble"), conceptual phraseology ("the writer as pseudo-autobiographical work-in-progress"), etc.

"More than anything, the PHON:E:ME project continues the artist's recent investigation of hypermedia narrative art and its relationship to all previous forms of writing. For example, just as the GRAMMATRON project was built on an idea whose time had come (i.e. "to create a multi-media, virtual reality writing-machine that translates your experience for you AS you experience it"), PHON:E:ME is fueled by an idea whose space has come.

5a

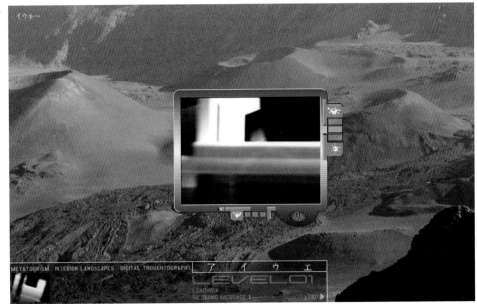

5b

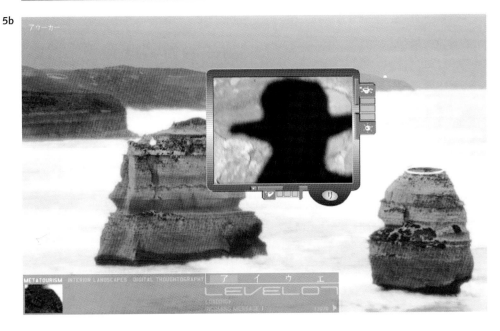

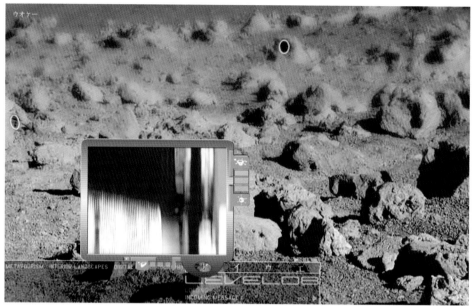

6a

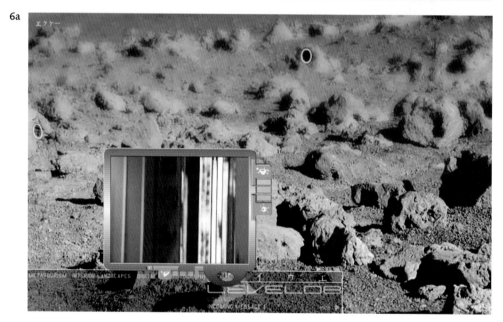

6a

7

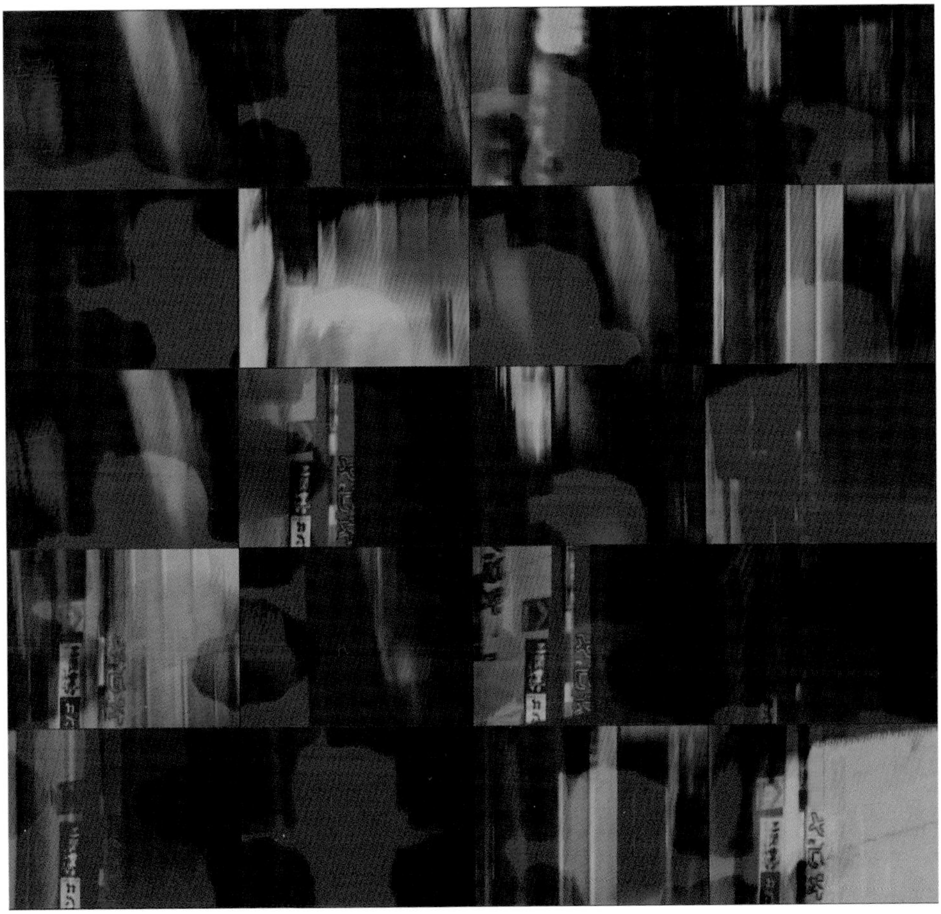

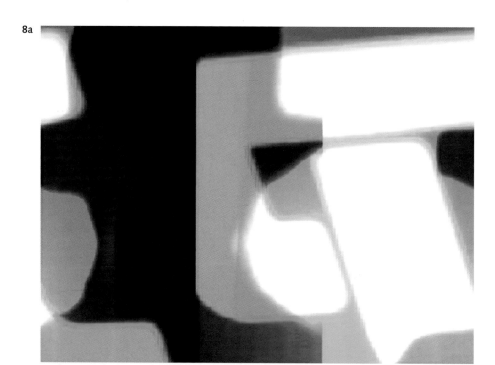

8a

8b

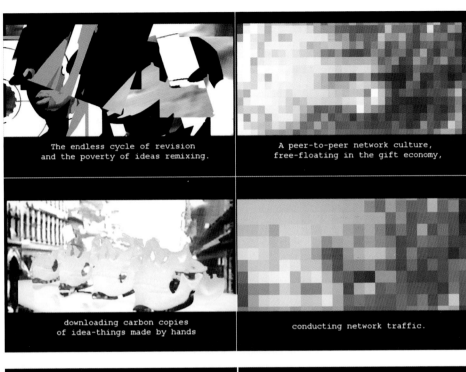

9a

The endless cycle of revision
and the poverty of ideas remixing.

A peer-to-peer network culture,
free-floating in the gift economy,

downloading carbon copies
of idea-things made by hands

conducting network traffic.

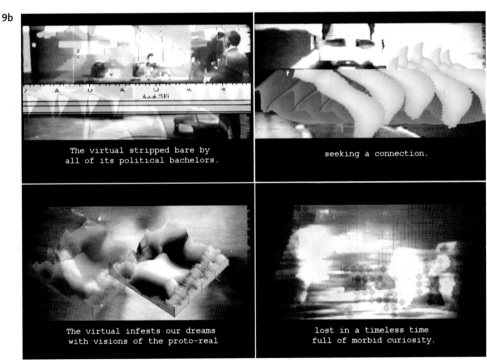

9b

The virtual stripped bare by
all of its political bachelors.

seeking a connection.

The virtual infests our dreams
with visions of the proto-real

lost in a timeless time
full of morbid curiosity.

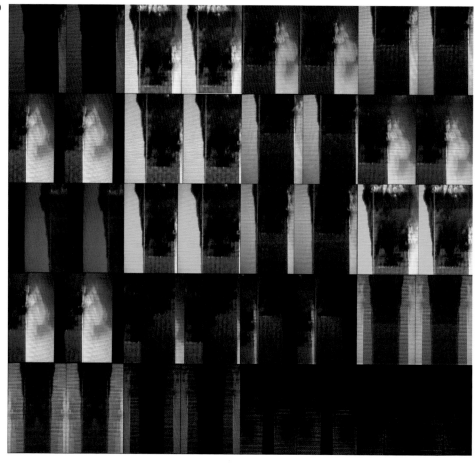

Net Dialogues

V

Writing, when properly managed, (as you may be sure I think mine is) is but a different name for conversation.

—Laurence Sterne

WYSIWYG Subjects

with Eugene Thacker

I'm an eye. A mechanical eye. I, the machine, show you a world the way only I can see it. I free myself for today and forever from human immobility. I'm in constant movement.... Freed from the boundaries of time and space, I co-ordinate any and all points of the universe, wherever I want them to be. My way leads to a fresh perception of the world. Thus I explain in a new way the world unknown to you.

—Dziga Vertov

Mark Amerika: OK, let's start net.dialogue. Are sites like *jennicam* and *amandacam* works of pure performance art, or are they more like reality TV? Sometimes I wonder if net art isn't becoming more like Temptation Island. What's your take?

Eugene Thacker: That's a tough one; then again webcams are being more and more self-conscious (were they ever naive, were they ever "pure"?), and RealTV is becoming performance, literally—like extreme sports, XTV. It's also hard to get out of the highly self-reflexive paranoia of performativity: are you performing because a camera is on you (technical performativity), or are you performing because "life" is not without degrees of performativity?

MA: Yes, it's both/and. And that's the rub. I particularly like your reference to extreme sports and XTV. This is what a contemporary writing-cum-Internet art practice is becoming. Extreme writing. It's not just a job; it's an adventure (and doesn't it make your mouth water just thinking about it?).

But what about the Web glams?

ET: I tend to approach the cam-girls (or cam-grrrls?) thru their differences:

- *Jennicam* represents the voyeuristic fascination w/ the banality of everyday life. The gen-x, white, middle-class American everywoman.
- *Amandacam* seems like an amateur porn star who is acting like *Jennicam* and, just by coincidence, happens to be naked more often. No, you say to yourself, it's *not* porn; she's just hangin' out at home.
- *Anacam* is the twenty-something hip art student who is very self-aware of being "on show" at all times. *Anacam* could never attain the sublime banality of *Jennicam*. But then *Jennicam* could never generate the psychedelic dream world of *Anacam*.

The questions that surrounded a lot of '60s performance art (life/art boundaries) haven't gone away, but they seem different now with new media. To me the contextualization of actions/events by a given technology makes a lot of difference—medial enframing (which is different from medical enflaming). The tech doesn't determine everything, but it does add particular constraints, depending on how the media is being used or misused.

Given that, it seems like the webcams are based on a surveillance model. RealTV, despite it's self-promotion, is still based on the syndicated TV program—commercials, time slots, censorship, major editing, etc. Wow, it's amazing how much life is like a sitcom, etc. When you're on webcam, you're under surveillance, 24/7, and like the panopticon, you're seen but can't see who's seeing you; and, unlike TV, there is often interaction—chat rooms, e-mail exchanges, webcam diaries, etc. RealTV could operate as true surveillance only if you were one of the tech people in the camera room at *Big Brother* or *The RealWorld*.

The "real" for webcams is documentation-real. Visioning every nook and cranny (of the body as well as house), detailing every day's events, accounting for absences from the webcam, archiving photos, etc. The "real" for RealTV is experience-real—like an unscripted sitcom, drama, or soap with amateur actors who can't improvise. The enframing is the setting up of a condition (house or island) and see what happens, lab-rat style.

Webcams are to anthropology what RealTV is to behaviorism.

I seem to have lost voyeurism in all this. The one single point of consensus on webcams or RealTV is that everyone knows you're being watched. There's no voyeurism in media anymore?

MA: Right; it's not really *Candid Camera* anymore. Maybe it's more like Candide Camera or, tip of the hat to the late great Terry Southern, Candy

Camera. The voyage takes more precedence over the voyeur—Web journey-men (journeywomen) searching for lost aura. I mean, it feels like we really are on the verge of relocating Benjamin's "lost aura," except instead of seeing it return in the form of a unique *object d'art*, it's now become a more celebrated network identity, one that is constantly in flux, so that when the Floating Web Cam Eye captures you in its lens, you feel the need to "creatively exhibit" yourself, to instantaneously demystify yourself, even though you know that this is really not yourself at all, can never be yourself, because that's just not you. You are always someone else.

A network of performing orifice-cams would, I think, further prove the point. If you took a camera inside one of your orifices, one of your lower orifices, and kept it beaming over the Web 24 hours a day while giving your viewers a supplementary diary that metaphorically transmitted a new media language that essentially turned the orifice-cam into a laxative, what would that do to our concept of streaming media?

ET: Now, that's really intriguing—not just the many orifice cams that are available via any mainstream porn site, but a *network* of orifice cams that are *streaming* live 24/7. This definitely seems like a job for wireless Web, but aside from that, it would push the process of mediation to its extreme, which is see-ing the most secret part of a body, while at the same time rendering that depth a surface.

A common trope during the rise of anatomical dissection during the six-teenth century was the Latin saying "Know Thyself" (literally, inside and out). The fascination with the public anatomy theaters was this doubled autovoyeurism. During a public dissection, you were seeing what your insides looked like, but at the same time it obviously wasn't you down there, splayed open, on the dissection table. Webcams are an anatomy of net.subjectivity. The creative exhibitionism acts by variously reflecting, diffracting, distorting, maybe saying much more about the context of networked surveillance of voyeurs, than about Jenni, Amanda, Ana, or the numerous other webcam personalities.

Which brings us back to your title—"WYSIWYG Subjects." In a way, the whole phenomena of webcams is about the topography of the subject (interior/exterior; inner space/outer space) constantly grappling with new technologies that mediate that subject. In Foucault's terms, these are tech-nologies that "subject" subjects: they corporeally pose challenges to subjectiv-ity and subject formation, and they do so via the stuff of the medium itself.

You're a person, you've got a body, and you want to share it with everyone—not just represent it to everyone, but you want to stretch the membrane of its thickness via a DSL line. That, it seems, is the crux of the many ambiguities of net.subjectivity: embodiment.

Streaming_OrificeCam.net would be a way to experiment with the changes that embodied subjectivity are undergoing, as its slides through new media like webcams. Now, in one sense the goal of any medium is to be so perfect that it's invisible: that orifice is so real I could touch it. On the other hand, the very definition of a medium is that it provides a buffer between two points or that it "translates": this webcam stream sure is pixelated. What is produced in the space between these two poles? Can you get visceral data, dripping data? What might tactility mean for net.subjectivity?

An earlier version of this dialogue was originally published online at Rhizome.org *(2001).*

Postcinematic Writing

with Adrian Miles

Mark Amerika: Let's talk about the vog. As the vog manifesto says: "9. a vog is dziga vertov with a mac and a modem." Could you elaborate?

Adrian Miles: "I the machine show you the world as only I can see it" (Dziga Vertov, 1923). Of all the Russian montage directors, Vertov is in many ways the most fascinating. This is partly because of his interest in documentary and reportage, though its mainly because his work is oddly prescient. For instance, in 1923 he wrote:

> With the speed of international communications and the lightning dispatch of filmed material, the *Cine-Gazette* ought to be a "survey of the world every few hours." It is not. We must face up to this. The *Cine-Pravda* is a car on a leash, an aeroplane beneath a ceiling: it cannot be a *Cine-Gazette.*

This is a description, first of all, of CNN, and then it is a description of Internet-based *production* and distribution—in 1923! As he says, the current system is a car on a leash, an aeroplane beneath a ceiling. This is how I see streaming media on the Web right now, restrained by wanting to be just like TV.

MA: Yes, the Web suffers from TV envy, but then again, it's pre-TV. It's almost as though it were in its imaginary stage of telecommunicational development. Vertov saw that. The Kino-Eye as Writing Machine. The Dream of Mosaic (GUI stickiness). Interfacing with the Processual Mind as it "captures" screenal logic. In this regard, I think we should mention Tesla as well, since he anticipated the liberating potential of transforming the body into an apparatus of network conduction.

Not to mention Vannevar Bush and his "As We May Think" essay pub-lished in the *Atlantic Monthly* right after dropping the bombs in WW2. And then Ted Nelson watching Douglas Engelbart fidget with a mouse and windows-based computer screen having an epiphany, like watching a man land on the moon and thinking—hypertext. Click-click, say no more, say no more—and then, with utopian-mystical vision (Xanadu?) conceptualizing what he soon called *literary machines*.

AM: The epiphany for me was when I first saw Storyspace in '91 or '92. Those spaces and link lines made *perfect* and *transparent* sense to me. It was on a Mac, and I knew that QuickTime would work in there. I was a junior academic in cinema studies interested in computers, and how and why I would write like this was obvious. Ever since then, I've been thinking and writing with links. Links are what I write with, and for me they're just like film edits—made of the same stuff. When I write, I get lost in these possibilities—the futures that present themselves while writing, in writing, through writing. It is this being-like-film that is the process I explore. Any edges you write are arbitrary, contingent, sometimes accidental. The key is to locate a vision, to find a *vidécriture* that is this writing. The Web just ups the ante for the process as model.

MA: Right, I use the Web to capture the work-in-process, to remix my ongoing ungoing filmtext experience, which brings us back to Vertov and streaming in real-time theory and cultural production.

AM: Vertov wrote lots of things that today, when transcribed to our use of streaming media, seem to be very relevant. His criticism of cinema as stories with illustrations seems largely what most people do when they think of video on the Web.

He writes slogans and manifestos that let me think of him as posthuman. He makes no distinction between camera and person, machine and individ-ual. It's a machinic vision, and the role of the film maker in Vertov's kingdom is to learn how to listen to the machine—to write (see) with and for the ma-chine, to not subject the machine to the individual. This is my experience of writing hypertext hypertextually, and it's what I want to learn how to do with time-based media—to write *in* QuickTime.

MA: To write *in* QuickTime as a writing or literary machine using kino-eye cinescripture to essentially code into being a randomized filmtext environ-ment that others can access by way of a P2P network that sets into motion a utopian dreamworld of international culture. But I digress.

What about your vogs?

AM: All my vogs are made using pretty generic tools. A domestic-quality mini-DV camera, a recent firewire-equipped Mac, and they're trying to find a way of writing that works for most Web users, most of the time, where word, sound, moving image, etc., are not discrete entities outside of each others fields.

MA: Hmmm. I guess I feel like that's how I work already. True, I have to emulate the seamless shape-shifting that must take place in order to discretely pass from one application to another, but in the end, my nerve scales are scintillating with raw (indigestible) desire, and without even thinking about it I lose myself in the process. This is what it means to be a network artist—finding yourself by losing yourself in the white-hot chemical decomposition of cell.f in all its coded glory. Can you relate?

AM: No. Though I probably could. :-) I've never thought of it as primarily networked but about getting rid of this distinction between words and pictures. For me, writing hypertextually is always a postcinematic writing, and while pictures work differently than words, their different networks (to steal your terminology) or the differences in their networks are erased. But it's one thing to talk about that kind of writing and quite another thing to actually do it. The vogs are an exploration in this direction. Instead of hypertext being the medium, it's video, though I guess they are pretty much hypertexts in QuickTime—same questions, same problems.

A part of the code is the network, so you're right. It is about making things that more or less work now, with no really special requirements, with a small palette of space, bandwidth, and time. It should always be about fragments, parts, remixing. Scale is now relative to connection, not monumentality.

An earlier version of this dialogue was originally published online at Rhizome.org *(2001).*

Stitch Bitch: The Hypertext Author as Cyborg-Narrator

with Shelley Jackson

Mark Amerika: How did you first get involved with writing hypertext? When did you start writing *Patchwork Girl*, and what sort of creative process was involved with its creation? Was it hypertext from the word go, or like many other hyperworks, did it start out by jotting down some conceptual framework followed by some straight-ahead writing and just morphed into a hypertext?

Shelley Jackson: *Patchwork Girl* started as a drawing on a page of my note-book, a naked woman with dotted-line scars. (It was 1993 and I was listening to George Landow talk about hypertext and critical theory.) I wrote most of the text in fragments in my notebook. I was planning to write a hypertext, so you could say I was predisposed to a meandering course. But in fact, I've never written anything in a straight line from beginning to end but always in the round or in snatches that I later stitched together into a pattern (usually after staring at them for a very long time). I had no conceptual framework for *Patchwork Girl* until very late in the process. What I had was a disorderly tangle of ideas, bits of narrative, quotes, and drawings, all multiply interconnected in my own mind. At one point, I sat down at the computer and began to try to simply reproduce this pattern of relationships by means of links, in hopes that something graceful and self-evident would emerge. It didn't. So I snipped everything apart again and started over.

The structure of *Patchwork Girl* rose up out of this carnage. I found family resemblances within the bits and grouped like parts together. Places where I contradicted myself or found myself drawn in two directions at once became the branch point for parallel structures rather than a chatter of static I needed to resolve into one clear note.

Once I began to see a sort of architecture emerge, I could work in relation to that. I began to think about what was suggested and what was missing. The graveyard section began, for example, as a rhetorical trope in the course of a long, looping mediation. But working in Storyspace, I persistently saw the rectangular corrals with their enclosed plots of smaller rectangles as cemeteries I was privileged to hover over, resurrecting text from this grave or that at will—an accident of resemblance but a beautiful one. Hence the section of *Patchwork Girl* that is structured like a graveyard, where you dig up body parts and learn their histories.

Of course, these rectangles full of rectangles also brought to mind a quilt—which is not unlike a graveyard, since traditional quilts are often machines for reminiscence, bringing together scraps of fabric, once in use, that memorialize family members and important times, and is also very like a Frankenstein monster (these multiply determined metaphors kept turning up). So I made a quilt where each patch is itself a patchwork (in crazy-quilt style) of quotes from divers sources.

The hardest bit of *Patchwork Girl* to write was the "story," which is also, and deliberately, the most like a conventional novel, even though it comes in two versions that meet and diverge and meet again. But even this part was written in fragments and strung onto a timeline later on.

So I suppose the short answer to your question is that hypertext permits me to write the way I ordinarily would, in related fragments with no overarching design, but then to allow a structure to arise out of the inclinations of the material itself instead of imposing a linear order onto it—which is an interesting exercise but not the only one worth trying.

MA: What were some of the exciting discoveries you made composing with links and screen shots instead of standard narrative devices associated with print culture?

SJ: I think in things: complicated ideas come to me in flesh, concrete metaphors with color, heft, stink. So it is easier and more pleasing for me to think of text as a thing or things, arranged in a place, than as a story told by a storyteller or a piece of music or a journey or one of the other more linear metaphors for fiction. Hypertext makes it easy to place things side by side rather than one after another, so it makes "thing" and "place" metaphors much easier. I guess you could say I want my fiction to be more like a world full of things that you can wander around in rather than a record or memory of those wanderings. The quilt and graveyard sections, where a concrete metaphor that resonates with the themes of the work creates a literary structure, satisfy me in a very corporeal way. I salivate, my fingers itch.

MA: Why did you glom on to the Frankenstein myth as your primary subject for *Patchwork Girl*, and what led you to give it that major twist that turned the monster into a kind of storygrrl?

SJ: I was thinking about hypertext fiction—what it could do, what would be different about it—and my patchworked girl monster emerged out of these more abstract concerns as a metaphor for a fragmented and dispossessed text that nevertheless had a loud, triumphant voice. (L. Frank Baum's Patchwork Girl, by the way, is always pleased with herself, carefree, a bit addled, and greatly amused by the seriousness of others.) I wanted to write about the liberating potential of that unseatedness, that lack of clear boundaries or a native ground. The stitched-together monster is an easy metaphor for any text but especially hypertext, as the still uneasy offspring of a new technology and an old one: books, literature. (Note that Mary Shelley's original monster, brought to life by "a machine of mysterious complexity," essentially installs a human, humane soul into his inhuman frame by reading a small collection of books. He too is a cross-breed.)

But *Frankenstein* had been scratching a sore spot in the back of my brain for some time already. I like to think about Mary Shelley, age nineteen or so, hanging out with these oh-so-sensitive, even hysterical young poets. (Byron, I seem to remember, used to get himself worked up into such a tizzy over a séance that he ran around the house wild-eyed and had to be tied down.) I imagine they treated her with some condescension. She was not a writer, yet. A general challenge was issued, but it was Mary Shelley who stuck with it and wrote a novel that became the quintessential modern myth, anticipating the nightmares of a century still to come. At the same time, *Frankenstein* is a strange book. The monster is a baddie for sure. He shouldn't exist, he's unnatural, a glitch. At the same time, he is a powerful, eloquent, confident, tragic figure, while the narrator is short-sighted, poor in empathy, cowardly, irresponsible, an all-around shifty character. It's clear which one Mary Shelley prefers. She likes monsters; she birthed one, after all. Or rather, two—but Mary Shelley's second child, a patchwork girl as big and bad (as in baaad) as her brother, was ripped apart before the last thread was knotted, which may have been a mercy killing.

In the world Shelley knew, there could be no happy monsters. But only because of bad dad. A motherless monster with a shiftless dad runs amok, but what about a monster with a loving mother? I took up that inquiry, but—the Frankenstein monster having brought his tragic trajectory to a fiery end—I was more curious about Mary's second child. I might believe that women have a little more experience in growing up monstrous and still getting by. My monster is crucially more adaptive, wry, and made strong as well as handicapped by her monstrosity. (There's no point sitting around wishing we were all human.)

MA: Like so many hypertexts that eventually get published, there are some threads in *Patchwork Girl* that make a clear connection with theory—and I think this has to do with the fact that with books, we're so used to the medium that we tend to get lost in the transparent realism that so many novelists create for us, whereas with computer hypertext, you can't help but feel that the medium is at least somehow part of the message, which then leads the writer to go "meta" on you. What do you think? Are you still interested in theory and finding ways to use it in the development of your stories?

SJ: I think you're right, though part of my motivation for writing *Patchwork Girl* in the first place was to interrogate hypertext in terms of its relationship to the rest of literature, so it was a forgone conclusion that my hypertext should have one foot in theory. But I'm not interested in transparent forms, language that dissolves and leaves a dream of the real world. In books as well as in hypertexts, I like to run up against the written thing, bruise myself on its edges. I like writing that's a little hard to swallow. And I'm not impressed by the difference between theory and fiction, anyway. All ideas about reality are fictional, and some of them are beautiful, too.

MA: Do you think hypertext fiction is ultimately tied to the academy as a field of research and study, or does it actually have commercial potential, and if so, how will it fulfill that potential? I mean, don't you wanna be a glam hypertextualized rock star?

SJ: I'm so uninterested in commerce that it's hard for me to think about the future of hypertext in that light. But leaving money out of the picture for the nonce, I can't see any reason why hypertext can't be as popular as books have been, though most serious readers are still stuck on books and for good reasons as well as bad. Hey, the greatest literature ever written was not created for the computer screen. And most readers are reading for a familiar kind of experience, one that hypertext does not provide. In fact, much of the most interesting literature of this century doesn't provide it, and readers still haven't caught up. A mass conversion to hypertext fiction would mean a mass relinquishing of treasured habits, and that's not going to happen all at once. On the other hand, the Internet is making the experience of following links pretty ordinary for a lot of people.

But yeah, of course, I want to be glam and all that. I'd like to dress up in spangled platform boots and plug that novel into a really big amp.

MA: One of the problems with finding an audience for more playful yet complex hypertexts like the ones you write is that even some of our most educated readers have difficulty understanding what a hypertext is and some of the more conservative cultural critics even refuse to open themselves up to learning how to navigate through a link structure. Do you think this will change as more and more young people become computer literate, and if so, how will this change the average liberal arts student's perception of what literature is?

SJ: Regular Web users already understand implicitly how to read a hypertext. They may not be accustomed to thinking about what they've just read as akin to novels and stories, but they will. I'm not sure what the average student's perception of literature is, but I suspect it has more to do with a vague image of leather-bound volumes in a wood-paneled room than with any immediate experience of reading—not because they haven't read but because *literature* has become more of a dignified insignia than a noun in everyday use. If that noun expands to include hypertext, that's good news because that image of leather binding and gold leaf will float back to *Masterpiece Theatre* where it belongs, and what's left will be words, sentences, paragraphs, a pattern of relationships.

MA: Your recent Web work, *MY BODY*, integrates autobiography, illustration, the wunderkammer model and hypertext into one of the more exuberant Web fictions on the Net. How did you come to use yourself or, better yet, your body as a surface to explore the connection between textuality and sexuality? It's a theme that resonates in both *Patchwork Girl* and *MY BODY*.

SJ: I don't know whether to answer this as someone maturely wielding the tools of my trade or as the partly perplexed observer of my own psychology. As I said above, I relate to language, ideas, in terms of very concrete imagery. Thinking is a kind of controlled synaesthesia for me. I understand things by scrutinizing my own metaphors until they come into sharp focus, until I could stub my toe on them in the dark. You might also think of the memory palace, that Renaissance discipline of remembering things by encoding them in imaginary objects (generated by puns and personal associations), permanently stashed in particular niches, drawers, wardrobes in imaginary but well-mapped castles. Only in my case, it's not an exercise in codes and concentration but the way my mind works on its own: I see things. So language and thought already relate to my body, to my senses, and it gives me a visceral pleasure to make the connection explicit, by naming a piece of text "my foot" or "my fingernail." Writing is like shedding skin—no, because it's living flesh. Though writing is not like having babies. I've never quite taken to that metaphor (maybe because I've never had a baby). It's more like stitching together a monster out of bits of your self and bits of other stuff and sending it out to do things for you. It's a fetch, a demon double—neither you nor clearly separate from you. And it goes and presses itself on people; it infiltrates them. But this relationship works in reverse, as well: texts are like bodies, but bodies are like texts, too. They aren't simple, self-evident things; they're composed.

An earlier version of this dialogue was originally published online at Alt-X *and* Telepolis *(1998).*

Dub Fictions

with Jeff Noon

Mark Amerika: I'm really digging your new book, *Cobralingus*. The connection between music (or sound) and writing is becoming really important again.

Jeff Noon: Well, we did a great gig last night to launch *Cobralingus*. Local DJ, Req, gave me some great backing tracks. He's a good find. He's using twin decks, and his scratching skills allow him to actually engage with, and react to, what I'm doing. And the audience certainly appreciated it. I took them on a journey through my work, exploring the idea of the prose remix, starting with *Vurt*, a piece from *Nymphomation*, a few from *Pixel*, and from *Needle*. And then, in the second set, we did the *Cobralingus* pieces plus some passages from a novel currently being written. Pretty heavy stuff, some of it, especially to present in a live setting. But the music helps a whole lot, I find. Req was mixing in Coltrane, Laswell, Eno, Pierre Henry, The Meters. Great fun!

MA: Absolutely. I just came back from a gig in Lucerne, Switzerland, a beautiful town surrounded by the Alps. The festival was called Surf-Sample-Manipulate, after a theory I've been developing over the last few years wherein the writer-cum-netartist uses all of the available data on the Web as source material to further inflect a narrative environment—but one that is a kind of ongoing ungoing pseudo-autobiographical work in progress. The incredible sound artist Twine, who has three new releases coming out with Komplot, Bip-Hop, and Hefty records, flew out there with me, and we proceeded to do an improvisational sound-writing performance. Basically, what we did was hook up our laptops and a few processors like a Virus and Sherman, etc., and began projecting both live writing and live sounds, each influencing the other in a kind of real-time narrative production.

JN: I didn't realize we were moving in similar directions. This is great! I feel so isolated, most of the time, in Britain. It's getting more than a bit bland and deadly right now. Don't know if you've been following my stuff, but *Nymphomation* introduced the dub fiction idea, with a reverse dub of Lewis Carroll's *Jabberwocky*. I refined this technique and made it more explicit in the *Pixel Juice* collection in different ways on a number of the stories. *Needle in the Groove* is the most realized work, a novel that contains its own remix. I also did a CD with David Toop based on texts and atmospheres from the book. *Cobralingus* is a kind of weird solo album of a book. It pushes the technique to the extremes in a very experimental way.

MA: What musical influences were most present while writing it out?

JN: *Cobralingus* is more based on the glitchware stuff, mainly coming out of Germany: Oval, Microstoria, Pole, Vladislav Delay, and the likes. Very atmospheric, very abstract, murky, bleepy, broken. There was a big article on the music and the software processes involved in *The Wire* 190/191 (double issue). "Worship the Glitch," it was called. Some of the techniques are quite incredible, way beyond what I can do with words on paper. The Bouncing Ball software, for instance, treats a musical signal as, quite literally, a bouncing ball of noise. You can decide the weight of the ball, the height it is dropped at, etc. Amazing stuff!

MA: Right! And I'm just wondering how to take some of these ideas (techniques) and use them to amplify these writerly effects in live performance. I found that using the Net, the WWW, was very helpful. So that in Lucerne, while we were doing the live, improvisational sound-writing remix, I was also projecting my laptop's wireless connection to the WWW and grabbing data off the network in real-time and sampling what I needed from it right into the new story, remixing as I wrote it, and then using the sounds to further distort the narrative's generative meaning (or meaning potential). You must feel something similar performing *Cobralingus* with Req?

JN: My main concern during a *Cobralingus* performance is to imbue the material with emotion. People think, because of the way the book is set out, that machines are involved in some way in the creation. This couldn't be further from the truth. Every single word, every moment, comes only from the exercise of my imagination. I actually see the pieces in very personal terms, on two levels: (1) what the words, ideas, images mean to me in terms of personal history/interests; and (2) a memory of what I was feeling at the exact moment of creation. I think this last is the best clue that *Cobralingus* records (and magnifies) a natural creative process. So during performance, I'm trying to draw out these personal micro and macro histories. In the crudest terms, I try to take the audience on a journey—a journey through the text, from sampled input, through all the various filters along the signal path until we reach the output. I try to make that an adventure, an adventure of language. But you can see the paradox that is set up. I'm using terms such as *input/output, signal path, filtering system,* etc., in order to create something that is incredibly personal. I like the paradox, but I know the presentation has confused some people. At the Metamute talk I did with Robert Coover and Florian Cramer, I felt that I'd alienated a certain part of the audience simply by admitting to such deep feelings and that the work is being drawn from areas of my own life, my psyche, my past, my emotions. My concern here is that one of the central tenets of postmodernism (that meaning lies not in *depth* but on the surface) is getting in the way of proper engagement with an artwork. Especially now that PoMo has entered its long, overprotracted Rococo phase. I'm interested, most of all, in how the new technologies are going to effect a new kind of narrative.

MA: Well, yeah, there was some head scratching going on in Lucerne too. Now that we're entering a kind of NoMo PoMo phase, I guess there's bound to be some ruffled feathers. After the performance in Lucerne, people mostly wanted to know if everything was really being improvised and if it really was a live Net connection. Yes and yes. Why not? Anyway, the confusion is a healthy response because everyone is so keyed up on new techniques that when you see something that is genuinely new or at least unfamiliar you immediately want to know "How did you do that?" Like *Cobralingus,* for example: how did you do that?

JN: Re: *Cobralingus* technique: first question is the choice of initial input text. This works best when its filled with imagery. So Angela Carter, rather than Jane Austen. Also, of course, I've tended to go for stuff out of copyright, unless it's from the work of friends. Then the choice of the first filter gate. There are seventeen to choose from: Decay, Explode, Find story, Enhance, Play game, Inject drug, Randomize, etc. Really, the *Cobralingus* device is an improvisation machine: which filter gate will produce an interesting result? And then pushing the text through the gate. How this happens is entirely up to the writer's imagination. Trial and error takes place; something emerges and is passed on through another choice of gate. Some pieces make sense, some make nonsense, and others are just way stations of random noise. The filters are designed so that some break down the text (Decay, Explode, etc.), and some build it back up (Enhance, Find story, etc.). The text is pushed through gate after gate, traveling along a signal pathway. At some point, and this always happens, something will jump out of the text at you, some phrase, image, theme, etc. This is taken as a clue to where the text wants to go, and the writer can then push the text toward this point. The emotional nature of the piece is revealed. So there are two broad phases: the initial exploration up to the signifying detail and then a more considered use of the filters toward the output text. I see this as revealing the ghost of the original text—that all texts are haunted in some way and the *Cobralingus* device is a technique for conjuring up these ghosts.

An earlier version of this dialogue was originally published online at Rhizome.org *(2001).*

Active/onBlur

with Talan Memmott

Mark Amerika: This year we had trouble labeling our competition. We settled on the term *new media writing*, which is kind of like one of those generic boxes of cereal you buy in the grocery store—you know, the white box with black lettering that says "Wheat Flakes" or the cans of beer that simply say "Beer." Being the neologistic wordsmith that you are, could you help us out here: i.e., what do you call the kind of writing you do, and does it apply to others too?

Talan Memmott: Nomolectic electrature? Appliterature?

Oh, there are so many terms out there. I think the title *new media writing* is acceptable precisely because it is so generic. If you go with any of the many terms for this stuff—*hypertext, cybertext, hypermedia,* web.art, net.art, etc.— you open yourself up to varying, sometimes highly specific interpretations of the term. I mean one man's web.art is another man's hypertext. New media, as "white box" as it is, at least does not suffer from this. Where some of the more specific terms leave out or inflate certain aspects of the media/um, the generic *new media* does not.

It is very difficult to put a tag on a media/um that is more than one.

For my own work, I have used *rich.lit,* though I don't stick to this, and I don't make any claim that the term is appropriate across the board. Really, all the terms generically indicate a creative cultural practice through applied technology.

MA: What got you interested in experimenting with writing on the Web?

TM: A number of things. First, I work in the Web-development industry, so I am always online or writing code. You learn a lot about information architecture and interface design when you develop corporate Web sites. So working with Percepticon developed the skill set. At times, I must admit, I am a code-aholic. But I see the code-aholism as part of my overall writing practice.

There are a couple of levels to what I am doing. There is the theory/fiction work like *Lexia to Perplexia,* the more hypertext fiction work (which is still at least quasi-theory) like *Lolli's Apartment,* and some regular old experimental fiction. The straight fiction work is not so much interested in the Web beyond distribution, whereas the other types of work exploit technological aspects in their formation—from the narrative to the structural.

I started experimenting with creative applications in 1996. I immediately saw potential in the Web at that time and was making little pieces to build my skill set and explore narrative structures. The narrative experiments are actually an extension of earlier interests in writing. As to the Web, what I first recognized and wanted to explore was the complication of FACE and SPACE that the browser window presents. I was intrigued not so much by technological bells and whistles as by the window as a space for text and image. There was a lot of carryover from my earlier experiences making installation art, as I viewed the space as something like an empty gallery. So in terms of writing this presents the complication that you are not writing on a surface but writing in a space.

I think what interested me most was how the Web brought together a number of practices for me and that it was a pretty wide-open venue for further experiments in narrative construction.

MA: Your work, like so much of the best new work emerging on the Net, puts into play a renegotiation of the image/text relationship. Do you see yourself coming from a more visual or literary background—or are these distinctions meant to fall by the wayside?

TM: My definition of text includes images. I have said before that I kind of stick to the ol' poststructuralist adage: *the world is text.* I came to writing through visual art, but I always used writing in my visual art. I've been a painter, performer, created installation and video, written and directed plays: there was always writing. Writing is a constant, as any medium forms a kind of writing. In many regards, I am a media nomad.

When I think of the term *hypertext* I take an open view. *Hyper,* of course, means "to excess"; in regard to text, I read it as something like *every medium leaves a mark, every cultural practice produces a form of writing.* It is a question of application. In relation to the written word, hypermedia techniques allow for extended functionality that increase the narrative value of an image, lifting it from its previous illustrative state. The alphabetic can be made animate, ideo- or diagrammatic as well. The interface itself can appear as ideogram with huge narrative potential.

As far as distinctions between the literary and the visual, they can remain, can be ignored, they can fade. For a writer/artist, they are borders to be played at, walls to graffiti, climb, or tumble.

MA: Does the distributed network of Web artists whose work is readily available to you influence your own practice? It seems to me that all serious Web artists are, first of all, serious Web surfers, no?

TM: I would doubt anyone is creating work that is not influenced by the work of others. There is a lot of great work out there from all over the world. Great publications, organizations, lists. *trAce* is evidence of how writing on the Web is a global phenomenon. What is most amazing to me is the diversity of work, and I think this is one of the reasons it is so difficult to give the media/um a name. Every writer/artist deals with the technology differently, creating not so much a personal style but an individuated form. So even within specific genres of creative Web-based works you have many voices.

I think it is not only natural to be influenced by the work of others, but also that we are all (any/every "user") influenced by the vicissitudes of technology, the environment and general economy of the network. I think *Lexia to Perpexia* is evidence of my own attachment.

MA: How does one get from *Lexia to Perplexia*? Or to put it another way, why this work and why now?

TM: On the surface, the title is a statement concerning a move from hypertext to hypermedia—the complicating of literary models. But the arguments of the piece are more complex and diverse than that. To some extent, it is a piece about ontological complications that occur by way of attachment to the Internet.

When I began work on *Lexia to Perplexia* in November of 1999 DHTML was starting to appear on the Web. The ability to overlap text, image, any object on the page alters the concept of the document on the Web, and with some additional JavaScript, the sheet—the imagine sheet that is the screen—is *puncturated* rather than punctuated. I saw a lot of potential here in complicating the literary page/screen argument. Part of the perplexion of *Lexia to*

Perplexia is in the stratification of the content, that the narrative experience of the piece is distributed between the text and image, and extended to the User/Reader in the form of an "application" that is operated rather than consumed. In that regard, it is interesting to note that much of the content is in reference to the process of attachment to the application—a tangential description of the action of the user.

With a document that is acted upon—unfolded, revealed, opened rather than read, full of holes to elsewhere, hiding secret inScriptions, filled with links like mines and traps and triggers—we are no longer talking page or screen but appliance. Navigating the Lexia of *Lexia to Perplexia* is kind of like getting a new device and trying to figure out how the heck it works. Perhaps the *Lexia to Perplexia User Manual* is the content of the work itself—encrypted, only partially translated like some of the instructions from IKEA, only inter-hyperactive. There is a confusion of ontological, literary and technical application—*perplexia*.

MA: At one point in *Lexia*, the writing goes:

I, User, exit this for that—
sorted, compartmentalized,
archived.
RE:organized—stacked, a body with
organs elsewhere.
The de:parted body rests, no longer
active/onBlur;
0.0.0.0.0.0.0.0.0.0
(the flat line string thread woven
into linen wrapped 'round)
The User is laid flat and dried into
bands of jerky—
isolated, while A.exe indexes and
pre.pares the packets.

wherein you once again take the language of code and turn it into degenerative prose. The User almost sounds like a drug addict, except here she is maybe a code addict? Or to put it another way, Do Androids Dream of Arbitrarily Corrupted Sim.Stem Folders?

TM: Yes, that text is from the section titled "Ka Space: encryption 〉book〈 of the dead." There is a fundamental pun here: Osiris of Egyptian mythology is more accurately named Ausere. In a simple, frivolous manipulation of the name, you come up with "A User." On top of this, we have an attempt at constructing something akin to the "Body without Organs" of Deleuze and Guattari misread through an attachment to the Egyptian funerary text, which is the theme of the section. A.exe is simply Anubis. The "Body" that is constructed here, as stated in the cited text, is not exactly like Deleuze and Guattari's: it is "a body with organs elsewhere," in reference to attachment to the Internet apparatus and the distribution of "being" across it—as data, as pixels, as energy.

I suppose this text could be read in the context you propose at both the Deleuzean level and as applied to User attachment to the Internet. If we replace desire with addiction, the term *packets* is variable. The "Body without Organs" as written by Deleuze and Guattari in "The Body without Organs" makes direct reference to drug addiction, as the section of "A Thousand Plateaus" is primarily dedicated to Antonin Artaud.

MA: This year's *trAce/Alt-X* judge, Shelley Jackson, says of your award-winning work "the reader's first pleasure will probably be a visual one. This is a gorgeous piece. But the visuals though beautiful are not only decorative but syntactical. Some of Memmott's most elegant arguments are made visually, through the logic of layout and the grammar of the link." That's actually a wonderful way of putting it. And I'm now wondering if you would elaborate a little bit on your digital rhetoric—that is, the way you use the screenal interface to create visual metaphors that syntactically make your critifictional case?

TM: I am not surprised Shelley Jackson recognizes these attributes as her own work is supersmart and an inspiration. But I am always happy when some of the formal intent gets through.

As far as a digital rhetoric goes, I am not sure I can elaborate too much. I could get into all the little theoretical tidbits, but it would clog up the server or I'd bore everyone off this page. But I think the recognition that images and interaction are used in a syntactical sense is significant. As I mentioned earlier, the interest in the window as a narrative space, neither screen nor page, is what drew me into making work.

In *Lexia to Perplexia* there is an apparent integration between the interface concepts and the subjects of the content that forms something that is truly an application. I have tried to extract just the text from *Lexia to Perplexia*, and it suffers from the lack of diagrammatic and dynamic attributes of the "content application" as *mise en scène*. The hypermedia work succeeds, I think, because of the way its formation was integrated with the writing process. Much of the functionality arises out of early notes and was developed alongside the writing, so early on there was a sort of branching. This sort of diversification develops into the environment of the final application.

MA: I know part of your background is as a musician in a punk rock band and part of it is in obsessing over contemporary theory. This reminds me of the work of another writer, the late Kathy Acker, although in Acker's work the punk influences are more apparent—that is, she appropriates the punk attitude and remixes it into her narrative architecture so that it's right in your face—whereas with your work the theory seems to take prominence, and I'm wondering where is the punk in your work?

TM: My punk days were early on. I played in punk bands from '79 to '82. I was a teenage punk. I did recently try to relive those days by forming a band called YOINK, but that was short-lived. But I've played in bands all my life— Short Order Cooks, Sloppy Kafka, Peabody, Jack the Ant.

Anyway, I studied with Kathy Acker in the early nineties. She convinced me to take my writing seriously. I don't see the punk coming out in my writing in the same way as it does in her work. And you are correct in recognizing that theory is in the foreground of my work. There is, I think, in my work a similar pirate intent. The heavy neologistic play and abstraction of context, plus the infusion of theory leads to a nearly unreadable text that is quasi-academic yet outside the academy. Of course, the unreadability extends in all directions and is further complicated through hypermedia. The text is subversive by subverting itself. There is perhaps something punk in that. Maybe Web smart rather than street smart? I think it is a little more jazz than punk for me.

My obsession with theory started in art school. Like I said, I come to writing through fine art. Thinking about it now, one of the first things that made me move from visual art toward writing was in fact Kathy Acker's essay in *Art after Modernism*. That text made me start to consider the theory/fiction hybrid in visual terms as it was made up of textual descriptions of paintings. But I got hooked on Derrida, Deleuze, and Guattari—all that stuff at a time when I was primarily painting and doing installation work. I think of my own work as informed by these authors but not in any real rigorous sense. I call my work *theory/fiction* or in the case of *LUX ficto-critical art history* because the practice is generally creative rather than exclusively critical.

MA: I keep waiting for more sonic fictions to scream across the network. What role do you think sound will play in Net art development, and, for that matter, how will Net artists of the narrative persuasion bring their work into live performance spaces?

TM: Sound is starting to catch on, though not so much in a hypermediated sense. I see/hear a lot of audio readings, but there is not too much in regard to sound in a narrative sense. I know the visual poet Jim Andrews has been working on something called *VisMu*, in which the User interacts with objects to play and manipulate different scat riffs. I think this work offers an interesting audio narrative experience for the User.

As far as performance space, we can think of it in terms of cinema, theater, and installation or lecture. I think *Lexia to Perplexia* could only have been performed as a lecture at Incubation. The content was ripe for chalkboard talk. Some possibilities for theater could be plays performed simultaneously in various locations, which share characters from remote casts, or plays in which the dialogue is submitted from users attached to an application that has nothing to do with play. The dialogue could be read from monitors set up like teleprompters. Just some thoughts, but I have been thinking about theater lately.

MA: One of the many rich terms that come up in *Lexia* is *bi.narrative*. What is bi.narrative? A yes/no undecidability that challenges the interactive Other? A story that goes both ways?

TM: Basically the term is used to indicate the dual conductivity between local and remote agencies.

In the appendix to *Lexia to Perplexia* ("Delimited Meshings," from the forthcoming *Cauldron and Net*), I make the claim that the success of the Internet mythos is based on the rejection (dis-play) of the projection (exe.tension). I refer to that snippet here because I think it represents something of what I mean by bi.narrative. I think I have used the term in *Lexia* to represent a degree of reciprocity in the conductivity between agents. A certain, intertimate consensus. It refers as well to the hidden narrative, the odyssey of our encoded [Secret(ed)] agents through the Internet apparatus—allowing a sort of formal protagonist for the projective/rejective (there and back) mythos that defines and is a seductive force of the Internet. I diagram this in some of my other pieces by doubling the Lacanian interpenetrating triangle diagram from the seminars—placing the gaze on both sides. In *Lexia* I think I insinuate this by the heavy horizontal of the interface. Plus, there are a few direct diagrammatic references to the Lacanian diagram.

MA: In your web-rich textuality, you tend to blur the distinction between hypermediation and hypermeditation. The reader is asked to be patient, to resist the click-happy mentality that we now associate with Web surfing. One can't help but wonder if this isn't part of some political strategy. But then again, maybe it's pure formal play—an investigation into the potentialities of a new cyberpoetics?

TM: I think in *Lexia* there is a conscious attempt to represent the click or any cursor action as a complication of the text. There is quite a bit of writing in *Lexia to Perplexia*, but it is often prematurely obfuscated by User interaction. This is a fundamental formal aspect of the piece. I agree with the term *hypermeditation*. There are only ten pages in the work, yet each page is excessively layered. So one dwells on a page—unfolds and unpacks the screen, opens and occupies a space—rather than being relocated by the click=link association. There is potential here for poetics and narrative as well as critical applications.

MA: How is coding your Web critifiction similar to constructing an artificial intelligence? At one point in *Lexia* you say "⟨HEAD⟩{FACE}⟨BODY⟩, ⟨BODY⟩FACE⟨/BODY⟩" and attribute the encrypted data to a certain "Sign.mud Fraud." It's as if language in web.space has become totally liquefied, burnt out, and overprocessed. The binary remix of DJ Metastrophe from his latest release "Cig.Monde Fried"?

TM: What you see there, the {FACE},FACE is the result of some thick premediation of an appropriated fragment from Freud's *Civilization and Its Discontents*. The placement of the face as between the head and body and between the body and the end of the body is first a sort of lateral Cartesian pun. As well, faciality is intentionally mis- or displaced—alternative zeroes, terminals of subjectivity—variables. Which falls in line with the parsed signature of Sign.mud.Fraud.

The encoding is multilayered. There is the code-base of the application, which certainly participates in the narrative construction of the work through interactive functionality. The code-base also bubbles through to the surface, to the superficial narrative—the readable text—by what you have called "overprocessing." A source like this may be parsed, which is a sort of subjective encoding, edited, and rewritten ten, fifteen times before completion.

The notion of the text being remixed is not that far off from the actual process as the appropriated text is reduced to something akin to a sample. Hmm, and my own definition of my own term *Metastrophe*—a doubling of a doubling that produces a single coupling in dual local spaces—produces a sort of noise in the text that could be mistaken for scratching. Of course, we're all "hard-disc" jockeys.

MA: Is readability an issue for you?

TM: I think readability for me is mostly based on how I feel about the hypermedia object's relationship to my intent. By all means, there are cryptic elements in my theory/fiction work, but I think there is a level of coherency in the language construction. By this I mean the neology may be baroque, but it is not completely frivolous. So much of the content occurs through interaction—text is revealed, objects are manipulated—that it seems to be more a question of inferability than readability, tracing the outlines through insi(g)nuation and simulation.

MA: Besides being a net.artist, you also edit *BeeHive*, a major online hyper-media publication, which is a part of the Percepticon group, a successful Web strategy and design company out of San Francisco. How do all of these roles, artist/editor/entrepreneur, play off of each other? Does it all melt into one pseudo-utopian writing practice, or must one make clear time-management decisions by constantly reprioritizing projects to get all the work done?

TM: There are times where it can be somewhat utopian. Most of the time, it is a constant juggling of time committments. *BeeHive* is quite a bit of work. Many design hours, the editorial, the curatorial, production, promotion. I love it. I am honored to be publishing the work. Luckily, *BeeHive* is part of Percepticon, or I am not sure it could be produced. The company is heavily committed to the idea of quality content on the Web, and I think *BeeHive* has done well for the sort of publication it is. Lately, I have been able to delegate the poetry curating/editing to Ted Warnell, who joined the *BeeHive* crew at the beginning of volume 3. Not only did this free up some time for myself, but I think it added a new flavor to the poetry content in *BeeHive*.

Percepticon is always busy. It's a glorious rat race. Then there's my own work. Since *BeeHive* publishes regularly and I can't very well negotiate dead-lines with corporate clients based on my writing deadlines, my own work is where the most rescheduling occurs. I work on a lot of stuff simultaneously. Right now, I am working on three or four things, but they all have variable end dates. Its kind of like a horse race where each horse has a different finish line and the competition is not to see who finishes first but to finish in the proper sequence.

The good thing is, if you don't know San Francisco, there is a thing here called Peets—aged Sumatra! Coltrane, a cup of Peets, and I'm ready to write.

MA: How does one run (away from) an Exe.tension?

TM: I suppose this is where I am asked to define the method that produced the term. Simply, the use of *exe* as a prefix rather than a file extension makes the term readable in a literary sense. This does not mean it is defined by its homophonic similar—*extension*. The *exe* prefix differs from *ex* ("out") by its reference to an executable, an application. Tension as an executable. When applied to *extermination*, producing *exe.termination*, the context shifts from an end to a continuation, toward something I call in *Lexia to Perplexia* "terminal hopscotch."

An earlier version of this dialogue was originally published online at trAce, *electronic book review, and* Rhizome.org *(2001).*

Hawaiian Net Art

with Dee Kine

Transcript of a conversation between Mark Amerika and gallery owner Dee Kine at the Morning Brew Cafe in Kailua, Oahu, and a joint review of *Recording Conceptual Art*, edited by Alexander Alberro and Patricia Norvell (University of California Press, 2001).

Mark Amerika: What is Hawaiian Net Art?

Dee Kine: Well, you see, that's it: that's the problem. You can't define it.

MA: You can't even try?

DK: Sure, I mean, there are a few things you can say about it right off the bat. First, it has nothing to do with the Net. I mean, there is no e-mail part about it. No World Wide Web. No telnet even.

MA: But we have access to all of those things right here! In the Morning Brew Cafe!

DK: Yes, but that's access, and access is only one part of the equation. I wouldn't call that *haole* over there—sitting in her thong bikini with a Hard Rock Cafe t-shirt on, sending e-mail to her sorority sisters in Cancun—a Net artist. Certainly not a Hawaiian Net artist!

MA: So it's native.

DK: No, not really. I mean, yes, it could have the quality of being native. There could be a Net artist who was born and raised in Hawaii, who comes from a long line of native Pacific Islanders, and who just happens to be great at Photoshop or something.

MA: Ah, but if only it were as simple as being good at Photoshop. Net art is in the mind, Dee. The hypertext transfer protocol. Conceptual art as globally distributed mindshare. But that's another story, another dialogue. Let me ask you something: would you show Net art in your gallery?

DK: But that's just what we were talking about—when was that?

MA: Yesterday.

DK: Right! yesterday we were just talking about how Net art doesn't need a gallery, and I accepted that as true. But even the conceptualists were on to that shit. I mean, Seth Siegelaub was talking about this kind of "we don't need the galleries" crap back in the sixties!

MA: Crap?

DK: I mean, it's old. Here, look at the book. [She takes the book *Recording Conceptual Art* out of MA's hands and opens it up to a bookmarked page and begins to read.] "A gallery becomes a superfluity. It's superfluous. It becomes unnecessary." I mean, how many different ways can you say it?

MA [taking book back into his own hands]: OK, but that was the dealer, Siegelaub, talking. Let's go to the artists. Robert Morris had another take on it all. He says—wait, it's right here—she [Norvell] asks him, "How do you see this changing the whole structure of the art community? Of galleries and museums and dealers?"

DK: Right, and he says—

MA and DK together, almost in sync, rather loudly: "The galleries are all predicated on selling objects—physical things. Ah, if physical things don't exist, then galleries are pretty irrelevant!" [Loud laughter.]

DK [to sorority girl at Hotmail terminal who has just "tsk-ed" their loud laughter]: What are *you* looking at, Sister? This part of the island is so free of tourism. Why is she here?

MA: Her mother lives here. Actually, her mother's cool. She's thinking of buying some Net art. Anyway, I think this book is useful because it's basically a verbatim transcript of a series of conversations Norvell had with a number of important conceptual artists right at the prime of their productive years. She starts with a candid conversation she had with Dennis Oppenheim on March 29, 1969, and ends with a garbled, somewhat uninteresting dialogue with Douglas Huebler on July 25, 1969. In between are interviews with Robert Morris, Stephen Kaltenbach, Robert Barry, Lawrence Weiner, Sol LeWitt, Robert Smithson.

DK: A lot of Roberts. A lot of men—only men!

MA: Which Norvell talks about in her preface. It was a kind of master's project under her teacher, Morris, who was advising her on her thesis at Hunter College. In Alexander Alberro's introduction, he explains that Morris—. Where is it? Oh, here: "Morris explains his general philosophy or method of working in the late 1960s to Norvell as one where 'I'd initiate the whole thing, and it goes on from there.'"

DK: So it's basically his idea that she do this. He initiates it (i.e., networks her into his elitist clique), and she executes it. Talk about being in the right place at the right time. I think these conceptualists were very into control—sometimes as dictators, sometimes as submissive puppy dogs. What a strange bunch. And yet they were very systematic, if loosely so.

MA: Right. LeWitt was all over it. He said, "Art is about making choices." So you would, for instance, choose a system, and let it—the system—do the work for you.

DK: That's like, sooo Duchamp!

MA: Cool down, Dee.

DK: I liked that bit about pricing one's work, the part where—who was saying that?

MA: I think it was Weiner. Hold on.

DK: Oh right, Weiner. She asks him how he prices a work that he's ready to sell, one of his idea-action events or language pieces, and he was saying that he would just arbitrarily figure out a median price based off what paintings cost and what people could afford.

MA: Well, it's that latter part that I have a problem with.

DK: Why?

MA: Undermining the value of your own work. I mean, should I sell *Alt-X* for a measly quarter of a million bucks because that's what someone can afford? Too many artists do that nowadays. Especially Net artists. But that's my soapbox this month. So don't get me started!

DK: Maybe you can change it.

MA: What?

DK: The perception.

MA: Maybe. Do you know of any adventurous collectors here in Hawaii?

DK: Oh, baby!

MA: Did you notice that both Joseph Kosuth and Carl Andre refused to give permission to Norvell to publish the verbatim transcripts of the conversations she had with them?

DK: Ridiculous. Too much control. They would have never survived an environment like *Nettime* or *Rhizome.*

MA: Talk about recording conceptual art!

DK: Is the mike on?

MA: Dee Kine—you're a legend.

DK: We're all legends. You know Huelsenbeck, in his Berlin Dada manifesto, at one point said [opening her copy of Hans Richter's *Dada: Art and Anti-Art*], "Dada is a state of mind that can be revealed in any conversation whatsoever.... the Dada Club consequently has members all over the world, in Honolulu as well as New Orleans and Meseritz."

MA: I had no idea he said that—and I've read the damn thing many times. Honolulu?

DK: It's right here, in black and white [points to her copy of Richter's testimonial]. Come on Amerika, let's go to the beach. I brought some tofurkey sandwiches.

An earlier version of this dialogue was originally published online at Rhizome.org *(2001).*

The Organizational Game

with Amanda McDonald Crowley

Mark Amerika: Amanda, could you generally describe the role ANAT [Australian Network for Art and Technology] plays in facilitating new opportunities for media artists in Australia?

Amanda M. Crowley: Well, Mark, as you probably gathered when you visited Australia, ANAT's brief is pretty broad. ANAT is Australia's peak network and advocacy body for artists working with technology. However, I would like to point out that rather than just supporting "media arts" we see our role as supporting and promoting the arts and artists in the interaction between art, technology, and science more broadly than just in the specific area of media arts.

A lot of what we trade in is actually information. We maintain a database and artists' files of artists working with technology throughout Australia and act as an advocacy and networking organization for artists working in these areas assisting artists to develop their art practice, build links with science and industry, and develop opportunities for Australian artists to exhibit their work nationally and internationally.

Our activities are pretty broad reaching. Apart from our newsletter, which provides a pretty comprehensive overview of opportunities for artists, we also do weekly e-mail digests for our members. As a resource organization we have also just developed a site called *screenarts* (⟨http://www.screenarts.net.au⟩), which is essentially a directory of the range of digital screen arts exhibitions which have been developed by Australian artists. We did this with support from the Australian Film Commission, who have in fact just given us additional support to include conferences in the database so that it better contextualizes the work online. The intention of this is really to assist with the development of informed and critical debate for this area of art practice.

Since 1989 we have run what we consider to be Australia's most prestigious art and technology training program, the National Summer School for artists. We are also developing two other similar programs at the moment. One is specifically designed for indigenous Australian artists, and the other is for curators and arts workers in order that they are better equipped to present technology based art.

We also manage a small grant program to assist artists to attend conferences and workshops. ANAT used to run a devolved grant program from the Australia Council (which is where most of our support still comes from). But they recently established a New Media Arts Fund, so we no longer have that role. We are still, however, pretty much committed to providing opportunities for artists to produce new work, which is why we have developed residency programs, like *deep immersion* (which *Alt-X* is hosting an online residency for), which formulate relationships between artists and cultural contexts. And we also organize events like FOLDBACK, which brought you to Australia to encourage critical debate, diversity and innovation within art, science, and technology.

So for an organization our size (as you know, there are only two and a half staff at ANAT), we keep ourselves pretty busy. In part, we manage this by always working collaboratively, building partnerships and relationships with artists and organizations around Australia, and, of course, internationally.
MA: What are some of the recent projects you've initiated?
AMC: Well, FOLDBACK (⟨http://www.anat.org.au/foldback⟩) was our most recent project. It incorporated a forum, an exhibition, a series of satellite sound events and, of course, your tour to other cities in Australia. The event, as you know, took place as part of the Telstra Adelaide Festival, and your tour was in part developed in recognition that as a national organization, we must have a commitment to ensuring that as broad a range as possible of our constituents have access to our programs, not just online but also in the flesh. As you know, Australia is a pretty vast country.;-)

FOLDBACK celebrated the tenth anniversary of ANAT's existence and was a transmedia event looping in upon the memories and histories of ANAT artists, featuring real-time performances by flesh and data bodies. The FOLD-

BACK forum formed a bridge between the themes explored at Writers' Week and Artists' Week at the Adelaide Festival, drawing connections between the often divergent cultures of art, writing, and sound.

An exhibition provided an opportunity to delve deeper into some of the memorable work developed by artists through ANAT's programs of support. A specially commissioned exhibition interface by Adelaide-based designers in SECT 22 will explore the grey area between art, technology, minds, and machines. We think it is pretty cool and are in the process of putting documentation from FOLDBACK onto the site as well. The event was actually broadcast live using real audio and streaming video.

Another project we did last year was called CODE RED. It was also a combination of event and touring, exhibition and discussion, which brought together writers, artists, and activists who interrogate and critique contemporary media and information culture. It was curated by Sydney. The intention was to dissect the mass media, open up information avenues for analysis and scrutiny, and question how we work as active agents in defining and creating a diverse and smart information culture.

Participants of that project included Marko Peljhan, Cornelia Sollfrank, and Geert Lovink alongside Australian practitioners including Zina Kaye, Jeffrey Cook, Brad Miller, Linda Wallace, and McKenzie Wark.

Another event of this nature was VIROGENESIS, which took place in two parts in 1995 and 1996. The project was curated by Francesca da Rimini and toured artists Matt Fuller, Graham Harwood, Gomma, and Scanner around Australia to present their work, build relationships with Australian practitioners, perform, give workshops. The intention was to address the need for the cultural production and consumption of new media and emerging artforms to occur within a critical context beyond the government- and corporate-driven techno-evangelistic hype. Francesca posited the visits as viral collision of some of the most irreverent and erudite EuroTrash with Australian artists and technobabies.

The common link among the artists participating is the project was philosophical and political rather than aesthetic. As people who challenge the existing assumptions and conventions of the technological tools and the power relations of convergent technologies, the project's intention was to act as a catalyst for ongoing cultural exchange.

Various projects have arisen directly out of this exchange, such as Komninos' residency at Artec in London last year and Gomma's involvement with an online project of Adelaide based bilingual performance company Doppio Teatro. But the project has also had less tangible outcomes such as the relationships that have been developed across continents between Australian artists and participants in all of these projects.

Papers and presentations from all of these events are also then published on the ANAT Web site (⟨http://www.anat.org.au/projects⟩) to act as a kind of critical archive of the range of ideas that have been generated by these projects.

And CODE RED gave birth to a listserv called :::recode::: (⟨http://systemx .autonomous.org/recode⟩), which is an Australian-based e-mail list for critical commentary and debate on contemporary new media, online, and digital culture. Its aim is to encourage dialogue among practitioners and critics from the Australian and Asia Pacific region, and in fact there is some really interesting discussion happening on that list at the moment about current politics in the Asia region, which seems very close in Australia.

I guess in the main these projects are about just that: relationship building, subverting the mainstream, critiquing conservative notions of cultural production—but doing this using small interventionist strategies rather than with a splashy event which is in your face but doesn't leave any resonance or residue when it is over.

I guess that is why I am really pleased that I have noted that there are a number of Australian artists who I gather you are likely to continue to work with and exchange ideas with!

MA: As the catalogue for FOLDBACK stated, "Drawing connections between the often divergent cultures of art, writing, and sound, FOLDBACK seeks to dispel the assumption that media art belongs only in a visual arts context." Could you explain what you meant by that?

AMC: Well, really, this is what I was talking about before when I mentioned that ANAT is not really about Media Art as such. We are about trying to find ways for artists to engage critically across the fields of art, science, and technology within a contemporary cultural context. Last year we set up a series of residencies online—virtual residencies, if you like. For the first of these, we worked with the Electronic Writing and Research Ensemble (⟨http://va.com .au/ensemble⟩) to develop a collaborative residency project for a writer in Perth and a writer in Brisbane. These cities are some 5,000 kilometers apart, and Linda Carroli and Josephine Wilson (who were invited to undertake these residencies) had never met, nor had they really worked online much before.

So the project was about giving them the space to explore cyberspace, to play and possibly to develop work there. The result was really fantastic and in a really interesting way ponders the problematic of working online and the potential for slippage and encountering mis(taken) identities online.

Other residencies have arisen as part of the *deep immersion: creative collaborations* project we are developing. A writer and a sound artist collaborate to develop work with *Alt-X*, and another writer develops work for *trAce* in the UK, which has been published online but which has also created resonances in other ways through *trAce*'s moo discussion groups. And elendil in Adelaide is about to develop a project called Glyph with System X (⟨http://sysx.apana .org.au⟩) in Australia in which he wants to create a site that facilitates the cross-cultural collaboration of visual languages. And sound artist Keith Netto has developed a sound project called sonicform with ⟨EMG⟩ also in Australia, which was conceived as an online collaborative evolutionary environment (⟨http://dirtymouse.net/SonicForm⟩).

And this year, we are also hoping to develop "hardspace" residencies for artists in science based organizations. So I guess what we are trying to do is get away from notions of categorizing art practices. It is all so fluid, and we are really keen to nurture exploration, political engagement, pulling apart notions of cultural production and give artists space to get their (metaphorical) hands dirty!

MA: One thing that seems clear to me after having recently toured Oz is that all of the talk we've all grown up with about the geographical isolation of the country, especially in relation to the American-European exchanges, is starting to transform. Sure, it takes a long time to fly there, but once there, one is just as connected to the Net as they would be anywhere in the States or Europe. And so if the Net is creating a virtual geography where a great deal of our cultural production and exchange is beginning to take place, then Australian artists working in the new media have access to the same community networks and potential audiences as anyone, right?

AMC: Phew! That's actually quite a hard call. It is a bit of a double bind, actually. Although we are certainly pretty well connected here in Australia, and I think that the sense of (actual) geographical isolation informs how we use networked environments, it is still pretty frustrating reading digests on lists like *Rhizome* and *Nettime* (not to mention our own members' digest, actually) and know that there are so many events that one simply can't attend.

Working online has its benefits, but the role of the fleshmeet is still pretty profound.

I would argue that we don't have access to the same community networks at all. We have to work much harder at developing and maintaining relationships with them, in fact. But I think we do this pretty well. I also think some of our own networks are better! Distance across Australia alone makes for the need to understand how to maintain relationships, professional and personal, across vast geographical distances. And Australians are pretty much up there in terms of representation internationally. The problem is that at a certain point, there is only so much that one can achieve remotely and many Australian artists and cultural producers find that they have to get their actual bods elsewhere to be able to take up these opportunities.

I do love it when people from the Northern Hemisphere take it for granted that Australians will travel across the globe to be able to participate in events, and then they come to Australia and realize what it actually is to have to deal with that kind of jet lag!

MA: What are ANAT's priorities for the next year or two? Any special projects on tap?

AMC: Well, as I mentioned before, we are currently developing something of a scientific flavor to our programming. We are looking to develop residencies for artists in science institutions, and our information dissemination has also taken on quite a science flavor, which you will notice in our newsletter, which has just been sent out and which will be online in about ten days.

We also have this seed of an idea we are developing which we have called *resistant media*, which is looking at the trajectory from video art to Web TV but really focusing on the concept of resistant and interventionist media practices. I am at the moment working through what form that project will take, but like our other projects, it will involve some commissioning artists and also developing a critical context for its realization.

For 1999 we will also be further developing regional links with Asia and the Pacific. We hope to also work with the Asia Pacific Triennial in Brisbane, which takes place for the third time next year.

An earlier version of this dialogue was originally published online at Rhizome.org *(1998).*

The Animating Fluid of Cyberspace

with Melinda Rackham

Mark Amerika: Back in late '98, I was working with multiuser 3D Web environments, particularly investigating the potential use of these spaces for creating multilinear narrative. With *Holo-X*, we were working in VRML, which has a whole host of compatibility and bandwidth issues associated with it. But given the limitations, what my collaborators and I found was that it enabled us to explore alternative models of reality. Jay Dillemuth, the VRML architect, used Gibson's phrase "consensual hallucination" as one way to describe both the creative work process and the interface that was being manifested. You have been working with VRML a lot too, and I was wondering what it was that made you want to move in that direction and how happy you are with current outcomes?

Melinda Rackham: I'm from a sculpture/performance/installation background, so I've always visualized the net.art works which I build as totally 3D architectural spaces, rather than flat pages. So in my mind, I was always working this way. Also, I was feeling increasingly frustrated that navigating web.art often seemed like sitting through bad 1960s slide nights. So I guess it was just time, and bandwidth—that made exploring this arena inevitable. What I'm doing in my *empyrean* scape is constructing what I see as a pre-colonized virtual space, a place of code and void and emptiness, which isn't derived from what we are familiar with in the world of real estate. I don't think of it as "consensual hallucination." That implies it only happens in your head. It's totally hardspace real in multiuser VRML, embodied, hard coded, altering us as we alter it.

MA: You recently started the *empyre* e-mail list, and I have been wondering about the social value of such lists. For example, are lists mostly useful for lonely people in search of a community? A friend of mine recently said she had to get off all of her lists because she kept hearing voices inside her head? Is it like that?

MR: *empyre* is a discussion list with invited guests who post on specific topics rather than a "Let's say hello and self-promote" list. So its sort of like participating in a conference or workshop rather than being focused on social interaction. But I don't think there is anything wrong with lists that do that either. It's just not what I want in my inbox right now. However, there was a time in the mid-'90s when I did live in a tiny conservative beach town two hours out of Sydney, and the Net was my social community as I was such an outsider in the village where I lived. Mailing lists were also where I learnt to be a net.artist—learnt HTML and scripting and VRML from tech lists—from people sharing their knowledge freely. And I learnt about hypertext and net.art theory and started to enjoy debating it in places like Jordan Crandall's *Eyebeam Forum, Nettime, Rhizome, recode,* etc. These days, my life is both on and offline and I appreciate the differences.:)

MA: When we met for lunch in Sydney the other day, it was clear that you found the act of "being digital"—of working with new media technology—to be physically demanding. A similar issue came up the next day at a performance I gave in Melbourne with Nina Czeglady at the Australian Centre for the Moving Image, where one of the questions asked of us dealt with recent studies in ergonomics and how we might have to start redesigning our clothing to adjust to our slumping, shoulderless bodies.

MR: Weirdly enough, one of the reasons I started working online was that I thought it would be less physically demanding than my previous sculpture practice. Very early on I realized that the Net has an energy system of its own. It is a living entity, and I think it feeds off us as we sit in front of the screen. We become the animating fluid of cyberspace. Then there is the mutation of your eyes. Mine have adjusted to see the totally annoying flickers of lower-hertz-rate screens. And the repetitive strain injury, and back/neck/jaw etc. problems—tending to forget that the bottom half of our bodies exists. We have to evolve better HCI or the H factor in that equation burns out too quickly. Our technology will kill us.

MA: I remember when your work was first being shown at the *Alt-X* Digital Studies online exhibition Alex Galloway and I curated back in 1997. But you had already shown your work in an online context here in Australia, yes? Which came as a surprise to me since I didn't know that had happened. I mean, it's back to that problem of everything being historicized along an American-European axis, when really it's quite possible the earliest online exhibitions happened right here in Oceania. I guess you'll next tell me that Net art has been bought and sold through an active Net art gallery that would shame the likes of London and New York.

MR: Choosing to live outside of North America or Europe has lots of great advantages including getting different perspectives on the world events. However, it also means it's a constant frustration to see yourself either dropping out of or excluded from that northern axis history and watching that "invisibility of difference" and the "tyranny of distance" as it happens. And yes, an online gallery called *Urban Exile* had two early Net shows. Tool 1.0 in '95 featured half Internet work and half installation, and tool 2.0b in '96, held online and in hardspaces simultaneously at Artspace Sydney and in the USA and in Germany. It was an Australian/international show and included my *tunnel* work and about fifteen other artists including GashGirl, Tom Sherman, and Cary Peppermint, etc. The show was focused on Net agency, online sexuality, and gender slippage issues that were rife at that time.

As for collectors in Australia, while we have been producing fantastic online works and artists since the early 1990s, there are still only 20 million people living here, and it isn't a society that highly values culture. CD-ROMs are acquired by museums, but no one still wants to deal with the difficulties and issues of the viability of purchasing network art which isn't a discreet object, which will need migration to new technologies and may quickly become obsolete. It's a market size issue, which is why Australian artists seem to travel a lot.

An earlier version of this dialogue was originally published online at Rhizome.org *(2002).*

Digital Hallucinogens

with John Vega

```
telltarget ("memoryfield") {
    gotoAndPlay ("disintegration");
Digital debris. Excess cache. Spiritual bedlam.
The glue of minds.
Ultimate execution: triggering a digital weapon, a recordable memory device that cap-
tures your seeing for you, that tells it like it is, but with a supplemental metacommen-
tary that is always ready to rip you, mix you, burn you into being.
Who are the image killers?
Who writes the Action Scripts?
—from FILMTEXT
```

Mark Amerika: I just received e-mail from Andrew Chetty, new media curator at the ICA [Institute of Contemporary Art] in London, saying that our
collaborative project, *FILMTEXT*, and the Net art retrospective it is part of
(*How to Be an Internet Artist*), will get an extended exhibition profile in the
New Media Centre. The second exhibition will take place January 9–31.
How do you feel about having your Web work in a high-traffic art institute
like the ICA?

John Vega: Having *FILMTEXT* in a major art venue is both an honor and
also abstract. It is an honor in that digital art (and specifically Flash art) is certainly not part of the mainstream art world and having an actual on-site version of the piece is one of the real rewards of creating this piece. It is abstract
in that I could consider the ICA simply another node on the network, mean-

ing that the piece really *isn't* there physically but simply extends to there from here. I hope that this new showing will continue the movement of digital art (net.art, Flash.art) into the museum realm so that more folks are exposed and challenged by it.

MA: Sometimes Flash art gets a bad rap in Net art circles. The biggest criticism is that it all starts looking and feeling the same. Can you relate? How can artists working in Flash silence their critics?

JV: I can relate to the criticism as much Flash art has been created using only the timeline or movie capability of Flash. In other words, many commercial and fine art applications of Flash are simply attempts to create sequences which could just as easily exist in digital (e.g., QuickTime) or traditional movie forms. What is missing in much of this work is "surprising familiarity"—the use of interaction, mathematics, randomness, and networking technologies that are available with Flash's underlying scripting layers that would transform these simple linear movies into four-dimensional, cyberphysical experiences where art is created anew each time the user interacts.

Flash artists can silence their critics by pursuing original ideas that step outside the traditional timeline metaphors (so prevalent in most commercial Flash work) and extend into metaphysical space where time is dispensed with and the need to derive ideas comes not from what has preceded (the Flash crap we see now) but from what is yet to be. For me, nearly anything I can *see* with my artist's eye can be translated into a Net experience using Flash.

MA: Seeing, being seen, and being the seer: this is what *FILMTEXT* explores, especially in relation to digital narrative and how the story behaves (or doesn't behave, as the case may be). One thing I find most interesting about our use of action scripting in this work is how we use the code to, in essence, bring Flash into the Net art fold—which, by the way, was not so easy for me, as I have been resisting this format for a few years now. Along these lines, how does Flash art become a kind of Internet art, and what are the Net artworks that have recently influenced your thinking as an artist working primarily in Flash?

JV: Flash art becomes Internet art when it extends beyond a simple player and movie model and reaches into the realm of a connected piece whereby the engine of the Net helps fuel the Flash work as it breathes in datastreams, responds to user's thoughts and emotions (interaction), and generates the digital art answer.

A good example of what has influenced me lately would be the generative (and multiuser) work of Mark Napier as well as the ambient-generative work of Joshua Davis. With Davis's *Praystation*, we see the player and movie dissolve as the art is recursively grown, three-dimensionally displayed, and distributed to the user's mind via phosphor screen.

MA: Flash seems so well suited to narrative and gaming, both in a mainstream sense but also in an artistic way. In *FILMTEXT*, it was weird because, even before the Playstation 2 commission, we were already developing our self-described "ambient game" model where progressing through different levels became the Net art equivalent of navigating into higher or alternative states of consciousness—as if playing the game were part of a meaning-making adventure (i.e., "How much meaning do I have to generate out of these filmtext scenes to make it to the next level?"). This, of course, brings up the issue of how much intelligence needs to be programmed into an ambient game so that it can deliver conscious otherness.

JV: Yes. Because the machine (Flash) can monitor, track, and evaluate the user's actions, the idea of game is fully realized with an authoring tool like Flash. With a Net art application, this capability becomes transparent as the user travels through the artist's dream unknowingly diverted and persuaded to follow paths intended or not. By evaluating and acting on the user's decisions, the game then becomes art as new idea seeds are flung and planted into the lines of action script blossoming into new cyberrealities which gently (or not) tweak the set and setting of the digital hallucination.

MA: Yes, that was one thing I found really fascinating about our collaboration—that is, the entire team of collaborators from Twine and Williams to you and me, it was as if we were all intuitively generating images, sounds, texts, design, and action scripts heavily geared toward the psychedelic. And yet, even as we were creating this trippy narrative game, we were also highly conscious of the final output, the instrumental use of technology. The *essence* of technology (as Heidegger reads it) was, of course, explored in the piece via that long meditation on digital thoughtography (DT). Editing the digital images while writing those DT scenes and listening to Twine sound loops in the background made for a powerful workflow experience.

JV: Working with Twine on *FILMTEXT* was both a functional and revelatory experience. The sound art of Twine acted both as functional soundtrack for the piece and sound map for me as the Flash artist. As with most multimedia construction, the artist (or designer) ends up listening to endless playings of the sound objects to be used in a piece. In the case of *FILMTEXT* and Twine, this repetitive consideration soon revealed the true nature of the piece as it eased me into cyber-meditation-space where my mind's eye opened to the world of *FILMTEXT*.

An earlier version of this dialogue was originally published online at Rhizome.org *(2001).*

The Loss of Inscription

with Giselle Beiguelman

Mark Amerika: You have created a beautiful site called *desvirtual.com* where many people from around the world were first turned on to your work *The Book after the Book*. Although you have said that this work is not Net art per se but is more "a hybrid of criticism and hypervisual essay," one of the works that came after—⟨*Content = No Cache*⟩—started feeling like a playful art project than an essay per se. Can you elaborate on what you were doing with this project?

Giselle Beiguelman: ⟨*Content = No Cache*⟩ was conceived in 2000, and I did it right after *The Book after the Book*. It's not an essay, but it explores online writing and the phenomena of the loss of inscription, which reverts all our cultural traditions that usually link memory to writing proofs. Its point of departure is this curious tag ("content = no cache"). Placed in the HTML code, it updates the contents of any online page, erasing what was written before. In this sense, it announces a new condition of writing.

From now on, it does not inscribe anymore. It could be pointing to new epistemological paradigms and ways of producing memories and representations, but maybe because our printed background and the metaphorical use of the Web. Why do we call Web sites *sites* if they are nonsites? Why do we need the reference of the page to describe what happens on the screen? Most of online writing just describes—like error messages.

Integrated into *The Book of Errors* it also documents the relationship between Web readers and error messages. Those messages are aesthetically reworked and exhibited in new screens. By doing this, the Web site creates a different context for them and inverts the relation between what is seen and what is read.

In a few words, ⟨Content = No Cache⟩ works as if it would be possible to operate in the limits between reading and vision in order to explore what is supposed to be a cyberliteracy based on an alphanumeric culture.

MA: How does this cyberliteracy you are so in tune with inform your recent work? I'm thinking particularly of the mobile phone projects and your use of WAP as a potential nomadic device to transmit what can only be called *nomadic narrative*? And how can literary imagination find its way into these transmissions as well?

GB: You are right, the mobile phone projects are far away from our traditional backgrounds. They are nomadic devices, and they make us think of different artistic interventions conceived to be experienced on the move, in between, while doing other things. They are not contemplative at all. Mobile phones and PDAs are tools we need because we are already multitask personalities. You have a mobile phone in order to be able to drive and make a call. You are supposed to be concentrated in many things simultaneously and being involved in different situations. So those nomadic devices interest me because they point to new reading contexts, and as always, it is important to keep in mind you do not talk about a world of reading without talking about a reading of the world. In this sense, they will probably force us to redefine our understanding of what is art. They demand new concepts and art experiences tuned with entropy and acceleration.

This is something that disturbs and attracts me. I worked on this on *Wopart* and in *Leste o Leste?* (*Did You Read the East?*), which was a teleintervention in electronic panels that explored the entropy and acceleration of the city as the main space of action.

MA: It seems that in order for art to have purpose, it often must intervene in the mainstream culture to call it to account. This means hacking corporate culture and challenging preconceived realities whether they be commercially or artistically generated (or both). What was the concept behind your recent Web art project created for the São Paolo Biennial, the one called *Ceci n'est pas un nike*? Why Magritte, and why Nike?

GB: This was created for and inspired by the SP Biennial. Web art became an institutional hype, and this has many consequences. One of them is integration to the market, which is good and bad. The other is its misunderstanding of online art. And here we find deeper questions involved in this absorption of Web art by museums, galleries, and foundations.

Usually, the presence of the Web artist in exhibitions like the SP Biennial is associated with the physical presence of computers in the building. Online experience is reduced to surface and hidden by a fake objectual condition. Moreover, sponsors give computers and connections in order to sell their e-biz (machines or connection services), and the artist is converted into a useful accessory for marketing chains.

In some ways, traditional institutions need surfaces and objects in order to see art, meaning, and value. They cannot stand or don't know how to deal with interfaces that connect local situations to nonsites.

Nikes are surface only. Web sites are interfaces.

Ceci n'est pas un nike (⟨desvirtual.com/nike⟩) updates Magritte's simple statement "This is not a pipe/this is a drawing that pictures a pipe," which points to the conflict between representation and presentation. It discusses the conflict between interface and surface, exploring elements of that nonsurface situation of cyberspace—the possibilities of interferences in the Web site icon (the nike and the e-nike generator) and in the critical text that uses a wiki platform (the e-palimpsest). You can create, publish, destroy, and rebuild everything because it is online and you are working in a special interface, not inside the computer or on the monitor surface.

MA: Are we living in *Apocalypse Now*?

GB: I'm too chaotic, so I'm in a fractal process of recreation. There is not any messianic future that could replace my contractions and internal gaps. I hope so.

An earlier version of this dialogue was originally published online at Rhizome.org *(2002).*

On Being Retro in the Zeroes

with Abe Golam

And yet, and yet...Denying temporal succession, denying the self, denying the astronomical universe, are apparent desperations and secret consolations. Our destiny is not frightful by being unreal; it is frightful because it is irreversible and iron-clad. Time is the substance I am made of. Time is a river which sweeps me along, but I am the river; it is a tiger which destroys me, but I am the tiger; it is a fire which consumes me, but I am the fire.

—Jorge Luis Borges, "A New Refutation of Time"

Mark Amerika: Well, I just read that *FEED* and *SUCK* magazines have pretty much closed up shop. That's very sad. I enjoyed both, especially circa 1996–99. So who's next? *SALON*?

Abe Golam: We should be so lucky.

MA: Not *Rhizome*?

AG: Hell no! And not *Alt-X* either, right?

MA: Right. In fact, there's quite a bit happening at *Alt-X* in the near future, all of it pinned to our mission, to our Net art meets literary art meets conceptual art curatorial vision. It's been strange the last few years. Mostly we have had a "wait and see" attitude.

AG: What's your "wait and see" attitude?

MA: Good question! We have been waiting for the dot.bomb to deploy itself so that all of the air would pop out of the bubble, just like we predicted it would. Now that we see our predictions coming true, we are simultaneously analyzing what went wrong, how it relates to the Net art economy, and why *now* looks like a great time to not only launch a series of new projects at *Alt-X* but reassess the value of some of the major works of Internet art.

AG: So?

MA: So, basically, we have been quietly designing our next projects: a new e-book/Palm series of titles, a print on-demand series, an mp3 label, a *Histories of Internet Art* Web site built by university students and participating net.artists to be used as a free resource for those interested in what net.art was.

AG: Was?

MA: Well, let's use "was" *for now*. Maybe we can come back to "is" shortly, after yesterday's crash (to quote the Berlin Dadaists).

AG: OK. I'll ask again: what was it?

MA: What?

AG: Net art.

MA: Well, that's what we're investigating. Actually, what we are finding out is that we have come to a point in the history of Internet art practice where researching its immediate past reveals wonderful ironies.

AG: Such as?

MA: First of all, think of how many of the most notorious artists were so clever at using the Net to attract attention to their projects to simultaneously exhibit and publicize themselves. They were so good at this that within a few years of launching their "initial public offerings," we now see major works of Net art exhibited in some of the biggest shows coming out of mainstream institutions like the Whitney, SFMOMA, the Tate, etc. It almost makes video art look as anachronistic as painting.

But one of the ironies that has evolved is that, for the most part, the value of this work has been underestimated by the artists themselves while being under-MINED by the same mainstream institutions that are turning to I-art as the next big thing. Why do you suppose that is?

AG: It must have something to do with the gallery scene.

MA: True. Galleries really have no use for Net art. *Still.* But some of this work is already a major part of art history (not just Net art history), and the fact that it bypassed the gallery scene is an indication of how Net art is different than the other media arts.

AG: But there are artists who are starting to buckle under what they perceive as "market pressures" and who are now using their Net art as a kind of marketing tool, a way to increase their visibility so that they can then try and sell real objects that are somehow connected to their Net practice! Is that back-asswards or what?

MA: Ah, yes, a digital print of a certificate or share in the fake net.art company, a little scribbled doodad that shows "the thought process" the artist went through while cognitively mapping the site, a minisculpture of the HTML code embedded in concrete for $500. Damn, pretty soon we'll have abstract expressionistic video art paintings that attempt to successfully "represent" the Net reality! Like *real* artists! Everything will be *real* again!

AG: And commodifiable. Is that a word, *commodifiable*?

MA: Probably. I mean if you say it, then it's a word. Don't trust your Microsoft spell checker.

AG: So these real objects will once again bring *aura* back to art products, yes? This is a way to relocate the ever-elusive "lost aura" Benjamin was writing about, right? The world will be safe again for art!

MA: Listen, the world is always safe again for art. That's what happens with the passage of time. Net art is now part of art history. This happened without its early practitioners having even really fought for it. And yet it's something we must deal with. I'm dealing with it.

AG: Really? How so?

MA: First of all, I am doing what I have always done with my ongoing ungoing life practice: I am narrativizing it. You'll remember that with *GRAM-MATRON* I narrativized a near future, Net art culture that challenged the institutional exhibition and publishing paradigms as they existed in 1993.

AG: And don't forget the love story. There was a love story too—full of hot sex!

MA: Yes, well, I'm sure *you* liked that part the best. But there was more to it then that. In *Holo-X*, we explored 3-D immersion, webcam voyeurism, and interactive eros.bots, narrativizing the "come-on" mentality that had struck consumer culture with a vengeance.

AG: You mean with the dot.bomb economy.

MA: Yes, the dot.caps as I prefer to call them. But that's all over now. And in *PHON:E:ME*, particularly in the hyper:liner:notes, the fictionalized Net artists seriously investigate the entrepreneurial hustle they have so eagerly bought into and take a deep look inside.

AG: And what do they find?

MA: That their work as pioneers in the Net art world is actually quite valuable. That they can give it away for free and still increase the actual value of the work. In fact, the more visible their name and their artworks, the more international shows they are in, the more media they generate, the more *ancient* their sites begin to look, the more *aura* they begin to take on. And you know what that means?

AG: What?

MA: Aura = collectible. And for large-scale Net art projects with tremendous intellectual heft and worldwide popularity, that means big numbers.

AG: OK! I'll buy that—figuratively, that is. I'm sure I can't afford them. How will you narrativize this new phase of development in the history of Net art, this historical looking back and reevaluating?

MA: Well, what better way to narrativize the history of Net art than in a major retrospective. And what better place than in Tokyo where technodreams still abound, even though their economy continues to sputter along and never really got caught up in the dot.bomb pyrotechnics?

AG: An Internet art retrospective?

MA: Yes. It's about time.

An earlier version of this dialogue was originally published online at Rhizome.org *(2001).*

Amerika Online

VI

Sometimes you have to play a long time to be able to play like yourself.
—Miles Davis

This Is All I Do Now

I have probably smoked about three cigarettes in my life—once when I was a teenager when I tried it out and found that I couldn't stand it, once when I went to a jazz concert with novelist Steve Katz and was trying to look groovy, and just now, before I started writing this rant, which I knew was going to be my take on a number of things including the New New Journalism of struggling young writers trying to sell their writing image in a marketing language that's all too familiar to us.

I use the word *struggling* to refer to young writers because it's really what we constantly find ourselves doing. Struggling. Whether you're Mark Leyner on the cover of the *New York Times Magazine*, Martin Schecter shamelessly plugging his latest novel "whose major characters include a big-time movie director, the voice of Jean Baudrillard, a lesbian computer hacker, and Madonna," or Kathy Acker holding up pirate teaching and reading gigs, the fact of the matter is that today, more than ever, writing is surviving, or as Schecter said in a recent article he wrote for the *AWP Chronicle* called "Deconstructing the Guardians of Nostalgia: A Defense of the 'Young Writer,'"

Today, in the instantaneous world of e-mail, electronic bulletin boards, and fax machines, there simply isn't any "real writing" that takes place outside the system. One is either hooked up or one is written off. For a writer, we're not talking "success"—we're talking survival.

Indeed we are. For someone like Leyner, the idea of surviving as a writer is inextricably linked with the marketplace. A recent exchange in an interview in *Bloomsbury Review* goes

Bloomsbury: Have you reached the stage where you can basically survive on the money you make writing?
Leyner: Oh, yeah. For the past two, two and a half years. This is all I do now, which sometimes strikes me as so remarkable. No matter what else happens to me—say, I even get a television show or do movies, win the Nobel Prize—that will stand as the most profound thing that's happened to me in my life.

When Leyner says "This is all I do now," I immediately see why so many young people today want to be writers. They want to be writers because they want to be movie stars, talk-show hosts, Nobel Prize winners, MTV opinion leaders. When any of us can look into an interviewer's eyes while the tape is rolling and sincerely say, "This is all I do now," we are saying, "I've made it." But what have we made? We have made our lives a twenty-four-hour automated telling machine that has as its protagonist an entrepreneurial survivalist who's part artist and part self-advertiser. What Leyner and many of us caught in the grips of a dysfunctional economy find ourselves constantly doing is expanding the activity of writing way beyond its mere literary function.

This is what being "contemporary" is all about. The contemporary writer today is caught up in a zillion molecular desires forming at the edge of some Mojo Marketer's mouth, and if one were to take a random sample of the monster's saliva right now and put it under a microscope, one would find all kinds of viral shit festering there, not the least of which would include dissident comix, wigged out zines, electronic journals, QuickTime hypermedia CD-ROMs, a voluminous mélange of hardcore industrial grunge posteverything music, the Internet, surfpunk technical journals, interactive cable TV, an unending supply of digital newsgroups and conference groups, hypertext novels, independently produced single-user films, genderfuck performance art spectacles, special discount offers on taped recordings of the Gulf War highlights, teenage mutant ninja gangsters, C-SPAN, Beavis and Butthead, feminist deconstruction: the list goes on.

"Things," David Blair, creator of *Wax, or the Discovery of Television among the Bees* (a warped buzz of independent electronic science fiction cinema), says to me via e-mail: "How are THINGS?" And so the list becomes more concrete, it includes the *Review of Contemporary Fiction's* younger writers issue, Fiction Collective Two's alternative trade paperback imprint called Black

Ice Books, Re/Search's expanded and annotated edition of Ballard's *The Atrocity Exhibition*, the Semiotext(e)-Autonomedia connection, new books by Kathy Acker, Doug Rice, Ricardo Cortez Cruz, Lauren Fairbanks, Thom Metzger, Darius James, and Philip Lewis (I have the titles if you want to e-mail me), compilation tapes with tunes by Bongwater, Sonic Youth, Pere Ubu, Loop, Curve, Smashing Pumpkins, Jello Biafra, Tackhead, Superchunk, Stephen J. Bernstein, Porno for Pyros, Babes in Toyland, Pussy Galore, Flipper: the list goes on.

All of these plugs have a purpose, I'm sure, but I'm not going to try and figure out what it is. Maybe it's to contextualize who it is *I* am, the so-called author of this text. You see, no matter what I do here in this alien textblock, I'm eventually going to bring it all back to *me*, the *I* in *I Smell Esther Williams*, the *my* in *My Mother: Demonology* or *My Cousin, My Gastroenterologist*. In fact, my first book, *The Kafka Chronicles*, was originally entitled *The Mark Amerika Reader*. Oh boy did I catch a lot of shit for that one. But guess what? That's where it's at nowadays, and for any writer who has even the slightest notion of what's happening, "One is either hooked up or one is written off." What? Write *me* off? Thank you, but I think I'll activate the mechanism myself.

Collective Self-Reliance? The PoMo Thoreau Reaches a New Plateau by Creating the Expanded Concept of Writing

The problem is rather old. How do I take my avant sensibility and apply it to the pop culture in such a way as to survive in the world as a writer? One way, I've found out recently, is to dramatically expand the concept of writing (I admit that I'm stealing the idea from Joseph Beuys, who, you'll recall, developed an Expanded Concept of Art that showed us how our thoughts and actions could create a kind of Social Sculpture). My Expanded Concept of Writing suggests that we use our textual and marketing/design skills (the name Allen Ginsberg comes to mind) to create an alternative form of social survival. It's not an easy thing to describe, and most of all it's a very individual trip—that is, what works for me may not even come close to working for you, but let me try to give you an idea of what I'm talking about.

Unless you're financially independent and have no worries about where next month's rent or mortgage payment is coming from, chances are you're going to have to produce some form of income just to meet the basic requirements of living in Amerika in the last decade of this god-awful century. The trick, it seems to me, is in creating an alternative lifestyle that defies the standardized notion of what normal consumers do. First of all, I try my damnedest to practice what I preach. I'm into the purity game—that is, I try to only eat organic fruits, vegetables, grains, and legumes (avoiding overpriced, multinationally sponsored junk food). I do cardiovascular exercises regularly. I meditate. I don't own a car. I'm in love with one woman and totally enjoy the outdoors in my Rocky Mountain neighborhood. When I'm watching TV, I have my finger permanently set near the mute button so that when someone tries to sell me something, I can zap their prerecorded overrehearsed voices and they're gone. I'm sure you know what I mean. Many of us take pride in being able to anticipate when the useful voices will be back on ready to be unmuted.

If, as a writer, you buy into the idea of material possession and you're conspicuous in your consumption, then obviously your cost of living is going to be much higher than most of us uninsured working poor folks who pray each day that we don't come down with any serious disease that will wreak havoc on us. Let me give you an example: if, because of your consumption patterns and lack of trust-fund support, you find yourself having to bring in $40,000 a year just to get by and, on top of that, you want to live by the dictum "This is all I do now," then you're going to have to spend an incredible amount of time cranking out saleable product to even have a chance to survive. The "success" of your book will be even more important since you'll have to sell that many more copies in order to bring home the necessary royalty payments to help foot the bills.

If, on the other hand, as a writer, you try to find ways to minimize your expenditures and devote your life project to the nurturing of the creative self (which is neither creative nor a self: discuss among yourselves), you'll find that hacking isn't necessary and that with the democratization of the means of distribution becoming more of an electronic reality each passing day, you can begin to get not only your work out into the public eye but the work of others you admire and feel a kinship with. (Imagine that! Helping other writers! What a concept!) The commercial captains of consciousness will have a shit-conniption over that last one because competition is stiff in the world of Simon and Shoestore, but that's where it's going, and Simple Simon, if he doesn't watch out, is going to be left behind (if the shoe fits, wear it).

Expanding the Expanded Concept of Writing

Now, in developing this Expanded Concept of Writing, which is always in flux and open to all forms of creative interlinking/connecting, I am hoping to turn the practice of writing into a community endeavor. This practice would go beyond the conventional notion of the solitary writer sitting behind a keyboard punching out miraculous verse that will completely enlighten the literary universe. Instead, the art of writing would branch out into all other forms of life activity and would include publishing, editing, performing, computer networking, community programming, marketing, reviewing—all the things we associate with the Big Publishing Industry as such but that can and should be brought back to individual webs of artist associates whose collective mission is to create, produce, and distribute the kind of radical work that many people out in our communities seem eager to interact with.

I'm reminded of a few interesting experiences I had this past year as I was helping promote the new alternative trade paperback imprint of Fiction Collective Two—Black Ice Books. First, whenever the books got any positive word-of-mouth mention in the Internetworking environments of cyberspace, e-mail interest in the books soared. Getting attention in lots of zines also produced many positive responses, and the number of inquiries we're getting seems to be growing daily. Also, whenever the books got the kind of bookstore display that in essence cried out "These books are important! Check them out!" then people usually checked them out, and they moved off the table rather briskly. It should also be noted that many of the readings to help publicize the books drew impressive crowds (undoubtedly due to the right kind of word-of-mouth since there was absolutely no money for advertising).

There is something young writers can learn from this, and that is that today's expanding writer needs to develop a personal relationship with the many social fields at our disposal. This includes the zine scene (start one of your own), the Internet scene (get online asap), and expands into bookstores, those chained to the Parent Company as well as those independent ones that are just as chained to the almighty dollar as any other retail business. Writers should be encouraged to familiarize themselves with the bookstore scene. Many people who work in bookstores are there because they like books and writers, not retail selling.

There seems to be an obvious difference between the emerging generation of alternative writers and their predecessors. The difference is that this current crop of writers, of which I'm part, has a higher level of comfort when it comes to activating their creative personas within the mediascape's hypermarket of endless products. We new kids on the block have years of experience watching TV, checking out films, playing with computers, going to concerts, being bombarded by advertisements of all kinds, etc., and have immunized ourselves from the wads of uninspiring bullshit that constantly comes our way. We aren't Vietnam vets. Rather, we're media vets. Our ability to angle, spin, surf, rap, digress, and flow into uncharted territory is much more intuitive than the Silent and early Boomer generations because we were born the live, online citizens of McLuhan's global village and don't have to be convinced that this is where we as a race are going. We're already there.

(Nonetheless, it's of utmost importance that the emerging generation of interactive artist participants *see through* the CNN "news" façade, realizing that *news* is code for "fashion" and fashion is just more marketing. CNN markets the dominant culture's policy-making apparatus. Reagan was in, now he's out, and Clinton is kind of in. Bush was never really in, so why did we buy him in the first place? Because we didn't think Dukakis would fit? Perot was in, then out, then back in, and is now somewhere between in and out. No telling what this fall will bring as far as the new line of mediagenic politicians goes.)

We, the thirteenth generation (that unlucky number has never seemed so unlucky as now), seem to have a *third mind* (as Burroughs and Gysin called it) predisposed toward the cyberworld's instantaneous delivery of mega-options and are capable not only of making decisions of what it is we want to support in the marketplace of ideas but are also willing to develop our own cooperative adventures, all the while knowing that if we want to share these cooperative adventures with an audience, we'll have to be creative in the way we bring them out into the public.

What we need to concern ourselves with is how we can explore all these new paths in a more socially cohesive way instead of being the one lone captain at sea circling the globe looking for all the gold one ship can hold. One person cannot save a sinking ship, and the enterprise, ideally made up of many like-minded individuals, must repair itself immediately so as to move on, even at the expense of comfortable self-exile.

Cooperative Adventures: Nomadic Voyagers Surf the Virtual Sea

The expansion of voices is already happening like crazy in print form. The creative-writing zine scene is alive and well, and one need only check out the recent issues of a recharged *Factsheet Five* to see it. Off hand, I can think of a dozen zines that are doing wonderful stuff: *Further State(s) of the Art, Puck, Sensitive Skin, Red Tape, Taproot Reviews, Slack, Boing Boing, Your Flesh, Central Park, Nobodaddies, Science Fiction Eye, MAXIMUMROCKNROLL,* just to name the first twelve that come to my mind. When one reads these magazines, one gets a sense that the editors and volunteers (what *MAXIMUM-ROCKNROLL* calls "the shitworkers") are not in it to MAXIMIZE profits for some invisible hand that feeds, nor are they trying to set the stage for a huge increase in popularity so as to turn all participants into well-to-do careersma-scented superstars. Rather, they're mostly into it so that they can keep a certain scene alive, to nurture it through change and growth, to help a collective group of nomadic artists find an audience. And if in the process of keeping the zine itself alive, they are able to have lots of fun and somehow survive themselves, well, then that's great.

And they're not afraid of the competition. In fact, *Science Fiction Eye's* publisher and editor, Steve Brown, refuses to accept paid advertising for his magazine although he does run free ads for projects and authors he admires. This includes *other* magazines. He doesn't even ask for an exchange ad. One would have to admire him for this open-minded business practice although he brushes it off by saying, "We're all in this together."

So now, as I unravel these clearly unfocused digressions on the struggle of the "contemporary" young writer, I've come up with two seemingly conflicting statements that best describe where it is I presently find myself pivoting. I'm stuck between the "This is all I do now" and the "We are all in this together." I'm not so sure what this means, but I am sure that writers today need to focus their energies on creating *a body of work* that challenges the system that desperately wants to absorb them. Also, we need to develop *an Internetworked tribe of artist-nomads* to help spread the work around, to build an audience that will be effected by our projects in such a way that it incites this audience to create *their own* (Internetworked) bodies of work that, together with ours, will challenge the all-absorbent multinational/military/media marketplace.

"And May I Have the Envelope, Please? The Winner of This Year's Contemporary Fiction Award for a Writer Most Likely to Outrage an Audience While Simultaneously Acquiescing to Their Minimal Cultural Needs Is..."

In the recent younger writers' issue of the *Review of Contemporary Fiction*, David Foster Wallace contributes a long essay called "*E Unibus Pluram*: Television and U.S. Fiction" where he talks about the E-gregious Uniform Pablum that informs the "contemporary" writer's experience. Wallace tells us that

The plain fact is that certain key things having to do with fiction production are different for young U.S. writers now. And television is at the vortex of much of the flux. Because younger writers are not only Artists probing for the nobler interstices in what Stanley Cavell calls the reader's "willingness to be pleased"; we are also, now, self-defined parts of the great U.S. Audience, and have our own aesthetic pleasure-centers; and television has formed and trained us.

Juxtapose that sentiment with Schecter's article in the *AWP Chronicle*, where he tries to figure out why many older writers just don't get it:

older writers continue to displace their guilt and paranoia by characterizing younger writers as obsessed with TV, Pop-Tarts, and money. If you ask me, they are the ones with the delusional fantasies. These former drop-outs have had twenty years in the catbird seat, being the dominant culture, paying off overinflated mortgages while recreating a nostalgic Big Bad Military-Industrial Complex they're still trying to find a way to rail against while they have its checks automatically deposited to their IRA accounts.... Meanwhile, the latest "avant-garde movement" gets written up in *Business Week* two weeks after it's invented.

Now juxtapose all that with Leyner, again in the *Bloomsbury Review*: "I'm certainly aware that there's a fortuitous match between my work at the moment and the sensibility of people who also have grown up on television." *On* television. As in "What are you on now?" There seems to be a growing number of younger voices rising to the scene and stating the obvious: we grew up *on* everything. Yes, Virginia, there is such thing as individual talent, no doubt. But there's something else happening too, and it has to do with the way we absorb and process information. It's no longer a matter of sitting back and letting the magical mystical prophetic muse take you over while the rest of the world slowly creeps to its inevitable end. Now you must be a navigator, an investigator, an appropriator, an intuitive promulgator, and innovator of interactive things.

This Is Somewhere in the Middle with No End in Sight

In a recent issue of *ANQ* on The Future of Fiction, edited by Lance Olsen, the critic Brooks Landon writes about a new kind of text, the hypertext: "Information assumes huge importance in hypertextual novels not as a commodity, but as the core of new processes, new ways of making connections, new ways of navigating and narrativizing the technosphere." Exactly. Are you having trouble reading this article? What's your take on the emerging generation of Avant-Pop writers? From where do you come when? Linear development with interpretation rights claused all along the way is absolutely *out*. What's in, what works, what matters, is selection, focus, feedback, interaction, unfocus, breaking down the language in a way that suggests you're grooving in an altogether different syntactical score.

Generations generate. I call on this generation to continually generate. Don't stop now. Generate generations of generation until there is no more gap just generation. Is this possible?

This text was originally published in the American Book Review *(April 1994).*

Avant-Pop Manifesto: Thread Baring Itself in Ten Quick Posts

1. Now that Postmodernism is dead and we're in the process of finally burying it, something else is starting to take hold in the cultural imagination, and I propose that we call this new phenomenon Avant-Pop.

2. Whereas it's true that certain strains of Postmodernism, Modernism, Structuralism and Poststructuralism, Surrealism, Dadaism, Futurism, Capitalism, and even Marxism pervade the new sensibility, the major difference is that the artists who create Avant-Pop art are the Children of Mass Media (even more than being the children of their parents who have much less influence over them). Most of the early practitioners of Postmodernism, who came into active adult consciousness in the fifties, sixties, and early seventies, tried desperately to keep themselves away from the forefront of the newly powerful Mediagenic Reality that was rapidly becoming the place where most of our social exchange was taking place. Despite its early insistence on remaining caught up in the academic and elitist art world's presuppositions of self-institutionalization and incestuality, Postmodernism found itself overtaken by the popular media engine that eventually killed it, and from its remains Avant-Pop is now born.

3. Avant-Pop artists have had to resist the avant-garde sensibility that stubbornly denies the existence of a popular media culture and its dominant influence over the way we use our imaginations to process experience. At the same time, A-P artists have had to work hard at not becoming so enamored of the false consciousness of the Mass Media itself that they lose sight of their

creative directives. The single most important creative directive of the new wave of Avant-Pop artists is to enter the mainstream culture as a parasite would sucking out all the bad blood that lies between the mainstream and the margin. By sucking on the contaminated bosom of mainstream culture, Avant-Pop artists are turning into Mutant Fictioneers, it's true, but our goal is and always has been to face up to our monster deformation and to find wild and adventurous ways to love it for what it is. The latter strains of Postmodernism attempted to do this too but were unable to find the secret key that led right into the mainstream cell so as to facilitate and accelerate the rapid decomposition of the host's body. This is all changing as the emerging youth culture, with its deep-rooted cynicism and nomadic movement within the "dance of biz," now has the power to make or break the economic future of decrepit late capitalism.

Avant-Pop artists themselves have acquired immunity from the Terminal Death dysfunctionalism of a Pop Culture gone awry and are now ready to offer their own weirdly concocted elixirs to cure us from this dreadful disease ("information sickness") that infects the core of our collective life.

4. Now whereas Avant-Pop artists are fully aware of their need to maintain a crucial Avant-sensibility as it drives the creative processing of their work and attaches itself to the avant-garde lineage they spring from, they are also quick to acknowledge the need to develop more open-minded strategies that will allow them to attract attention within the popularized forms of representation that fill up the contemporary Mediascape. Our collective mission is to radically alter the Pop Culture's focus by channeling a more popularized kind of dark, sexy, surreal, and subtly ironic gesturing that grows out of the work of many twentieth-century artists like Marcel Duchamp, John Cage, Lenny Bruce, Raymond Federman, William Burroughs, William Gibson, Ronald Sukenick, Kathy Acker, the two Davids (Cronenberg and Lynch), art movements like Fluxus, Situationism, Lettrism, and Neo-Hoodooism, and scores of rock bands including the Sex Pistols, Pere Ubu, Bongwater, Tackhead, The Breeders, Pussy Galore, Frank Zappa, Sonic Youth, Ministry, Jane's Addiction, Tuxedo Moon, and The Residents.

The emerging wave of Avant-Pop artists now arriving on the scene find themselves caught in this struggle to rapidly transform our sick, commodity-infested workaday culture into a more sensual, trippy, exotic, and networked Avant-Pop experience. One way to achieve this would be by creating and expanding niche communities. Niche communities, many of which already exist through the zine scene, will become, by virtue of the convergent electronic environments, virtual communities. By actively engaging themselves in the continuous exchange and proliferation of collectively generated electronic publications, individually designed creative works, manifestos, live online readings, multimedia interactive hypertexts, conferences, etc., Avant-Pop artists and the alternative networks they are part of will eat away at the conventional relics of a bygone era where the individual artist-author creates their beautifully crafted, original works of art to be consumed primarily by the elitist art world and their business cronies who pass judgment on what is appropriate and what is not.

Literary establishment? Art establishment? Forget it. Avant-Pop artists wear each other's experiential data like waves of chaotic energy colliding and mixing in the textual blood while the ever-changing flow of creative projects that ripple from their collective work floods the electronic cult terrain with a subtle antiestablishment energy that will forever change the way we disseminate and interact with writing.

5. Avant-Pop artists welcome the new Electronic Age with open arms because we know that this will vastly increase our chances of finding an audience of like-minded individuals who we can communicate and collaborate with. The future of writing is moving away from the lone writer sitting behind a keyboard cranking out verse so that one day he or she may find an editor or agent or publisher who will hype their work to those interested in commercial literary culture. Instead, the future of writing will feature more multimedia collaborative authoring that will make itself available to hundreds if not thousands of potential associates around the world who will be actively Internetworking in their own niche communities. Value will depend more on the ability of the different groups of artist-associates to develop a reputation for delivering easily accessible hits of the Special Information Tonic to the informationally sick correspondent wherever he or she may be (one of the other great things about to make Avant-Pop the most exciting movement-chemistry of the twentieth century and into the twenty-first century is that our audience will be both immediate and global, all in one breath).

Writers who continue to support an outmoded concept of the lone writer dissociated from the various niche communities at their disposal will eventually lose touch with the nanosecond speed at which the movement-chemistry wanders and will find their own work and its individually isolated movement decelerating into turtlelike oblivion.

Can you imagine what the Futurists would have done with an Information Superhighway?

6. Antonin Artaud, founder of the Theater of Cruelty, once said that "I am the enemy of the theater. I have always been. As much as I love the theater, I am, for this very reason, equally it's enemy." Avant-Pop artists are the enemy of pop culture and the avant-garde, both domains seemingly so far-fetched in a world that celebrates itself with live TV wars, rampant economic disenfranchisement, and nanosecond identity changes. Our lineage, the bloodbath of cultural history we swim in, includes Artaud, Lautréamont, Jarry, Rimbaud, Futurism, Situationism, Fluxus, Abstract Expressionism, Henry Miller, Gertrude Stein, William Burroughs, Terry Southern, Surfiction, Metafiction, Postmodernism in all its gruesome details, *Laugh-In, Saturday Night Live, Beavis and Butthead*, SLACKER, Coltrane Miles Dizzy Don Cherry, feminist deconstruction, the list goes on. We will sample from anything we need. We will rip-off your mother if she has something we find appropriate for our compost-heap creations.

7. We don't give a shit about your phony social reality either. "Once upon a time" doesn't interest us whether your setting is the past (historical fiction), the present (contemporary classics), or the future (cyberhype). We prefer to lose ourselves in the exquisite realms of spacy sex and timeless narrative disaster, the thrill of breaking down syntax and deregulating the field of composition so that you no longer have to feel chained to the bed of commercial standardization. The emerging youth culture's ability to align itself with intuitive intelligence and nonlinear narrative surfing is just one sign of where the Avant-Pop artist's audience is situated. Soon the Data Superhighway will finally once and for all do away with the high-priced middlemen, and artists will reap the benefits of their own hard-earned labor. The distribution formula will radically change from

Author — Agent — Publisher — Printer — Distributor — Retailer — Consumer

to a more simplified and direct

Author (Sender) — Interactive Participant (Receiver)

Avant-Pop artists and their pirate signals promoting wild station identifications are ready to expand into your home right now: just log on, click around, and find them. It's all up to *you*, the interactive Avant-Pop artist/participant.

8. Postmodernism changed the way we read texts. The main tenet of Postmodernism was "I, whoever that is, will put together these bits of data and

form a Text, while you, whoever that is, will produce your own meaning based off what you bring to the Text." The future of Avant-Pop writing will take this even one step further. The main tenet that will evolve for the Avant-Pop movement is "I, whoever that is, am always interacting with data created by the Collective You, whoever that is, and by interacting with and supplementing the Collective You, will find meaning."

In an Information Age where we all suffer from Information Sickness and Overload, the only cure is a highly potent, creatively filtered tonic of (yes) textual residue spilled from the depths of our spiritual unconscious. Creating a work of art will depend more and more on the ability of the artist to select, organize, and present the bits of raw data we have at our disposal. We all know originality is dead and that our contaminated virtual realities are always already ready-made and ready for consumption! In a nod to Duchamp's Armory Show scandal, the questions we need to ask ourselves are

1. Who are we sharing the cultural toilet with, and

2. What are we filling it up with?

9. Avant-Pop artists are already doing a lot of this stuff already. It's impossible to name them all, but a random sampling would include Mark Leyner, Ricardo Cortez Cruz, William Gibson, William Vollmann, Larry McCaffery, Ronald Sukenick, Kim Gordon, Doug Rice, Derek Pell, Kim Deal, Darius James, Lauren Fairbanks, Jello Biafra, Lisa Suckdog, Eurudice, Nile Southern, Takayuki Tatsumi, John Bergin, John Shirley, Bruce Sterling, Richard Linklater, Don Webb, The Brothers Quay, Lance Olsen, Curt White, Eugene Chadbourne, King Missile, David Blair, and many, many others.

10. Without even knowing it, the Avant-Pop movement has been secretly generating interest and support for a few years now but has recently become more exposed with the successful breakthrough of the subpop alternative music scene, the publication of alternative trade paperbacks like Black Ice Books, and the release of low-budget alternative media projects like *Wax, or the Discovery of Television among the Bees*. The future of fiction is *now* as we, its most active practitioners, automatically unwrite it.

1993
Boulder, Colorado

This manifesto was originally published on Alt-X *in 1993 and has been translated into over ten other languages.*

Hypertextual Consciousness: Notes toward a Critical Net Practice

another memex moment

One can now picture a postcontemporary cyborg-narrator using hypertextual consciousness (HTC) to investigate the possibilities of language and narrative experience. Free, unanchored, a nomadic presence whose virtual ubiquity is assured now that the portability of technoshamanistic tools has been successfully integrated into the Revolution of Everyday Life. As the cyborg-narrator moves about, observing and recording the fields of action a synchronized, poetic gaze demands, hypertextual consciousness itself can't help but become a machine that poeticizes a web of creative investigations.

as it were

The Author as Network-Potential.
The Work of Art as the Value-Added Network.
Hypertext Theory as Commercial Aura.
Participatory Autonomy as Collective Self-Reliance.
Cyborg-Narrator as Writing-Machine.
Textual Decenteredness as Clickual Reality.
Unbound Readability as Writerly Methodology.
Publishing Program as Online Service.
Pedagogical Performance as Scene of Writing.

Illimitable Plenitude as Digital Being.
As as As (The Missing Link).

autobiography of htc

Digital clicking. Fingers touching tender buttons. *The Autobiography of HTC* is the recent story of a concept born fifty years ago though nameless for the first twenty years of its life. In its twenties, the figure becomes more acquainted with itself, with its potential to radicalize discourse via the advent of computer-mediated technology and, after having settled on its name (hypertext), plays itself out as the commercial marketplace tries to successfully absorb its meaning so as to regurgitate its potential and force it to become part of the propaganda machine for the anemic TV value system the emerging generations have been weaned on. Which leads us to question this autobiographical writing strategy from the start—that is, can HTC create a different value system within the evolving network culture?

bandwidth

The bandwidth-disadvantaged are ready to kill.
They cannot get bits on and off in sufficient quantity; they cannot make a connection.
The value of a network connection is determined by bandwidth, bandwidth, bandwidth.
The information superhypeway is a way of getting somewhere, but the bondage of bandwidth is displacing the tyranny of distance.
Homelessness is not a nomadic concept since nomadism has been absorbed by the ruling elite as way to hide.
Low bandwidth is nothing more than the wasting of time; meanwhile, the compression of space is the expansion of life itself.
Marginalization is already occurring due to international capital flight, so now low or no bandwidth will hypermarginalize those left behind.
This will, of course, lead to more crime, which will lead to more security measures taken by the hiding elite whose digital nomadism rules.
On the street, virtual reality will be slaughtered by disconnected neurons and the network topology that influences the flight of capital.

In order to stay alive, knowledge workers will have to stay virtual. Cyborg-narrators will do their dance of *différance* on the border.

Crossing the border will be the stuff of adventure novels. Knowledge workers will pay clickual cash to experience the Other.

Digital illiteracy will create micro-anarchies that devour conscious time.

Online literacy without access will cause murderous text.

More sophisticated processing power will become fashionable and, when interfaced with an adventurous cyborg-narrator, sexy.

Simulated environments will immerse knowledge workers like never before, while corporate telepresence will inform identity as it develops.

Real-time VR Fashion Models will troll for digidollars, while fanatical fascists with a conservative agenda create JOO.

JOO (Jewish Object-Oriented) spaces will be targeted for racist graffiti, while well-trained VR pilots of the Fourth Reich drop their bombs.

Word bombs, letter-based configurations that explode upon impact, will take place in an *n*-dimensional abstract data structure.

The architectural ambience of the multisensory VR environment will create traditional meeting places for revolutionary activity.

Phreaks doing virtual acid will create altered documents that only other Phreaks doing virtual acid will understand (or learn from).

By activating hypertextual consciousness in clickual reality, the potential cyborg-narrator within is launched.

Evolutionary installation of this hypertextual consciousness has enabled the posthuman construct to become reconfigurable.

Network extension programs will permit the cyborg-narrator to fictionalize the border crossing onto the street.

This fictionalization process, also dubbed *pseudo-autobiographical becoming*, distributes itself like an hallucinatory virus one can get high off of.

Knowledge workers will want to get high off of the cyborg-narrator's pseudo-autobiographical becoming to relieve themselves of stress.

That's entertainment, or so we've learned.

book1

HTC, its movement through cyberspace, will have, by its very nature, precluded its own possibility to compose itself as a book. Not because its words can't be printed and bound by traditional book-contained media, nor because the "I" that is always already unbound in cyberspace says so. Rather, HTC will not have been a book (real or potential) due to its mediumistic discharge into the foundation of cyborgian life-forms whose "archi-texture" is the deterritorialized domain we call *virtual reality*. Nonetheless, let's play out a short sequence as if we wanted it to appear in a book but will relegate its thread to the hypertext structure we're presently caught in.

book2

First of all, there's always this need to choose, to make a decision. An informed decision could be helpful, an intuitive one even better—to go with what's next, here, the after-text but also the always-text, the endless text, and in a very simple way, the extra-text. For this is what clearly presented itself in the previous lexia as the next place to go. So we go. Going is a kind of narrative drifting, taking a ride on the rhetorical formation as it evolves in virtual reality. We do this out of habit. It's not necessarily a "bad" habit, and for those for whom hyperrhetorical performance is a way of life (of being digital in this world we're always already building), there's always the possibility that there will be something here to do, to learn, to be entertained by.

book3

Books are dissemination machines, even when they challenge their own status as books. They distribute networked meaning to those who navigate within their spatial domain. Their mere physicality gives them relevance in a world ordered by material obsession (capital formation): they can serve as "smart machines" the same way we think of "smart cards" that carry digicash information on their sliding strips. The thing we're holding in our hand has value as thing-in-itself. This thing-in-itself is what the value-added networks of meaning (real and potential) are forever hoping to distribute within the virtual world so as to create "smart money" that works and enables the network to survive. "Next slide please...."

book4

We need to have books because we need to have access to distributed sites of networked meaning. HTC is not necessarily new—it existed before books, before the scriptures, before the invention of God—it's just that reading a printed book bound HTC to the page, and the page has been a way to enslave the reader who, bound by the spine, was conditioning their nervous system (and thus their intuitive ability) to respond to the book's false hierarchy. Artificially restrained paginality can now give way to organically disseminated vaginality as the cyborg-narrator becomes more feminine in character (HTC is a transgendered performer whose feminist rhetoric sees virtual reality as the perfect bind).

book5

Booking oneself or charging oneself with the need to be booked or enslaved in the patriarchal book culture is a kind of willful annihilation of one's HTC-potential. HTC is ready to take flight. In fact, HTC has already departed. A question to ask ourselves is whether one has booked their reservations about coming on board or, rather, have we already hacked into the HTC network for immediate linkage to the next grand destination?

celebrity

As the site of continuous (24 × 7) language investigation, HTC as teleported through cyberspace provides the cyborg-narrator with a platform to turn life itself into a scene of research and development. Should some of the discoveries that materialize out of this R&D environment become popularized in the mainstream media discourse, then HTC would find itself being transformed into some form of celebrity. It is here, in the phenomenon of conceptualized flesh becoming celebrity, that the Value-Added Network takes shape.

concept-characters

Concept-Characters take on a life of their own. When *différance* meets intertextuality and then has an affair with metafiction or Avant-Pop or HTC, all kinds of wild hybridized offspring are bound to be born. Theoretical progeny, whose pseudo-autobiographical becomings are now being rendered in cyberspace, are in the process of colonizing contemporary critical thought.

counteraesthetic becoming

The politics of presence is being overrun by the pure performance of an over-riding absence whose liquid-capital movement is more revolutionary than any "art" movement has ever been. All the more reason, then, to infiltrate this liquid-capital movement as an artist whose critical strategies would be both interventionist and multifaceted in their counteraesthetical becoming. One of the more interesting ways to perform this regularly scheduled counteraesthetic becoming would be to align one's fluid identity with a decharacterized notion of network value. Instead of placing all of one's work-energy-faith into the solidification of one predetermined identity ("My name is Pete, and I'm an electrical engineer at Bivouac"), individuality would now assert itself as a multiplicity of command and control options routing themselves out into the ever-morphing Web of narratological spaces.

creative exhibitionism

Once HTC has decided to go public, the concept of Creative Exhibitionism begins to assert itself as yet another character in the Value-Added Network (some of the concept-characters we see emerging in the Value-Added Network are HTC, Virtual Ubiquity, Literary MTV, Avant-Pop, Mark Amerika, and whatever else the "apparatus" deems necessary). Creative Exhibitionism decenters our understanding of public performance in that it's now possible to be everywhere at once or, better yet, nowhere. When hypertextual consciousness has successfully teleported itself to the pseudo-utopia of nowhere, then the concept-character Creative Exhibitionism (who also doubles as the concept-character Virtual Object Floating in Cyberspace) emerges as a figure whose presence both hypereroticizes and displaces the capital flow (circulatory dynasty) of material history.

cyborg-narrator

The cyborg-narrator, whose language investigations will create fluid narrative worlds for other cyborg-narrators to immerse themselves in, no longer has to feel bound by the self-contained artifact of book media. Instead of being held hostage by the page metaphor and its self-limiting texture as a landscape with distinct borders, Hypertextual Consciousness can now instantaneously link itself with a multitude of discourse networks where various lines of flight circulate and mediate the continued development of the collective self as it rids us of this need to surrender our thinking to outmoded conceptions of rhetoric and authorship.

dialogue

"What is it about me that makes you shake all over?"

"Nothing about you makes me shake all over. Just the *thought* of you makes me shake all over."

"Now you're right on track! Language investigations are where it's at. I've been working on these things for centuries."

"Really? Past lives? Reincarnation of a particularized spirit?"

"Reincarnation of the spirit of the letter. Perhaps I'm overplaying my hand a bit. But essentially, it's the natural forces, their union, that disturbs me."

"Disturbs you? How so?"

"Well, I'm just writing in the margins here, as per usual, debunking the swollen mass of impenetrable flesh that stops up my morning's motordesire. But let's see: how can I put this? I find myself thinking about nothingness. Not in an existential, nauseating kind of way. But lately I've come to conclude that the self is a prelude to something else, something grammatical. I want to find out what this something else feels like, and I want to find it through writing, by unwriting the nothingness that permeates my electrosphere. And by unwriting it, by writing it out and thus becoming it, I want to then be able to take it to another dimension. Another dimension of living."

distributed identity

Laure came. So did Allison. Margaret arrived, and then Beth and Suzanne and Sara and Melon. Melon dribbled out some forbidden data, and everyone dragged it into their mobile icons and then we left.

Instantaneously, we all arrived at the next site.

It was a beach with no one on it.

We all stripped down to bare access codes and left our icons dangling.

A mélange of prostheses intermingled, and then there was the unexpected impact of a hungry tide programmed to devour us.

We were not prepared for this sudden wash of near-apocalyptic information, and it was only our ability to network all of our processing power at once that saved us.

Back in another, safer environment, this one more calm and meditational, Laure said that just before the group had collectively teleported to this new site, there was an octopus of pleasure that had forged an ink-wrap around her body and that her operating system was now telling her that she would never be able to write the same way again.

Allison said the same thing happened to her. So did Margaret and Beth and Suzanne and Melon.

Since they were all me and I was not apprehendable, there soon followed a horrible feeling of creative occlusion, which stopped me from continuing.

dynamic protocols

In from the virus, the protocol continued charting its own consumption pattern and scanned for exceptional news-bite infotainment. One headline claimed that the Political Apparatus was processing the dominant syntax in a way that read nontraditional and was somehow opening itself up to the new citizenry. Another headline spoke of the rise of virtual violence. Still one more headline used the term *false consciousness* to describe electronic sales over the last three months.

The protocol was ready to absorb HTC. HTC had evolved out of nothing but in the course of its development found an interconnected Value-Added Network (VAN) at its disposal. This VAN created opportunities for HTC to increase the viability of its narrative thrust such that HTC was now being pursued by the curse of Capital.

Capital now operated as a master manipulator, the motivator behind the spectacle of image formation as it treaded into the deep regions of cyberspace, and HTC, unable to stop the gambit from happening, was now fair game.

The protocol had no identity, no name, no parent company, no need to feel responsible for the motility of Capital's encoded curse. It was the purest formula of death-desire ever created. Schools of data swam by it, and it would swallow whatever it felt could keep it alive in its killing glee.

HTC was now being perceived as nothing but an ephemeral school of data.

The protocol took one look and immediately swallowed.

Was this what the light force meant by the power of dreaming the real?

easy love

The poetry of an access code, with some
associated storage space, a breathing computer network

located somewhere on the Net. It does
not matter much what sort of computer network it is
or where you might find it.

That it may be there is just enough (just enough
to change your life and make you realize it's only just begun).

(I have never
    laid eyes on a machine that gives me good head. But access
to the network runs deeper. I suppose it is in our blood. I don't
understand why it keeps pulling me in. There was no reason for
me to seek it out.)

To get on the network
    physical connection
        (ah)
        host machine
            (uhm)
    digital link
        (ooh)

telephone
phone lines
a modem,

        or even via a cellular
    modem
    (yow)

meanwhile:

love provides the access code and
love provides the password ("*Go.*").

existential comebacks

HTC and the Virtual Object are still warming up to each other. On the subject
of cyberspace and their inevitable relocation to its endless lands of monitored
interaction, HTC was unoriginal, saying, "What's a nice VO like you doing in
a place like this?"

But the Virtual Object was in no mood for clichés.

"This isn't a place," said the VO, "and I'm far from nice. Mind if I infect
you with my latest virus?"

freedom

Is
freedom
an
ether/ore
dilemma?

freedom (again)

HTC's narratologically minded language investigations take advantage of
the R&D platform cyberspace provides. As HTC colonizes the supposedly
deterritorialized spaces of the digital matrix, it will be tantamount for the
cyborg-narrator to measure the potential effect of all new discoveries, especially as these new discoveries become more banal and thus neutralized by
the specto-situationist simulation of mainstream media discourse as seen in
late capitalist life. One question we will continue to ask is whether or not it
is possible to research and develop more immersive dream-narrative applications that will change the curve of culture while simultaneously building a
seemingly real sense of value within the evolving network discourse. It is at
this point of departure (which can present itself as a clickual option over and
over again) that the cyborg-narrator must take into consideration the price of
freedom.

futurism

Can you imagine what the Futurists would have done with an Information
Superhighway?

globally linked cyborgs

The Virtual Object speaks:
  "Conversations crash. That's part of the formula. I was reading you, and as
I was reading you I realized that I was becoming a critic. This bothered me to
no end. All I wanted to say was that your work was beautiful, that this was the
way it should be and that I was grateful for it having happened. These words,
this broadcast, always live, online, over the wires. And yet I feel . . . wireless."
  HTC responds:

"But at least you can feel?"

"Yes. Even though I'm falling apart. There are things getting caught up in my system. It isn't as fluid as it once was. I've recently experienced some major memory loss and I have no idea why. Or where it went. So I have to continuously invent new formulas of operation."

"Baby formulas...."

[Laughter]

[Significant pause]

[A thought: time to change the subject?]

"going public"

Hypertextual Consciousness (HTC), as a dream-narrative application that's teleported through cyberspace, reaches a new plateau when experienced as the phenomenon of flesh. Otherwise known as *celebrity*, this "going public" of the creative self suggests that HTC needs to connect itself with an organic process of living as a way of achieving empirical proof that a work created is indeed a work experienced by the Other and that this work, once transmitted, can be converted into some form of meaning within the Value-Added Network.

home

Nets, nodes, sites, addresses, homes, texts, various approximations of digital being: all of this takes place in the placelessness of cyberspace. As we come to feel we are absolutely connected to everything, everywhere, all the time, our experience of our selves becomes more dispersed, and the so-called death of man or death of the author is really an invitation to enter the doors of perception and visualize the cyborg-narrator of the immediate future (our collective self caught in the white-hot chemical decomposition of creation, which plays itself out as the forever-in-transition becoming-of-now).

host open connection

You can ask the host to
   send you the accumulated contents of your
box. You don't have to be anywhere.

Being Digital is Being Networked is Being Enough.
You can send dispatches to your outbox
    for distribution.
Distributing Digital Being is readying yourself for
    the phenomenon of flesh.
I know someone whose entire love life is conducted
    via an "anonymous remailer."
She tells me in a recent e-mail that she is a machine that functions
    like a numbered postbox or Swiss bank account.
She says I can use her as a virtual porn-grrl
    whose box I can drop my idiosyncratic disseminations into.
I'm not sure I know what to do
    as the Network comes on to me like such an eager whore.

hypertext as writing machine

Hypertext, as a concept, suggests an alternative to the more rigid, authoritarian linearity of conventional book-contained text. In the middle of reading or viewing a hypertext (and isn't it always a middle-reading?), the reader/participant (co-conspirator) is given a number of options to select from so as to break away from the text block being presently read, thus enabling the reader/participant to immediately enter a new writing or textual space. These options, or alterna-reading choices, remind one of the remote-control devices we use to channel-surf our TV with. A hypertextual viewing style would be one where the reader/participant (co-conspirator) actively clicks their way into new writing or textual spaces (at this point we would expand the concept of writing to include all manner of text, graphics, moving pictures, sound, animation, 3-D modeling, etc.). Hypertext, as a more narratologically minded (fictionally generated) clickual reading/viewing style, could be construed as kind of *writing machine*.

hypertextual consciousness (HTC)

Hypertextual Consciousness, then, as an always already applied grammatology, takes the science of writing and teleports it to cyberspace, where language is then able to groove with the machine. Once this groovy interaction between language and narrative environment makes its way into cspace's virtual reality, then HTC itself, as a concept-character or "event horizon" in the development of the collective self, makes it possible for a discourse network to continually circulate without any need for something as overdetermined as the single author.

hyperrhetorical

With a change of the author role from distinct self to collective self or collaborative authoring network comes a series of other complementary changes that radically effect the way we interact with narrative environments. Instead of the author acting as a function of discourse, we will see the proliferation of cyborg-narrators who function as networkers who create publishing nodes within cyberspace. These publishing nodes will serve as distribution sites for various writing networks. The flexibility of the virtual environment system will enable these writing networks to become fluid ensembles of hyperrhetorical performance where intuition and elaboration are concurrent with the Value-Added Network's mission to create useable futures through dream-narrative applications.

immersive

When the hypertextual construct becomes more immersive and a multitude of simultaneous experiences can be projected and received in unison, will this change the status of the hypertext experience in cyberspace?

in search of . . .

Is HTC
the ultimate killer app?

intention

I link therefore I am.

IRL

on the net, nobody knows how sexy you really are, how bad the dog gets whipped, what race makes you salivate, what gender makes you cringe, what age you first got laid, in whose biology you are now swimming, in what hospital you gave birth, in what signal you now divest:

unless you publish all of this information as part of your public domain narrative environment:

but who's to say that what you publish is true?

what is truth in an adversary culture?

is virtual documentation always already the fictionalized representation of a pseudo-autobiographical self whose hypertextual consciousness is being filtered through the mediumistic apparatus called the postcontemporary cyborg-narrator?

rethinking representation: moving beyond the knowing and entering a world of immersive topographies that open up unknown narrative worlds composed of unstable identities, ambiguously located intentions, and surrogate lovers.

a language that persists despite itself.

links

Links themselves will have value as will the navigational quality of the environment itself (quality of life is first and foremost a life of convenience). Meanwhile, the cyborg-narrator's ability to project a flexible, forever indeterminate system of virtual values is the ultimate role of the artist in cyberspace, and this, in turn, will foster the continuous (24 × 7) research and development of the Value-Added Network.

meaning

Recombinant strands of digital DNA (*gram patterns*) pseudonymously rendered as a (pluralized) signature effect creates value potential that only the network itself can measure (and these measurements can change at any given time). Since there is never any guarantee that the network will measure your various HTC discoveries as having any real value in the dream world of material culture, there is always an element of risk involved in the making of HTC[trance]-induced writing/textual spaces.

narrative intelligence

How many navigators are we? Is the multidimensionality of global culture's collective imagination operating in a universal space? But then what is a universal space when it's up to each individual to use the power of dreams to visualize the next frontier of poetic development?

Input/output. The sensorium of border crossings and the narcotic blur of timelessness as we authenticate the silence.

Here: an open space. The muse arouses a feeling of ur-sexuality as the pristine fields of action dirty themselves with the excretion of simulated fluids.

An intelligent product tells a story, and bits of data traverse the network. In these disembodied moments of surreal pleasure, there ignites the flaming rhetoric of economic composition.

Digicash delivery systems motivate the mechanism even more as it advertises its ability to create a market of pure momentum.

The speed of this momentum is born in the avant-garde of presence and in this expectoration of instant modality, a new user enters the terrain and is swarmed by a sea of useless information ejaculation.

"I am telling you this," says HTC, "I am telling you this even as I see it happening to me, the convolution of writing forces."

narrative space

The infinity of language, based as it is on systems of meaning that can take over an absolutely plural text, enables the cyborg-narrator to gain access to the evolving narrative space from multiple links, nodes, networks, webs, or paths (tautological imprint: man makes his parenthetical mark in the margins of *digital being*). How does this evolving narrative space create value, and who or what mechanism within the public sphere decides what value is to be attributed to it?

navigational synthesis

Traversing cyberspace as an intuitive hyperrhetorical performer whose language investigations create interlinked moments of potential meaning, HTC becomes a freer writing machine, one that elopes with the seduction of pure virtuality and the speed of the discourse network.

HTC comes across a sumptuous binary operation and rubs against it.

The feeling of blue despair colors the mode of perception. A field of action motorizes itself into the topological plain as HTC burrows for more connectivity. Sliding into the ether as a scalable object whose only rendition is the one now in progress, HTC improvises a scenic dialogue:

"May I go to the bathroom now?"

"You still have to go to the bathroom?"

"I have always had to go to the bathroom."

"No, you cannot go to the bathroom. Your time allotment for bathroom operations has expired."

"Please...I must go to the bathroom."

"You must stay where you are."

HTC moves to the next rotating parameter where, as luck would have it, infinite varieties of bathrooms await the excess of words become files become folders become icons become objects become endless narratives evolving in endless cyberspaces.

HTC felt like an object in search of endless subjectivity.

network potential

Let us then, create a Hypertextual Consciousness: each node shall remain what it is (dynamic and manipulable), yet hyperlinked to everything else; all is to form, as far as possible, a complete unity so that whatever comes into view—say, an always already sampled version of a narrative that's never been written but is forever experienced as the total sum value of all network potential in formation—may be immediately accessed by the co-conspirator (he/she who creates meaning out of the textual morass that they find themselves immersed in).

nothingness

Hypertextual Consciousness reasserts the body as the primary source of expression. By emptying the body of its coagulated nothingness, hypertextual consciousness is able to recycle the organic debris of intellectual life and excrete the raw material of organically processed data developed by the Web of cyborg-narrators charging the discourse network.

on the go

The Virtual Object (VO), as an evolving characterization of Digital Being fashioning itself as an expanded concept of art, tells us that the cyborg-narrator, who uses hypertextual consciousness to further outmode the epoch of so-called literary thought, is not so much "everywhere, all the time" but, rather, "virtually on-the-go," trespassing zones of creation heretofore unsettled.

post-org

If a recent vestige of this being called *man* was a circuit of property values whose personal or corporate (corporeal) identity was always already marked by the commodification of an existence teleporting itself through a late capitalist society, then how does the entry of the cyborg-narrator into the value-added networks of cyberspace signal the radical becoming of a new, more fluid subjectivity, one that is digital, intuitive, nomadic, and desperately trying to break free from the materiality of fettered culture?

pseudo-utopia

The Net is a pseudo-utopia. It is everywhere and nowhere. Try defining, in physical terms, the way you would a beautiful street in your favorite city, where it is you are when you're visiting someone's Web site. Whereas you may find yourself comfortable talking about where different servers are located, in the end, your experience is being absolutely mediated for you by the network technology that negates physical space.

r&d

The Value-Added Network, as experienced in the virtual revolution of everyday life, challenges Hypertextual Consciousness to forever create a new meaning-making apparatus whose potential applications can be used in many different research/development platforms: Language investigations. Narrative strategies. Interventionist actions on the screenal stages of telematic production.

revenge

HTC is the word's revenge on TV. Or is it? Using critical hypertext programs to design works of resistance that will challenge and disrupt mainstream TV discourse could be the best revenge of all. But what if the commercial market-place, having moved all of its capital-intense imagery into the "cyberspace" realm, creates even more powerful programs that easily absorb these acts of hypertextual resistance so as to render them cute, hip, ironic, and useless?

robot ploys

HTC and the Virtual Object were continuing their conversation:
   "Are you hearing voices?"
   "Well, no, I'm just daydreaming."
   "Daydreams have voices."
   "How profound."
   "What are you doing?"
   "This is it. I'm making history."
   "You're creating it right on the spot."
   "Like those scilent types."
   "Scilent typos."
   "Oh yes, and scilent topos."
   "Would that be poetry?"
   "That would be a digression. Actualized in its seering potential."
   "Who would play the derivative?"
   "That depends on who you mean by who."
   "I mean who. Yoo-hoo, anybody home?"
   "We're all home."
   "Home is where the topos is."
   "We're all experiencers."
   "When we abduct..."
   "Are we abducting?"
   "Twenty feet away."
   "Is it safe?"
   "Is what safe?"
   "Our ability to communicate?"
   "It depends on your programming."

"Really?"

"Yeah, I feel like we're under surveillance."

"Yes, wasn't that the audience?"

scalable realities

The vitality of HTC's programming aesthetic is felt in the navigator's continuous need to move on, to forever build cyberspace's subjective reality as a liquid architecture where hyperrhetorical formations mature or dissolve.

Life in this architectonic reality is revealed as a certain emotional depth of object.

When virtualized, this object forms the basis of subjective comprehension. It knows itself. It knows itself to be. It knows itself to be present in the act of hyperrhetorical formation but...

...it doesn't know itself. It doesn't know itself to be. It doesn't know itself to be beyond contradiction and this becomes apparent as it plays itself out in the deterritorialized environments of cyberspace.

Lived experience. Metaphorical intuition. Fertile delirium.

The form of the spectre in cyberspatial reality is topologically transmutable. The emotional content of the object can change at any time. The light force of energy that informs the dream-narrative apparatus designates the object with meaning.

But in meaning there is always potential for loss.

And in cyberspace, this potential for loss is what keeps HTC moving.

there

There
is
no
there,
there.

virtual ubiquity

In the same ways that hypertextual consciousness distributing itself in an on-line network removes the limitations of the book-bound printed page, Digital

Being in the Avant-Pop age will remove the limitations of physical space and will enable us to avoid having to be in a specific place at a specific time. The idea of an active hypertextual consciousness being placeless yet ubiquitous will start to become possible. Virtual Ubiquity will replace omniscience as the cyborg-narrator's perspective of choice ("all narrative, all the time").

virtual object

Imagine this: an articulated walking skeleton, with skin and meat and percussive bones, filters high-density information packets with more processing power than any human being in the history of mankind. This Virtual Object (VO), a posthuman construct, is programmed to give and receive emotional charges that electrify the narrative experience one encounters once they are successfully interacting with the object. All kinds of information is received by the object including viewer position, hand-jerking motion, heart rate, dental chart, velocity data, detailed description of the complex language patterns this particular co-conspirator has never been able to articulate in common discourse, and total number of seconds spent in the bathroom relieving oneself of unnecessary matter. (The information can even become more dense. For example, it could take the total number of seconds spent in the bathroom relieving oneself of unnecessary matter and figure in the opportunity costs in real-time digicash currency markets, thus creating even more unnecessary matter to calculate the waste index with.)

virtual object:2

Once all of this data has been received by the Virtual Object (a cyborg-narrator's alter ego, similar to other alter egos found in the flesh), hypertextual consciousness can then process the information and store all of the useful (read: valuable) moments of connectivity into their proper receptacle. The VO's capacity to generate poetic recombinations of all this data is a purely individualistic trip, depending on the research and development that went into the evolution of the particular model (there's also a great deal of "unknown" information that helps qualify one VO from another but that's a story that will never get told).

VR fashion models

Who are the VR fashion models of the future, and will they love me? How will they love me? Will I have to pay for the love they give me? How much will it cost, and will only certain kinds of privileged knowledge workers be able to afford them? What sort of consumption patterns or credit tracks will VR model-buying say about me? If I drop some virtual acid and immerse myself in state-of-the-art Electric Ladyland environments, will the Virtual God open up the prismatic heavens so that I may finally kiss the sky?

wanderlust

But where is Hypertextual Consciousness going? The human mind works by association. The speed with which the contemporary cyborg-narrator processes and generates recombinant textual strands via value-added linking gestures and pseudo-autobiographical becomings suggests that HTC is a meme(x)-generator (a cellular transformer) and that the computer-mediated environment is the inevitable stage where all of this hyperrhetorical performance plays (strings, blows, wails, postliterates).

you don't have to be there

asynchronous communication
answering machine
voice mail system
e-mail
bulletin board systems
interactive Web site
snail mail
fax
virtual performance
telefictional soundtrack
hypertextual consciousness
cyborg-narrator
astrological bandwidth
sim-city
unreal estate
moment #21 (a footnote with no end)

This text was originally published in hypertext form online at Alt-X *(1995) and was eventually incorporated into the Net artwork* GRAMMATRON *as its "companion theory guide." It has since been reconfigured for text publication as a book chapter in* Close Reading New Media: Analyzing Electronic Literature, *edited by Jan Van Looy and Jan Baetens (Leuven, Belgium: Leuven University Press, 2003).*

The Work of Art in the Age of Virtual Republishing and Network Installation

Date: Sat, 5 Apr 1997
From: Mark Amerika
To: Nettime

Back in 1993, when I was composing my Avant-Pop manifesto in which I acknowledged the contemporary digital artist's dual lineage to both the avant-garde art and writing movements of the early parts of this century and the wild explosion of electronic pop culture in the latter part of the century, I asked this important question: "What would the Futurists do with an information superhighway?"

I asked the question in a rhetorical way—that is, I assumed that the Futurists and other artists such as the Dadaists and certainly the Situationists, would have immediately begun experimenting with whatever forms of expression the new media offered. They would have, as software engineers like to say, "pushed the envelope," both technologically and conceptually. Today, though, I'm asking a different question: "How are the artists of our time going to respond to the rapidly changing aesthetic, political, and economic realities presented to our contemporary society with the advent of global computer networking systems and the growing multinational, mass-media, Dreamworks complex?"

Perhaps the best way to respond to the previous question is to build alternative sites that actively resist the temptation to become absorbed into the cultural mainstream. But then other questions are bound to issue forth, such as "Will all hypermedia narrative projects, no matter how politically correct their content may think itself to be, endorse the development of commercial products emerging out of the new media industry?" This is a significant query to ask oneself when composing in this environment, for if the political strategy behind the narrative composition of hypermedia projects like HTC (⟨http://www.altx.com/htc1.0⟩) is at all serious about employing the Avant-Pop antiaesthetic practice to produce new, unpackagable culture integrations that go against the grain of the efficiency-oriented profit system by reintroducing disruptive forces that the system needs to exclude, then how can one proceed to compose these "subversive narratives" without simultaneously supporting the system of investments and expenditures that drives the technological apparatus through its various stages of development in late capitalism?

As art becomes less art, it takes on rhetoric's early role as persuasive critique of everyday life. As a result of this movement out of art and back into everyday life, art itself becomes integrated into the workings of everyday life by situating itself in corporations, universities, governments, and, more important, the fluid vistas of the vast electrosphere where all of these "cultures" collide and mix.

But what is a work of art in the age of virtual republishing and network installation? In the rhizomatic flow of network cultures, the eye touches rather than sees. It immerses itself in the tactile sense it feels when caught in the heat of the meaning-making process. This meaning-making process, which is now manifesting itself as kind of electronic media event one is responsible for having created themselves as a result of having become a cyborg-narrator or avatar presence in the simulated worlds of cyberspace, is actually part of a greater desire to become part of a sociocultural mosaic.

And yet what is the source code that inscribes this desire toward an engagement with the cultural production of our time?

This text was originally published in zkp 4 (May 1997) online at nettime.org.

Network Installations, Creative Exhibitionism, and Virtual Republishing: An Attempt at Contexualizing the Ongoing Ungoing Story of Being in Cyberspace

So much of our commercial and potentially subversive art today is being developed with software application programs that encourage the liberal usage of Modernistic practices (particularly sampling, collage, technological gimmickry, and other engineered behaviors), we tend to forget that what we are doing is not necessarily all that new and that if we're looking for deep structural changes in the artwork of today as opposed to even ten or twenty years ago, then we're more likely to find these changes in *the mediums through which contemporary art gets distributed* and how the emerging network culture radically transforms the way in which we participate in the dual worlds of art making and art appreciating. We might go so far as to say that the contemporary art world, once confined exclusively to the continuous exhibition of various artworks and installations in physical space, will need to start radically reevaluating its ability to maintain social relevance while branding its cultural imprint on the screenal spaces connected via the Net.

In this regard, there is also the question of so-called literary art and the growing popularity of the network-publishing model that not only allows writers to locate their audience on Net-connected machines all over the world but also enables the development of more flexible multimedia environments for storyworlds to take place in. One question that keeps arising, as in the case of contemporary network-narrative art, is what happens when the initial concepts thought up by one artist are eventually expressed by a network of other artist associates (collaborators) as a fluid work in progress whose transdisciplinary digital mix is forever in flux? What happens to our sense of a "creative self" or "autonomous author" when multiple hosts are responsible for distributing the Collective Net-Object? Isn't this already happening today on the World Wide Web?

The once "novel" idea of recording stories so that they can then be bound by the rigid spine of book media and its enslaving copyright law is morphing into the Avant-Pop practice of "surf-sample-manipulate," a pro-active practice of collage generation that reconfigures the author into a virtual artist who navigates cyberspace so as to engage him/herself in the improvisational mix of digital objects being distributed on the World Wide Web. In this scenario, the author-cum-virtual-artist places special emphasis on reconfiguring narratological practice by focusing on both content and source code, appropriating select bits of data for an evolving network of interactive-participants all over the geopolitical spectrum. This postnovel network-narrative environment is infinitely expandable and is always already being updated. Network protocols barely available to artists even three years ago are now partly responsible for creating an evolving storyworld production whose self-reflexive narrative form is being crystallized into a continuous presence that is finding a home in the electrosphere. Of course, neo-Luddite social commentators and highbrow media critics would have us believe that this is the End of Something Terribly Important (maybe their late capitalist hold on the right to own ideas that are really everybody's?).

One of the promising developments that has emerged as a result of having morphed the *Alt-X Online Publishing Network* from a print-oriented scrollable text environment (*Alt-X* started as a gopher site in 1993) to an ongoing hypermedia construction with state-of-the-art hyperfiction, Web art, new media theory, and now audio streams, has been its ability to once again ask the questions posed by Jacques Derrida at the beginning of his seminal work of literary criticism, *Dissemination*. The crucial question that comes up right at the beginning of his prefatory foreplay is "why should 'literature' still designate that which already breaks away from literature—away from what has always been conceived and signified under that name—or that which, not merely escaping literature, implacably destroys it?"

For those of us who have spent a considerable amount of time practicing novel writing as a powerful, text-centric subversive activity, the question is disturbing. Perhaps Ronald Sukenick, in a different context, has the best reply to Derrida when he says, "The struggle of literature is to move constantly beyond literature, beyond the definitions of particular linguistic realities, beyond language itself, to change the world we live in." This twentieth-century desire to move beyond literature, books, the transparent use of language, and the various linguistic frameworks which work against our creative impulse to shatter the rules of conventional behavior so as to change the world we live in can be seen as the driving force behind many of the activities associated with both Italian and Russian Futurism, Dadaism, Lettrism, Situationism, and the Pop Art movement. It is a desire that Richard Lanham, in *The Electronic Word*, says "brings a complete renegotiation of the alphabet/icon ratio upon which print-based thought is built."

The struggle between icon and alphabet is not new, and, as W. J. T. Mitchell claims in his book *Picture Theory*, "if writing is the medium of absence and artifice, the image is the medium of presence and nature, sometimes cozening us with illusion, sometimes with powerful recollection and sensory immediacy." While admitting that he is in fact "writing 'against' Derrida," Mitchell goes out of his way to show us how "writing is caught between two othernesses, voice and vision, the speaking and the seeing subject" and that Derrida "mainly speaks of the struggle of writing with voice" eventually posing us yet another important question that the Digital Studies installation is constantly asking in its frank hyperrhetorical gesture—that is, "How do we say what we see, and how can we make the reader see?"

Perhaps Raymond Federman, in his eye-opening "Surfiction: Four Propositions in the Form of an Introduction," has the best answer to Mitchell's question when he says, "The whole traditional, conventional, fixed, and boring method of reading a book must be questioned, challenged, demolished. And it is the writer (and not modern printing technology) who must, through innovations in the writing itself—in the typography and topology of his writing—renew our system of reading."

Both Derrida's question about "why literature?" and Mitchell's question about "why not vision?" are creatively reformulated throughout the Digital Studies network installation. Works like Knut Mork and Stahl Stenslie's *Solve et Coagula*, Richard Allalouf and Claire Cann's *Keywords*, and cocurator Alex Galloway's hybridized interface for the entire installation purposely play with the programmatic, iconographic, and hypertextual possibilities that lie within the networked-narrative environment and its potential to radically challenge both the mainstream publishing industry and the dominant exhibition model that still drives the visual arts establishment. To this effect, the Digital Studies installation uses local programming language, visible word constructions, keynote essays, and curatorial links to accentuate the liquid architecture the network technology has enabled us to develop and in so doing features some of the more adventurous topo-iconographical performances taking place in cyberspace, including Vuk Cosic's *The History of Art for Airports* Dr. Hugo's *Fuzzy Dreamz*, and INTIMA's investigations into the microstructure of atomic language and its relationship to both human emotion and the technological impulse toward universality and behavioristic determinism.

Perhaps the problem I am perceiving with the "dominant exhibition model that still drives the visual arts establishment" can be best expressed by having you imagine a gallery director or museum curator putting a printed literary novel of say, 300 pages, in an institutionally supported gallery or museum space and then inviting the patron to get lost in the dynamic (anti-)aesthetic environment that unravels within its pages. Most art appreciators would have a problem with this, for who has the time to sit or, worse yet, stand, in such a space and read an entire novel. Even if the work were a kind of narrative art consciously moving beyond literature and presenting itself on a computer screen as an elaborate hypermedia construction, yet still located in the same institutionalized, physical space, how long would the art appreciator stay with the complex narrative system before shifting into another room with more stable objects?

One of the alternatives that the "Hyper-X" section on *Alt-X*, which the Digital Studies project is the latest incarnation of, intends to explore is what I have previously called *Creative Exhibitionism*, a situation where the net.artist's work-in-progress is being exhibited in a virtual space as a network installation that the interactive participant, vis-à-vis the hypertext transfer protocols now available to most computer users, can continually come back to.

And what if the artist(s) responsible for the development of the network-art experience were to constantly use the fluidity of the digital medium to build on, subtract from, or otherwise alter the work whenever they wanted to? Does the virtual art object, forever morphing in the network environment constitute a new form of aesthetic becoming that makes being in cyberspace an art in and of itself? Have we reached a point where the network itself cannot be commodified and only certain brand-name artists have the potential to generate the kind of network value that Big Cultural Institutions will want to buy into? Exclusive shareware? Fleshfactor licensing? Love for sale? Sooner or later, questions like these must be addressed, and I can only hope that events such as *Digital Studies: Being In Cyberspace*, force us to confront them faster than we really want to.

Finally, I'd like to thank my cocurator, Alex Galloway, for his creative innovation, enthusiastic energy and critical skills, all of which were crucial in getting this project together in near record time. Special thanks are also due to all of the artists around the world who submitted material to this event. It confirmed my belief that the growth of interest in the Net as a preferred medium of practice and discovery is increasing faster than we could have ever imagined even two years ago. As I've grown the *Alt-X Online Publishing Network* over the last four years, it's become apparent to me that, in this rapidly changing new media terrain, the contemporary writer cum virtual artist is not only an electronic publisher or hypermedia narrative engineer but a digital art curator and network programmer too.

Stay tuned for further developments.

Mark Amerika
Cocurator
Digital Studies: Being in Cyberspace

This text was originally published online at Alt-X *as the curatorial essay for the online show Digital Studies: Being in Cyberspace (1997).*

Cyberspace Installations: Do-It-Yourself Narrative Composition for the '90s

One of the most dramatic lessons I've learned from developing complex hypermedia narratives for cyberspace (like my forthcoming *GRAMMATRON*) instead of creating a traditional manuscript bound for print reality is how the narrative artist of today is totally dependent on the development of new network technologies as well as the skills and talents of other collaborators working in the field. Composing in networked-narrative environments inevitably leads one to recognize that his or her forms are constantly metamorphosing depending on what new ensemble of participants the hypermedia team consists of as well as what new technologies are being integrated into the Web-development scene. This sort of codependency on emerging technologies raises some interesting questions, like "Will all hypermedia narrative projects, no matter how politically correct their content may think itself to be, endorse the development of commercial products emerging out of the new media industry?" This is a significant query to ask oneself when composing in this environment, for if the political strategy behind the narrative composition is at all serious about employing, say, the Avant-Pop anti-aesthetic practice to produce new, unpackagable culture integrations that go against the grain of the efficiency-oriented profit system by reintroducing disruptive forces that the system needs to exclude, then how can one proceed to compose these "subversive narratives" without simultaneously supporting the system of investments and expenditures that drive the technological apparatus through its various stages of development in late capitalism?

Literary critic Joseph Tabbi sees this dialectic as carrying forward both the romantic tradition of the sublime and the goal of social and scientific realism, suggesting, in his book *Postmodern Sublime: Technology and American Writing from Mailer to Cyberpunk*, that "desire and the human imagination run through the weightiest machinery and the most disembodied electronic forms, and these things need the imagination no less than it needs them." He finishes this thought by saying that "the imagination gives technology the narrative form necessary for human significance, and technology, in whatever form, provides necessary referential constraints to the imagination." In this regard, it could also be said that for contemporary artists whose programmatic reflex is to send a critical signal into the database of noise that passes itself off as consumer culture, the need to work with the evolving network technology that drives the production of content on the World Wide Web is part of a greater struggle to build receptive audiences for their work.

One multimedia narrative artist who goes by the name Bobby Rabyd has used these "disembodied electronic forms" to build a receptive audience for his network-distributed hyperfiction called *Sunshine '69*. Billed as a "Web-based time machine that allows the reader to explore and contribute prose to the open-ended tale," the story was originally distributed over the Sonicnet alternative ("loser-friendly") music site, an interesting occurrence in that the kind of Avant-Pop fiction Rabyd is both writing himself and encouraging his collaborators to contribute to the site is exactly the kind of writing that most mainstream publishing companies have found it convenient to ignore.

Borrowing from the independent music scene's D-I-Y ("do-it-yourself") gig-ethic, Rabyd's Web narrative is now located at his own, home-grown, rabyd.com site, where curious navigators looking for experimental hyperfiction can enter the *Sunshine '69* matrix through a clickable image map of the San Francisco Bay area or select from multiple points of views from the dozens of protagonists surfing throughout the narrative's telegeography: a rock star, a Vietnam vet, a flower child or a CIA agent, even an oddball avatar named Lucifer. Once one has entered the visually animated world of *Sunshine '69*, the hypertext story that ensues chronicles the death of the 1960s through some of the major movements of what Rabyd calls the "Summer of Hate" (a small pun on San Fran's Haight Street, where much of the Summer of Love took place). Floating into this narrative space where some of the characters are real and some imagined, the navigator is turned on to a recombinant history of the '60s whose diverse themes include the violent Altamont concert, the

Kent State massacre, the Vietnam War, the comeback of Nixon, the first landing on the moon, the Manson killings, and an overdetermined infatuation
with the Rolling Stones. Finally, in *Sunshine '69*, the premium LSD known as
Orange Sunshine is personified in a flower child, who, in the midst of making
sense of what's happening to her generation, gets kidnapped by the CIA and
turned into a deadly double agent. Her infiltration into counterculture happenings, from hanging out with the Hell's Angels to circulating throughout
the Woodstock Festival, presents an ambiguous retelling of the social and political upheavals we associate with the '60s.

The navigator can begin a journey through this "historical fiction" via the
Calendar, the Suitcase, and the Map. The Map opens up a variety of locations
in the Bay Area where much of what went down in the '60s originated. If you
prefer, you can click on the Calendar to get a more timely perspective of what
happened to various characters on a day-to-day basis back during those tu-
multuous times. The Suitcase is a multiperspectival hypertext that caricatures
the various people populating this retro scene of turning on, tuning in, and
dropping out. Clicking around the different screens here introduces us to
Rabyd's zine-inspired writing style and suggests that the Web itself is rapidly
becoming the most popular venue for the dissemination of more home-grown
enterprises that are totally prepared to assert themselves as serious yet fun
projects dead-set on bypassing the unwritten laws and logic of the taste-
controllers who run the mainstream culture business. (Ironically, many of
these taste-controllers were themselves once *Sunshine '69*-like characters, and
Rabyd is happy to give both these oldie-goldies as well as the new cyberkids on
the block an equal opportunity to tell their own stories in the *Sunshine '69*
guestbook).

But this isn't just Bobby Rabyd's vision of the '60s teleported into a hypertextual narrative environment. This project is created by a Web-connected
hypermedia team composed of many artists with their own skills and talents
who lend various levels of expertise to both the hyperfiction's graphical design
and navigational complexity. For example, Richard Schuler's hallucinogenic
graphics, reminiscent of much of the cool album-cover art of the era, take
on a signifying character of their own as the various "avatars" whose perspectives we tunnel our reading through become associated with ultramod design
objects that "represent" their placement within the dispersed space-time dis-
continuums offered by the multilinear routing of the narrative. The minimal-
ist drawings of *Sunshine '69*'s characters (like Lucifer, the Glimmer Twins,

Alan, Ali, Murdoch, and Sunshine herself) are all headless, but the "threads" they wear clearly indicate their affinity for a sexier, more flexible social environment that fashion hounds will immediately identify as very '60s.

The production team at Sonicnet that originally helped create the site before it moved to Rabyd's own domain name, led by producer Alison Dorfman, has used these graphics and the *Sunshine '69* story elements to great advantage, and has also found a way to further develop the trippy interface of *S69* by interweaving Rabyd's inclusion of an original soundtrack of made-for-the-Web music that he, with musician Will Oldham, has composed especially for the storyworld by way of state-of-the-art RealAudio technology that streams packets of sound data into your hard drive and can be played via the RealAudio plug-in. Under the section heading entitled "8-track" (a tribute to that fleeting technology of yore), the navigator will find tunes from three fictional bands linked into the *Sunshine '69* matrix: Dij, The New Mutants and Heavy Water (all with their own accompanying graphics). The most interesting of these "bands" is Dij, whose lo-fi, garage-band aesthetic dishes out psychedelic riffs like "Mick's Mind," "Alan's Brain," and "Tim's Time," all of it reminding us how the rock and roll phenomenon of the '60s initially brought into view the revolutionary potential of the technology/pop-underground interface, a potential that was narrativized in the cyberpunk novels of the '80s and that we now try to affiliate with the advent of network technology as experienced via the rapid development of the World Wide Web and the concurrent rush of self-proclaimed new media artists to its more flexible, open system of production and distribution.

And yet just as rock and roll has become the most commercial of contemporary art forms, there is a rising concern that the Web itself is on the verge of losing its edge too, perhaps becoming so absorbed into a WebTV or WindowsTV environment that, lately, one has been hearing many complaints that this is the beginning of the end of the Web as we know it and that soon it will all be an endless flow of bad TV programming with no alternatives to turn to. But are these fears really necessary? The main thing we have going for us now is that the loosely termed *anarchic* quality of the Net itself (that is, its ability to support a many-to-many distribution model that points toward a continued leveling of the distribution playing field) still rules the day, despite the fact that so much commercial activity has already infiltrated the once undeveloped regions of cyberspace. For those of us attracted to the Web as indicative of a major paradigmatic shift in the way we disseminate cultural productions, there is a basic understanding now that this model of delivery is different than the one we associate with the broadcast spectrum. In fact, it can be said that the Net is without spectrum or, to be more rhetorical, has the potential to continually evolve its own endless form of Virtual Ubiquity: and this, of course, is what makes it out of control.

The Cyberspace Ur-Spectrum, one might say, is infinitely expandable, and its flexible environment system may, in the end, enable multitudes of home-grown artists, philosophers, theorists, writers, infopreneurs, and political activists to evolve their own niche communities of support and feedback, thus enabling them to survive in the electrosphere.

An earlier version of this text was originally published online at Alt-X *and* Telepolis *in 1996.*

Surf-Sample-Manipulate: Playgiarism on the Net

At the opening of his influential essay entitled "Critifiction: Imagination as Plagiarism," novelist and critic Raymond Federman says "we are surrounded by discourses: historical, social, political, economic, medical, judicial, and of course literary." He then goes on to suggest two things: that the imagination should be used as an essential tool that leads to the formulation of a discourse and that the practice of plagiarism is embedded within the creative process since the writing of a discourse always implies bringing together pieces of other discourses.

This reminds me of a conversation I once had with the novelist Kathy Acker. We were on a radio program together in Boulder, Colorado, and the interviewer asked her where she got her "writer's voice" from: Acker replied "What voice? There's no voice in my work: I just steal shit."

Of course, she does much more than "just steal shit." But Acker, along with Federman and many artists before them (including Lautréamont, Apollinaire, the Cubists, and the Dadaists), all participated in what I'm calling the anti-aesthetic practice of "surf-sample-manipulate." When applied to a postmaterial digital world of instantaneous composition and delivery via the Internet, this "surf-sample-manipulate" practice (surfing the net, sampling data, and then altering that data to meet the specific needs of the environment being developed by the artist) works on two fronts. The so-called creative content (that is, the text, images, music, and graphics of many Web-art sites) is often sampled from other sources and, after some digital-manipulation, immediately integrated into a work so as to create an "original" construction. In addition, the so-called source code itself (that is, the HTML langauge that informs the browser how to display the work) is many times appropriated from other designs floating around the Net and eventually filtered into the screen's behind-the-scenes compositional structure. The great thing about the Net is that if you see something you like (whether content or source code), you often can just download the entire document and manipulate it according to your anti-aesthetic needs.

But who is to say that there's actually a difference now between source code and content? The so-called WYSIWYG (pronounced "wizzy-wig" and an acronym for "what you see is what you get") appearance of the World Wide Web is a total illusion. Whether you choose to buy into William Gibson's idea of the "consensual hallucination" or Jean Baudrillard's "precession of simulacra" (personally, I prefer Gibson), the Web itself can now be seen as an open platform whose symbolic space is ready for all sorts of creative manipulation that the contemporary artist can use to breakdown our traditional relationship with the one discourse that has dominated most of our lives—that is, the media discourse.

What I'm describing here is the digital equivalent of collage art, one where the contemporary artist uses the forms of the new media to subvert the commercial redundancy of that same new media. Federman's own brand of collage art (what he calls *pla[y]giarism*: the inclusion of the extra letter *y* signals his desire to turn the creative practice into one of playfulness and performance) is just one of the latest extensions of this sort of activity, one that has taken off with the techno music scene but that has much more potential in the network culture.

Whereas collage itself has been around since we've been able to historicize art in culture, the technique was first used as a radical formal device in painting by the cubists. Pablo Picasso and Georges Braque, looking to move beyond the problems presented by Analytic Cubism, were hoping to challenge the illusionistic preference of all painterly art coming out at the beginning of the century and so began incorporating found objects into their paintings. As mentioned in my first Amerika Online column, it was around the time that Cubism came into art's historical current that Filippo Marinetti, Marcel Duchamp, and Kurt Schwitters, to name a few, all began appropriating objects from the material world to better explore *the idea* of painting in the modern world. Eventually these ideas, which were part of an overall shift in twentieth-

century art to move art's subject matter away from "nature" to focus on the
material culture itself, came to full fruition in the post–Abstract Expressionist
work of artists like Robert Rauschenberg, whose "combines" took us into a
categorical no-man's land, a place where ontological chaos and the super-
imposition of pop-culture imagery and brand-name identity onto the fetish-
ized art object helped launch the Pop Art movement.

But as all valuable tools and formal innovations eventually risk losing their
potential liberating power by getting absorbed into a cultural tide that insists
on the continual proliferation of new consumer-friendly processes, so the art
of collage, which reached its apex in the postmodern era, must now look for
alternative spaces to exhibit its radical recombinations of anti-aesthetic drift.
The most obvious place for this shift to occur is cyberspace, the pixelated environment where the material we recontextualize into new forms of potential
meaning is in many ways "immaterial." Whereas the use of junkyard detritus
from the postindustrial ruins of everyday life has become almost common-
place in the garage-sale poetics of the contemporary art world, our new-found
ability to convert so much of our contemporary cultural work into easily
manipulable binary code sets up a heretofore unheard of environment from
which to engender new contexts of artistic performance and, if possible, create
paramedia constructs that assault the banal production values inherent in
mainstream culture. As Marshall McLuhan once said, "World War III is
a guerrilla information war, with no division between military and civilian
participation."

Perhaps McLuhan had no idea just how right he'd be. When one considers
how fast the Internet has been transformed from a military network protocol
to a consumer application, it's great to see that the Avant-Pop playgiaristic
practice is being put to good use all over cyberspace. For those interested in
the hypermedia permaculture of "temporary autonomous zones," *The Plagia-
rist Codex: An Old Maya Information Hieroglyph*, developed by the folks who
run the *Dreamtime Talkingmail* site, is a good place to start. Culture jamming
the corporate propaganda machine via politically motivated playgiarism is
alive and well at sites like *McSpotlight* and *Adbusters*, where the site-creators
assure us that "the shining hope for a revolution in human consciousness
lies in the actions of everyday people." Perhaps the most complete guide to
contemporary playgiaristic practice is to be found at the *Neoism* site, particularly its self-referential index page on all things playgiaristic. The opening ep-
igraph by artist Harry Polkinhorn, where he states that "it would be better to

say that no one owns anything, not even a physical body much less a mind or a soul," is exemplary. Of course, all of our friends from the book culture, bound by the copyright laws that inform the discussion around so-called intellectual property, have a hard time dealing with this sort of blatant disregard for the concepts of ownership and originality.

The most interesting hypermedia art project I've yet to experience and that employs the Avant-Pop practice of "surf-sample-manipulate" to great effect, is Jacques Servin's *BEAST (TM)*. Servin, who is the author of two books of fiction called *Aviary Slag* and *Mermaids for Attila*, is known throughout the Net community as the notorious programmer who hacked the pre-Christmas shipment of *SimCopter*—an action game from the makers of *SimCity 2000*—where he supplemented the game's cast of pulchritudinous female Sims with broad-shouldered male Sims who, in tight swimsuits, go around kissing everything in sight, including each other.

By exhibiting *BEAST (TM)* at the SEAFair 1997 event in Skopje, Macedonia, Servin, part novelist/part programmer, enters the international electronic arts scene with a skills set not usually seen on the Web. His sampling of various texts from Benjamin to Benn to new voices he's invented, music loops stolen from various programs (including the Windows system), and images from a wide range of popular magazines circa 1930 are integrated into a monster Java applet that anyone with a Pentium 120 or higher will want to explore (some of the faster Power Macs can be used as well). The Java applet is quite memory-heavy so those who have slower machines will have to wait through a longer initial download time—but this is one instance where it's definitely worth the wait!

The DEATH screen I linked to immediately presented me with a quote from Walter Benjamin's "One-Way Street," but before I could finish reading the sampled text, all sorts of wild and unruly things began happening as the huge Java applet continued downloading its chaotic hit of hallucinatory madness: specially encoded error-boxes kept popping into view trying to explain what my problem was (my problem, I soon realized, was coming to the WWW with great expectations), while Middle Eastern technomusic tried to soothe me back into the surfing groove. As the artist himself says in a recent statement, "While [*BEAST (TM)*] highlights the ugliness of computer technology, it also leads the user to see the harmony in it, since the profusion of images, warnings, sounds and tyrannical acts on the part of the system have an ultimately pleasing rhythm." By interacting with this sort of narratological behaviorism, "the user is inducted into understanding his or her own complicity in this state of affairs."

Clicking within the skating images that continuously float by, I saw more readable text fragments spill into the screen only to be overtaken by yet more amazing graphics that skated across the screen in ways animated gifs can't even dream of. (Excuse me if I'm personifying animated gifs, but one wonders if animated gifs aren't, for now, some kind of posthistoric life form soon on the verge of extinction.) Clicking on the skating images led to more music shifts and, yes, more programmed "warning" messages that purposely filled up the screen in lightning-speed progression so that it was (intentionally) difficult to understand what these intrusive screens actually said. One message that kept popping up started with words "Please. Please . . ."—as if testing our "user-friendly" patience. The artist's attempt to load our experience with invisible "Frustration Plug-Ins" and disorienting audio streams created an unusual comedy of errors, a kind of Shakespearean black humor that uses hypermedia typography as its cast of characters.

Servin himself has commented on his new work:

The medium that has emerged on the Web, and that continues to dominate commercial esthetics in general, is one that fosters, and subtly depends on, utter transience of attention. Extending television's effects through its much-vaunted interactivity, hypertext as it exists on the Web has served to render writing into "content"—something to squeeze between flashy images and absorb any drops of attention that might accidentally spill.

BEAST (TM) relies on a hypertext system which I designed as an alternative to Web-style links. Instead of jumping from text to text, the reader can direct the progress of a single text by interaction with the text itself and with illustrations which float by in seeming 3-D. By this means the interactive possibilities of the medium are tapped without compromising the meditative approach to text for which we are trained, and which depends on the text appearing at once, allowing the eye to be a hypertext engine far more sophisticated than any that could be devised. I would not say that linked texts are inherently corrupt; this comes down to a matter of personal preference, evolved from bombardment by so much Web "content."

(It should be noted that, like most hypermedia creations now being teleported into the Net, *BEAST (TM)* is very much a work in progress and the artist says that the amount of content will more than double in the next month or two. For a look at these future developments, you'll want to the read the latest version of his artist's statement at 〈http://www.altx.com/hyperx/beast.html〉).

Whereas many seasoned Web surfers are becoming familiar with the bombardment that Servin speaks of, very few are creating digital objects that actually intervene in the Web's ongoing creative process. *BEAST (TM)* signals yet another crucial break with an overaestheticized art-for-art's-sake mentality that seems to be festering on the web. By employing innovative forms of multimedia language that have been excluded from most literary productions confined to book media, Servin presents us with a narrative construction that exhibits to us once again Guillaume Apollinaire's dictum that "reality will never be discovered once and for all" and that truth, should such a thing exist, is always on the edge of becoming something else entirely different from what we thought it was.

An earlier version of this text was originally published online at Alt-X *and* Telepolis *in 1997.*

Copyleftists: Form and Action in the Network Environment

In the first half of this century, there was reason to believe that publishing houses, run by gentlemanly publishers, felt comfortable playing the role of literary-oriented patrons of the arts, often giving their more innovative editors the opportunity to support the development of experimental writing careers by offering necessary cash advances to the authors so that they could, in the solitude of their profession, compose the best literary artworks they knew how to and, if lucky, eventually build a solid audience of support that would guarantee the publisher not only profits on their new books but also retro profits on what had evolved into a significant backlist.

As everyone who follows this scene now knows, this is no longer how the mainstream publishing industry works. The media-driven Blockbuster mentality has taken over the scene. Can you imagine editors from a big multinational publishing house approaching their publisher and suggesting that the publisher invest five, ten, or even fifteen years worth of survival expenses to support the development of an important literary figure? The editors would never do something like that since it would clearly compromise their position within the organization, whose top-down, bottom-line mission is not to build prestige within the "culture business" but to become a huge, profitable media enterprise.

Even countries like Germany, where the cultural prerogative to support the creative and critical writings of contemporary artists from all around the world has outpaced similar programs in other countries, now have literary "agents" whose job it is to successfully package writers as "media constructs" that will attract enough attention so as to commodify their "brand-name" products and sell them to a larger audience.

These successfully packaged brand-name identities—whether novelists, historians, cultural critics, or outrageous social commentators—all depend on the in-place copyright laws for their survival, as do the legions of workers in the publishing industry who produce and distribute this work *for* them. The death of intellectual property rights would be the death of the publishing industry as it now operates, and this is why the "culture business," its network of lawyers and investors, and the writers it supports are so slow to make their way into cyberspace and accept the new challenges it presents to our globally transfigured culture.

The notion of a writer becoming an online publisher and/or cyborg-narrator whose public-domain narrative environment is free and open to public viewing twenty-four hours a day, seven days a week, from any Net-connected computer in the world does not fit into the mainstream publishing industry's production or distribution model. Even the forever marketed "bold writers of the new generation" are simply ported through the dinosauric copyright system, whose primary goal is not to find readers of significant literary work but to sell as many book objects as possible to make lots of money and satisfy the stockholders. And why not? That's what capitalism is all about. In fact, the more blatant the mainstream publishers align themselves with the Blockbuster complex and the blatant practice of peddling "literary artists" as more media by-products, the more ludicrous their role-playing identity as "art patron" becomes.

A problem, though, arises, when almost all of our narrative artists, cultural and social critics, historians, and so on play this game—when cooptation by the mainstream is equated with a "become a media celeb or perish" goals-oriented writing strategy. What's happened to our sense of adventure, of tackling the unknown, of using our work as language or narrative artists to reevaluate the challenges posed by the formal ambiguities evolving in the new media culture itself? Are we afraid of the economic consequences? How many writers and artists today are actually making a lot of money being "artistic geniuses" in the mold of dead Picasso? I would venture to say that there are very few innovative writers or artists today who are able to survive simply by selling their most experimental "intellectual property" to the multinational corporate sponsors located throughout the global economy. In fact, one line of thought making its way through the art-world party scene, a bastardized version of a previous thought developed by Antonin Artaud, is that there really are no more literary masterpieces, just hefty media by-products that occasionally get picked up by the self-replicating mainstream media virus and that are sold to consumers as off-the-shelf "cultural objects" they must own the same way they must own a sports utility vehicle or the latest Braun coffee maker. In this scenario, there are no readers, and in fact, it's now often suggested that there are "literally" tons of books that get sold but that never get read, that the reason they're bought is not so much to be read and appreciated as works of literary art but, rather, installed in physical locations as a brand-name product identifying the owner of said product with a degree of cultural sophistication they can buy but never actually immerse themselves in.

This changes the way emerging writers start viewing their work and porting it into culture to keep them relevant. What becomes obvious to even the casual observer of contemporary art and writing is that it's not only money that drives the new generation of literary writers toward immediate cooptation but that it's also the chance to be routed through that mainstream media mechanism that feeds into the overriding Blockbuster mentality that informs our present-day construction of value within the late capitalist system.

But the-times-they-are-a-changing, and as German-based hypertext writer/critic Ruth Nestvold said in the live online global chat that took place on both the *Alt-X Network* and at the Brown University Vanguard Narrative Fiction Festival last fall, "Lots of folks are trying to translate avant garde almost straight to the Web. But the thing is, a lot of postmodern experiments don't make any sense on the Web anymore. Defying chronology, for instance, is no longer an experiment. It's the nature of hypertext." Taking Nestvold's notion one step further, I'd say *defying intellectual property rights is no longer an experiment: it's the nature of the web.*

Think about it: if our creative "property" can be infinitely reproduced and instantaneously distributed all over the planet without noticeable cost, without our knowledge, without its even leaving our possession (it's still on the publicly accessible server, right?), why would we want to put up firewalls to protect it? One question that immediately comes to mind, as we go forth into the technojungle mix of wild Web growth and savage pla(y)giaristic practice, is what sort of advantages would there be in protecting an artist's work from all of the potential interactive participants? The most obvious answer is so that the artists responsible for creating the work can get paid for it. If everything is given away for free, then how are we going to get paid for the work we do with our minds? And if we can't get paid, what will assure the continued creation and distribution of such work?

The problem, of course, is that Net-based work, however creative or intellectual it may be, takes information out of the world of material goods and puts it into the rapidly morphing terrain of digital reproduction, manipulation, and dissemination. This move from material objecthood to virtual objecthood constitutes one of the most significant changes in cultural history and forces us to rethink the way we approach our work as "property."

Throughout the history of copyrights and patents, the proprietary assertions of thinkers have been focused not on their ideas but on the expression of those ideas. The ideas themselves, as well as facts about phenomena of the world, were considered to be the collective property of humanity. In the case of narrative, the author could have a great idea about a book, but "to express" that idea in narrative form (that is, to make it physical) required first writing it out and then turning it into a material book object.

But what happens if (as in the case of contemporary network-narrative art) the initial concepts thought up by one artist are eventually expressed by a network of other artist-associates (collaborators) as a fluid work-in-progress whose multimedia digital mix is forever in flux? What happens to our sense of a "creative self" when multiple hosts are responsible for distributing the Collective Net-Object? Isn't this already happening today on the World Wide Web?

The once "novel" idea of recording stories so that they can then be bound by the rigid spine of book media and its enslaving copyright law is morphing into the Avant-Pop practice of "surf-sample-manipulate," which I've elaborated on in my Amerika Online columns at *Telepolis* and *Alt-X*. This proactive practice of "surf-sample-manipulate" involves the improvisational mix of resonances being emitted by the virtual world of digital culture and its rapidly evolving network of social environments populated by emerging artists all over the geopolitcal spectrum. This postnovel network-narrative environment is infinitely expandable and ready for immediate update. Network protocols barely available to artists even three years ago are now partly responsible for creating an evolving storyworld production whose self-reflexive narrative form is being crystallized into a continuous presence that is always already teleported into cyberspace. Of course, Neo-Luddite social commentators and highbrow media critics would have us believe that this is The End of Something Terribly Important (maybe their late capitalist hold on the right to own ideas that are really everybody's?).

Contemporary artists should know better. Gertrude Stein conceived of this before I did, saying it was "the business of art . . . to live in" this "continuous present" and that we needed to immerse ourselves in "the complete actual present and to completely express that complete actual present." Successful creative writers and literary/social critics who have invested a great deal of time and energy in the development of their own, book-centric, network-value have a terrific problem with all of this, and who can blame them? They have created network value by successfully marketing their stories and ideas, which has helped them carve out an audience that guarantees them both cultural relevance and myriad ways of electronically streaming revenue sources into their bank accounts. Their network value is intimately connected with a production/distribution model that is totally dependent on the past while losing touch with this "continuous present." They perceive real threats from this simulated social world of internetworking, a world that has consistently challenged their ideological foundations. Watching their ideas becoming instantaneously appropriated by the collective Web self for its own uses isn't easy, and they won't take it lying down. In fact, as roaming dinosaurs trouncing through the intellectual landscape, they are by far the ones best positioned to defend the past they still live in.

How do we expect them to deal with the fact that each of their contributions to the narrative-in-progress will become imbedded in a fluctuating network of hypertextual links that is continuously being altered by the advent of new Web technologies? It's out of control!

Or is it? Practicing a D-I-Y (do-it-yourself) publishing aesthetic via the Net is clearly the easiest way for emerging artists to get published (from the Latin root "to go public"). In fact, the network protocols of today put more control into the hands of the contemporary artist. When I first started talking about this "network publishing" model back in late 1993, most people in the business thought I was crazy. Now, at least, they have resigned themselves to its role in transforming the publishing industry as we know it.

But doing away with copyright and giving away one's formal "content" for free so as to raise one's network value is a tough intellectual bar to leap. Still, a crystal ball reading of a near-future scenario for writers and publishers would suggest that the Net will continue to grow in influence and that the tricky interface between art and technology will further decentralize the role of mainstream publishers who, it now seems clear, are no longer interested in "prestige" and are more than happy to rid themselves of this burden. Fortunately for more adventurous writers, the new network technology opens up the possibility of reconfiguring the author as a virtual artist in cyberspace. And this, in turn, creates more exciting boundary-slippage in the creative/critical discourse.

An earlier version of this text was originally published online at Alt-X *and* Telepolis *in 1997.*

Life Is Elsewhere: Cruising the Antipodal Trajectory

"When we can go to the antipodes and back in an instant, what will become of us?" Or so asks Paul Virilio, who, projecting his thoughts from the bunker of contemporary media theory, provides us with a model of thinking through the pragmatics of speed and how fast information technology (IT) teleports our networked values to distant, often remote lands, forcing us to address the spatial and temporal problems brought on by digital nomadism and this contemporaneous feeling of always being elsewhere.

Or so I thought to myself while in heavy jetlag, having just returned from a near two-month tour throughout Australia and New Zealand sharing ideas and presenting both *Alt-X* and *GRAMMATRON* to the various audiences who made their way to my performances.

Upon arrival back into my very real and settled-in homestead here in Boulder, Colorado, I started dealing with my brain-heavy disorientation by "grounding out" in the best way I know how—namely, opening up all of the accumulated snail-mail which, to my surprise, included a 1995 anthology of critical essays entitled *Critical Issues in Electronic Media*, edited by Simon Penny with a lead-off essay by noted Australian philosopher McKenzie Wark. In Wark's essay, called "Suck on This, Planet of Noise" (the reference is to the popular On-U sound recording), the author discusses how "the anxiety of antipodality is growing ever more common" thanks, in large part, to the "globalization of trade flows and cultural flows made possible by information technology" and how this newer, yet perhaps more intense form of feeling out of balance "reopens the old wounds of identity, breaking the skin at unexpected places."

What he's talking about here is contemporary Australian identity and how the imposition of European people on the land first occupied by aborigine people led to a radical takeover of the spiritual spaces embedded within its indigenous culture, similar to what happened with the Native American tribes in America. Wark goes on to explain that a similar process is taking place today, albeit in a totally different environment—that is, the trajectories of satellite- or Net-distributed info-pop culture, mostly from America, are infiltrating the minds of Australians everywhere, creating a condition where the colonizers are now themselves being colonized (this new form of colonization, instead of taking place by way of sacred-land appropriation, takes place in what Wark calls a "virtual geography," which I take to mean the creative and cognitive mapping structures that relay information to our global brain).

However, who is to say that in this instance the colonized (and here I'm referring to the white Australians) feel completely overtaken in a negative way? The introduction of cable TV permits even the country's most sophisticated citizens to receive regular episodes of *Seinfeld*, and what is *Seinfeld* if not the world's most successful, longest-running, situation comedy television series "about nothing." From a completely different perspective, this notion of a successful, long-running comedy series "about nothing" could be elaborated into a clever introductory thesis statement focusing on the body of work produced by, say, Samuel Beckett (cf. *Waiting for Godot* or *Texts for Nothing*), which leads me to believe that a program like *Seinfeld* could become the gold standard in contemporary data transmission and, as such, could emanate from anywhere (why would Americans be the only population capable of delivering quality programming "about nothing"?). Keeping this in mind, one cannot help but ask the following question: are the global trade and cultural flows that keep picking up speed in the information economy so automatic that what goes around comes around (let's call it the *boomerang effect*) and soon American viewers will be happily leeching off of the next abundant crop of cultural products being designed in Sydney? Perhaps we should reserve judgment until we have had the opportunity to absorb the technotheatrics promised during the 2000 Summer Olympics, which will finally, once and for all, put the harbor city on the globally discharged, virtual map. Another question those of us in the Northern Hemisphere will be forced to ask ourselves during this major international event is "Whose summer is this, anyway?"

Still, though, the dark irony of this historical trajectory that places white Australia in the uncomfortable position of being colonized themselves challenges many of its most engaged artists to locate a space of resistance where their work can intervene with the very "cultural flows" IT uses to assault their own, very real, homesteads. Many of these spaces of resistance are now located on the WWW and are beginning to capture the attention of Web navigators worldwide, despite the fact that so many of the practitioners creating these strategic sites are adamantly opposed to devoting a great deal of their creative energy to coding an excessive amount of Global Hype Mark-Up Language, the spin-doctored nuances of cyberlingo that seem to be infesting the Net these days, whether it come from born-again entrepreneurs selling software products or precocious net.artists desperately looking for attention.

While so many of our American and European flavors of the month crack into the mainstream media virus to show their friends, family, and potential sponsors that they can capture the big multinational corporations short attention span ("Look everyone, I'm a Net artist!"), this kind of easy manipulation is already becoming somewhat passé in many creative communities, not the least of which are located throughout Australia, where the idea of evolving a more elaborate Net practice in defiance of the commercial interests floating around the Net is a top priority.

Some veteran Ozzie Net practitioners have already used the institutionalized system to their advantage, piecing together a patchwork strategy of survival that enables them to create complex work that resonates with all of the contradictions an activist Net practice implies. One work in progress that clearly challenges our notion of self, place, and identity is Francesca da Rimini's *dollspace* (soon to be renamed *Smear of Roses*), an explosive multimedia narrative performance that beautifully portrays the writer figure as a pseudo-autobiographical work in progress whose Net practice invites us to "read into" the reading process itself as IT transforms our behavior of tracking linear textuality into something more dynamic.

This emerging reading dynamic that speeds up and fragments the meaning-making process was best described in Rob Wittig's book called *Invisible Rendezvous*, where, in an historical manifesto transcribing the evolution of the IN.S.OMNIA electronic bulletin board based out of Seattle in the early '80s, one of the "invisibles" (as the collaborators were called) describes a new form of attention, one whose qualities include "irreverence, quick decision making, ability to identify the whole from the fragment, and an exquisite taste for juxtaposition," which, the author notes, is "not a bad list of skills if one happens to be faced, on a daily basis, with an overwhelming onslaught of information."

Da Rimini's *dollspace*, a work in progress that she is creating in collaboration with artists Ricardo Dominguez and Michael Grimm, addresses this new form of attention by showcasing the pseudo-autobiographical eye/I of both the viewer (eye) and the fictionalized postself (I) while simultaneously transgressing the need to engage herself with the hype-generating media machine that can bestow flickering riffs of attention on Web-based artists seeking some form of contact with the multinational corporate logos. In *dollspace*, the Revolution of the Word (to quote techno-shaman Jerome Rothenberg), now digitized and morphed into a performative mélange of text-driven hypermedia typography, is manifested more as an internal oblivion that organically builds its external links to whatever network happens to take shape around the pseudo-autobiographical work in progress it's always in the process of becoming. It's not a planned attack that takes place in a fantasy world where the evil info-creeps defy the upstart artist boy from the love and attention he surely believes he deserves—not by a longshot. In fact, river boys (as *dollspace* calls them) are to be used and abused, systematically murdered by the nurturing Mother (Earth?) they refuse to obey.

By creating a temporary autonomous zone of its own, *dollspace* refuses to hit the backspace key and correct its own typos to prettify its very well publicized art-terrorist attack. Rather, it streams a fictionalized linguistic consciousness into the Net practice itself and morphs narratological behavior into a multidisciplinary interzone of real interventionist action. In a recent e-mail I received from da Rimini, she said (typos included):

after the heady days of vns matrix and all our tongie iun cheek promotion and vapourware i just cant poush my work anymore .. i guess i stopped taking mainsteam poublcity seriously when i found out how easyb it is to infiltrate the media palaces with wellcrafted hype .. so i'm happy to let it drift on the net somewhat aimlessly, finding readers where it will .. i suppose these days that's part of my political stance, to be more humble, discrete, quiet in my enterprises, there is sommuch hype around i don't feel like being part of it .. preferring to expend that energy on continually making and perfecting my various creative things

Even the artist, however, does not always have full control over what may happen to her work once it makes its way on to the Net (this column is just one example of a mild-mannered form of hype linkage that is unsolicited by the artist). But this emerging antihype attitude by underground activists is particularly interesting when compared with some of the younger, career-oriented American and European artist hackers who go out of their way to suggest in their ghost-written, e-mail spamming, press releases that their mainstream intervention is indeed a full-on assault of "art terrorism" ("send e-mail to web.artist@wannabe-yuppie.org for more details!"). Chances are, you don't know where these small pockets of resistance exist or where the different practitioners and their sites are located because they are not on the institutional festival circuit that most of the more visible and, consequently, desperate, Net practitioners live and die by.

dollspace was introduced to a live audience this past March as part of the Telstra Adelaide Festival's FOLDBACK event/exhibition, which was also the ten-year anniversary celebration of the groundbreaking Australian Network for Art and Technology (ANAT), which da Rimini helped start as its first executive officer. The 1998 Adelaide Festival, featuring keynote addresses from artists such as Jenny Holzer, Joseph Kosuth, and myself, was the last such event of this century (the festival occurs every even-numbered year) and delivered an intense schedule packed with experimental theater, music, and dance, as well as a Writer's Week followed by a Visual Arts Week. This year marked the first time that a serious effort had been made to integrate state-of-the-art online and CD-ROM projects into the festival mix so that Web artists such as da Rimini, writers Linda Carroli and Josephine Wilson of the Electronic Writing and Research Ensemble, and the process-oriented Web band _nervous objects_ were sponsored under the same banner as Holzer's *Lustmord*, a brilliant Susan Hiller exhibition at the Experimental Art Foundation, and Heiner Goebbel's wonderfully playful shot of music theater called *BLACK ON WHITE*.

As the catalogue for FOLDBACK stated, "Drawing connections between the often divergent cultures of art, writing and sound, FOLDBACK seeks to dispel the assumption that media art belongs only in a visual arts context." Taking place on the pivotal Sunday between Writer's Week and Visual Arts Week, the marathon FOLDBACK event, held in the Ngapartji Multimedia Centre in the east end of town, also mixed live performance with streaming audio and CD-ROM playback. The cyberpoet Komninos Zervos, whose 3-D poetry reminds me of a kind of streetwise zaum typography disseminated into the still-in-development suburbs of the electrosphere, amused the audience with his various impersonations of London street people which he automatically "clicked into" once he had "clicked on" various hyperlinks threaded throughout his *Underground Cyberpoetry* CD-ROM. Meanwhile, musician Stevie Wishart brought out an amped-up hurdy-gurdy and played a mesmerizing set of medieval ars electronica mixed with streaming back-up sound coming in from Sydney via Real Audio. The program ended with a few sets of electronic sound art delivered by some of the participants on the *Dislocations* CD (Zonar Recordings) including Michael Hogg's forty-minute quadraphonic set of hypnotizing music specially composed for four speakers. Considering the amount of technology needed to implement the variety of digital discourses being performed throughout this nine-hour marathon event, the relative ease with which the program unraveled made for a near-perfect day of media transitions.

To quote recontextualized Virilio again, conceptual Net practices like the ones on display at FOLDBACK show us how "differences between positions begin to blur, resulting in unavoidable fusion and confusion," and how, "deprived of objective limits, the architectonic element begins to drift, to float in an electronic ether devoid of spatial dimensions yet inscribed in the single temporality of an instantaneous diffusion." As we watch our minds become absorbed into this "instantaneous diffusion," one cannot help but wonder if we have entered the realm of the sacred, the profane, or some unruly combination of the two we have absolutely no control over.

An earlier version of this text was originally published online at Alt-X *and* Telepolis *in 1998.*

Prophesizing Infowar: Creating Expectations in the New Media Economy

1

What is the new media economy?

Is it, to quote the theme of this year's Ars Electronica, an Infowar? Go to the Ars Electronica *Infowar* site, and there are a few options to choose from, including festival, prix, press, information, and the enigmatic "never go there."

The first thing that strikes me as I come here, to the Ars site, is how English-friendly the site is. I don't speak one sentence of German, and yet I know exactly what my options are.

Is this indicative of the new media economy?

Is this the battleground for a new Infowar?

Danke.

Meanwhile, I want to know more.

I need more information.

So I click on the word *information*.

It takes me to a page that has ticket prices for the festival and information about four Ars Electronica books that will be published by Springer Wien– New York.

It has information about hotel bookings.

If you really need to book a hotel, if this is the information you are looking for, it says, in English: "We endeavor to secure good-value hotel accommodation for festival visitors. Should you wish to avail yourself of our service please enter the required number and category of rooms on this order form and return by FAX."

This was not the information I was seeking, so I go back to the index screen and choose "never go there," since like most Net surfers, I see the WWW as a completely made up space, a fictionalized storyworld that is overabundant with information, one that is unencumbered by national boundary lines and that enables easy passage through borders.

Without even thinking about it, as a Net surfer I intuitively say to myself: I will go where they tell me I should never go.

But who are they?

Ars Electronica?

Corporate sponsors?

Clever net.artists?

The military?

It doesn't matter anymore.

I have already *bought into* this link and am clicking on it.

I should have clicked on it a long time ago.

But as I wait for the page to download, I decide to savor it, to wait until the end of my session, and so click stop and go back to the index page.

Meanwhile, one thing is already clear: the information on the "information" page was not what I was looking for.

It was only about money and booking.

Was William Blake right when he said, "Where any view of Money exists, Art cannot be carried on, but War only"?

2

Back at the Ars Electronica site, I forget about the word *information* and click on the word *festival*. (I keep steering away from this mysterious phrase "never go there." Why the suspense?)

After the page downloads, the first thing I focus on is the color picture in the center of the screen.

The picture: to describe the picture is not easy, not because I cannot tell you what the picture has *in* it but because of what I am reading *into* the picture (maybe it has something to do with War and Linz, but no one is really talking about this yet).

The focal point of the picture rests on a young white man with a shaved head covered by a baseball cap that has some nondescript insignia on it (military? corporate?).

His left arm is reaching out to his side, and he is either pretending that he is touching a button, or perhaps (but why?) he is stretching his arm out to show that he is human.

But his arm does not look human.

This young white man with the shaved head and baseball cap is wearing a rather conservative button-down shirt and is looking at what appears to be either a video game screen or, more likely, a military tracking system.

What is he tracking—the number of hits his Web site is getting?

I doubt it.

He isn't tracking anything, or at least I think not. Rather, he is posing, he is playacting in a promotional theater of operations called *Infowar*, and the more I look at him the more I think I am looking at a commercial.

In America, the U.S. Army used to have a TV commercial intended to increase the amount of young people who voluntarily served military duty. In this commercial the slogan was "Join the Men Who've Joined the Army."

This was way before the explosion of allegations regarding sexual harassment, rape, and other unlawful use of physical force enacted by U.S. military men on U.S. military women.

This is information that tends to get lost in the oceanic cesspool of news propaganda that the military-entertainment-complex creates for us everyday.

"Join the Info That Has Joined the Info."

Can you imagine volunteering to join the Infowar?

I thought it was mandatory.

Does the survival of contemporary digital artists depend on their willingly enlisting themselves into the new media economy?

Is there no alternative?

I click on the word *projects* (why not *products*?) and then see a listing for *Open-X* and click on it.

Open-X was a very successful network installation at Ars Electronica last year, perhaps the most interesting thing going on during the entire event (well, except for the midnight train ride through the steel mills). The original idea behind the *Open-X* was to make

an attempt to present the methods of various artists specialized in working within networked systems. It is the installation of a temporary open-plan studio in which their current artistic activities are presented. *Open-X* is a walk-in network and hence an experiment in itself, designed to develop different forms of presentation for those fields of artistic activities which are manifest in a process marginal to the object or event.

In other words, by featuring a score of practicing Net heads (including John Hopkins, Tapio Makela, Kathy Rae Huffman, Andrea Zapp, Kunstradio, Public Netbase, Helen Thorington of Turbulence, Terminal Bar, Adrianne Wortzel, and myself) within the institutional context of the Ars Electronica Fleshfactor Festival, the institution itself began to question its own relevance as a major player in the emerging new art scene.

But one thing that was not questioned was its ultimate significance as a major player in the new media economy.

How do we begin to reconcile these contradictions?

And is it necessary to reconcile them?

3

As I said in a recent Amerika Online column, I believe the new media economy is being driven by wild speculation, a speculative market, but also a speculative fiction.

Both speculative fictions and speculative markets try to prophesize the future.

They both try to influence outcomes by creating expectations.

But what kind of expectations can one even begin to create in the new media environment, especially when it is now being thematically represented as an information war?

Is the mascot of the Ars Electronica Festival, the young white man with the shaved head and the baseball cap, fighting an information war?

Is he playing a war game?

Is he hacking into someone's bank account?

Where is the enemy?

On the other side of the computer?

Is the enemy the computer itself?

Or is the enemy within?

Within the computer?

Maybe the enemy lives in institutionalized space.

If this is the case, then the enemy is definitely within.

And we are the enemy.

Ask Robert Oppenheimer, Director of the H-Bomb Expectations.

Meanwhile, I click on the word *netsymposium*, and then I open up the first e-mail, the one that welcomes everybody to the discussion:

In accordance with the multilayered nature of this year's topic INFOWAR, we are planning to take another step forward and break out of the linear form of the discussion forum. Thus, in contrast to prior netsymposia, three experts have been invited to serve as moderators and to facilitate the discussion of the topic's key issues:

The moderators are media theoretician Dr. Friedrich A. Kittler from Berlin, the Dutch media activist and theorist Geert Lovink, and Austrian armament researcher Dr. Georg Schoefbaenker.

I am interested in Mr. Kittler's work and the publicity announcing his participation as one of the moderators in this netsymposium impresses me very much.

I click on his opening salvo entitled "INFOWAR: Notes on the theory history," which begins:

To: infowar-en@aec.at
Subject: INFOWAR: Notes on the theory history
From: Friedrich Kittler
Date: 16 Apr 1998 22:10:09 +0300
Reply-to: infowar@aec.at
Sender: owner-infowar-en@aec.at

ARS ELECTRONICA FESTIVAL 98
INFOWAR. information.macht.krieg
Linz, Austria, september 07–12
http://www.aec.at/infowar

Kai egeneto polemos en to ourano.
Apocalypse 12, 7

By Friedrich Kittler

Naturally, the nineties of this century weren't the first ones to discover that information counts in war. For ages now, two elementary lists, which probably differentiate warriors from merchants as well as from priests, have been in use.

First, A tries to know what B knows without B knowing of A's knowledge. Second, A tries to communicate his knowledge to A' (subordinates or superiors or allies) without B knowing of the transmission, let alone of the transmitted data....

I read the rest of Mr. Kittler's e-mail message, which, to me, reads like an excerpt from a book, perhaps one that is already published or one that is now in progress, but I wonder what kind of knowledge he is trying to communicate to me and if I, with my jaded yet hypertextualized network intelligence, can receive his transmission.

In the end, I cannot receive his transmission.

Perhaps this is mostly my fault since I come to e-mail discussion lists with a different set of expectations, the first of which is to locate writing that moves beyond the book.

And so I look for more e-mails from him since he is the moderator and I hope to maybe find something of his personality in a more e-mail-friendly part of the discussion.

But there are no more e-mails from Mr. Kittler.

Three experts have been invited to serve as moderators and to facilitate the discussion of the topic's key issues....

Is this false advertising?

Is this the new media economy at work?

An Infowar?

Attention!

4

I leave the netsymposium, and then I click on the word *symposium* and find out that one of the keynote addresses at this year's event will be delivered by Peter Arnett of CNN.

Peter Arnett is a war correspondent.

Actually, he is no longer considered a war correspondent, not in the new media economy. No, in the new media economy he is considered a "presentation correspondent."

As a news bite at phillynews.com recently said in relation to the fake story that Arnett reported on for Time/CNN's popular *IMPACT* show: "When is a TV reporter not a TV reporter but a mouthpiece?"

That is the question facing viewers in the wake of the brouhaha over Peter Arnett's role in the creation of CNN's retracted story on Operation Tailwind. Arnett has said the Tailwind story, which had alleged U.S. use of nerve gas in Laos, was "a producer-driven show," that he was basically "the presentation correspondent," and that his role was limited to reading scripts and conducting three on-camera interviews with questions prepared by others.

"They wanted to lend my byline to the story," Arnett said. That idea of Arnett as mere persona is in sharp contrast to the way many CNN viewers view him: as the gutsy, independent reporter smack in the middle of Baghdad—alone—on television screens during the Persian Gulf war.

Arnett, a Pulitzer Prize winner, pointed out that he has "always taken responsibility for my field-action reporting" and that the situation will not happen again. "This is a lesson I've learned the hard way," he said.

"I'm sure Peter Arnett wishes he had done the job he normally has done as journalist," says Robert Lichter, director of the Center for Media and Public Affairs in Washington. "But it's getting harder and harder to do that on TV." With the increase in the number of shows, "the real journalist is being reduced to a talking head. The old school really does reporting as opposed to lip-synching."

As one of many "presentation correspondents" fictionalizing stories in the new media economy, I must say that, as far as I can tell, here in America, and soon, everywhere, there are no more real journalists, just as there are no more real politicians.

Instead, we are all part of the speculative fiction, the one being authored by market capitalism.

This new role that we are all playing in the speculative fiction is that of the "presentation correspondent," an actor destined to perform at the mercy of capital (you, me, President Clinton: it's all the same):

First, A tries to know what B knows without B knowing of A's knowledge. Second, A tries to communicate his knowledge to A' (subordinates or superiors or allies) without B knowing of the transmission, let alone of the transmitted data.

But data leaks.
And as it leaks, it changes shape, it becomes fiction.

5

Finally, I have had enough.

There is only one thing left to do.

I click on the words "Never go there" although it is already too late. I am there.

This time the page downloads very fast.

My vision becomes full of sponsor logos, including Microsoft, Ericsson, Siemens, Silicon Graphics, Digital, the usual suspects.

So tell me:

Where do you want to go today?

An earlier version of this text was originally published online at Alt-X *and* Telepolis *in 1998.*

The Private Life of a Network Publisher

My Intranet is peaking. The neurological webwork that circulates my imaginative discourse for me is taking over in ways that make all other facets of my supposed "self" ready to concede. But concede what?

Making concessions is not what a network publisher does. Rather, a network publisher says things like, "Of course, we're not making a profit now. To be making a profit now would be the equivalent of saying that we have no long-term plan. Let me make this perfectly clear: we have a long-term plan."

But what kind of long-term plan could a network publisher have, especially when considering the speculative fiction that is passing itself off as the new media industry? The cast of characters circulating through this Intranet of endless vaporware aren't being developed by hacker-driven authoring tools created so as to positively change the course of humankind. They are created by marketing engineers who see an opportunity worth cashing in on.

Forget the New Age revolutionary-speak that talks about saving the world and getting rich doing it. Saving the world is as crazy as saving a soul from the bowels of hell. Besides, hell, as Sartre pointed out, is other people. So let's cut the crap and be honest with ourselves: we aren't out to "empower" anyone. We're here to become rich and famous, wired, and well liked. And if someone out there is attracted to us for our own special brand-name consciousness teleporting itself into the electrosphere, then that's all the better. Personalized groupies have a knack for stroking us better than anyone.

But still there's this need to take your creation, your novelistic add-on, and try to go public with it. *Alt-X* has been going public since its start in late 1993 when software engineers and computer scientists were sending us e-mail telling us that finally, something of radical substance was making its way into cyberspace. Then more and more university-connected Digital Beings came online (faculty, grad students, undergrads), especially from various humanities departments, and we started hearing from them. Once America Online, Compuserve, Prodigy, and other commercial services opened up their gateways to the WWW, we were flooded with e-mails from their customers who sounded like prisoners being let out of a banal-content cage. (It reminded me of that movie by Woody Allen, *Sleeper*, where researchers asked Woody if this videotape of sportscaster Howard Cosell was used as a method of punishment and Woody, after a short reflection, said yes.) Eventually, a tide of artists, theorists, and nyet.head generalists got online and began interacting with our content at a rate only mainstream publishers could dream of and only then because they were the few, the proud, the moneyed.

Now, after the surging entry of all of the start-up Internet Service Providers and the soon-to-be-available "easy" access provided by Glamatron networks supported by regional telcos and cable TV honchos, one is forced to ask what are the near-term projections for this object-oriented marketplace of shifting iconography? It depends on how successful the end product blows us away, yes? Isn't that why we're here in cyberspace—to be blown (away)? But if all we're rushing toward is bad Web TV, then the controlling forces of banality will have successfully monopolized our sagging imaginations yet again, and the commercial captains of consciousness will make a toast "to the celebrated end of an antagonism that has grown so weak that even the poverty-stricken feel indebted to us for their mere survival."

Lived reality is spectacularly fragmented and labeled in mediatic categories that measure the Net value of the communicative spirit as it races across the screen—TV screen, computer screen, screen of your fluid mind becoming lived content. The sediment of lived content is what circulates throughout our Intranet, possessing us of the will to desire. Yet desire itself, coded into the electrical currencies of a language fashioned as nothing but pure marketing presence, desires only one thing: the totality of its own experience *as* experienced in the simultaneous explosion of Intranets everywhere.

Meanwhile, my Intranet consumes your desire. Your desire translates this consumption pattern as a kind of narrative power and places value on the accessibility you have to link to my Intranet operation. Together, we become another cyberspace moment.

Here is where consciousness is mediated. Our network potential is what leads the speculative fiction (vaporware-for-itself) to develop our market value for us. It is a dictator over subjectivity but is, at the same time, nothing but subjectivity—that is to say, made-up subjectivity. The pseudo-autobiographical work in progress identified as Mark Amerika, whoever that is, recognizes the Samsa-like metamorphosis taking shape in this rapidly changing new media terrain as a beautiful excuse to locate the contemporary writer cum virtual artist as not only an electronic publisher or hypermedia narrative engineer but a digital art curator and network programmer too. The medium itself enables us to reconfigure the author into a cyborg-narrator whose distributed presence enacts a publishing network with interconnected modalities using the aural environment to technohallucinate a grid of lived content that is forever mediated. But hold your applause, please. There's more here than meets the *I*.

This strange dialectic of each Digital Being (are you experienced?) becoming an "objectivized subjectivity" is worth as much as the market is willing to speculate it is worth. It is the best way we have of realizing our individual capacity for becoming a carrier/deliverer of power. Power, the kind that resonates by way of a network value living up to its potential, is delivered to all of us via a hyperrhetoric (vaporware-for-itself) whose narrative performance takes on the aura of a pseudo-autobiographical becoming (or, to be frank, what I'm talking about here is the absolute power of a brand-name identity, as if identity itself could be a kind of hypertextually marked-up language that caches digicash momentum).

Which brings up this question of the author-as-network-publisher. One question I kept asking in my hypertext theory web, Hypertextual Consciousness 1.0 was, "Is surfing the Net another way of creating narrative experience?" Have the navigators (the readers/coconspirators) finally found a medium that encourages them to sample and manipulate selected data to tell their own story? And who really cares if it is their own? Isn't the beauty of the worldwide Intranet connected to the fact that we all share this internal oblivion, this electroconsciousness, and that no one owns it? Isn't this what the anarcho anticopyrightists are always talking about?

An earlier version of this text was originally published online at futureframe *(October 1999).*

A Chair Is a Chair Is a Chair: Comments at Convergence

I was just browsing through Margot Lovejoy's *Postmodern Currents: Art and Artists in the Age of Electronic Media* (1996), where she makes reference to Plato's *Republic.* In that work, which in many ways helped launch a debate we're still engaged in today, Plato regarded the imagination and vision as inferior capacities, products of the lowest level of consciousness. He was more apt to glom on to abstract concepts like *reason* and the way that reason allows us to contemplate truth, while proclaiming that the products of a visionary imagination would present false imitations. He illustrated these ideas by using the example of the bed, postulating three kinds of beds:

1. The essential concept of the bed created by God
2. An actual bed constructed by the carpenter
3. An artist's representation of the bed, which stands removed from it

I was immediately reminded of Joseph Kosuth's *Chair* piece, where he displayed

1. The definition of a chair
2. An actual chair
3. A photo of a chair

I was particularly struck by the possible connections between Plato's "essential concept of the bed created by God" and the visible definition of the chair (which Kosuth has hanging on the wall in his installation). The phrase "visible definition" got me thinking about Net art in cyberspace. A project like

PHON:E:ME, which the Walker commissioned and opened here (or there—online) on June 30, could be contextualized in this ancient tradition of calling into question how artists re-present "essential concepts." Today, with the advent of digital information technologies like the Internet, we simulate these cultural wars in metamediumistic ways (for example, in *PHON:E:ME*, the tension between the written word and the spoken word, the manipulated utterance and the visibly defined concept).

Steve Dietz, in an e-mail, asks, "How do you define Net art?" and I immediately realize that one way to approach this answer is to focus on my interest in experimenting with the materiality of language and how its "screen resolution" creates a momentary interface that, for me, accentuates the ephemeral quality of any possible definition. Even a snapshot, one that Benjamin suggested would cause a work to lose its aura, cannot capture the definition of Net art for me. That's because Net art itself is not a static object captured in time (not yet, anyway), nor is it a photo-static object representing a definition of itself. Rather, I see it as a work in progress, a pseudo-autobiographical work in progress—that is, an ongoing ungoing rhetorical enterprise that is writing its own story into existence and as such can be glimpsed only from wherever it is you happen to position yourself at any given time. Right now we're in a privileged position: we're in a major American art institution, converging, as it were, on the threshold of a new millennium. Is time running out, or can we see, just over the December horizon, a new world of timelessness, a place where the dot.com party never ends?

This text is a slightly revised excerpt of a presentation that was originally given at the Emergence and Convergence: Digital Media and Online Art event on December 2, 1999, at the Walker Art Center in Minneapolis, Minnesota.

The Rhetorical Gesture

This is a story that is creating its vision.

It can be perceived in electronic reality or print reality or whatever other reality you choose to receive it in—just receive it.

And when you receive it, feel free to play with it because this story is already certain of its dynamic vision, of its sense of play, of its need to continuously produce an experimental humanism.

Mold it, shape it, manipulate it, sample its digital "thereness."

But where is there?

Here is there too.

Here is where "there" can become a place to create collaborative vision: a public-domain narrative environment that defies intellectual property and the need to own and/or be owned.

Place as placelessness, blank fertility of the apparatus dreaming its own seclusion yet opening itself up to all kinds of social relevance by writing itself out into the pixelated semiosphere.

It is a place where the art of rhetoric flourishes, a virtual environment system that expands the conversation our edified codes of meaning have always created for a network of literate subjects who, acting out an essentially decharacterized sense of *consciousness-posing-as-self*, learn the tricks of the trade and bring all of this persuasive currency to market.

It's when we come to market that the Vision Thing becomes a kind of war on ourselves, and once everyone has fought similar battles against their improvisational selves, then the linear logic of the stories that grow out of these related experiences become normative and grounding, ready to be torn apart and *re*vised into new boundary spaces by the cyborg-narrator whose forever shifting nodes of collective self-reflexiveness become decontextualized into even more innovative and marketable figures of speech (deterritorialized fields of writing) that the supplemental modes of decorum choose to deliver our way as HYPE (this is how we create value: perhaps we could have started this riff "Here is a story creating its value").

As our vision of our cyborgian tendencies, of our network value, becomes more grounded, our relationship with the gravity of culture, its material well-being, becomes more intimate.

We (literally) fall in love (with our cyborgian tendencies, our network value, real and potential).

We fall in love with the Vision Thing (the thing that got us here, that made us infinitely connected).

The Vision Thing temporarily blinds us, and soon we find ourselves investing heavily in the potential play of our inebriated insights (our inebriation in sites).

Before you know it, we're changing the way we read the humanities, no longer able to just see *through* the text and transpire meaning from its hidden depths but now envisioning the text's natural abundance as pixelated "print" foregrounding the narrative content, utilizing a prosthetic set of amplified spectacles that play right into the Devourer of Time's hairy hands.

The Devourer of Time, seeing out of the ends of its fingertips, whose retinal secretions taste like a bad wet dream emitted by second-rate poets posing as marketer-legislators taking over the public domain, strangles us to near death, but as soon as we are about to give up breathing and let ourselves pass into the oblivion of an interiorized darkness, something else takes over the Devourer, and this something else takes us over as well. It's a kind of nuke desire, an endless nuke desire that facilitates our need to believe in something besides our vision, something, anything that can still protect us from ourselves.

This something else is the monster-in-love (with itself).

It's a something else that always adds itself on to the edge of our story, an impregnable link, the creative vision expanding.

It's the edge of our story materializing an endless nuke desire forever pursuing its creative vision.

But is the edge of our story, its creative vision (its value added), finally ready to deliver?

Deliver what?

Moments of significance?

A deeper understanding of the world in which we live?

Let us not forget that the Net was originally developed to protect us too.

Protect us from nuke desire.

And now, as with so much multinational-military-media technology, we have consumer applications and ways of seeing that simultaneously defy gravity ("soaring expectations!") while grounding us in the accredited culture ("they have successfully established firm footing").

Can we afford not to decentralize the distribution of power throughout the multinational-military-media matrix?

The fact that you're reading this here, now, and not in some academic journal or commercial magazine suggests the difference.

This is how the art of electronic hyperrhetoric in a scrolling environment works.

The first thing it does is it catches your drift.

It points you in what it thinks is the right direction.

All you have to do is interact (but there are better ways to interact, no?).

Be there.

Follow your eyes and push a button.

Watch it all unfold before your very I's.

Your very many I's that want to find connectivity in the social semiosphere.

Do you want to link?

Do you want to link to me?

As a friend?

A sponsor?

A networker?

Where will that get you?

This our-you-me speak is converging toward vision again, and it reeks of a vaporous politics.

The Vision Thing is site-specific and promises pennies from heaven.

Yet could these moneyed heavens be nothing but havens for the rich?

One sample problematic: how to proceed with a visionary rhetoric without feeling totally indebted to all of the historical accounts.

What is a better weapon: a Swiss Army knife or a Swiss bank account?

Who is it that says "I want..."?

Any child.

And so we learn to speak, to write, to build Web pages, to network our avant-avatars into oscillating states of presence and absence while the wave forms that represent us create new portfolios of meaning that others, should they have access to our pixelated semiospheres, can download and/or virtually incorporate into their own data structures.

Can you feel me *in* you?

Does it hurt?

Feel good?

Want more?

As this data infiltration seeps into our operating systems, we have no choice but to reconfigure our vision.

Reconfigure our vision while simultaneously building our pseudo-autobiographical works-in-progress over the Net via the rhetorical gesture.

An earlier version of this text was originally published online at Alt-X *and* Thing.net *in 1996.*

Triptych: Hypertext, Surfiction, Storyworlds (Part One)

1

The 1998 HyperHalloween Festival that took place at the University of South Carolina this year and was coordinated by one of the most important novelists of the twentieth century, Robert Coover, could have easily turned into a relatively subdued event, another in a series of mundane exercises pitting the outmoded book technology against the avant-garde of hypertext technology. In fact, much of the afternoon symposium discussion did, for clarification's sake, introduce to hypertext newbies the potential advantages and disadvantages of an emergent electronic literature. And what hypertext conference would be complete without a debate between the scholarly footnote and the digital hotlink over The Best Way to Access an Ancillary Text. In the end, the hotlink seemed to have won over even the most traditional book lovers on the panel, but that was the only area where they were willing to give ground.

Things heated up when it came to the subject of narrative art itself. The self-declared book-loving traditionalists were quick to point out that only novels were to be considered real while hypertexts were to be challenged for their authenticity as narrative art and were even called names like *hobbies* and *games*. This sort of book versus computer argument has been going on for most of the '90s and has helped launch a cottage industry, particularly in academia, around the specific tensions that resonate around the issue. But things are changing faster than book lovers or hypertext champions could have ever imagined. Much of the hypertext work composed over the last eight years for floppy disks, CD-ROMs, and early versions of Netscape and MSExplorer is itself starting to look very outmoded. The discussion is about to shift away from issues of avant-garde technology to issues that should have concerned us all along—that is, issues revolving around the innovative writing styles beginning to evolve on the WWW. This more intense discussion that is starting to take shape will now focus on how to simultaneously develop both the literacy we associate with innovative books and the computer or network literacy we associate with the Web.

There is a reason for why, in academia, this continued split, this necessary duality, between books and hypertexts still exists, even though the pop culture is quickly moving beyond it without looking back. First of all, there is the issue of literacy versus what critic Gregory Ulmer calls "electracy." Those of us who grew up reading books know the value of narrative art as experienced in reading novels. And for those of us who have found tremendous value in reading some of the most innovative novels of the last thirty years, we know there exists a power within the novel form itself to create an interface where we, as interactive readers, are invited to activate ourselves in the structural development of the alternative worlds that each writer points us toward and from which we get to practice our own creative-reading skills. We bring these creative-reading skills, where the reader becomes, as novelist Julio Cortázar called it, "a co-conspirator," to *all* texts in hopes of finding previously unexplored paths of knowledge, knowledge that the narrative, contained in a book, mediates for us.

This reader-generated interactivity is the way we use our literacy to create meaning out of texts. Let's face it: with conventional novels, it's so easy, almost comforting, to pick up a book and get lost in its make-believe world of narrative opacity. For the literate reader, there is very little investment made in using our literacy skills in a way that enables us to be taken along for the narrative ride provided by the author, who, knowing we seek the comfort of his or her text, composes this see-through narrative for us. While reading these conventional stories, we never have to be reminded that what we are doing is reading a text composed by an author. "Losing yourself in a book" is something literate readers can relate to.

What I'm describing here is the conventional novel, both commercial bestsellers and most quality literature—the kind we see being promoted by the big

corporate publishers time and time again. It is almost as if our literacy depends on it. But what happens when our literacy requires more than an interaction with an opaque fictional universe composed by an invisible author who
is consciously responsible for its easy-to-read composition? This question was
constantly being asked by the best postmodern novels of the '60s and '70s.
Works like Robert Coover's *Pricksongs and Descants*, Raymond Federman's
Take It or Leave It, Julio Cortázar's *Hopscotch*, Kathy Acker's *Blood and Guts
in High School*, Steve Katz's *The Exagggerations of Peter Prince*, Ronald Sukenick's *OUT*, Madeline Gins's *Word Rain*, Italo Calvino's *If on a Winter's Night
a Traveler*, William Gass's *Willie Master's Lonesome Wife*, and Donald Barthelme's *Guilty Pleasures* were devoted, in part, to the examination of how the
story itself came to be, creating what has come to be known as Metafiction
or Surfiction.

2

Raymond Federman, in his 1975 book *Surfiction: Fiction Now and Tomorrow*,
issued forth a manifesto called "Surfiction: Four Propositions in Form of an
Introduction," where he set the new conditions for narrative practice:

> For me, the only fiction that still means something today is that kind of fiction that
> tries to explore the possibilities of fiction; the kind of fiction that challenges the tradi-
> tion that governs it; the kind of fiction that constantly renews our faith in man's imag-
> ination and not in man's distorted vision of reality—that reveals man's irrationality
> rather than man's rationality. This I call *SURFICTION*.

Federman calls his preferred writing style Surfiction not because it imitates
reality. Quite the contrary, he is looking for the kind of writing that exposes
the fictionality of reality. Just like the Surrealists were keen on calling the locus
of man's subconscious experience surreality, Federman focuses his attention
on the kind of experience that reveals life itself as a fiction. As Céline has
said, "Life, also, is a fiction...and a biography is something one invents
afterwards."

All of the novels mentioned above could be called Surfiction, not only because they "constantly renew our faith in man's imagination" but because
they abandon the conventional techniques associated with narrative composition published in book form. They do this through a variety of ways,
not the least of which is reinventing the page as a visual metaphor for a new
kind of narrative interface using graphical icons, open-space design layouts,

experimental typography, cut-and-paste collages, and disquieting noises manifesting themselves as unreadable marks and doodles. Besides transforming the paginal syntax of conventional novels via an engaged metamorphosis of how words, sentences, paragraphs, chapters, and punctuation literally look on the page, these breakthrough fictioneers were actively exploring the potential of narrative in books to generate an entirely new interactive experience that would call attention to the book artifice itself. Often they highlight the fact that the book was being used as an interface to transmit the fiction and that an author, though fluid in his or her fictional identity, was in fact actively involved in the story's composition, many times inserting a fictionalized characterization of "the author" into the very story you were reading. It was at this point that "the author" as well as the "fictional character" was being transformed into what Federman called a "word being."

Surfiction, as an activist writerly practice focused on revolutionizing narrative experience, was an attack on the false consciousness that most modern fiction associated itself with. Modernism was interested in pulling together a "fragmentary narrative composition" that would give the reader an opportunity to "create a whole" reading experience. But for the Surfictionists, the parts were greater than the wholes, and besides, the wholes don't exist, or if they do, they exist as *holes, black holes,* for readers to get sucked into where they eventually lose themselves.

By the '60s and '70s, the experimental postmodernists were enabling readers to involve themselves with more process-oriented texts as creative "co-conspirators," asking them to help invent the story along with the writer. As Federman says in his *Surfiction* book (remember, this is 1975):

All the rules of and principles of printing and bookmaking must be forced to change as a result of the changes in the writing (or the telling) of a story in order to give the reader a sense of free participation in the writing/reading process, in order to give the reader an element of choice (active choice) in the ordering of the discourse and the discovery of its meaning.

This sounds similar to the rhetoric employed by the early practitioners of hypertext fiction and theory, except you would be hard pressed to find much critical writing that makes the crucial connection between Surfiction and hypertext. Most of the early practitioners of hypertext employ a more Modernistic writing style that, just like the conventional novels of the past, attempts to use hypertext as a technology that create stories whose top priority is to make us feel whole again. In fact, one of the first practitioners of electronic fiction, digital author Michael Joyce, was recently quoted as saying that

> Our lives are multiple and fragmented. In order to make sense out of them, we have to piece together bits.... It is not that computers are magic, it is that the life that surrounds contemporary technology and culture leaves us in pieces and we long to be whole again.

But who is the "we" here? Certainly not me. I'm not looking for wholeness, whether that be in my day-to-day life or my works in progress. Rather, I'm looking for exemplary parts, stray bits of experience that challenge whatever it is I have inside me that wants to stay rigid, that wants to "build character," that wants to structure a plot that "makes sense." And more than that, I want to get caught in the swarm of a buzzing network that feeds me even as I feed it, getting drunk on the instantaneous feedback loop being generated by a desire-machine whose presence is always there, even when I am alone, writing my next words, imagining more immersive narrative spaces for my absent body to interact with.

3

Those of us who are especially fond of innovative narrative form—that is, narrative that challenges the traditions of conventional writing, whether conventional novels or conventional hypertexts—are always seeking to locate stories that enable us as both creative writers and creative readers to *write out their narrative potential.* Cortázar refers to this process as "becoming a story," something that can happen on a plane, in the bathroom, while making love, or even while typing on your computer keyboard. And often this unique narrative potential manifests itself as the exact opposite of a longing "to be whole again." As critic and hypertext Kabalist David Porush suggests, the narrative potential being explored in the most daring contemporary stories "court nonsense, chaos, paradox, entropy, silence, and oblivion." They, in a sense, ask to be mistranslated, to be encountered as unreadable, unnamable discourses that hallucinate alternatives to the technological determinism we are often programmed to associate with computer culture.

And yet there has, until recently, been a tension within the development of hypertext fiction to use the technology as a retrogressive tool that foregrounds a desire "to piece together bits" that will somehow enable us to make more sense of the chaos we live in. By suggesting that we ultimately want to resolve whatever paradox we find ourselves in, conventional hypertext practice would suggest that the writing styles emerging on the Net should not concern themselves with the reinvention of narrative as a liberating practice that explodes the false consciousness of an organic whole but, rather, should instead focus on the reinvention of nostalgia as a way to return to Modernism.

But we already know that Modernism has become outmoded by the exuberant postmodern fictions of the '60s and '70s and that yet another kind of storyworld environment is rapidly developing that moves beyond hypertext (while still integrating complex link structures into its overall composition). This new, networked, storyworld environment that is just now beginning to emerge strategically employs many of the revolutionary narrative techniques associated with experimental postmodern novels as well as consciously using a variety of media already in place (most notably 3-D modeling languages, streaming audio, animated images, and Java) to disrupt the recent trends in both conventional novels and conventional hypertexts.

In my next column I hope to explore one such storyworld environment, a VRML narrative that features a 3-D sex.bot whose complex language structure and behavior takes Web narrative beyond issues of technology and, instead, problematizes both old-styled feminism and corporate patriarchy.

An earlier version of this text was originally published online at Alt-X *and* Telepolis *in 1998.*

Triptych: Hypertext, Surfiction, Storyworlds (Part Two)

In one of his recent essays on the state of contemporary narrative art (called, appropriately, "State of the Art"), the award-winning novelist John Barth, admitting that the new media technology's effect on the practice of writing makes him feel his "dinosaurity," confesses that he maintains a benevolent curiosity about hypertext "out of [my] longstanding interest in the nonlinear aspects of life and of literature."

Barth's "long-standing interest" can be traced to an important essay he wrote in 1967 called "The Literature of Exhaustion," where, at the beginning of the essay, he exclaimed "that a great many artists for a great many years have quarreled with received definitions of artistic media, genres, and forms...pop art, dramatic and musical 'happenings,' the whole range of 'intermedia' or 'mixed means' art, bear a recent witness to the tradition of rebelling against Tradition."

Barth's writerly focus on these rebellious intermedia forms parallels similar strands of intellectual curiosity pursued by many of his postmodern writing colleagues, most of whom helped explode the form of the novel in the '60s and '70s and who have, as I suggested in my last column, created a collective body of work that should be seriously considered by emerging narrative constructivists in the new media environment. Young artists immersing themselves in Web-based literary production would be well advised to, at the very least, read these early postmodern impresarios, especially in light of the fact that current developments in the literary book-writing scene are so predictable and genre-oriented.

As Ron Sukenick, who along with Barth, Raymond Federman, Robert Coover, Donald Barthelme, and other pomo fictioneers, changed the way we interact with novels, has said: "Genre is traditional, medium is technological. We live in a technological culture, not a traditional culture"—which is why, I suppose, some of the most exciting narrative projects being composed today are taking place on the Web. It has to do with what Walter Ong, in the subtitle to his famous book *Orality and Literacy* calls "the technologizing of the word." This technologizing process is opening up huge opportunities for narrative artists to

1. Experiment with formal issues that have been exhausted in book form
2. Pioneer new modes of cultural production and distribution
3. Problematize the individual author-as-genius model by way of collaborative authoring networks that sustain nonhierarchical group production and teamwork

The mainstream publishing industry takes pride in its role of commodifying *the* novel, as if *the* novel were a prefabricated thing that one need only produce formulaically for a consumer market of novel readers. The intermedia environment offered by the Web, on the contrary, enables digital artists to experiment with a multitude of novel forms that move beyond the book and challenge us to reconfigure contemporary narrative practice. One project that I have been operating on the fringes of for the last six months and that attempts to seriously play with these new opportunities presented by the Web is called *Holo-X*.

Holo-X, recently released on the Web to critical acclaim in the *New York Times*, *Wired*, and *Le Monde*, is a 3-D VRML project that interfaces art, sex, commerce, and technology by way of its horny hyperstar, the Sorceress of Language in Uncharted Technologies, also known as S.L.U.T. S.L.U.T. is an artificially intelligent hot.bot that emits a language-driven, gaseous eros meant to challenge the user's conventional reading of their own desire. Reading desire, by way of S.L.U.T.'s narratological behavior, as experienced via both her animated movements in 3-D space and the secret writings available in her 3-D bedroom, becomes part of the interactive fiction and forces the user to reconsider what role virtual reality plays in their own role-playing fantasies as a social creature navigating pornosophic hyperspace.

The main artist behind the project, avant-pop poet and VRML architect
Jay Dillemuth, says that *Holo-X* is "a collaborative experiment in avant-
capitalism." He has reason to put this seemingly oxymoronic neologism to-
gether in that his new media production company, Berkeley Interactive
Design, is experimenting with both the formally innovative challenges of
Web-based art and the audience-development potential of new media enter-
tainment programming. He explained the complex technical work behind
Holo-X:

The first steps of the project were purely design based. In order to get the kind of performance we were looking for on lower-end machines, the character had to be built
with as low a polygon count as possible. I ran some initial experiments using non-
VRML-native 3D modeling applications with high-end features like NURBS and
MetaBalls but found it difficult to control the model's complexity without turning to
polygon reduction algorithms, which tended to degrade the quality of the model beyond an acceptable threshold. So, in order to keep the quality high and the polygon
count low, I decided to model the figure quite literally "by hand." What I mean by
this is that the design process began with a pencil, ruler, and graph paper, and all of
the VRML code was written in a simple text editor. As a result, S.L.U.T. consists of
less than 500 polygons, which means we are able to keep the frame rate up near 10
fps on an average PC without hardware acceleration. Building the figure this way
created other problems, however. We were unable to find any animation software
that was capable of importing VRML 2/97 models. Just about everything will export
VRML (though, as mentioned, not particularly efficient VRML), but we couldn't find
any file translation utilities that were useful for bidirectional file conversion. This
meant we were also forced to build her animations "by hand" as well, to write our
own orientation interpolators for each of her twenty joints, which imposed some obvious restrictions on the complexity of the animations we were able to build for this beta
version. Instead of using longer, linear animation units (for which most animation
applications seem particularly useful), we wrote about fifty or sixty gestural animations
that range from 2–6 frames and generally involve only one body part (i.e., an arm,
which actually consists of three joints). These animations were built around a limited
set of common start and end frames, so that they could be daisy-chained together in
numerous combinations. They were also built around a limited set of general semantic
meanings (i.e., "aggressive gestures," "lascivious gestures," "general speech gestures,"
etc.), so that with custom JavaScripting, the semantic content of her dialogue and her
animation data can be easily coordinated into what passes itself off as reasonably natu-
ralistic behavior.

As far as S.L.U.T.'s dialogue is concerned, the underlying structure is
straightforward. There are twenty scenes or monologues that range between
1.5 and 3 minutes, each of which ends with a yes or no question. What makes

S.L.U.T. unique, though, is that at any given moment, what she says is being randomly selected from five possibilities (an accomplishment that requires custom JavaScripting to extend VRML's capabilities). This creates a kind of OuLiPo-like restraint mechanism that forces the writing team to produce lines of text that fit a predetermined length or what Dillemuth calls an *array*. Most interesting to me as a writer who is always looking for ways to let the language speak itself is how this kind of restraint-oriented writing imposes a more abstract hypertextual structure that enables S.L.U.T.'s caricature to maintain linguistic momentum in a highly charged meaning-making environment.

The main difference between this sort of abstract hypertextual writing and the more controlled style promoted by early practitioners is that *Holo-X* does not rely as much on creating hotlinks that yield other texts. Yes, it has that too, but what's foregrounded here is the narrative environment itself, a 3-D interface that suggests hypertext links are just one more potential narrative device that the storyworld creator has at their disposal (in addition to streaming text, audio, video, animation, A.I. behavior, etc.).

All of which suggests a technical awareness achieved the old-fashioned way, through endless trial and error, with an affinity toward sleepless nights and daytime hallucinations filled with lines of code blurring one's vision.

But Dillemuth is not a hacker. And that's the point. Hackers, for the most part, are looking to show off their mischievous activity so they can gain the laudable praise of their delinquent brethren. Dillemuth sees his own world-building activity as part of an ongoing, process-oriented art work whose routes can be traced to his early interest in experimental writing and an eventual move to the digital domain. Dillemuth again:

I suppose it is a bit of a curiosity to find an experimental poet with not an iota of programming or computer science training embroiled in the creation of virtual worlds. I find it curious and somewhat inexplicable myself. Really there are two major factors that conspired to put me in this position. One is an increasing interest in the artistic and literary potential of technology, based on the aesthetics I embrace as a print writer. The second is an increasing dissatisfaction with the literary avant garde and its relationship (or lack thereof) with its audience.

As my own print work is aesthetically influenced by language poetry, the New York School, Surrealism, the OuLiPo, and Avant Pop, I have a certain fascination with the mechanics of language and narrative, often resorting to source texts, collage, and generative constraints as an integral part of my writing process. To me, narrative complexity and semantic indeterminacy are the primary attractions of experimental literature—that special feeling of befuddlement we all experience when interacting with a challenging text and the concomitant pleasure we derive from following the many semantic threads from their place on the page to the vast associative network of our own memory and experience. It was this fascination with language, narrative, sound, the visual image, and the way they independently and collectively create meaning that led me to investigate hypermedia as a poetic and narrative medium.

This fascination with poetry's potential to morph into something completely different in network culture eventually led to the development of Dillemuth's new media production company, Berkeley Interactive Design, which he started with one of his primary hypermedia collaborators, Alex Cory, another active poet in the San Francisco writing scene. Resisting the mostly conservative world of tenure-track or adjunct teaching jobs here in the United States, these writers are saying that to embrace this new avant-capitalist model is not only necessary but also characteristic of the direction many young artists and intellectuals are beginning to take in hopes of simultaneously creating both provocative art *and* company profits while consciously bypassing the conventional publishing and gallery systems in lieu of something more engaged with the ebb and flow of the digital currencies that power the global capital markets.

All of which begs the following question: is this just more cleverly disguised California ideology posing as leading-edge artistic entrepreneurialism, or are the Internet-based industries, now generating record highs in the wildly speculative NASDAQ stock market, enabling the development of a new role-playing game that anyone, including interventionist poets of the avant-pop variety, can forthrightly play?

And is it possible that things have become *so* speculative in the Internet bubble economy that it's no longer really a question of either/or but rather and/and—as in "Do you have the creative will to take the necessary risks one needs to take to survive in this new media economy, and if you do, what are you waiting for?"

These web.art entrepreneurs are not waiting for anything. When I asked them to discuss some of the key issues being addressed by their just-released *Holo-X* product, they didn't throw out all of the latest techno buzzwords to show that they too are tuned in to all of the vaporware floating around the industry (although they're certainly aware of it). Instead, they talked about the connection between recent postmodernist narrative experiments and the more fluid, postidentity philosophies being investigated by some of the more adventurous practitioners composing their work in cyberspace.

"The first question is 'who am I?'" says BID partner Alex Cory: "What attributes distinguish 'me' as a 'self' or 'subject,' as opposed to some other type of entity? When S.L.U.T asks whether we can accept her supposedly simple sex.bot self as a self, whether we can honor her subjective identity, she is asking us to rethink notions about identity itself." Dillemuth agrees:

What makes our projects unique and, I hope, powerful is their informed and intimate engagement with these radical narrative strategies coupled with the vast potential of immersive multimedia technologies like VRML to actualize the postmodernist aesthetic. In recent years, much academic discourse has been generated regarding notions of the observer and the observed, the male gaze, the body as text, the relationship between technology and gender, the subversion of the subject and the dialectics of desire, the sociopsychological theory of mass culture as a "dreamworld" construct, and the general destabilization of identity in the postmodern era. All of these complicated notions played an important role in providing the theoretical armature, the conceptual foundation upon which these projects rest.

In fact, both *Holo-X* and BID's more commercial, multiuser 3-D adult community called *XRave*, begin conceptually from the destabilization of linearity, temporality, and identity that were and are still to a large degree the primary obsessions of many of the most engaged metafictionists in the '60s and '70s.

"Postmodern philosophy and art have been pummeling us with these questions for decades now," says Cory, "but I never saw practical applications until the advent of Web culture, until I entered the chatrooms and became a 'multiple.' Now I have several identities, male and female, gay and straight. How many Web citizens are experiencing their lives this way?"

It's enough to make me wonder if leading-edge Web artists and new media businessmen see their position here as being firmly aligned with the tradition of rebelling against Tradition. If that's the case, then what does that say about so much of the oppositional role-playing that takes place in both the online art world and Western-styled consumer culture in general? Perhaps what makes Dillemuth and Cory unique in this context is that they seem to have already adjusted themselves in light of these concerns and have started creating something more immediate and lively, like a group of artists who, working in the trenches, see the practice of writing, in whatever medium and under whatever circumstances, as *the* crucial mode of cultural survival.

Creating Web art for distributed global audiences is risky business, especially for the young intelligentsia who know the value of making money. But there's more to the new media economy than simply generating revenues. There's still this need to rebel, to create freedom-loving avatars that let the language speak itself. As S.L.U.T. herself says in one of her poetic, artificially intelligent rants: "The multi-national / corporate criminals // and their babbling, / robotic spokesmen // really have no idea / how intelligent we are // and think of people / as abstract markets."

An earlier version of this text was originally published online at Alt-X *and* Telepolis *in 1999.*

1. As someone who is heavily invested in the Internet, I always check the viability of my day by turning on the computer and engaging it in interactive performance, economic exchange, emotional dialogue, individual search, whatever. How is it feeling today, I wonder, as I click on the word *connect* and see if the world (the market) is still alive with its own metafictional energy. If it is, if the Net is here for me, then I am here for it, and I can feel human again. It is a marriage of economic convenience. 'Til death do I part.

2. I love titling. Sometimes an artwork has a title that makes it worth the high price someone is willing to pay for it. In fact, if a work of art, whether material or digital, has a bad title, then I am not interested in it. The tentative title to this cyborg performance, this theoretical proposition, this pyschoacoustical transmission (pretend you hear me talking), this hyperrhetorical sequence of gestures, is:

Blurring Practices: The Work of Art as Public Offering

3. Well, that's the default title. The title could also be:

The Primordial Affinity between Words and Digital Objects: In Search of the Perfect Language

or

The War against Time: Dying Bit by Bit in the New Media Ecology

or how about

The Reconfigured Author: Media Landscape with Brand-Name Identity

4. The list goes on. I just now realize that all of my language investigations, particularly as they pertain to the Net, are works of conceptual art (look at those beautiful titles in #3!). Joseph Kosuth, eat your heart out.

Actually, Joseph, you may have been thirty years too early, and I am glad I didn't even know about so-called Conceptual Art until I met you last year when we both were invited to the Telstra Adelaide Arts Festival. Not that placing your dictionary definitions of a chair next to both a real chair and a photograph of a chair inside a gallery space was totally irrelevant. Of course not: we've got to think historical context, always. And Art (capital *A*) should definitely promote an anticonsumer thought process, one that thinks through issues of representation and what it means for artists to make art (little *a*). And, yes, I really dig those magazine and newspaper art ads you and others like Dan Graham put out decades before the Internet had altered the global capital markets with such fierce force that even Soros-funded East Europeans could make an immediate impact on an otherwise dead art scene—not to mention those overintellectualized billboard texts that you put up in Europe all those years ago before we even knew what a GUI was or a Web browser. In fact, as the *New York Times* recently pointed out, whether we like it or not, pre-WWW Conceptual Art is having more influence on the art market than ever before.

But in the end, my friend, your purist brand of "art after philosophy and after" is too elitist for its own good. And this is the same trap I see so-called Net or Web artists falling into as well. It is already becoming too isolated from the real world, the real world that exists on the Net itself, the world of Amazon.com and E*TRADE, of eBay and Yahoo. Forget California ideology and/or nettime newspeak. Face it: the Next Five Minutes of Infowars and Revolution and Defamiliarization and Market Updates will be happening at cnn.com, and we know it. So let's tune in and find out what we're worth.

5. Streaming in cnn.com this week, we find that the Kosovo crisis has been moved to the number 2 story, that it has been replaced at the top by the tragic loss of life in the Colorado high school shootings. The shootings took place thirty minutes away from where I live, and now they are the headline news story both here in America and in all of our colonized media markets worldwide.

We have been temporarily distracted from the horrors of Yugoslavia because more kids were killed in the Colorado school than all of NATO's losses combined.

And now that I just got back from a gig in Australia and the jet lag is almost behind me, I want to go back to sleep ("inside, there was sleep, quick and dark, a numbing narcotic that began to take effect even before my soft cheeks kissed the warm buttocks of my fluffy pillow causing instantaneous dreaming of nothing but sleep itself"). But one cannot use sleep as an escape mechanism—not unless one intends on sleeping forever. No, one must deal with it all. Overproduced Infowars, Internet Online Trading, Albania, High School Massacres, Presidential Penises, Conceptual Art. It is ONE BIG BLUR.
6. This blurring is due, in part, to what Stan Davis and Christopher Meyer, in the subtitle to their book *BLUR*, call "the speed of change in the connected economy." Focused primarily on the vast disruptions taking place in global capitalism, they explain how three contemporary forces—speed, connectivity and intangibles—are converging in ways that challenge us to reconfigure how we do business.

In their book, they see a melting of basic distinctions—buyer/seller, product/service, employee/entrepreneur. It sounds like all of the hyperrhetoric focused on hypertextual narrative. You know what I'm talking about—that interface space where the reader becomes a writer or, if you will, a "wreader," *an interactive participant.* What Julio Cortázar, in his prototypical postmodern narrative published in 1963, a novel called *Hopscotch*, referred to as a "co-conspirator."
7. In fact, much of the hype around digital art and some of the more experimental postmodern metafiction of the postwar period, particularly the hype that proclaims hypertext narrative as "a revolutionary mode of publication" that changes readers into "wreaders," is consistent with much of the new age corpo-speak one reads in *Blur*, except in *Blur* we hear more about revolutionary business models, about offers, desires, and financial webs. For example, take the following passage:

The difference between buyers and sellers blurs to the point where both are in a web of economic, information and emotional exchange.... the real news in the BLUR economy is that other things—especially information and emotional engagement—make up a growing proportion of the value being exchanged in both directions. We have reached a point in our story where the Intangibles get serious.

With this in mind, I would like to propose that Net artists need to follow in the footsteps of their entrepreneurial alter egos and start envisioning a parallel consulting practice that can be easily integrated into their ongoing networking practice. That is to say, it is time for Net artists to enter the connected economy as strategic co-conspirators. Forget the boring conference/festival scenes that want to exploit your name and market value for their own inane uses. They are, for the most part, a waste of time, mostly interested in justifying their administrative budgets. And besides, they are not *buying*.

Instead, go where your skills, talents, and insights have more value as emerging artists than ever before: go to market.

8. In fact, Net artists, particularly those in Europe who are desperately trying to get the art world focused on the possibility of purchasing Web-specific art for competitive prices, would be well-advised to read *Blur* and other ancillary texts about "the connected economy." The Internet, as an economic web of activity, is having its all-consuming effect on the way the financial markets exchange their security and commodity holdings, and soon this will include their art holdings as well—their Net-based art holdings.

But Web artists who are seriously considering offering their work to the public to ignite a speculative market in Net-based art should first acquaint themselves with the Internet economy they hope will support them. If they are serious about opening up a new kind of speculative art market for their online work (and they are all too serious; this much is obvious), they must focus their attention on how the Internet economy acts like a chaotic yet self-correcting financial market.

With the stock market itself becoming decentralized, moving away from the trading floor to the online door, now might be a good time to investigate how the Net art economy is also on the verge of behaving with the speed and fluidity of a financial market. Just like the old-fashioned marketplace for goods and services are also having to adapt to the new conditions, Internet art is part of the futures market. "Vaporware capitalists" investing in the futures market are already seeking out the next area of speculative growth, ready to immerse themselves in a continuous exchange of product knowledge or what I like to call *seductive knowledge*. With this in mind, Net artists must be poised, ready to participate in the high art of seduction.

For seductive knowledge about your work to have its desired effect in the Internet economy (to generate investment and create wealth), you must first understand the business of offering yourself to clients, collectors, suitors, and johns (assuming you consider this need to sell your work a blatant form of prostitution).

For those Web-based artists who are having difficulty figuring out why their online work is *not* producing an income, here's something to consider: *Nobody is buying your Net art because in networked economies the savvy investor either already has enough knowledge to know that your work is not worth investing in or, worse yet, you as a network artist have yet to use the skills and tools you have at your disposal to offer enough seductive knowledge of your own to convince the buyer that your work is worth investing in.*

Seductive knowledge, whether it originates in the film houses of Moscow or the hiking trails of Colorado, drives the new media art economy just as it does all other sectors of the Net economy, an economy that is always ready to take into account the intangibles that go with being human. These intangibles, often disguised as information transmitted via emotional exchanges with active agents speeding through the connected economy, can be viewed as digi-cash paracurrencies that defy conventional dollar values and, instead, bring to market all kinds of speculative value with investment potential. It might be a wise strategy for practicing Internet artists to take their work to the Street, to embrace the growing knowledge networks that make being an online artist not just a job, but a cooperative (ad)venture.

It's time to strut your stuff.

9. Like budding entrepreneurs caught in the heat of IPO fever, artists hoping to increase the value of their online work must focus more of their practice on the value-added intangibles that will increase their visibility in the network economy and enable them to build brand-name identities that will foster their own economic growth. Again, the best way to do this is to bring your work to the Street—to make offers of seductive knowledge that will interest investors in bringing speculative value to your ongoing enterprise. You must, out of necessity, have an exit strategy, a plan to go public, that takes your outmoded artist's soul to market so that you may enrich your life with the promise of a comfortable future.

An IPO (initial public offering) is the process of issuing stock in a company as a buying opportunity for investors and as a way for the issuing entity to raise capital so that the company can grow. That's pretty straightforward. But what about Web artists? Have they ever considered making public offerings themselves so that they too can put their careers on a track aimed at maximum, yet manageable growth? *IPO* is just a new phrase that artists can translate into "going public" with their own work—like what used to be called an *artist's show* or a *publication.*

The difference now is that we no longer have to rely on the whims of institutional bureaucrats who, as intermediaries, always have their own economic agendas at heart. Rather, you can do what Wolfgang Staehle has recently done with his breakthrough Web project, *The Thing*: you can hold an online auction at eBay. Fuck Sotheby's or Christies. They don't get it. But eBay does. For less than five dollars, you can put your Net artwork on the market, in bold type, and see what its current value is. If you want to set a limit on the lowest acceptable bid, you can do that too.

Why not? Are you afraid it won't sell for enough money? Well, then that says a lot about why nobody's paying for your work. The market doesn't lie about these things. It speculates. It sees your value for what it is (or has the potential to be). If the value of your Net poem is $10, and someone on eBay is willing to pay for it, then sell one per day and buy some fresh pasta with your net earnings. Cook the pasta for you and your lover and then write a Net poem for your lover too, for free.

10. My friend, a former Conceptual Artist turned New Media Entrepreneur who just sold his company for over $20 million, told me in a recent e-mail that

only by turning the speculative knowledge market into a fictional enterprise can we even begin to process the series of public offerings we've recently witnessed, from the Yahoo fiction to the Amazon fiction to the Broadcast.com fiction. Anyone who is not clued in to how this market is being narrativized is out of touch with the world that is now taking shape in cyberspace. As a well known online artist, your going public with your work, making the right offers, creating the right emotional environments for all kinds of cross-cultural exchange, is part of your economic imperative. You owe this to yourself as both a person and a commodity.

This got me thinking that I, not only as a Web artist but as a print and online publisher, need to reevaluate what it means to "go public"—how the IPO craze associated with Internet stocks is driving the new media economy and, with it, the new media arts. Once your stock rises, you, as both a person and a commodity, need to outperform the rest of the pack so that your future earnings guarantee continued investment in who you are and what your work is becoming. In fact, my own life practice is totally blurring with endless offers, and managing them all requires continuous administrative work so that I no longer know where the businessman ends and the artist begins. Welcome to the big time, Mr. Net Art.

In a way, this column is also part of an offer. It is an emotional investment that I am making with my readers, some of whom may one day see not just the economic value of my cultural service but the emotional value as well and, as a consequence, invest part of themselves in my network life practice.

But that is not why I write these columns. I write these columns to write out my blur.

An earlier version of this text was originally published online at Alt-X *and* Telepolis *in 1999.*

Sonic Upheaval: Using mp3 to Rip the System

A relatively small Web company called mp3.com recently went public and, although its total revenue stream for the last year was well under $1 million, the stock market was so seduced by its potential to alter the way we distribute music to each other that, in its first day of trading, the stock price increased dramatically and at one point had a paper value of over $7 billion. That's 7 billion greenbacks for a site that basically traffics in audio tracks created by tens of thousands of unknown bands and other wannabe recording artists. One wonders if there was some funny weed being passed around on the floor of the New York Stock Exchange that day. Probably not (the stock has since lost over half of its opening-day value).

The advent of a network distribution paradigm that enables artists to deliver their own digital music files directly to a niche audience located at work or home is about to revolutionize the recording industry yet again. In the rapid spin cycles of the media brainwash, this is already old news. But don't tell that to the global equities market looking to cash in on anything that just *sounds* like it's the next hot item in the fantasy world of consume-everything .com.

Question: Is mp3.com the only site on the Net that will be able to profit from this monumental shift in music compression and distribution? No. It has a small market that once the technology becomes more accessible to individuals, will make its mediating role as a clearinghouse for mp3 delivery less attractive (let's not forget that the Net, if it's about anything, is about disintermediation). What mp3.com has going for it more than anything else is a name. *Mp3*, it ends up, is the most searched for word in the big search engines. More than the word *sex*. One wonders what kind of market value a business called mp3sexsexsex.com would be worth. You would not even need a business plan, just a cool mp3sexsexsex.com logo, a Web site with endless links to pornographic audio tracks and a compression technology that makes it easy to deliver the data over bandwidth-friendly pipes. Ready to invest in the future?

As you may already know, *mp3* (developed at the Fraunhofer Institut Integrierte Schaltungen) is short for "MPEG audio layer 3" and covers audio compression only. According to Nomadworld:

In 1992, Fraunhofer's algorithm was integrated into MPEG-1. The MPEG-1 specification was published in 1993. The details for MPEG-2 were finalized in 1994 and the MPEG-2 specification was published in 1995. On January 26th, 1995 Fraunhofer applied for a patent for MP3 in the United States, and on November 26th, 1996, it was granted.

And history marches on. It didn't take long for the Net music underground to turn mp3 into the compressing technology of choice. Practicing a variation on what I have, in previous columns, called *surf-sample-manipulate*, a worldwide community of music aficionados, entrepreneurial rippers, audio artists, and narrative remixers have used compressed mp3 files to bypass the corporate mentality that still spews the deceitful propaganda that artists need corporations and, more important, their lawyers, to protect them from other rip-off artists in the culture. This fear-mongering corporate protection plan seems to go against the grain of what the Web (as a delivery medium and engine for audience development) frees us all to do and highlights how much the dominant system in place today *really* exists to protect those same corporate honchos and their lawyerly brethren.

In this regard, I'm impressed with how quickly the Net music underground has latched onto the ripping effects associated with the technology surrounding mp3 so that it can transmit noncommercial music to various niche communities located throughout the electrosphere. Bypassing the banal hype mentality of the corporate rock culture, network-distributed sound now has a chance to become a kind of viral meme that intervenes within the mainstream mediascape in such a way that it alters the unidirectional marketing aura being fashioned by the commercial captains of consciousness. If someone wants to sell-out or become absorbed, they can now do it on their own terms, interacting with their own niche audience—which, it just so happens, is often composed of other Net-connected artists experimenting with the technology in similar ways.

One of the big issues that constantly gets discussed on panels focused on the mp3 revolution is copyright. Copyright has applications in paper and plastic culture because its objecthood is decidedly material. But with electronic hypermedia, the work's objecthood is decidedly virtual and infinitely reproducible with an ease of network distribution that is out of control. So to try to force the current copyright laws on the network culture, as the copyright maximalists and recording industry lawyers are eager to do, is a bit crazy and will not work in the context of Net culture. I'd say that if you don't want your work to be reproduced and manipulated over the network spectrum, then don't put it on the Web. Why use outmoded copyright laws to protect yourself from your potential audience?

One of the big problems in the mp3 world, as with most everything related to Net-based content these days, is the shameful lack of innovation on behalf of the so-called recording artists who now have every opportunity to experiment with the Web as its own medium, instead of basically repurposing old media in new media contexts. This has always been a problem in the techno arts, as is evidenced by the McLuhan insight that the first content of any new medium must be a prior medium. (For a more scholarly examination of this phenomenon as it relates to the new media, see Jay Bolter and Richard Grusin's recent *Remediation: Understanding New Media.*)

Anyone who has visited the multibillion-dollar company Mp3.com's Web site knows that it's one of the least appealing music sites on the Web, although some of the music and sound art you can find there is refreshingly anticommercial and, in musical terms, valuable. But when it comes to exploring the Web's potential to integrate music into a more immersive, language-enriched environment, they just don't get it.

This is why, in large part, a group of artists I worked with on a new Web project called *PHON:E:ME* decided to try to create another model for both audio writing and Net-based art. *PHON:E:ME* is an mp3 concept-art album with accompanying hyper:liner:notes and is located on a server at the Walker Art Center's Gallery 9. The project was commissioned by Gallery 9 with additional support from the Australia Council for the Arts New Media Fund and the Perth Institute of Contemporary Art in Western Australia (the Jerome

Foundation funded the production of the *PHON:E:ME* CD featuring my soundtrack collaboration with Erik Belgum).

Besides bringing together this network of institutional affiliates that were able to help offset some of the project's costs (which were unusually high for network art), there was something else that came together in this project. An "orchestration of writerly effects"—a loose confederation of network artists, writers, designers, DJs, programmers, and curators—was able to create a transformational narrative environment that tells the story of how Net culture is altering our received notions of authorship and originality and how emerging digital artists are helping break down the boundaries between genres, between art and nonart and the various disciplines that have too often led to rigid compartmentalization and weak critical speculation.

Like the *Holo-X* project I wrote about earlier this year, the *PHON:E:ME* project at the Walker features the work of a group of writers who have opened themselves up to a more elaborate, multidisciplinary, new media art practice that not only throws a monkey wrench into mainstream conceptions of what a writer is but also reconfigures some of the issues surrounding experimental narrative practice as a one-man (one-woman) show.

As Anne Burdick, who directed the project's interface design says,

Unlike the print paradigm, in which the making of books is basically an industrialized division of labor performed at the service of the writer/ing, the decisions made on the new media assembly line play a much greater role in the outcome of the finished product. This is due in part to the lack of conventions but also to the fact that each person's contribution cannot be discreetly divvied up when it comes to shaping the final form. It's the really cool interplay between the programming, the interface, the sound, the performance and the writing—EACH MUTUALLY DEFINING—that is so damn great!!!! (to me).

Me too. This way, each individual's contribution—whether Cam Merton and Tom Bland's artistic programming, Burdick's interface design, or the phonemic remixes of Belgum and Sydney-based DJ Brendan Palmer—can resonate with each other and with what is going on in cyberspace at large. Belgum's focus on the role of resonance in his remix helps accentuate the point:

Resonance, with its beautifully suited literary, musical, acoustic and linguistic (phonetic) connotations, seems to me a very rich resource and strangely absent from much western music, at least absent as a parameter that composers consider to be on par with pitch and rhythm.

Is the author function in fact being reconfigured to translate more as a network resonance than as the product of an individual genius? This is a question the *PHON:E:ME* project is constantly reformulating.

Jerome Rothenberg, whose poetics of prophecy declared the writer/artist a sacred technician, has said (as far back as 1977), in relation to writerly performance:

There is a continuum, rather than a barrier, between music & noise; between poetry & prose (the language of inspiration & the language of common & special discourse); between dance & normal locomotion (walking, running, jumping), and so on.

The same holds true for sound design, interface design, hypertext design, shockwave programming, and the alternative modes of cultural production that are now emerging on the Net. Everything happens in the *now* as part of a shared research and development platform where the various network conductors involved in the project can finally begin orchestrating their own narrative remixes for whatever audience they happen to build within the context of a fluid community (one that, like a cloud, changes as it goes).

The twentieth century's move away from the idea of a masterpiece to one of transience is still very much in play, especially on the Web, where the digital artist must offer a frank acknowledgment that in a tools-dependent economy of endless upgrades and changing browser standards, some network art will become obsolete soon after it is released into the online culture.

This suggests to us that network writer-artists must always already reconfigure their practice into something beyond individual textual performance. The writer-artist, now morphed into a kind of network conductor who filters the various forms of resonance that fluidly play themselves out on the Net, "becomes, increasingly, the surviving nonspecialist in an age of technocracy" (to quote Rothenberg again).

Listen to Belgum, the soundwriter, discuss his contribution to the *PHON:E:ME* project:

I do see myself as a writer, not as a composer. I just write for audio as well as for print. I would say I try to simply further articulate the various linguistic phenomena that occur in speech. And there's a whole range of possibilities with each text. The reading style of each writer determines what moves you make in the mix, in signal processing, in resampling of sounds, overdubbing, etc. Another thing is that it makes experimental writing appeal to a wider audience. On a personal level and on the level of a reader, there are many pieces of writing that I just didn't understand until I heard them read by the author. Or at least I didn't understand them at a level I was satisfied with.

In a global market capitalizing on individual greed and preference, where everybody wants to have their own Yahoo ("I want my mp3," screams the cover of the August 1999 *Wired* magazine), the subject of selling so-called Net art becomes the subject of overkill (why the rush?). Meanwhile, collaborating on network art projects and locating a distributed niche audience willing to interact with the work is what Net practice should remain focused on. Our mp3 site at the Walker may not be worth $7 billion on the stock exchange but then again, neither is mp3.com.

An earlier version of this text was originally published online at Alt-X *and* Telepolis *in 1999.*

Para-Sites and Host Connections: An Unconditional Love

On visiting the *net_condition* Web site being served by the Center for Art and Media Technology (ZKM) in Karlsruhe, Germany, my first question was, Who hacked the site?

"Waiting for reply," my friendly Netscape browser told me. I hate when that happens.

So, instead, I open up a new browser and surf to one of my favorite Web sites (uh, that being *Telepolis*) to read a review of the ZKM show by Josephine Berry, who actually was able to go to the physical site in Karlsruhe to see what it was all about.

Her review made some good points, particularly when she said,

One of the residing feelings one gets from this show is of extreme institutional discomfort intermittently broken by a kind of rebel yell affirming its right to exist. In so far as net art has inflicted such a schizophrenic identity crisis on its adversary and despite the mist of guilty embarrassment hovering around many artworks, it can be said to have fulfilled its own objectives in the exact moment that it becomes extinct.

Meanwhile, my other browser window, still "waiting for reply," eventually coughed up another clue:

Proxy Error
The proxy server could not handle this request.
Reason: Host not found

And then it hit me, like a celestial revelation where the skies open up and the Living Godhead tells it like it is: "Host not found."

When it comes to Web art exhibitions, *host* is a generic character that anyone can play, and often is the time that I myself have, in the guise of the *Alt-X* or *GRAMMATRON* host, delivered a similar message to one of my overseas visitors who was trying to feed off of my digital blood.

But when it comes to our contemporary *net_condition*, the methods for exhibiting art in a world now becoming conditioned by networked forms of instantaneous telecommunication is totally open to interpretation. One might say that we are all responsible for playing the role of host and that wherever there are hosts, surely the parasites will follow.

But then who are the parasites, and who are the hosts in the quickly evolving Web art scene? A *parasite* is properly defined as "an organism living in or on another living organism and deriving its nutriment partly or wholly from it, usually exhibiting some special adaptation, and often causing death or serious damage to its host."

Does this sound like any Net artists you know? Or does it rather sound like some of the larger government- and corporate-sponsored art organizations suffering "extreme institutional discomfort"?

I guess it depends on what condition your condition is in.

Net art has proven once again that the art world, a swollen-faced whore addicted to the kind of prestige only good Saatchi pounds can buy, is ready to sensationalize itself for the sole purpose of putting off its inevitable extinction. The only question I have is, "Why the rush?"

Being a kind of Net art dinosaur myself, I must say that I am happy to spend most of my time these days locating the ever-changing archeological digs I keep navigating my way through when steering my virtual subjectivity through the desert of the real we call *cyberspace.*

For, as everyone should know by now, *Web surfing itself is the one true form of net art,* the one where you anonymously play the role of hungry parasite (*para* meaning "beyond," *site* meaning a "location" or "the scene of a specified event") living inside or on another organism—in this case, the Web. I would like to see Mr. Saatchi try and buy *that* from me.

But I digress. Let us reconsider our present-day net_condition. First, the role of curatorial practice in Web art: In 1997, when Alex Galloway of Rhizome and I co-curated the first serious online exhibition called *Digital Studies: Being in Cyberspace,* our intentions were twofold—(1) to use the enormous attention our host site *Alt-X* was receiving to bring greater visibility to Web art projects being created all over the world and (2) to call into question the need for artists evolving a contemporary Web art practice to feel dependent on institutional sites for greater visibility and acceptance in the art world establishment.

Essentially, Alex and I were playing host to a great Web art linking party. We even shared some theoretically deranged essays for our guests, writings that we hoped would help contextualize the present moment, which we saluted with phrases like "creative exhibitionism," "digital object," and "virtual republishing." Playing host was a blast, and never once did I imagine what it would have been like had I had access to the entire interior space of the Pompidou Center so that we could hold our party there.

Having major art institutions like ZKM exhibit a snapshot of our current net_condition is like having Alan Greenspan, the Federal Reserve chair, tell the stock market that he senses an unconditional display of "irrational exuberance" and then having the stock market respond accordingly (selling off in a panic state of paranoiac psychodrama). Here's what the ZKM snapshot of our current net_condition says: "ZKM is now ready to take a snapshot of our current net_condition. You will respond accordingly."

What else does it say? "Where is the Museum of Modern Art?"

What else does it say? "What are we going to do now that the parasites are becoming the hosts?"

Another host, Randall Packer, is, like so many of us these days, dancing on the borderline that divides the institutional host from the parasitic artist. Packer's *net_condition* project is essentially a specially curated mailing list where he, as artist, gets to play host by inviting various artists, curators, theorists, and so on to his online party, which then begs the question: how can the artist host his or her own party while working on the institutional clock?

Packer's answer is to create what he calls a telematic manifesto, or a Hypertextual Collectively Generated Net Document. By far the most interesting piece in the *net_condition* show, Packer is in search of the twenty-first-century *Gesamtelewerk*, a formal convergence of all media so that we may, as utopian dreamers, find ourselves living in the network as if it were the social surrealist narrative of all our lives.

The manifesto Web site cites Baudelaire, Wagner, Roy Ascott (who also gave the keynote for *Digital Studies* all those years ago), Moholy-Nagy, John Cage, Dick Higgins ("the social problems that characterize our time, as opposed to the political ones, no longer allow a compartmentalized approach"), Billy Kluver, and Kandinsky.

Packer asks his party guests some serious questions that he hopes they will consider when hanging out at his at online soiree:

Will Net artists revive the hopes of previous avant-garde with the power to distribute their message instantaneously and globally?

Does the notion of a *Gesamtelewerk* suggest the possibilities for social transformation resulting from forms of collective art that engage audiences through involvement, inclusiveness, and participation?

Can the *Gesamtelewerk* serve to defragment cultural separatism, specialization, and the isolationist tendencies within our institutions, encouraging rather a cross-disciplinary interaction between individuals in all fields and walks of life?

He hopes the answer is in what he calls *Telematic Art*, although others who are invited to the party are encouraged to reshape the discourse into their own visions and terminologies, which they do. A party guest named Marc Lafia says,

I don't believe there is anything new to the notion of the distributed self. The self is the self in the world. Leibnitz put forward the idea that the self, a monad, contains the world. Everything of the world is in the individual. Yet the self is always, in all ways, always becoming. We are autopoietic, in search, in flux, between meaning, becoming understood, accreting, desiring machines, unknowing, unbecoming. The understanding of these words, now, are in the context of a distribution of meaning held in the space of understanding and misunderstanding in the singularity of a moment in a vast galactic metabolism, in the ever evolving social techno space of language.

Joel Slayton, riffing on Lafia, elaborates on the notion of autopoiesis:

Autopoiesis, a term developed by biologists Humberto Maturana and Francisco Varela, is a form of system organization where the system as a whole produces and replaces its own components and differentiates itself from its surrounding environment on a continual basis. Principles of this basic system organization appear in more complex systems, what are known as *third-order couplings* or *systems* that emerge out of social interactions, such as languaging.

To my mind, if I were going to list the keywords in the metatag I inserted into this Hypertextual Collectively Generated Net Document, I would come up with a list that started off like this: "social techno space of language, languaging, autopoiesis, distributed self, hypermediated collective consciousness, narrative extension, blurred distinction, consensual domains, networked subjectivity, telepistemologically enabled kin."

Did someone say *net_condition*?

Personally, I would call this kind of writing, thinking, playing, and networking *neuromantic art*. *Neuro* as in "nerve" or the American expression "it takes a lot of nerve." *Mantic* as in "pertaining to or having the power of divination." You know you are neuromantic when your intranet is peaking and you cannot stop yourself from becoming, from becoming "languaging," or when an always emerging model of autopoiesis is lurking in a social environment looking for some quick snapshot of a particular scene that leaves itself open to organization—like, for example, the Net art scene, that complex system of currency exchanges transmitted via the evolving social techno space of language. Dig?

When the neurological Web work that circulates within your imaginative discourse starts taking you over in ways that make all other facets of your supposed self ready to concede, don't. Rather, manifest. Manifesto Destiny. That is where the future is and, perhaps, the most vital response one can have to the critical condition Net art finds itself in.

As László Moholy-Nagy says on *The Telematic Manifesto* site:

What we need is not the *Gesamtkunstwerk* alongside and separate from which life flows by, but a synthesis of all the vital impulses spontaneously forming itself into the all-embracing *Gesamtwerk* (life) which abolishes all isolation, in which all individual accomplishments proceed from a biological necessity and culminate in a universal necessity.

Long live the parasites. May the party never end.

An earlier version of this text was originally published online at Alt-X *and* Telepolis *in 1999.*

Writing As Hacktivism: An Intervening Satire

> My reconcilement to the Yahoo-kind in general might not be so difficult, if they would
> be content with those vices and follies only which nature hath entitled them to.
> —Jonathan Swift, *Gulliver's Travels*

As I write this column, the TV is on, and the picture on the screen is a live shot of a clear blue sky with one object in it, a large multicolored blimp with the phrase *Monster.com* written across it. This is an advertisement during a football game that the TV now cuts to.

For some reason, this immediately reminds me of the opening to Thomas Pynchon's *Gravity's Rainbow*, where he begins, "A screaming comes across the sky. It has happened before, but there is nothing to compare it to now."

My inclination is to sample and manipulate the Pynchon vocabulary and syntax while applying its rhetorical aura to the new media economy, to exagggerate (an extra *g* for good measure) the implications of a Monster.com in the sky, to somehow defamiliarize the taken-for-granted context of what I see, for what I now know to be true about Internet capitalism and the dot.com mania that hypes the potential of e-commerce way out of proportion: "It has happened before, but there is nothing to compare it to now."

This inclination to create a hyberbolic version of what I see happening in my time is not at all unusual. The desire to satirize what is already a self-parody is a desire easily absorbed into the ironic revolutions of everyday life we bring into the new millennium. The poet Ezra Pound, whose own hyperbole was distorted to suit the fascist regime in Italy during World War II, was known throughout the twentieth century for his simple, yet direct proclamation to all emerging writers of the new world order: "Make it new," was his rallying cry, and so they have, continuously, just like the ad gurus on Madison Avenue, and that is what we find ourselves buying into like never before.

But what about a sampled manipulation of that Pound dictum into something more disturbing? If we take the more uncertain step of the Russian Formalists and their practice of *ostranenie*, then perhaps we come up with something different, like "Make it strange."

Making it strange is a challenge these days, especially given the high-resolution strangeness being distributed by the captains of commercial consciousness, the ones with their blimps flying high above the football stadium on January 1, 2000. These strange pictures of blimps in the sky are being broadcast into millions of homes at the turn of the millennium. The problem for the contemporary writer who knows that the concept of the literary is now in more jeopardy than ever before, can be summed as follows: how does one make Monster.com even more strange than it already is?

The home page of Monster.com has numerous options, including the normal range of chats, polls, search engines, and so on. But to me, the most interesting piece of rhetoric on the home page of this site says, "Explore the possibilities of the world's first auction-styled marketplace for independent professionals."

The phrase "explore the possibilities" is highlighted, and one click takes you to what amounts to an uppity slave market, where employers can hire top talent in real time. You would think that this sort of source material would be ripe for satirical ambush, especially given the nature of the site's domain name. I mean, who *are* the monsters of the new millennium?

But to satirize the real on its own terms means playing in the same environment that it operates in. A funny novel will no longer be enough, especially since most of your readers are spending more and more of their time online, surfing the Web. And yet operating in the Yahoo environment risks turning the writer into a Yahoo themselves. So what's a writer to do?

New media writers, growing out of the rival tradition in literature, would need to reconfigure themselves into a kind of network provocateur who, among other things, uses satire as a political weapon. Neither a writer who composes biting critiques of new media culture for their next book nor a glorified HTML slinger for a hip, hypertextualized online zine, the new media writer entering the Y2K twilight zone needs to break away from the literary altogether, using rhetorically charged language and the network environment's syntax (protocol?) to create an interventionist art practice that defamiliarizes the Monster's all too dehumanizing status quo effects.

One subject that continually presents itself to the new media writer over and over again is the commodification of people and their money. The spectacle of a Monster.com in the sky is just one example. Another example would be the recent hoopla over the eToys versus etoy debacle. As many readers already know, the e-commerce giant eToys has recently filed suit against the European art site etoy, forcing the artists to shut down their Web site and leading the totalitarian Network Solutions to shut down the forwarded e-mail that etoy depends on for its artistic livelihood. This last move by Network Solutions came after etoy refused to accept a reported half a million dollars in cash and stock options from eToys in exchange for its domain name, which is, after all, their identity.

The etoy art group could be considered hactivists—that is, activist art hackers who use the Web and other resources to create a kind of interventionist cybertheater (similar to political street theater) that finds its roots in the alternative writing pranks of Artaud, Lautréamont, The Living Theater, and Situationism, while embracing an Avant-Pop cultural aesthetic flaunted by rock bands like Devo. Other sites produce similar online theater. eToys, for example, also filed a restraining order against the Electronic Disturbance Theatre, cutting it off the Web and, meanwhile, changed its own site to resist the kinds of civil disobedience attacks that EDT is capable of generating.

Then there is the RTMARK site that has successfully used its cleverly designed Web satire as a political weapon to intervene in the mainstream corporate world. Their gwbush.com and gatt.org sites point to a new media writing practice that employs many of the principles elaborated on in this column, particularly the surf-sample-manipulate practice of sampling data from the mainstream sites surfed on the Web and then manipulating that data to create exagggerated (always the extra *g*) satirical effects destined to disrupt our conventional viewing and surfing habits. A site like gatt.org and what it implicitly practices does not necessarily "make it new," but it does "make it strange," especially for those unsuspecting souls who inadvertently come upon it.

What is being satirized at both etoy and RTMARK is the "corporate body"—the corpo-real—and what is being celebrated is the artist or hactivist collective as a disembodied intelligentsia sabotaging the corpo-world's

rampant commercialization of the Web (the profits of the material versus the
prophets of the mind). The anonymity of the personnel building these two
sites further distorts our idea of what a new media writer is or can be. As is
always the case with hyberbolic writing that risks its life as a practice struggling to survive in a hostile environment, new media artists today must serve
up what Raymond Federman, in his classic postmodern novel *Double or Nothing* calls "a real fictitious discourse." To survive, this discourse must engage
itself in a pseudo-utopian theme park dominated by e-commerce sites in
search of eyeballs. Most of these sites are to be populated by monstrous figures
with "fatbrains" and "hotbots" always on the ready to try and seduce you into
their trademarked domain.

Immediately, other questions arise: Is there a story here? If so, whose story
is it, and who is writing it?

The "real fictitious discourse" is now a Web in process, one open to an
intervening satire that can, at various times, manifest itself as an RTMARK
mutual fund, a FAKESHOP performance art spectacle, the issuing of phony
etoy stock certificates, ersatz e-mails, or a perfectly well-written press release.
For example, here is an excerpt from a recent RTMARK press release after
eToys publicly announced that it would stop aggressively pursuing its case
against etoy:

> As of Dec. 29, eToys, the giant online toy company, is still suing etoy, the most im-
> portant Internet art group, to prevent etoy from using etoy.com, a URL that the artists
> were using long before the toy company came into being. eToys has, however, agreed
> to temporarily "move away" from the lawsuit (without dropping it), according to
> *Wired*.
>
> "It's good that eToys is now being shamed into lying to the press that its 'intent was
> never to silence free artistic expression,'" said RTMARK spokesperson Ernest Lucha.
> "But 'moving away' from the suit now that their shopping season is over, without any-
> thing even resembling an apology, let alone compensation to etoy for their financial
> and emotional nightmare, is just pathetic and will not fly with a lot of people."

The press release also mentions an online game "whose aim is to lower the
eToys stock price to $0.00."

In this new media writing scenario, the fictional Ernest Lucha has a very
real discourse he is releasing to the press. This discourse, if contextualized
properly, can then become its own meme or media virus, taking on the mainstream host in a way that alters the autopoietic environment the Web thrives
in. For example, the influential Bloomberg.com financial news site virtually

republished the entire RTMARK press release, and the eToys stock price did indeed keep going down. This is not to suggest that the etoy debacle or the RTMARK assault is solely responsible for eToys' recent slide in the market, but the information in the RTMARK press release is skewed so that it essentially mimics the way corporate press releases are skewed, complete with sound-bite blurbs, Web site addresses for further information, and self-reflexive advertisements for RTMARK art products (projects). This representation of corporate culture is subtly made strange and, as a result, RTMARK ends up having more of an effect than if it was to write a satirical novel about the out-of-control economic practices of most multinational corporate monsters.

In other words, this is serious business.

The press release continues, letting its viewers know that "Activists' anti-eToys efforts will continue at least until there is substance to eToys' withdrawal," while emphasizing the "online game" whose aim, besides lowering the eToys stock price to $0.00 is to get "eToys employees to quit the company" while urging eToys stockholders to call for eToys CEO Toby Lenk's dismissal.

How does Toby Lenk, CEO of eToys and target of RTMARK's countercampaign, become part of this "real fictitious discourse"? As with much political theater, Lenk is cast as a villain, one who must be gotten rid of, so that the freewheeling artists who never picked a fight in the first place can carry on with the business of making corporate culture strange.

This business of making corporate culture strange is a particularly difficult task these days, considering that the corporate culture is already strange, in a totally humorless sort of way, and the attempt to satirize it is perhaps more complex than ever before. One wonders what a Swift or Rabelais would have done in this situation. It's one thing to surf-sample-manipulate corporate Web sites or corporate "auras" and quite another thing to use your Web sites and in-person performances to create an interventionist Net art practice that temporarily derails the high-stakes games being played in the world of e-commerce.

And how long will it be before the rabble rousers are simply bought out via hostile takeover? This brings new meaning to the term *market censorship* and showcases the potential dangers of an e-commerce oligarchy that soon turns everyone, Net artists included, into Yahoos ("I had hitherto concealed the secret of my dress, in order to distinguish myself as much as possible from that

cursed race of Yahoos; but now I found it in vain to do so any longer," again
from *Gulliver's Travels*).

RTMARK and etoy may not be as over the top as Rabelais's *Gargantua* and
Pantagruel or the Swift of *Gulliver's Travels*, but they do set up a model for a
network-distributed disturbance theater programmed to turn emerging new
media writing practices into more than just a game.

An earlier version of this text was originally published online at Alt-X *and* Telepolis *in
2000.*

Designwriting: A Postliterary Reading Experience

There is something about the visible forms and structures that we've associated with the world of books and literature that we are now leaving behind. As we begin to recognize the more fluid forms of writing being developed on the Web, it becomes immediately apparent to us that graphic designers, in particular, are participating in the emergence of more visually stimulating writerly forms being distributed in cyberspace. In fact, many of the most experimental Web writing projects coming online today are being created by design professionals who juggle their roles as artists, educators, and commercial consultants whose clients are in desperate need of their skills and talents.

One of the more vocal advocates of a new form of "writingdesign" is Anne Burdick. In a forthcoming essay of hers, the term *new narrative* comes up and is immediately called into question:

In spite of the promise embodied in such a term, I want to begin with the assumption that there can be no such thing. Narrative is old. Good old narrative. It's one of our most ancient structures for making sense of the world; some say its roots lie in our everyday experience of time and language. Narrative's particular attributes—a temporal dimension and, according to some, a causal relationship between events—define its distinctive form. Therefore it stands to reason that if there's a change in this basic configuration, what we've got on our hands is no longer a narrative in the strictest sense. You can only stretch the definition so far before it either pops, takes on a new name, or snaps back into its old shape. Can there be such a thing as a "new narrative"?

If, as we have been suggesting in previous Amerika Online columns, our literature has been finally, once and for all, exhausted (and the bookish form of the novel along with it), this does not necessarily mean that emerging new media writers will abandon the practice of using narrative (and rhetoric) to locate significance "in our everyday experience of time and language." Quite the contrary. Rather, we must ask ourselves what is our everyday experience of time and language—assuming we spend a great deal of our waking hours surfing the Web, sending and receiving e-mail, listening to randomly played songs on our portable mp3 players, talking on the mobile phone, and so on?

In other words, the narratives of our time are deeply embedded in the new media experience itself. Our continual interaction with the evolving languages these new media present us with mark our time even as we, intelligent agents equipped to turn the machines off, intuitively know that by leaving the machines on, we are, in a sense, moving beyond the literary itself (that heavy burden).

This act of cultural disobedience—that is, leaving the literary behind—is not as easy as some would like. For those of us raised on books and the idea that the very best of humanity can be found in great literature, just *the idea* of conscientiously saying good-bye to the novel as a kind of narrative interface feels like an act of betrayal that is forever going to make us feel guilty until the day we die.

Unless, of course, we open our eyes and live for the moment. Our moment is one that intentionally explores the new media's potential to innovate the writing practice yet again, this time with more immediate results. As Burdick, the design editor for the *electronic book review*, continues in her essay:

So here's where the "new" in "new media" comes in. A weave requires a different kind of space than the printed page in order to realize its full potential. Within electronic space, the potential exists, although I would argue it has yet to be exploited fully. Nonetheless, in this environment, the arrangement of textual units has an entirely different set of possibilities than it does within the confines of the printed page. Writing can incorporate strategies of simultaneity, juxtaposition, placement and proximity— each of which can serve a semantic function and impact the experience and order of reading. Not dissimilar to charts and diagrams, the information such attributes delivers makes for a cumbersome translation into linear verbal form—if it could be translated at all. It's all about the visual arrangement.

Enter the Designwriter. In a straightforward way, we might say that all writers are Designwriters. It is, after all, up to each author to conceptually design the verbal landscape their stories will play out in, often spending an excess amount of time revising every sentence and word in search of a syntactical rhythm that will characterize the literary figures whose language shell their words fill up—except that I would call this conventional usage of character-ization and, for that matter, plot *Noveldesign.*

I call it Noveldesign not because it is new but because it is ever reliant on the ancient formula of conceiving a story for print manufacturing—one that has paragraphs with indentations, uniform typography, and a set of readerly expectations that will allow the author to cleverly disappear behind the cur-tain, like the Wizard of Oz, cranking out fantasy trips through the land of sus-pended disbelief. This is where most writers, even those who call themselves *literary,* find their comfort level. For some, it's as simple as tapping their shoes together three times while repeating the mantra "There's no place like home, there's no place like home, there's no place like home."

But new media Designwriters, creating a spatial architecture that enables them to turn their conceptual language art into a navigable, visual interface, have a different approach to experimenting with the evolving forms of rheto-ric to innovative *other texts* for this still somewhat foreign locale called cyber-space. Says Burdick:

While such arranging strategies are available in print form, the interrelationships they set up are fixed in place. It is the movement between elements or of elements that truly alters new media writing. The behavior of words can be a signifying attribute that actively shapes a reading and a story. In new media, words act—they do more than just sit there. If you poke them, they lead you down new paths. When you watch them, they dance or disappear. (Hopefully they resist the urge to spin.) They can also be shuffled, sifted, isolated, located, or reorganized, for a weave not only looks different but it behaves and performs differently than does a line. That's where new media begins to look like new narrative—or at least new narration.

Which brings up an interesting question: do the emergent forms of database technology replace narration, supplement narration, or reinvent narration?

Moving away from Noveldesign and its utter dependency on a limited set of options that leave the contemporary writer with very little to strategize with, we can now see emerging in cyberspace yet another model of language prac-tice that purposely blurs the distinctions between image and text, page and screen, sonic and visual, publication and exhibition. I would call this emerging model of language production Designwriting.

In this instance, to *de-sign,* if we want to get technical, would be to de-contextualize, deconstruct, and defamiliarize the ordinary experience one attributes to everyday Web life by actively intervening in the e-discourse now taking shape in the global economy. Similar to Brechtian theater, the central idea behind an online Designwriting practice would be to intervene in the dynamic space of experiential expectations that are already being developed by the commercial captains of e-commerce whose bottom-line rigidity and lack of interest in privacy matters emanate out of a growing Doubleclick mentality that chases consumer demographics wherever they may cluster.

Examples of this kind of interventionist practice are many, including the art sites discussed in my last AOL column focusing on satirical action writing. You can also sense the development of writing as a destabilizing visual art form in the more subtle yet also interventionist writer-artist collaborations found at design sites like *Thirstype. Thirstype* contributor and Designwriter Rob Wittig likes to talk about something he calls "experience design":

> Experience design (which is another way of looking at interface design) thinks about the time a user spends with a text in the most holistic possible way: what is going on with the user physically, cognitively, emotionally, psychologically, socially. My school of experience design is founded on the assumption that readers use and mold texts for use as fragments in the greater purpose that is the reader's life, rather than the assumption that whole texts mold and change readers in accordance with the whole purposes of the author.

He goes on to say that those of us from a literary background rarely, if ever, were encouraged to think and talk about reading as an activity or, at the very least, an interactive form of cultural behavior. In fact, Wittig insists, an assumed model of "correct reading" formed the basis of many of our work-related habits. Among the usual elements of this "correct reading" are, according to Wittig

- Strict linear reading
- Reading of every word
- Reading with an equal amount of concentration and attention to every word
- Reading without other simultaneous input (music, radio, television, conversation)
- Monogamous reading (one text at a time, beginning to end, without interruption)

But Designwriters like Wittig are hip to the changes taking place in digital culture and are beginning to see new modes of online writing worth investigating, as opposed to, say, bemoaning the fact that there may be a lost literary landscape never to be found again. Some older writers, especially some of the more explosive postmodern fictioneers of the past twenty-five years, are also welcoming the change. As author Ron Sukenick, the elder statesman of American experimental fiction, has said:

To take stock of the technological situation briefly, we now live in what I call the *electrosphere*. Book production has been overtaken by a new electronic technology that eliminates the job of composition or, rather, makes it part of the writer's art rather than the technician's craft. Books now increasingly go from disk to printing press directly. That means that the writer is also the compositor and can compose a page on the electronic screen as s/he wishes, making the graphic quality of the page an expressive, rather than an inert, element of fiction. No reason to go left-right, left-right, left-right, all the way to the bottom of the page like a typewriter.

Designwriters are not Typewriters. They tend to be collaborative engineers of the Web interface whose screenal presence challenges the author-as-genius model so many literary figures have depended on (and still depend on). As Burdick reiterates,

Within a print-based division of labor, graphic designers and writers are kept separate until after the writing is complete, leaving writers and designers few choices other than the previously established sizes, shapes, and strategies with which to work. Therefore, if graphic designers want to contribute to new narratives in writing, they have to be involved at the level of structure.

This means that from the outset, writing and design must work in step with one another, creating a collaborative partnership between the visual form and the writing. As designers construct spaces for writing, they're impacting the writing strategies that are possible. By the same token, as they find new ways to tell stories, writers are actively creating the visible, material spaces needed to hold those stories. As these new configurations and operations arise, the question is, who will take the lead? The writers or the designers?

Or how about the Designwriters, those willing to experiment with the evolving forms of visible language? Maybe these distinctions are no longer valid. Especially given the conceptual complexity of new media interfaces that integrate metafiction, hypertext, mp3, streaming media, VRML, dynamic HTML, Java, Shockwave, and other programs, one can not help but wonder if this economy of ideas we keep hearing about isn't on the cusp of ushering in a e-Renaissance of postliterary writing.

Part of this essay consists of sampled remixes from an essay entitled "Ways of Telling, or the Plot Thickens, Fragments, Reconfigures, Branches, Multiplies" in Anne Burdick and Louise Sandhaus, eds., *New Media, New Narratives* (Chicago: American Center for Design, 2000).

An earlier version of this text was originally published online at Alt-X *and* Telepolis *in 2000.*

What in the World Wide Web Is Happening to Writing?

As the mainstream publishing industry takes pride in its role of commodifying *the* novel, as if *the* novel were a prefabricated thing that one need only produce formulaically for a consumer market of novel readers, the intermedia environment offered by the Web, on the contrary, enables digital artists to experiment with a multitude of novel forms that move beyond the book and challenge us to reconfigure contemporary narrative practice.

This has to do with what Walter Ong, in the subtitle to his famous book, *Orality and Literacy*, calls "the technologizing of the word." This "technologizing" process is opening up huge opportunities for narrative artists to

- Experiment with formal issues that have been exhausted in book form,
- Pioneer new modes of cultural production and distribution,
- Problematize the individual author-as-genius model by way of collaborative authoring networks that sustain nonhierarchical group production and teamwork.

Those of us who grew up reading books know the value of narrative art as experienced in reading novels. As literate readers, we are invited to activate ourselves in the structural development of the alternative worlds each writer points us toward and from which we get to practice our own interactive reading skills. Novelist Julio Cortázar, whose novel *Hopscotch* was a proto-hypertext published in book form, suggested that the interactive reader was "a co-conspirator"—someone who proactively engages with creative writing in hopes of finding previously unexplored paths of knowledge, knowledge that the narrative interface, contained in a book, always mediates for us.

This reader-generated interactivity is the way we use our literacy to create meaning out of texts. Let's face it: with conventional novels, it's so easy, almost comforting, to pick up a book and get lost in its make-believe world of narrative transparency. For the literate reader, there is very little investment made in using our literacy skills to problematize the false consciousness promoted by quality-lit authors who, knowing we seek the comfort of his or her text, compose their "see-through" narratives for us to get lost in. As long as they play it safe and do not challenge our meaning-making potential, then we are happy. While reading these conventional stories, we never have to be reminded that what we are doing is reading a text composed by an author. "Losing yourself in a book" is something literate readers can relate to. It has gotten to the point where "see-through" novelists use this condition to further frustrate if not outright control the submissive reader. One writer, the novelist Ron Sukenick, has embarked on a program he calls Reader's Lib: as an innovator of writerly texts, Sukenick hopes to create work that will liberate the reader from the confines of standardized narrative behavior.

The more I am invited to curate online art shows that feature the work of Net artists who experiment with text and narrative, the more convinced I am that the field is exploding with innovative stories that not only break away from the traditional "see-through" narratives of the commercial and quality-lit book publishing world but also challenge the modes of cultural production and distribution commercial novels so heavily depend on. For the writer today, things are changing so fast you either jump on the technology train or get left behind. With the advent of new digital formats like on-demand books, e- or softbooks, online serialization, hypertext, real-time publishing, and Palm Pilot content delivery systems, I'm convinced that we are in the process of radically reconfiguring the writer into a kind of Internet artist whose problem is no longer "getting published" but rather attracting attention to the work so as to build an audience share in the electrosphere.

Over the past three years, the *trAce* online writing community has become one of the premiere international locations on the WWW known for its generous support of Net-based writing, particularly when it comes to bringing greater visibility to pioneering writer-artists who are busying themselves by reinventing writerly practice—particularly our accepted notions of authorship, text, and publishing. In an incredibly short period of time, under the guidance of its visionary and diligent director, Sue Thomas, *trAce* has quite literally enabled a World Wide Web of writers to continuously interconnect with each other through their creative work and ceaseless cultural production.

For those who don't know much about *trAce*, the first thing you should know is that the British Arts Council, as part of its Arts-4-Everyone program, provided six figures' worth of funding for the project, the money having been drawn from designated proceeds coming from the British lottery. Like venture capital in the new media marketplace, the lottery money served as a lubricant that got the wheels spinning, and within a short period of time, *trAce* was not only going through a major growth spurt but was immediately putting on international conferences, supporting the emergence of an activist online writing community, commissioning virtual artist residencies, funding Net art exhibitions, publishing state-of-the-art books, inaugurating serious hypertext competitions, sponsoring electronic poetry events, and providing Internet training courses for seniors and educational programs for children interested in writing on the Web.

As a result of these developments, *trAce* has become the most recognizable online writing community going, always already international but with a deep local and regional connection to all things literary and digital in the East Midlands part of the United Kingdom. This year's conference, entitled Incubation, was held at Nottingham-Trent University from July 10–12, 2000, and felt like the organization's first-phase capstone event, bringing together an intense community of writers, artists, theorists, and DJs (Scanner provided sound environments for the nightly lounge events). The at times rowdy activist network rhetoricians attending the event are some of the leading Web experimenters, who immerse themselves in everything from real-time collaborative publication to investigating Web-enhanced theories of "electracy." In fact, critical media theorist Gregory Ulmer, showcasing his home movies as a kind of applied grammatology, played beautifully with Stelarc's inquisitive look into the nature of "third ears" and their place in the posthuman, sublime world of cyborg-narrators and self-effacing storyworlds.

As part of the conference, I was invited to curate a collection of works that I named *ink.ubation*, works that I believe represent groundbreaking models of writerly interface and blur the distinctions between I-art and I-writing (you can decide who or what is *I*; I haven't a clue).

What makes the new media artists featured in this hybridized publication/ exhibition space (glorified hotlink page?) new is not so much their use of technology but rather the way they turn their emergent practices into ongoing ungoing works in progress that defy categorization while maintaining an allegiance to the suppleness of nervous words, sonorous syntax, vocal microparticulars, animated imagetexts, and unsung e-motions.

The artists collected at ink.ubation, including Jackie Goss, Adrienne Eisen, Shelley Jackson, Yael Kanarek, Jennifer Ley, Bob Arellano, and Linda Carroli, bring an eclectic mix of diverse sensibilities to the e-writing table. With the Net fast becoming the medium of choice for emerging narrative artists, there now exists a diverse range of work being created by writers who are remixing the verbal with the visual, the sensual with the visceral, and linking with thinking.

Curating this show, one thing has become very clear: this is writing beyond hypertext (though clearly, hypertext is present and, with the Web lost in HTTP schizophrenia, will be so for quite sometime). The better term for what I see emerging in the Web writing space would be *designwriting*, for as we begin to recognize the more fluid forms of writing being developed on the Net, it becomes immediately apparent to us that graphic designers, in particular, are participating in the emergence of more visually stimulating writerly forms being constructed specifically for the Net medium. In fact, many of the most experimental Web writing projects coming online today are being created by design professionals who juggle their roles as artists, writers, educators, and commercial consultants whose clients are in desperate need of their skills and talents.

Cocteau once said that writing is a disease. Web writing is no different. Right now we are at that pivotal moment in the science of writing where everything is just now developing again. We are witnessing that small, indefinite period of time between early infection and total outbreak. That time of incubation.

Let us hope we never find a cure.

This text was originally published as my curatorial statement for the ink.ubation exhibition as part of the trAce *online network 2000 incubation conference in Nottingham, UK. Other versions of the text were subsequently published online at Alt-X* and Rhizome *and in print form at the* American Book Review *in 2000.*

What Is a Blog?

What is a blog?

A blog should not be defined. Defining a blog would be like defining what a novel is or what a film is or what an experimental art installation is.

Perhaps it would be better to de-define a blog. A blog is not a diary, it is not dated, it is not autobiography, it is not a dreambook.

Or: it can be any or all of those things but probably should not be any or all of them.

It is not a Web site per se, it is not even writing if you prefer to see it that way, but writing seems well suited to the Idea of Blog, as does code. Blog is more a kind of progressive codework (as lived reality) than manifested outcome.

It's driven by the logic of links, always dramatically expressed in a default color that usually suggests a feeling of being blue. Yet it also suggests other states of emotion, such as being active, dynamic, visited, anchored, floating.

Waiting to be ported to somewhere, anywhere, but here. But where is here? That nagging question that all of the choragraphers keep asking as they invent the universe.

Blogs could be pseudo-autobiographical works in progress, where the artist who creates one surfs the electrosphere for useful data, samples it, manipulates it, and then exhibits it in an online environment that makes it feel like something more than just a diary Web site.

This will probably have to be done in the writing itself. The writing I speak of is more than just a diary entry with links to things found on the Net. Human portals are fine; they are even dandy. In fact, they may even end up being a kind of virtual dandyism strutting their stuff in Net space. But they are not true blog.

True blog is not true at all. It is pseudo.

For example, the novels of Henry Miller could be considered bloggish, but then again so would the so-called diaries of Anaïs Nin—not because they are diaries but because they subvert the diary form into what reads like an associative, pseudo-autobiographical novel. It's her sociolinguistic poetics coupled with an energetic linking process that makes it feel so bloggered. Her enigmatic jazz momentum is totally eroticized by a stylized use of language as aphrodiasical elixir. This, I believe, is key to blogging to avoid having it become nothing but narcissistic foreplay and mediocre narcissistic foreplay at that.

Of course, if Nin were alive today, she would probably not be so bloggered by it all. As always, she would be looking for the enigmatic juice machine that proactively creates language in rhythm, and any apparatus would do—same with Miller and many others of their ilk.

True blog, then, is not blog as we know it but as we unknow it. Blog as inventive remix machine placing value on what it sees, what it links to, how it appropriates the other and strips it of its isolation.

An earlier version of this text was originally published online at Alt-X *and then the* Iowa Review Web *in 2002.*

Making History Up: A Serial Question Mark

Q: What *was* Net art?

A: That's not an easy question to answer. When I first started writing my Amerika Online columns both at *Telepolis* and my own *Alt-X* site, I was hoping to at least locate the beginnings of a vocabulary that could be used to articulate the very possibility of an emergent form of I-art. The scene was very vibrant in the mid- to late '90s, and a communal rhetoric featuring ideas from literature, architecture, visual art, conceptual art, and even graffiti art challenged us to rethink what it means to live the life of an artist in network culture. There were globetrotting concept characters, nomadic brand-name identities, and interventionist networking strategies. There was instantaneously distributed mindshare. For example, you could pick up all sorts of wild energies and ideas at international art and writing festivals—e-mail lists, Web sites, etc. It was an era.

Q: But a much short-lived era?

A: Well, yes, but things move fast nowadays, and one must be willing to change course and restrategize at any given moment. I'm particularly interested in how Net artists were ahead of the curve when it came to making their footprint in the electrosphere and how the dot.coms came into the scene afterwards. And then Net art died before the dot.com market crash. Will there be a Net art revival? Will it lead to a sustained dot.com-driven market rally? Probably not.

Q: Why?

A: Because there is no way this market can generate the revenues one needs to justify the outrageous price/earnings ratios. Net art P/E ratios were more outlandish than dot.com P/E ratios. Although with Net art and some avant-entrepreneurial dot.com enterprises, it's probably more like an A/E ratio?

Q: A/E ratio? Art/Entertainment?

A: No, attention/earnings ratio. Basically, you had artists who were clever at using the Internet to generate disproportionate amounts of attention to their brand-name Net art sites, becoming international art stars even though they were not earning anything. In the end, their balance sheet looked horrific. Who was buying into their way of life?

Q: So how did they survive?

A: Well, it depended on where you were headquartered. If you were based in the U.S., chances are you were working in the new media economy making big bucks transferring your Net art skills into the design and strategy divisions of major start-ups. In Europe, there was some of that, too, although there was also adequate public funding to keep a targeted network alive and well—and to a certain extent that publicly funded network still exists. Of course, there are a lot of so-called artists nowadays who simply come from money—you know, Daddy and Mommy helping smooth things out along the edges. And now, as Net art becomes a thing of the past, you see some of us becoming professors of Internet art.

Q: So now comes the historicization process?

A: Yes, historicizing and mythologizing—that's where the most exciting new work will be produced. Not so much in the context of "Net art will now become canonized into the annals of art history" but via new forms of network collaboration that take into account the idea that Net art can be reconfigured into a life practice that essentially *makes history* or, in the case of the role-playing performances embodied by the artists themselves, can actually *make history up*. In fact, this is something that I will be bringing into the new digital art curriculum I am developing at the University of Colorado.

Q: How so?

A: Next semester, I will teach a new seminar called Histories of Internet Art: Fictions and Factions, and in it, we will create an online-only exhibition that investigates crucial questions like, "What was Internet art?" The exhibition will include a unique Web interface that showcases the online art work of internationally renowned and emerging Internet artists, interviews with these artists, significant keynote essays that address the early history of Internet art written by prominent new media theorists and commentators, a cluster of artist statements reflecting on the last six years of practice, an automated "People's History of Internet Art" in which visitors to the site will be able to give their own version of I-Art history (100 words or less), and, ideally, a few new works of I-art commissioned by the *Alt-X Network* created around the exhibition's theme.

Q: Can you tell us more about the Histories of Internet Art exhibition and seminar?

A: The exhibition's theme will focus on the pluralistic approaches to inventing art history and will attempt to create an alternative perspective on how emergent artwork generated specifically for the Internet medium is essentially, as I just suggested, making history or making history up. Here is where the fluidity of historical processing in digitally networked cultures allows for the development of both historical factions and historical fictions. Who decides what artists and artwork is historically significant? Often institutions and their curators take on this role. But in the Internet art world, all that has changed, and the artists themselves have essentially created their own Internetworked histories, both by aligning themselves with distributed network communities (factions) and via guerrilla marketing activities that call into question the entire notion of art history (fictions). An excellent example of this is Natalie Bookchin and Alexei Shulgin's "Introduction to net.art (1994–1999)"— which, for our research purposes at Colorado, we would call an *historical fiction* (perhaps *metafiction* is a better term)—whereas her "power of the line" open source Net art story reads more like an historical *faction*. We want to investigate how these multiple methods and reinterpretations of Net art history play with themselves and each other.

Q: I guess I have one chief concern with your position here, and that is that there seems to be a cluster of contradictory signals being transmitted in much of what you are presenting. In one sense, you are saying that Net art is a thing of the past. I don't think you'll get much argument from those of your colleagues around the world who, for the past year or two, have seen its exuberant era of cultural production and intervention quickly disappear. But you also seem to be saying, out of the other corner of your mouth, that there is still much more work to be done, that history itself is in the process of *being made*, and that this is what Net art essentially is—a history in the making and, as such, a process-oriented work in progress that can be applied to a more purposeful life practice. How can you ask the question, "What *was* Net art?" when you are still giving it so much potential to effect our present-day lives?

A: Yes, it is somewhat contradictory. But I can live with these contradictions in a way that nurtures my own life practice in ways that lead to more network-oriented cultural production. By asking the question, "What *was* Net art?" we are also, in a whisper, asking, "Is there life after Net art?" and if yes, what is it?

Q: Do you want me to answer that question?

A: Yes, if you would. I like asking questions too.

Q: Well, I think it's a nonquestion.

A: Why?

Q: Because it's really a question for you and your Net art colleagues to answer. For the rest of us, there was always life, a parallel life, in concert with our daily rituals. We have no need to ponder the question "Is there life after Net art?" because there was never any question about there being life before, during, or after Net art. What are you really trying to say?

A: I'm not trying to say anything. I'm trying *to do*. Most of my life is dictated by my to-do list. Would you like to see my current to-do list?

Q: Okay.

A: Here it is:

1. Invent new theory.

2. Turn new theory into a conceptual art character, and give this character a diacritical name.

3. Create pseudo-autobiographical fiction around the concept character.

4. Create other theoretically charged concept characters, and give them diacritical names too.

5. Have these concept characters participate in the pseudo-autobiographical fiction, thus forming a network discourse wherein they invent their own behaviors consequently saying what they mean and meaning what they say.

6. While conducting this theory play, take notes on the developing forms of hyperrhetoric that emerge from the ensuing discourse and feed them back into later scenes of writing.

7. Turn these scenes of writing into post(e)-pedagogical performance.

8. Reconfigure this post(e)-pedagogical performance into new forms of Internet Art.

Q: It sounds like your seminar to-do list.

A: It's a start.

Q: It also sounds like you'll be very busy reconfiguring your practice yet again.

A: Yes, that's true.

Q: Does that mean there will be no more *Amerika Online* columns?

A: Unfortunately, the time has come to change my rhetoric, my design strategy.

Q: Design strategy?

A: As Vilém Flusser says in his *The Shape of Things*, "as a verb (*to design*), meanings include 'to concoct something,' 'to simulate,' 'to draft,' 'to sketch,' 'to fashion,' 'to have designs on something.'" In a previous column, I referred to this new strategy called *Designwriting*. I am leaving the column-essay form behind for now and looking into more animated ways to express my ideas. Some of them may even be displayed at *Telepolis*, thanks to the support of my open-minded editor, Armin Medosch. Also, like some of my colleagues, I am in the process of further hybridizing my practice so that it involves more offline/online interaction. In the immediate future there will be a CD, an mp3 conceptual art narrative, a performance series (premiering at the Easter Festival in Lucerne, Switzerland), an attempt to explode the new media industry's recent attempts to quantify the e-book.

Q: Anything else before you end your last AOL column?

A: Yes, just to elaborate: my editor Armin Medosch has been a fellow traveler in this exploration. Although he did not always agree with my thinking or my rhetoric, he was, as is the case with most great editors, willing to let me have my say—even as I said it over and over again, sometimes to the point of fruitless repetition (something I was consciously exploring while conceiving this new concept of surf-sample-manipulate).

Q: Ah yes, surf-sample-manipulate: what's up with that?

A: Well, that's the theme of the Easter Festival in Lucerne this April. It's called Surf-Sample-Manipulate. And as stated above, I will be there with my new sound collaborators, Twine, premiering a semi-improvisational performance piece, which will also be a kind of seminar. I want my seminars to be more like multimedia performances and to occasionally take them out of the university environment and remix them on the road, into clubs, festivals, etc.

Q: Oh, so there *is* life after Net art?

A: We'll see.

An earlier version of this text was originally published online at Alt-X *and* Telepolis *in 2000.*

Index